ABOUT THE F

Seán Healy and **Brigid Reynolds** are directors of the the Conference of Religious of Ireland (CORI). For the past 20 years, they have been active on issues of socio-economic policy. They have worked on a number of government bodies and task forces, dealing with a wide range of social policy issues. They have played an active role in securing social partnership status for the community and voluntary sector in Ireland. They have also written and published widely. This is the tenth in a series of books which they have edited on social policy issues.

The Conference of Religious of Ireland is a voluntary umbrella organisation for Religious. While serving the needs of its affiliated members, its principal focus is on leadership, not only in its member organisations, but also in the wider Irish society. It is one of the social partners in the community and voluntary sector.

SOCIAL POLICY IN IRELAND

Principles, Practice and Problems

Edited by
Seán Healy
Brigid Reynolds

Oak Tree Press
Dublin

Oak Tree Press
Merrion Building
Lower Merrion Street
Dublin 2, Ireland

A catalogue record of this book is
available from the British Library.

ISBN 1-86076-089-9

The publication of this book was made possible
through sponsorship by AIB Investment Managers Ltd.

Printed in Ireland by Colour Books Ltd.

CONTENTS

LIST OF CONTRIBUTORS

John Baker is a lecturer in politics and equality studies at University College, Dublin, and author of *Arguing for Equality*.

Ursula Barry is an economist and lecturer in the Women's Education Research and Resource Centre, University College, Dublin.

Noel Cahill is an economist with the National Economic and Social Council.

Tim Callan is a research Professor at the Economic and Social Research Institute, Dublin.

Sara Cantillon lectures in economics at the Equality Studies Centre, UCD, and has worked as an economist and social policy advisor at the Department of the Taoiseach.

Charles M.A. Clark is Professor of Economics at St. John's University, New York, and was formerly visiting Professor at the National University of Ireland, Cork.

Michael L. Collins is an economist in the Department of Economics, National University of Ireland, Cork.

Patrick Commins is with the Rural Economy Research Centre, Teagasc, specialising in socio-economic aspects of rural development.

Donal de Buitléir is Chairman of the National Social Services Board.

Tony Fahey is a Senior Research Officer at the Economic and Social Research Institute.

John Healy is an economist working on research and evaluation within the PAUL Partnership, Limerick.

Kieran Healy is a sociologist in the Department of Sociology, Princeton University.

Catherine Kavanagh is a lecturer in economics at the National University of Ireland, Cork.

Brendan Kennelly is a lecturer in economics at the National University of Ireland, Galway.

Kathleen Lynch is a lecturer in equality studies and education at University College, Dublin.

Terrence McDonough is a lecturer in economics at the National University of Ireland, Galway.

Brian Nolan is a research Professor at the Economic and Social Research Institute, Dublin.

Donal O'Brolcháin is Secretary of Drumcondra 2005, a group of seven residents' associations in north Dublin.

Rory O'Donnell is Jean Monnet Professor of European Business at University College, Dublin.

Patricia O'Hara is a consultant with Callaghan Associates and lectures at University College, Cork.

Eamon O'Shea is a lecturer in economics at the National University of Ireland, Galway.

Francis O'Toole is a lecturer in economics at Trinity College, Dublin, and his research focuses on tax reform and the economics of competition policy and regulation.

Patrick Riordan SJ lectures in political philosophy at the Milltown Institute and is currently President of the Institute.

John Roden is Managing Director of Kompass Internet Limited.

Damian Thomas is a Newman Fellow in Industrial Relations at University College, Dublin.

Tony Varley is a lecturer in political science and sociology at the National University of Ireland, Galway.

Sean Ward is a public sector analyst working in the civil service.

FOREWORD

Social Policy in Ireland: Principles, Practice and Problems has been produced to mark the tenth anniversary of the Conference of Religious of Ireland's first social policy conference. In that ten-year period, policy-making in Ireland has been much discussed. While specific issues such as poverty and unemployment have been addressed in detail, there has also been an emerging, broader focus on the framework within which these discussions take place.

Since its establishment in the early 1980s, this framework has been a central concern for CORI's Justice Commission. While the Commission has always dealt in great detail with the specific issues being considered, we have consistently emphasised the importance of this policy framework and the underlying paradigm which shape the discussions. We have argued constantly for the inclusion of all groups in the policy-making process.

The policy-making framework and the underlying paradigm determine, to a great extent, which issues are discussed and which ignored. Realities can be taken as inevitable, assumptions made and policy initiatives legitimated as a result of the unquestioned acceptance of the paradigm which underpins society's understanding of itself. The same can be true if there is a "cosy consensus" that accepts that some people have a right to be included while others are excluded from the discussions out of which policy decisions arise. A different paradigm and framework would, at least, open all of these to question. CORI's Justice Commission has long argued for a broadening of approach in the policy-making process, so as to incorporate ongoing discussion of this paradigm issue, and the inclusion of the socially excluded in these discussions.

In each of the past ten years, we have held a conference focusing on a specific issue or aspect of policy and published a book containing the papers of each conference. These conferences have dealt with topics such as work, income, participation, rural development, citizenship, progress and taxation. Papers have been produced on each topic by a wide range of policy analysts, focusing on the present situation, how it emerged, how it should be adjusted and what could be done in specific policy terms to address the problems identified.

CORI has sought out detailed solutions to specific problems identified in these conferences. In many cases, it has been involved in developing and piloting creative initiatives to tackle these and other issues. It has also argued for the inclusion of groups such as poor people, unemployed people and women in the policy development process.

This book continues the tradition of CORI's previous social policy publications. Some of the following chapters look at issues of principle, some analyse practice, while others focus closely on specific problems. Many of the issues covered over the last ten years are revisited, in many cases by the same authors. Other issues are identified and analysed for the first time in this publication, while others still are omitted for want of space, although we intend to return to them in future years.

CORI is an organisation of religious women and men. It seems appropriate that it should be concerned not just with the specifics of problems, but with issues of principles, paradigms and guiding values. The religious quest, after all, seeks to deal with ultimate issues. We in CORI's Justice Commission have always seen this quest, however, as deeply rooted in the struggle to move the world from where it is towards a better place. For us, this involves a number of things. It involves detailed analysis, linking of this analysis to the experience of people, articulating of viable alternatives and identifying pathways to move towards such alternatives. It also involves ongoing dialogue on these issues with as wide a range of groups, organisations and people as possible.

We do not claim to have all the answers. We do, however, argue that the issues we identify are important and need to be addressed in a comprehensive way if there is ever to be a world where human rights are respected, human dignity is protected, human development is facilitated and the environment is respected and protected. For CORI's Justice Commission, these are the core elements of a just society and all of our work is focused on developing such a world. We offer this book as a contribution to the public debate we believe is urgently required if Ireland is to develop as a just society.

We wish to express our deep gratitude to the 29 authors who have produced the 20 chapters that follow. They contributed long hours and their obvious talent to preparing their chapters. A special "thank you" is due to Tony Fahey of the ESRI, who had the original idea for this book, and who has been unstinting in his advice and support through the months of its development and production. Our gratitude is also due to Sinéad Fuller of the Justice Office; to David Givens, Brian Langan and the team at Oak Tree Press, who saw the book through to publication quickly, calmly and with great professionalism; and to AIB Investment Managers, whose financial assistance made this publication possible.

Seán Healy and Brigid Reynolds
February 1998

Chapter 1

PROGRESS, PARADIGMS AND POLICY

Seán Healy *and* Brigid Reynolds

We live in a world which promotes constant economic progress. Wealth, employment and production are growing steadily. The conventional economic wisdom argues that continuing on this path for the foreseeable future will produce a world in which everyone has a stake and where the good life can be accessed by all. It presumes that everyone, in a world population twice as large as it is today, can reasonably aspire to and achieve the high-consumption lifestyle enjoyed by the world's affluent minority at present. This is seen as progress.

This conventional economic vision of the future is unattainable. Environmental degradation, encroaching deserts, unemployment, starvation, widening gaps between rich and poor, exclusion from participation in either decision-making or development of society: these are the global realities confronting decision-makers today. Economic globalisation and environmental stress are accompanied by social inequality and endemic deprivation. Millions of people in the richer parts of the world recognise these problems and are seriously concerned about the plight of the billions of people on all continents whose lived experience is one of constant exclusion from the resources and the power that shapes this world.

People feel powerless. The media present one vision of the future and assume it is the only desirable or viable future. Politicians, more concerned about the next election, rarely discuss the fundamental causes of, or long-term solutions to, the issues and problems they confront every day. It is crucial that questions be asked concerning the core assumptions that underpin and support the present situation. What model of development is being followed? Is it likely to produce a good life for all the world's citizens? What constitutes progress? What are the underpinning values on which decisions are made in shaping the future? Are we at ease with these values and the structures that flow from them? Is it possible to envision a future where everyone really would have a stake, be respected, have meaningful work and an adequate income, where all could genuinely participate? These are the questions addressed in this chapter.

Ireland is at a major crossroads. It has the resources and capacity to choose a wide range of different options. Decisions made now will have major effects on the generations of the future. Consequently, it is essential that the questions addressed here be examined by policy-makers. The authors offer their views on these issues as a contribution to the public debate which is so badly needed at present.

PARADIGMS

The source of many of the problems lies in the development paradigm being followed and in its view of progress. A paradigm contains core beliefs and assumptions. It is a model or framework from which analyses, decisions and actions flow. "The world is flat" is a good example of a paradigm. If one accepts this, then one holds certain values, takes certain actions and expects certain results. On the other hand, if one's paradigm is that "the world is round", then one holds different values, takes different actions and seeks very different results. Moving from a framework which sees the world as flat to one that sees the world as round is a paradigm shift.

Paradigms are extremely powerful, as they determine one's "world-view". They underpin decisions concerning what constitutes a problem, how it should be approached, what action should be taken and what the desired outcome might be (Healy and Reynolds, 1993). History shows that if a paradigm is producing negative results, however, it is not always changed immediately. Thomas Kuhn (Kuhn, 1970) analysed how paradigm change was effected in the natural sciences. Changes did not occur through a process of cumulative research which brought people ever closer to a final solution to the problems encountered. "Rather it happened through a 're-volution' in which a small group of scientists recognise that the existing frame of reference is inadequate for the resolution of newly emerging problems" (McCabe, 1997). They seek out a new paradigm. Change, however, is resisted and the transition is never smooth

(Dunne, 1991). As the existing paradigm becomes more recognisably inadequate, the new one attracts more and more support until the old one is finally abandoned. Tension and conflict are usually part of the transition process, as are rearguard actions in defence of the outdated paradigm. Total acceptance of the new paradigm can take a long time, as was the case for example in the world of science in the shift from the Copernican paradigm to the Newtonian one and again in the later shift to the Einsteinian one.

The dominant paradigm underpinning public policy-making today is mechanistic. It first emerged as a direct response to the scientific and philosophical revolution of the seventeenth century.

Isaac Newton formulated the fundamental laws of physical reality. Philosophers and sociologists followed in his wake, drawing on his approach and seeking to discover the basic axioms and principles of social reality. The machine was used as the basic model and was applied both to the state and to individuals.

> Mechanistic physics became the dominant paradigm of the modern world. It has had many positive effects and opened up great new possibilities ranging from the development of technology to the emergence of liberal democracy. But it also has had dramatic limitations which were unseen by the thinkers and policy-makers who adopted it with enthusiasm. (Healy and Reynolds, 1996)

These limitations are especially obvious to people encountering current global problems. The ecological crisis, the emphasis on hierarchy, addressing the issue of difference through conflict and confrontation, defining work in a very narrow way: these are simply a few, very varied, effects which flow from adoption of this mechanistic paradigm. Its key, however, is in its impact on the understanding of progress.

PROGRESS

Economics accepted Newtonian physics as the dominant paradigm. Progress came to be seen principally in terms of economic growth. Gross Domestic Product (GDP) became the measurement used by policy-makers. Growth in GDP came to be seen as the key indicator of progress. Everything with a market price which was paid for was assumed to add to the national well-being. The family and the local community are accepted by most people as essential components of their well-being. These are omitted, however, from this indicator. The natural environment is also accepted as being crucial for human survival, yet its plundering and destruction are added to this measure of progress as a plus, while costs, such as the consumption of finite resources, are not deducted.

The adoption of an economic indicator as the widely accepted measurement of progress also had another side-effect: economists became the ultimate authorities on most areas of public policy. We see this clearly today in Ireland, both in the context of Government decision-making and of media commentary. Over and over again, the views of economists are accepted, often unquestioned, unless economists disagree among themselves. If there is no disagreement, their views are given the status of absolute truth!

The end result of all this is that growth in GDP, which is a measure and means of policy, became an end of policy in itself (Cobb, Halstead and Rowe, 1995). Because GDP growth was seen as the key to progress, other aspects of policy development were not considered or given any real priority. Alternative analyses or ideas were often dismissed without any serious consideration. The policy-making process assumed that everything people needed or wanted would follow, once economic growth was sustained. Once growth is maintained, according to this approach, jobs will emerge for everyone seeking them. These in turn will produce adequate income which will see the end of poverty and the emergence of the good life for all.

There are some very serious problems with this approach, however. At the global level, economic growth has been dramatic, yet the number of people living in poverty has never been higher. The redefinition of work as paid employment, which has accompanied this approach, has resulted in ever-larger numbers of people being excluded from meaningful work. Nor do the vast majority of people benefit from the growth which is produced. In fact, poverty, unemployment, exclusion, poor healthcare and inadequate accommodation are the lot of an ever-larger number of people on this planet.

After decades of increasing unemployment in Ireland, the last few years have seen a reversal in this trend. Economic growth has been dramatic and unprecedented. The benefits of this growth have gone, however, principally to those already better off. Budget after Budget produced by successive Governments has seen little being made available to those in poverty or on lower incomes, while substantial gains were provided to the better-off. The only difference between Governments tended to be the scale of the disparity in the allocations to the two ends of the spectrum. This skewing of the benefits towards the better-off is justified on the basis that they are the ones who produced the growth and who will re-invest their gains in generating further growth in the economy. Meanwhile, the poor are told to wait!

ALTERNATIVES NEEDED

The paradigm underpinning decision-making in the social policy area is not adequate to the present situation. Likewise with the generally accepted measurements of progress. Alternatives are required. Finding agreement on what these should be, however, is not easily achieved. What should provide the anchor for an alternative paradigm, framework or model? What could serve as a fundamental reference point when evaluating the present situation and making decisions concerning future directions? What should guide the choice of real progress indicators?

The present authors have long argued that underlying the guiding paradigm or the choice of measurements of progress lie sets of values. The existence of such values is sometimes accepted, more often denied. Daly and Cobb summarise this situation and its implications succinctly:

> One of the central limitations of the academic disciplines in contributing to wisdom is their professed aim of value neutrality. That there is here a large element of self-deception has been pointed out frequently and convincingly. The ideal of value neutrality is itself a value that is generally highly favourable to the status quo. Which economic questions are taken up and in what terms, even within the range allowed by the disciplines, often depends on the interests of the economists or even of someone who has commissioned the study. More objectivity is in fact obtained by bringing values out into the open and discussing them than by denying their formative presence in the disciplines . . . as long as the disciplines discourage any interest in values on the part of their prac-

> presence in the disciplines . . . as long as the disciplines
> discourage any interest in values on the part of their prac-
> titioners, they inevitably discourage the ordering of study to
> the solution of human problems. (Daly and Cobb, 1990: 131)

A similar position is enunciated by Fritjof Capra:

> . . . there can be no such thing as a "value-free" social science.
> . . . Any "value-free" analysis of social phenomena is based on
> the tacit assumption of the existing value system that is im-
> plicit in the selection and interpretation of data. . . . Economics
> is defined as the discipline dealing with the production, distri-
> bution and consumption of wealth. It attempts to determine
> what is valuable at a given time by studying the relative ex-
> change values of goods and services. Economics is therefore
> the most clearly value-dependent and normative among the
> social sciences. (Capra, 1982)

Uncovering the underpinning values and having them discussed,
scrutinised and evaluated is crucial if there is to be any agreement or
consensus on what constitutes real progress (Wogaman, 1986). This
is an issue that arises in many spheres and is the often-unarticulated
question at the root of people's concerns.

In Search of a World Ethic

Despite frequent references to the Celtic Tiger and the economic
boom being experienced, there is much unease. People are searching
for security. The awareness of rapid social change causes great insecurity. People want assurance against the future. Even news media
feel the need to speculate about what is going to happen, rather than
report on what has happened. Those in leadership give assurance
that the future is under control. Labels like "New World Order",
"Post-Industrial Age", "Information Age", "World Government",
"Global Village", etc., are used to give an impression of inevitable
benign and manageable progression.

The future is not inevitable. It will be determined largely by the
decisions that are being taken now. What are these decisions? Who is
taking them and on what basis? What values underpin the decision-
making processes? How are questions like: "What constitutes the
good life for citizens?" or "What makes a life a good one for the per-

tionship of ethics to decision-making (Mieth and Vidal, 1997). In a pluralist society, are universal values possible?

Michael Walzer, in his reflections on various events which have evoked international response (Prague, Beijing, Bosnia, Rwanda), shows that there is something like a "core morality" — a whole set of elementary ethical standards, which include the fundamental rights to life, to just treatment (also from the state), to physical and mental integrity (Walzer, 1994; Curran, 1998). While it is possible to identify similar responses from people living in different geographical and cultural areas, is it possible to devise a process which would arrive at an agreed articulation of this "core morality"? We can take heart from the efforts of eminent and committed international bodies to formulate a global ethic. Worthy of particular note is the work of the Council of the Parliament of the World's Religions in Chicago (Kung and Kuschel, 1993), which was supported in principle by a report of the InterAction Council of Former State Presidents and Prime Ministers under the chairmanship of former German Federal Chancellor Helmut Schmidt (1996). These former world leaders are convinced that there will be no better global order without a global ethic.

The core of a global ethic adopted by this body has two basic principles:

- Every human being must be treated humanely!

- What you wish done to yourself do to others.

On the basis of these principles, the InterAction Council affirms four irrevocable directives on which all religions agree:

- Commitment to a culture of non-violence and respect for all life — the age-old directive: You shall not kill! Or in positive terms: Have respect for life!

- Commitment to a culture of solidarity and a just economic order — the age-old directive: You shall not steal! Or in positive terms: Deal honestly and fairly!

- Commitment to a culture of tolerance and a life of truthfulness — the age-old directive: You shall not lie! Or in positive terms: Speak and act truthfully!

- Commitment to a culture of equal rights and partnership between men and women — the age-old directive: You shall not
  commit sexual immorality! Or in positive terms: Respect and love
  one another!

In 1992, the United Nations Organisation Commission on Global
Governance was established. In its report in 1995, entitled *Our Global
Neighbourhood*, it highlights the connection of rights with responsibilities. Reflecting on this report, Kung (1997) first summarises the
rights of human beings as:

> . . . the right to a secure life, equitable treatment, an opportu-
> nity to earn a fair living and provide for their own welfare, the
> definition and preservation of their differences through peace-
> ful means, participation in governance at all levels, free and
> fair petition for redress of gross injustices, equal access to in-
> formation and to the global commons.

Having noted that "hardly ever has it been stated in an official international document that concrete responsibilities, human responsibilities, are associated with human rights", Kung goes on to quote
the report (Commission on Global Governance, 1995):

> At the same time, all people share a responsibility to:
> - Contribute to the common good;
> - Consider the impact of their actions on the security and
>   welfare of others;
> - Promote equity, including gender equity;
> - Protect the interests of future generations by pursuing
>   sustainable development and safeguarding the global
>   commons;
> - Preserve humanity's cultural and intellectual heritage;
> - Be active participants in governance; and
> - Work to eliminate corruption. (Quoted in Kung, 1997: 226)

He notes that responsibilities were formulated long before rights:

> . . . in the debate on human rights in the French Revolutionary
> Parliament of 1789 the demand was made: if a declaration of

the rights of man is proclaimed, it must be combined with a declaration of the responsibilities of man. Otherwise, in the end all human beings would have only rights which they would play off against others, and no one would any longer recognise the responsibilities without which the rights cannot function. (Kung, 1997: 99)

Kung discusses the relationship of law with rights and responsibilities and concludes that:

no comprehensive ethic of humanity can be derived from human rights alone, fundamental though these are for human beings; it must also cover the human responsibilities which were there before the law. Before any codification in law and any state legislation there is the moral independence and conscious self-responsibility of the individual, with which not only elementary rights but also elementary responsibilities are connected. (Kung, 1997: 103)

For Kung, law has no permanent existence without ethics, so there will be no new world order without a world ethic, which he defines as:

the basic moral human attitude, understood individually or collectively . . . a basic consensus on binding values, irrevocable criteria and personal basic attitudes, without which any community is sooner or later threatened with anarchy or a new dictatorship. (Kung, 1997: 105)

RELATIONSHIPS

What should be the basis of this "world ethic"? What should be the fundamental paradigm to replace the present mechanistic one? We argue it is right relationships. Developments in "new physics" give huge support and credibility to the centrality of relationships in the universe. Einstein initiated two revolutionary trends in scientific thought (a) the theory of relativity and (b) electromagnetic radiation. He believed in nature's inherent harmony.

The universe is no longer seen as a machine, made up of a multitude of objects, but has to be pictured as one indivisible, dynamic whole whose parts are essentially interrelated and

can be understood only as patterns of a cosmic process".
(Capra, 1982: 66)

Experimental work showed that, not only were atoms not solid particles, the sub-atomic particles were nothing like the solid objects of
classical physics. These subatomic units had a dual aspect. Sometimes they appeared as waves, sometimes as particles. Capra explains this very complex reality as follows:

> Subatomic particles, then, are not "things" but are inter-
> connections between "things" and these "things" in turn are
> interconnections between other "things", and so on. In quan-
> tum theory you never end up with "things"; you always deal
> with interconnections. This is how modern physics reveals the
> basic oneness of the universe. It shows that we cannot decom-
> pose the world into independent existing smallest units. As
> we penetrate into matter, nature does not show us any iso-
> lated basic building blocks, but rather appears as a compli-
> cated web of relations between the various parts of a unified
> whole. (Capra, 1982: 69, 70)

Newton's work in developing the general laws of motion in the late
seventeenth century was adopted by philosophers and opinion-
formers of the time. The universe was seen as one huge mechanical
system operating according to exact mathematical laws. As pointed
out earlier, this view influenced all disciplines and policy-making. It
was a static view of a world made up of parts which could be treated
in isolation — a view where change was measurable and predictable
and hence could be controlled and managed.

This world-view did facilitate much progress in various areas.
However, we must recognise its limitations. While it has facilitated
increased specialisation, it has also resulted in increased compartmentalisation and isolation. A new world-view is required which
recognises that not only living systems but also inanimate matter are
interconnected. This idea of interlinkage calls us to form relationships. Human development is about forming right relationships.

Approaches to understanding human existence in the social and
psychological sciences see it as made up of a series of relationships.
These relationships can be divided into four categories which correspond to different levels of human existence:

- Relationship with self and God *(interior life)*: By getting in touch with self and the Transcendent, we grow and become more human;

- Relationship with people *(social life)*: Our humanity is developed and enriched through our relationships with people;

- Relationship with institutions *(public life)*: If institutional structures and relationships are right, human development is facilitated by social institutions and structures;

- Relationship with the environment *(cosmic life)*: Each of us is related to all the generations that have gone before us and to the generations that will follow us. Also, we have a relationship with all other people living at this time and with the environment. Life itself depends on basic elements like air, water and minerals to survive.

We grow as persons through these four sets of relationships. A just society is one that is structured in such a way as to promote these right relationships so that human rights are respected, human dignity is protected, human development is facilitated and the environment is respected and protected.

CITIZENSHIP

How might this new paradigm of right relationships and our earlier comments on the development of a global ethic and the balancing of rights and responsibilities be incarnated in a meaningful and tangible way? It is essential that this be done. Otherwise, these ideas may be deemed interesting or worthy but ultimately be ignored for want of a concrete means of accessing them. We suggest the concept of citizenship as the key to this end. Citizenship is hardly a new concept, but it is one which is argued about and understood differently by different groups today.

Historically there are two major traditions (Heater, 1990; Oliver and Heater, 1994; Held 1987). One sees citizenship in terms of rights (Marshall, 1950; Doyal and Gough, 1991; Ginsburg, 1994). This comes from the liberal political tradition which emerged in the seventeenth century. It views civil and political rights as the means by which the state guarantees the freedom and formal equality of individuals. The second tradition sees citizenship in terms of obligation (Mead, 1986; Novak et al., 1987). This emerged from the civic republican tradition of classical Greece. It goes back as far as Aristotle and views political participation as civic duty and emphasises responsibilities. These two different approaches have been conceptualised as "citizenship as a status" versus "citizenship as a practice" (Oldfield, 1990). The first of these prioritises the individual citizen, while the second emphasises the wider society (Heater, 1990).

Those who support the first of these approaches include classic liberals, who restrict citizenship to the formal and political rights needed to protect individual freedom. They also include people in the tradition of Marshall who see social rights as necessary in terms of promoting freedom (Marshall, 1950). Those who support the second of these approaches include those who argue that the real citizen is actively involved in political and civic affairs (present-day followers of civic republicanism). They also include those who insist on the obligation of (some?) citizens to take up paid employment or to engage in some service of the community. Those who argue for more responsible attitudes to the environment can also be placed in this approach.

Marshall identified three sets of citizenship rights: civil, political and social. These have underpinned the development of the dominant understanding of citizenship in Europe in the second half of the twentieth century. In the US, however, civil and political rights were highlighted while social rights were not emphasised (Turner, 1990; Fraser and Gordon, 1994). Discussion on the nature of rights and the status of social rights have become a major issue again in more recent years with the emergence of the new right which gives priority to property rights over all other forms of citizenship rights. This new debate is rooted in different understandings of freedom. The new right sees freedom in negative terms as the absence of coercion and interference. If this were accepted, then the role of government would be confined to protecting the freedom of individual citizens. Involvement by government in promoting an understanding of freedom as the ability to participate in society as full citizens is rejected by the new right. The new right's understanding of freedom is too limited. If one asks what this freedom (as the absence of coercion and interference) is for, it is to enable people to pursue their own ends. But this cannot be separated from the ability to pursue those ends.

Consequently, the freedom and the ability to pursue chosen ends are inextricably linked (Plant, 1988). The right to participate in decision-making in social, economic, cultural and political life has been urged by Gould (1988). Seven clusters of rights — health, social, cultural, civil, economic, pacific and political — have been identified by Held, who argues that these are crucial in facilitating free and equal political participation (Held, 1987; 1989).

However, this emphasis on social rights as central to citizenship is often downplayed today and in its place far more emphasis is placed on duties under various headings. For example, there has been a movement which identifies taking up paid employment to support their families as the prime obligation faced by social welfare recipients (Mead, 1986; Novak et al, 1987). This approach has been gaining ground in some countries and many of the more recent welfare-to-work and workfare programmes reflect this change of priorities. The obligation to work is often presented as uniting all citizens in making a contribution to the common good. However, its application varies in practice. Those with sufficient wealth or income from other sources can ignore this obligation if they so wish. Those targeted by welfare-to-work and workfare programmes are very often poor and the jobs available to them are usually low-paid, often dirty and unpleasant. Consequently, people's right to work is turned into an obligation (to take up whatever paid employment is available) which has to be met only by those already experiencing exclusion. What this does in practice is to reinforce the existing inequalities in the interests of the better-off (Jordan, 1989).

So we see that citizenship has two historical roots based in the traditions of liberalism and civic republicanism. One views citizenship as status, carrying a range of rights. The other views it as a practice, involving both obligations and political participation broadly defined. Ruth Lister (1998) argues that "while the rights and participatory approaches to citizenship remain conceptually different, they do not necessarily have to conflict; indeed, they can be seen as being mutually supportive, even if tensions between them remain". She draws them together in a critical synthesis around the notion of human agency (Lister, 1998). She argues that:

> to act as a citizen requires first a sense of agency, the belief
> that one *can* act; acting as a citizen, especially collectively, in

turn fosters that sense of agency. Thus, agency is not simply about the capacity to choose and act but it is also about a *conscious* capacity which is important to the individual's self-identity. (Lister, 1998: 38)

Citizenship, then, both as a practice and in the relationship between practice and rights, can be seen as a dynamic process. We believe this synthesis provides the basis for putting flesh on the new paradigm that we have argued is necessary. It also enables the issues we raised concerning core moral values to be placed within an integrated framework. We recognise that the outline contained here needs substantial development. We are constrained by space from writing further on the issue, but we believe it offers great potential for useful investigation. The new relational paradigm we propose is consistent with the global ethic we outlined. It is also consistent with developments in the scientific field. Acceptance of this paradigm would open up new frontiers for full citizenship for all people (Healy and Reynolds, 1993).

NEW PROGRESS INDICATORS

One issue remains to be addressed here. If full citizenship for all people is the ultimate goal, then how should progress be measured?

On this issue of measuring progress, Erikson (1993) argues that

> . . . welfare — or level of living — should be defined in terms of resources and conditions and is best measured by use of descriptive indicators. And to the extent that welfare research is coupled to societal planning . . . I find it quite essential that descriptive indicators should be used. The data for planning should refer to factoral conditions and planning goals should be formulated in terms of such conditions. People's opinions and preferences should influence societal planning through their activities as citizens in the democratic political process, not through survey questions and opinion polls.

The need for respecting differences in traditions, cultural background and social context of the society in question has been highlighted and an argument made for ensuring a wide-ranging debate about societal preferences and priorities (Scott et al., 1996).

We believe that much work needs to be done in this area. Progress indicators should be developed in four key overlapping areas and at a number of different levels. These four areas are: economic, political, cultural and social. In the area of economics the traditional indicators could be maintained. However, some modification would be required in measures such as GNP, to ensure they included costs as well as benefits. Also, further indicators need to be adopted in this context. These would include measures of poverty, of income distribution and of wealth distribution. We have argued previously that every person has a right to have sufficient resources to live life with dignity (Healy and Reynolds, 1996). Indicators are needed to monitor this area.

In the political area new indicators are needed which would identify the real participation levels of people, both in public decision-making and in the development of society. If interdependence is to have any meaning, then indicators are also needed to measure how progress in one nation is affecting development in other countries. New forms of governance are beginning to emerge which seek to find a balance between representative democracy and a more participatory process of democracy (National Economic and Social Forum, 1997). Progress indicators are needed in this context.

In the cultural area, a wide range of indicators is needed. We accept the definition of culture developed by UNESCO:

> culture may now be said to be the whole complex of distinctive spiritual, material, intellectual and emotional features that characterise a society or social group. It includes not only the arts and letters, but also modes of life, the fundamental rights of the human being, value systems, traditions and beliefs (UNESCO, 1982).

Consequently, progress indicators could be developed on the quality of life and work, on media, language, education, youth and popular culture, recreation, sport (Kelly, 1989). This may seem very wide-ranging, but it could be done by developing a national cultural policy and developing indicators to measure progress in this area.

In the social area, progress indicators are needed on equality, most notably in the context of gender (Lister, 1998). In this context, the conceptual framework outlined by the National Economic and

Social Forum (1996) would be most useful. This comprises four stages:

1. Equality of formal rights, opportunities and access

2. Equality of participation

3. Equality of outcome or success

4. Equality of condition.

These are not exhaustive and it is clear that the areas overlap. However, it is useful to focus on progress indicators in this way as it helps identify all the areas for which progress indicators need to be developed. It also helps to identify the policy areas within which these indicators should now be incorporated.

There is also a need to ensure that progress indicators are developed for different levels of society, ranging from the local to the global. One of the reasons for this is interdependence. The mechanistic view of the world and of society has resulted in increased compartmentalisation and isolation. Integration has not been a priority and its absence has produced many problems which could have been avoided.

One final point needs to be emphasised in this context. A wide range of groupings should be involved in choosing meaningful indicators and in deciding how these should be applied. It should not be acceptable that only professional elites or powerful institutes have the right to decide what constitutes progress or development (Healy and Reynolds, 1996). Agenda 21 (1993) recognises a range of major groups. These are women, children and young people, indigenous people, farmers, local authorities, workers and trade unions, business and employers, the scientific and technical community, and non-governmental organisations. This list provides a good starting point. We would add poor people and unemployed people.

CONCLUSION

In this chapter, we identified major problems facing society today. We argued that the source of many of these problems lies in the development paradigm being followed and in its inadequate understanding of progress. We highlighted the limitations of (a) the dominant mechanistic paradigm and (b) the emphasis on a narrow understanding of economic growth as the key measurement of progress. Having argued that alternatives are required, we suggested what some of these might be. A global ethic is required and we suggested some elements which might form the core of such an ethic. We proposed that right relationships would be a better paradigm to underpin development than the current mechanistic one. Having outlined some of the key dimensions in such a paradigm, we showed how these were linked to the building of a just society.

If this new paradigm, underpinned by a global ethic, were accepted by policy-makers and others, we suggested that the most tangible way of incarnating this, and ensuring the balancing of rights and responsibilities, would be in a broader understanding of the concept of citizenship. An argument was made for the development of genuine progress indicators in the (overlapping) economic, political, cultural and social areas, as well as at different levels of society ranging from the local to the global. Having outlined what some of these indicators might be, we argued for the involvement of a wide range of groupings in choosing meaningful indicators and in deciding how these should be applied. We believe a public debate is urgently needed around the issues of progress, paradigms and policy. We offer this chapter as a contribution to that debate.

REFERENCES

Agenda 21 (1993), *The Earth Summit's Agenda for Change*, Geneva: Centre for our Common Future.

Capra, F. (1982), *The Turning Point*, London: Fontana Books.

Cobb, C., T. Halstead and J. Rowe (1995), "If the GDP is Up, Why is America Down?", *The Atlantic Monthly*, October.

Commission on Global Governance (1995), *Our Global Neighbourhood*, Oxford: Oxford University Press.

Curran, C.E. (1998), "Absolute Moral Norms" in Bernard Hoose, (ed.), *Christian Ethics: an Introduction*, London: Cassell.

Daly, H.E. and J.B. Cobb (1990), *For the Common Good*, London: The Merlin Press.

Doyal, L. and I. Gough (1991), *A Theory of Human Need*, Basingstoke: Macmillan.

Dunne, J. (1991), "The Catholic School and Civil Society: Exploring the Tensions" in *The Catholic School in Contemporary Society*, Dublin: CMRS Education Commission.

Erikson, R. (1993), "Descriptions of Inequality: The Swedish Approach to Welfare Research" in M. Nussbaum and A. Sen (eds.), *The Quality of Life*, Oxford: Clarendon Press.

Fraser, N. and L. Gordon (1994), "Civil Citizenship against Social Citizenship" in H. van Steenbergen (ed.), *The Condition of Citizenship*, London: Sage.

Ginsburg, N. (1994), "Agendas and Prognosis for Social Policy " in R. Page and J. Baldock (eds.), *Social Policy Review 6*, Canterbury: Social Policy Association.

Gould, C. (1988), *Rethinking Democracy*, Cambridge: Cambridge University Press.

Healy, S. and B. Reynolds (1993), "Work, Jobs and Income: Towards a New Paradigm" in B. Reynolds and S. Healy (eds.), *New Frontiers for Full Citizenship*, Dublin: CMRS.

Healy, S. and B. Reynolds (1996), "Progress, Values and Public Policy" in B. Reynolds and S. Healy (eds.), *Progress, Values and Public Policy*, Dublin: CORI.

Heater, D. (1990), *Citizenship*, London: Longman.

Held, D. (1987), *Models of Democracy*, Cambridge: Polity Press.

Held, D. (1989), *Political Theory and the Modern State*, Cambridge: Polity Press.

InterAction Council (1996), *In Search of Global Ethical Standards*, Vancouver: InterAction Council.

Jordan, B. (1989), *The Common Good: Citizenship, Morality and Self-interest*, Oxford: Basil Blackwell.

Kelly, A. (1989), "A Cultural Policy for Ireland", *Administration*, Vol. 32, No. 3.

Kuhn, T. (1970), *The Structure of Scientific Revolutions*, Chicago: University of Chicago Press.

Kung, H. (1997), *A Global Ethic for Global Politics and Economics*, London: SCM Press.

Kung, H. and Kuschel (eds.) (1993), *A Global Ethic: The Declaration of the Parliament of the World's Religions*, London.

Lister, R. (1998), *Citizenship: Feminist Perspectives*, London: Macmillan.

McCabe, M. (1997), "Clashing Paradigms: Leadership in the Church Today", *SMA Bulletin*, Christmas, pp. 1–12.

Marshall, T.H. (1950), *Citizenship and Social Class*, Cambridge: Cambridge University Press.

Mead, L. (1986), *Beyond Entitlement: The Social Obligations of Citizenship*, New York: The Free Press.

Mieth, D. and M. Vidal (1997), *Outside the Market No Salvation?* London: SCM Press.

National Economic and Social Forum (1996), *Equality Proofing Issues*, Dublin: NESF.

National Economic and Social Forum (1997), *A Framework for Partnership — Enriching Strategic Consensus through Participation*, Dublin: NESF.

Novak, M., J. Cogan, B. Bernstein et al. (1987), *A Community of Self-reliance: The New Consensus on Family and Welfare*, Milwaukee: American Institute for Public Policy Research.

Oldfield, A. (1990), *Citizenship and Community: Civic Republicanism and the Modern World*, London: Routledge.

Oliver, D. and D. Heater (1994), *The Foundations of Citizenship*, Hemel Hempstead: Harvester Wheatsheaf.

Plant, R. (1988), *Citizenship, Rights and Socialism*, London: Fabian Society.

Reynolds, B. and S. Healy (eds.) (1993), *New Frontiers for Full Citizenship*, Dublin: CMRS.

Scott, S., B. Nolan and T. Fahey (1996), *Formulating Environmental and Social Indicators for Sustainable Development*, Dublin: ESRI.

Turner, B. (1990), "Outline of a Theory of Citizenship", *Sociology*, Vol. 24, No. 2.

UNESCO (1982), World Conference on Cultural Policies, Mexico.

Walzer, M. (1983), *Spheres of Justice: A Defense of Pluralism and Equality*, Oxford: Oxford University Press.

Walzer, M. (1994), *Thick and Thin: Moral Argument at Home and Abroad*, Terre Haut, Indiana: University of Notre Dame Press.

Wogaman, J.P. (1986), *Economics and Ethics: A Christian Enquiry*, London: SCM Press.

Chapter 2

EQUALITY

John Baker[1]

On the face of it, equality is just another of those principles which Irish society is happy to endorse on ceremonial occasions, so long as it doesn't impinge on real life. There it is in the Easter Proclamation: "The Republic guarantees . . . equal rights and equal opportunities to all its citizens, . . . cherishing all the children of the nation equally." The Constitution also pays its respects: "All citizens shall, as human persons, be held equal before the law" (Art. 40.1). Meanwhile, back in the real world, Ireland is a deeply unequal country, marked by one of the most unequal distributions of income in Europe, massive class inequalities in educational participation and entrenched intolerance towards minorities such as Travellers. So equality seems to be no more than a pious aspiration, an idea which is fine for the Constitution, so long as it stays there.

This picture is complicated, however, in two major ways. First, despite the widespread complacency with which privileged people view Ireland's gross inequalities, the issue refuses to go away. Groups that have been oppressed and marginalised — women, Travellers, disabled people, gay men and lesbians, working class communities and others — continue to assert their claim to equal treatment. The second complication, and the main concern of this chapter, is that equality has more than one meaning: there are many different types of equality (Rae, 1981). So it is not enough to demand "equality": we need to know what kind of equality we want.

---

[1] This paper represents work in progress as part of a collaborative research project within the Equality Studies Centre. I am grateful to other members of the Centre for their ideas and suggestions.

In this chapter, I set out three different definitions or conceptions of equality, which I call basic equality, liberal equality and radical equality. I try to show that these different ideas of equality place very different demands on Irish society (and by implication on the relation between Irish society and the rest of the world). At the same time, I argue that it is not easy to believe in basic equality without believing in liberal equality, or to believe in liberal equality without taking the next step to radical equality.

Over the last century, there have been many attempts to define equality and to classify types of egalitarianism. The framework developed here is only one alternative, which I think is particularly relevant to contemporary Irish society. I try to relate it to some of the major theorists of equality, but they do not all fit in very neatly. This is because the categories are meant to distinguish broad approaches to equality rather than to analyse particular theories, and broad classifications always involve a certain amount of simplification and generalisation. Theorising about equality is constantly challenged both by new academic work and even more importantly by social movements of the marginalised and oppressed. The framework below is meant for now, not forever, and is intended to be open enough to allow for different interpretations and perspectives.

BASIC EQUALITY

The idea of basic equality is the cornerstone of all egalitarian thinking: the idea that at some very basic level all human beings have equal worth and importance, and therefore are equally worthy of concern and respect. It is not easy to explain quite what these ideas amount to, since many people will claim to hold them while defending a wide range of other inequalities, including the view that some people deserve more concern and respect than others. Perhaps what is really involved in basic equality is the idea that every human being deserves some basic minimum of concern and respect, placing at least some limits on what it is to treat someone as a human being. At any rate, that is how I will define basic equality here.

The minimum standards involved in the idea of basic equality are far from trivial. They include prohibitions against inhuman and degrading treatment and at least some commitment to satisfying people's basic needs. In a world in which rape, torture and other crimes against humanity are a daily occurrence, and in which millions of people die every year from want of the most basic necessities, the idea of basic equality remains a powerful force for action and for change. Yet taken on its own, it remains a rather vague and minimalist idea. On its own, it does not challenge widespread inequalities in people's living conditions or even in their civil rights or educational and economic opportunities. It calls on us to prevent inhumanity, but it does not necessarily couch its message in terms of justice as distinct from charity. These stronger ideas only arise in more robust forms of egalitarianism, of the sort to which the rest of this chapter is devoted.

It is surprisingly hard to provide any *arguments* for basic equality. That is partly because it is an assumption of our age and therefore something we do not feel any need to justify, and partly because the people who reject basic equality in practice do not have any interest in arguments. (In fact, they commonly pay lip service to equality at the same time as they are wielding the knife.) Most people willingly accept that there are such things as inhuman treatment and human needs; these ideas seem to be built into the very idea of morality. They are in any case the common assumptions of all modern political outlooks. I will not survey all of these outlooks here. Instead, I will concentrate on two which are particularly important for our times and which can both claim to be genuinely egalitarian.

LIBERAL EQUALITY

The idea of liberalism has itself been interpreted in many different ways, all of them embracing basic equality, but varying quite a lot in terms of the other types of equality they believe in. I mean to include under the idea of liberal equality only those forms of liberalism that move well beyond basic equality in terms of social, economic and political equality — positions which might be called "left liberalism" and which are often found in social democratic political movements. But liberal equality still covers a range of outlooks.[2]

---

[2] The paradigm case of liberal egalitarian thinking is Rawls (1971; 1993). Other authors whose work falls largely within the realm of liberal egalitarianism are Dworkin (1981a; 1981b; 1987; 1988), Walzer (1985) and Williams (1962). Important contributions to liberal egalitarianism have also been made by Barry (1995),

A key assumption of liberal equality is that major inequalities of income, status and power will always exist. The role of the idea of equality is to regulate these inequalities so that they are fair to everyone. Broadly speaking, we can say that liberal equality involves both strengthening the basic minimum to which everyone is entitled and regulating the competition for advantage by means of the idea of equal opportunity. But in spelling out these ideas it is helpful to use a number of different headings.[3]

1. Basic Rights

The most central and long-standing idea within liberal egalitarianism is the protection of basic civil and personal rights. Such rights include the prohibition of slavery, of torture and of cruel, inhuman or degrading punishment. They include equality before the law, protection against arbitrary arrest and a right to the due process of law. Also included are such rights as freedom of movement, the right to own property, freedom of thought, conscience and religion, freedom of opinion and expression and freedom of association. These civil and personal rights are familiar features of modern liberal regimes and can be found in such documents as the American Bill of Rights (1789, except of course for its acceptance of slavery), the Universal Declaration of Human Rights (1948), the European Convention on Human Rights (1950) and the International Covenant on Civil and Political Rights (1976). Quite what is included in these rights and how they are specified and interpreted has varied, the prohibition of slavery being the most glaring example. But taken overall, they are one way of setting limits on the degree of inequality any society should tolerate.

A related feature of liberal egalitarianism is the distinction it makes in the name of personal freedom between those aspects of human life that are subject to social and legal regulation and those

---

Arneson (1989), Cohen (1989), Sen (1992) and Van Parijs (1995), although these authors are to varying degrees more radical in their egalitarianism.

[3] The headings are chosen for ease of exposition and to provide a coherent framework. The first, second and third headings correspond to the three types of principle set forward by Rawls (1971; 1993). The third, fourth and fifth correspond to the classic and ultimately inescapable Weberian trio of class, status and party (Weber, 1958). Redistribution and recognition form the framework for Fraser's (1997) analysis.

which are protected against any such interference, a distinction sometimes phrased in terms of the "public" versus the "private".[4] Arising in the wake of religious wars in Europe, one of the cornerstones of liberalism was the recognition of religious belief and practice as a private concern beyond the reach of public regulation. Another less explicit exemption was the realm of the family, allowing for male dominance of family affairs regardless of the degree to which women were able to achieve equality in other areas. Neither of these exemptions has been absolute — religions aren't allowed to perform blood sacrifices, husbands aren't allowed to murder their wives. But the public/private distinction has protected important spheres of life from egalitarian challenges.[5]

2. Liberal Equal Opportunity

Another central and long-standing liberal egalitarian idea is equality of opportunity, the principle that people should in some sense have an equal chance to compete for the better positions in society. This principle has two major interpretations. The first, non-discrimination, is expressed in the French "Declaration of the Rights of Man" (1789) as the principle that all citizens "are equally eligible for all positions, posts and public employments in accordance with their abilities" (Art. 6). In our own times, many states have anti-discrimination legislation which makes it illegal to deny education or work to people because of their religion, sex or other specified characteristics. Some states also prohibit "indirect" discrimination, which is the use of irrelevant criteria which favour one group over another. An example would be the requirement for employees to be a certain height, if there is no job-related reason for this, because this indirectly discriminates against women.

---

[4] In fact, liberalism makes several different public/private distinctions. The distinction discussed is the one most relevant to basic rights.

[5] The liberal protection of the family as a private sphere has in recent times been used to defend a wider variety of family forms, such as one-parent families and single-sex couples. Two key issues distinguishing a liberal egalitarian from a radical egalitarian position on such questions are whether this variety should be "tolerated" or "celebrated" and whether such family forms are viewed as exempt from or open to critical scrutiny.

Non-discrimination is a weak form of equal opportunity, because it does not consider how people come to have their educational or job-related abilities in the first place. A stronger form of equal opportunity insists that people should not be advantaged or hampered by their social background, and that their prospects in life should depend entirely on their own effort and abilities. This principle, which Rawls (1971: 73) calls "fair equal opportunity", implies that the educational system should try to compensate for the obstacles people from working class and other disadvantaged backgrounds face in developing their talents as compared to people from privileged backgrounds.

Since most educational systems do little in this regard, another implication of fair equal opportunity is the development of "affirmative action": policies for helping members of disadvantaged groups to compete for and obtain education and jobs. The reasoning is that if members of these groups are under-represented in, say, universities or the professions, this must be because they have not had equal opportunities to develop their abilities. Affirmative action is a way of improving the balance at a later stage, ensuring greater equality of opportunity in the end. A strong form of affirmative action is the use of quotas to ensure that disadvantaged groups are represented at all levels of society.

A useful framework for testing the degree of fair equal opportunity in a given context is provided by the ideas of equality of access, participation and outcome (Equality Studies Centre, 1995). The clearest way to deny opportunities to the members of a particular group is to deny them *access* to education, jobs, political influence and so on, by erecting legal, bureaucratic or other barriers. Opportunities can also be limited by making it harder for them to *participate* on an equal footing with more privileged groups. Ultimately, the strongest test for whether or not a group has achieved full equality of opportunity is in the *outcomes* of participation: have its members succeeded at the same level as other groups? Only when groups are achieving roughly the same levels of success can we be reasonably confident that they have had the same opportunities to succeed (O'Neill, 1977).

A common feature of both non-discrimination and fair equal opportunity is the assumption mentioned earlier that the world will always contain major inequalities. The role of liberal equal opportunity is to ensure that the competition for advantage is as fair as possible.

3. Redistribution: Anti-Poverty Focus

A third key element of liberal equality, though of more recent vintage, concerns what might be called the economic or more broadly the material condition of people's lives. The material condition of a person's life has a number of different components — not just their income and wealth, but also other factors such as their social and physical environment, their access to public services and local amenities and their working conditions. For example, the material condition of disabled people is strongly affected by an environment designed to serve non-disabled people.[6] In addition, the same circumstances can have a different impact on different people because of their different needs. This complexity sometimes makes it hard to compare the material condition of specific individuals, but it does not prevent us from seeing that some people are materially much better off than others.[7]

Broadly speaking, the liberal egalitarian position on material inequality is that it should be cushioned at the bottom, that there should be a safety net or floor below which no one should be allowed to fall. This is a logical extension of the basic egalitarian commitment to satisfying human needs and a central idea of the modern welfare state.[8] Quite where the floor should be and how it should be defined

---

[6] Equalising the incomes of disabled and non-disabled people would certainly be an advance in a society like Ireland, where most disabled people live in poverty. But it would still only be addressing one aspect of their disadvantage. How to analyse the disadvantages faced by disabled people is itself an important issue on which liberal and radical egalitarians disagree, with liberals tending to employ a medical model of disability and radicals employing a social model. A relevant discussion is Smith and O'Neill (1997).

[7] This issue is closely related to the "equality of what?" debate. Some relevant sources are Sen (1992), Nussbaum and Sen (1992), Dworkin (1981a; 1981b) and Cohen (1989). "Material condition" is not a wholly satisfactory terminology because the needs in respect of which it is partly defined are not all "material" needs, but I hope it is reasonably clear for present purposes. It is meant to be open to interpretation rather than to take too definite a stand on "equality of what?".

[8] There has always been some tension between this idea and the liberal belief, embedded in the principle of equal opportunity, that people should take

is a continuing issue for liberal egalitarians, illustrated in debates about whether poverty is an "absolute" or "relative" idea and whether it can be defined entirely in terms of income or must include other factors. The key point here is that liberal egalitarians are more concerned with eliminating poverty than promoting material equality.

A more demanding liberal egalitarian principle, at least in theory, is John Rawls's "difference principle", which states that "social and economic inequalities" should work "to the greatest benefit of the least advantaged" members of society (Rawls, 1971: 83; 1993: 6). Like other liberal egalitarians, Rawls assumes that there will always be major social and economic inequalities, explaining that "the function of unequal distributive shares is to cover the costs of training and education, to attract individuals to places and associations where they are most needed from a social point of view, and so on" (1971: 315). But rather than aiming simply at bringing everyone above the poverty line, the worst off should be brought as high up the economic scale as possible. How far this approach takes us towards full equality depends on the degree of inequality necessary to perform the function Rawls sees for it. So it is hard to judge in practical terms quite how far the difference principle departs from an anti-poverty position.

4. Recognition: Tolerating Differences

A fourth element of liberal egalitarianism is its commitment to "social" equality in the sense of tolerating individual and group differences, so long as they respect basic rights. This toleration is embedded in freedom of conscience and opinion and in the protection of the private sphere from outside interference. But it extends to the idea that people have very different views about what matters in life — different "conceptions of the good", as it is sometimes put — and that society should as far as possible be impartial among these different beliefs.

---

responsibility for their own lives and should bear the costs of their own failures. Although some liberal egalitarians, emphasising equal opportunity, take the view that individuals who deliberately squander their advantages deserve no help from society, I think it is more accurate to the liberal egalitarian tradition to distinguish between equal opportunity and the safety net and to acknowledge the tension.

5. Power: Liberal Democracy

On the face of it, liberal egalitarianism has a stronger commitment to equality in the political sphere than in the economic. The principle that every citizen has an equal say through the ballot box, and the extension of this principle over the past two centuries to all social classes, to women and to ethnic minorities, is clearly an egalitarian idea, and one which plays an important role both in reducing economic inequality and in expressing the equal status of all citizens. But we need to contrast these equal political rights with the fact that economically and culturally dominant groups have much more influence on public policy in all liberal democracies than disadvantaged groups. Liberal democracy also assumes that there will necessarily be a power gap between ordinary voters and the people they elect. Elections are seen, primarily, as a method for choosing and limiting the power of decision-makers rather than as a means by which the people engage in self-rule in any meaningful sense. A further feature of liberal democracy is its concentration on what is generally considered "politics", neglecting power inequalities in the economy, the family, religion and other areas.[9] Liberal democracy and the conception of political equality that goes with it are thus themselves in line with the general idea that liberal equality is about regulating inequality rather than eliminating it.

6. Reform of Existing Social Structures

The discussion so far has concentrated on the key principles of liberal egalitarianism, but the picture would be incomplete without discussing how liberal egalitarians conceive of these principles being implemented: what social structures or institutions are necessary to put these principles into practice? Liberal egalitarianism's vision of the world and of the possibility of change seems to be based on the assumption that the fundamental structures of modern welfare states are at least in broad outline the best of which we are capable. In saying this I do not mean to imply that liberal egalitarians think that we live in the best of all possible worlds or that there is little we can do

---

[9] There is a close connection between this limitation and the public/private distinction mentioned earlier, but in this case even the economy is brought within the idea of the private.

to improve the way we manage our societies. But I think they are convinced that certain key features of modern welfare states — including representative government, a mixed economy, a developed system of social welfare, a meritocratic educational system, a specialised and hierarchical division of labour — define the institutional framework within which any progress towards equality can be made. The task for egalitarians is to make various adjustments to these structures rather than to alter them in fundamental ways. It is partly because these structures inevitably produce inequality that liberal egalitarians think that inequality is inevitable and that the egalitarian agenda must be defined in terms of regulating inequality rather than eliminating it.

Justifying Liberal Equality

Liberal egalitarianism represents a tremendous challenge not just to the inequalities of pre-capitalist societies but also to the entrenched inequalities of the contemporary world. Can this challenge be morally justified? Many of the arguments put forward by liberal egalitarians are rooted in the idea of basic equality, the claim of every human being to basic concern and respect. If we are to take the ideas of concern and respect seriously in the context of modern societies in which people have complex and diverse needs and differ profoundly in their moral and political beliefs, we must surely take steps to protect their personal freedoms, to enable them to participate in decision-making and to tolerate differences. The ideas of concern and respect also support the principle that everyone should have a decent standard of living, including the resources necessary to exercise their rights and freedoms. The most novel idea of liberal egalitarianism, equal opportunity, can be seen as a way of showing basic respect and concern for human beings as rational agents with differing talents and ambitions. None of this amounts to a compelling *argument* for liberal egalitarianism, but it indicates something of the way in which many authors have attempted to construct one. In any case, the tenets of liberal egalitarianism are in fact widely accepted in contemporary welfare states (Miller, 1992). But is liberal equality enough? I shall argue that it is not.

RADICAL EQUALITY

Radical egalitarians challenge the liberal assumption that major inequalities are inevitable and that our task is simply to make them fair. Our aim should be much more ambitious: to eliminate major inequalities altogether, or at least massively to reduce the current scale of inequality.[10] The key to this much more ambitious agenda is to recognise that inequality is rooted in changing and changeable social structures, and particularly in structures of domination and oppression. These structures create, and continually reproduce, the inequalities which liberal egalitarianism sees as inevitable. But since social structures have changed in the past, it is at least conceivable that they could be deliberately changed in the future. Exactly how to name and analyse these structures and their interaction is a matter of continuing debate, but one way or another they clearly include capitalism (a predominantly market-based economy in which the means of production are privately owned and controlled), patriarchy (systems of gender relationships which privilege men over women), racism (social systems which divide people into "races" and privilege some "races" over others) and other systems of oppression.[11]

This emphasis on social structures in explaining inequality affects the way radical egalitarians understand equality as well. In contrast to the tendency of liberal egalitarianism to focus on the rights and advantages of individuals, radical egalitarianism is also sensitive to the rights and advantages of groups. In contrast to liberal egalitarianism's tendency to concentrate on how things are distributed,

---

[10] Among radical egalitarians I would include Schaar (1967), Carens (1981), Nielsen (1985), Norman (1982; 1987; 1991), Baker (1987), Okin (1989), Cohen (1981; 1989; 1991; 1995; 1997; n.d.), Young (1990) and Fraser (1989; 1997). There are of course many differences among these authors but my aim is to draw together their most important insights.

[11] These oppressive systems include structures which systematically exclude people with impairments from participating fully in their societies, structures which socially construct a division between "heterosexual" and "homosexual" persons and privilege the former over the latter and systems which privilege dominant over subordinate ethnic groups. No attempt is made here at a complete list of oppressive relationships and no inferences should be drawn as to their relative importance. The key point here is that radical egalitarians tend to have a more sociologically informed understanding of the causes of inequality than liberal egalitarians.

radical egalitarianism pays more attention to how people are related, particularly through power relations. In contrast to the tendency of liberal egalitarianism to treat individuals as responsible for their successes and failures, radical egalitarians are more likely to notice the influence of social factors on people's choices and actions. These contrasts should not be overstated, but they do affect how radical egalitarianism operates, as will become clearer by looking at its central ideas.

1. Personal and Group Rights

Radical egalitarians retain the liberal commitment to basic civil and personal rights, including the right to personal private property. They recognise, however, that the general right to private property enshrined in some declarations of rights, including the Irish Constitution (Arts. 40.3.2 and 43), can be used to protect capitalism, and they therefore adopt a more limited definition of what this right involves. Radical egalitarians also point out that the systematic oppression of social groups may sometimes be countered by creating group-based rights, for example the right of a linguistic minority to educate its children in their first language or the right of an ethnic minority to political representation. Such group-based rights are a natural extension of individual rights in response to group-based oppression.

A significant shift between liberal and radical egalitarianism concerns the definition of the "private" sphere, the area of life that ought to be protected from regulation by either law or social convention. Radical egalitarians are not opposed to the very idea of a private sphere, but they point out that how that sphere has been defined in the past has protected certain forms of oppression: in particular, the oppression of women and children inside both families and religions (Okin, 1989; Cohen, n.d.).

2. Radical Equal Opportunity

Discussions of equality sometimes contrast the liberal idea of equality of opportunity with the idea of equality of outcome. In my view this is not really valid, since radical egalitarians are also keen to ensure that people have a wide range of choices rather than insisting that everyone should end up the same. The difference is in how equal opportunity is understood. Liberal equal opportunity is about fairness in the competition for advantage. It implies that there will be winners and losers, people who do well and people who do badly. An "opportunity" in this context is the right to compete, not the right to choose among available alternatives. So two people can have equal opportunities in this sense even if one of them has no real prospect of achieving anything of value. For example, a society in which only 15 per cent of the population attend third level education could in this liberal sense give everyone an equal opportunity to do so, even though in a stronger sense it would clearly be denying the opportunity for third level education to 85 per cent of the population.

Radical equal opportunity is about opportunities in this stronger sense, what might be called *real* opportunities or *real* choices. In the field of education, it means ensuring that everyone is enabled to develop their talents and abilities. In the economy, it means that everyone has a real choice among occupations that they find satisfying or fulfilling. This is not the same as an open admissions or hiring policy, through which anyone can walk into any course or job regardless of their preparation or ability. It is about helping people to develop the skills necessary for pursuing worthwhile educational and career choices, and about reforming the structure of education and employment so that every alternative is worthwhile.

3. Redistribution: Equality of Material Condition

For radical egalitarians, economic or material equality means much more than satisfying basic needs or providing a safety net, although these are clearly urgent priorities.[12] It means aiming for a world in which the economic or material conditions of people's lives are roughly equal. Because of the multi-faceted nature of material condition, equality here does not mean that everyone should have the same income, but it does involve a dramatic reduction in the scale of

---

[12] A complication which I cannot pursue here is that basic, liberal and radical egalitarianism tend to operate with increasingly wide lists of needs. Basic egalitarianism tends to concentrate on subsistence needs, liberal egalitarianism on the idea of a decent standard of living and radical egalitarianism on what people need for a full human life, raising issues about the "neutrality" of political principles between conceptions of the good life.

income inequality. In adopting this view, radical egalitarians reject the liberal belief that substantial material inequalities are inevitable.[13]

In thinking about economic equality, it is natural to start off by looking at inequalities between major social groups: men and women, disabled and non-disabled people, members of dominant and subordinate cultures, and so on. This is partly because economic inequalities between groups are symptoms of a lack of "fair equal opportunity". Focusing on groups also helps us to avoid difficult issues about comparing the material condition of different individuals. But equality between social groups does not excuse inequalities within them. Ultimately, equality of material condition is about the condition of every person, not just of groups.

4. Recognition: Celebrating Difference

One of the great strengths of the liberal tradition is its commitment to respecting and tolerating differences. However, radical critics of liberalism have pointed out that toleration is not quite what it seems, since the very idea of toleration suggests a superiority of the tolerant over the person tolerated, and therefore a fundamental inequality of respect. It is only dominant cultures that "tolerate" subordinate ones, not vice versa. The dominant view is still seen as the normal one, while the tolerated view is seen as deviant. There is no suggestion that the dominant view may itself be questionable, or that an appreciation of and interaction with subordinate views could be valuable for both sides.

For these reasons, radical egalitarians prefer to talk about the appreciation or celebration of difference. Differences from the norm are to be welcomed and learned from rather than simply permitted, and the dominant culture itself needs to be critically assessed, particularly if its sense of identity depends on belittling others. But the celebration of difference does not mean that subordinate cultures have to be accepted uncritically, either. In fact, by redrawing the line between public and private, radical egalitarians are likely to widen the scope for criticising and transforming both dominant and subordinate cultures. How to conduct such criticism can be a difficult

---

[13] A major question here is the alleged need for incentives; see Carens (1981), Baker (1987: Ch. 9) and Cohen (1991; n.d.) for relevant discussions.

issue for radical egalitarians, particularly in cases where the view from outside a particular culture seems to conflict with the values of those within it. Without wishing to avoid this issue, it is worth noting that there is often resistance within oppressive cultures. It is not always a conflict between insiders and outsiders.[14]

5. Equality of Power

As discussed earlier, liberal democracy has a strictly limited impact on power inequalities, leaving dominant groups largely unchallenged in the political sphere and neglecting many other types of power altogether. Yet it is precisely these power relations which sustain inequality between privileged and oppressed groups. Radical egalitarianism responds to these limitations on two fronts. First of all, it promotes a stronger, more participatory form of politics in which ordinary citizens, and particularly groups who have been excluded from power altogether, can have more control over decision-making. Strengthened local government, closer accountability for elected representatives, procedures to ensure the participation of marginalised groups and wider access to information and technical expertise are some of the elements of this radical democratic programme.

The second aspect of equality of power is to challenge power in other areas, such as the economy, the family, education and religion. The agenda here includes democratic management of individual firms and democratic control over key planning issues for the local, national and global economy. It involves rejecting the power of husbands over wives and questioning the power relations between parents and children. It means a democratic, co-operative model of education. It implies that the power structures of religious organisations are just as open to question as are those of the secular world.

In both cases, the aim is to promote equality of power rather than to contain inequalities of power, recognising that power takes many forms, is often diffuse and has to be challenged in many different ways.

---

[14] There are some useful discussions of this issue in Parekh (1996; 1997), Nussbaum and Sen (1992) and Nussbaum and Glover (1995).

6. Challenge to Existing Structures

It seems clear enough that the radical egalitarian agenda challenges the basic structures of contemporary societies. A predominantly capitalist economy continually creates and reproduces inequalities in people's real opportunities and material condition; it relies on and perpetuates inequalities of power. Many of the key structures of the welfare state, from the welfare office to the "caring" professions to the prison system, marginalise and disempower the very people they are supposed to help. The ways in which Irish and other societies are structured around gender differences — in the organisation of the economy, in the family, in religion, in education and in other areas — systematically limit women's opportunities, material well-being, status and power. Societies pervasively and systematically disable and disempower people with impairments and members of ethnic and "racial" minorities. Liberal democratic politics protects and sustains inequality.

Radical equality would require quite different economic, political and social institutions, developing socialist, participatory, inclusive, enabling and empowering ways of co-operating in all areas of life. This is not the place to pursue these issues, but they represent perhaps the most challenging questions for radical egalitarianism.

Justifying Radical Equality

Radical egalitarianism represents a radical challenge to existing attitudes and structures, but many of the arguments in its favour come from basic and liberal egalitarianism. The most general way of putting the case is that the aims of both basic and liberal egalitarianism are thwarted by inequalities of wealth, status and power which they refuse to challenge. On the face of it, it seems a simple enough task to ensure that everyone in the world has access to clean water and decent food, but layers of entrenched inequality make it quite possible for the privileged to resist this minimal goal. On the face of it, it seems easy enough to ensure that everyone's basic rights are protected, but in practice the rights of powerless and marginalised people are easily violated. Liberal egalitarians are eloquent proponents of equal opportunity, but equal opportunity is impossible so long as privileged people can deploy their advantages on behalf of themselves and their families.

Other arguments for radical egalitarianism arise out of the internal tensions and contradictions of liberal egalitarianism. We have seen how the idea of toleration embodies the very inequality of respect it purports to reject. There is a similar contradiction in the "incentive" argument for inequality, namely that when privileged people demand an incentive for helping the worse off, they are taking resources away from the very people they pretend to be concerned about (Cohen, 1991). Another tension arises in arguments for liberal equal opportunity. This principle is often justified by appealing to the interest each person has in "experiencing the realisation of self which comes from a skilful and devoted exercise of social duties" (Rawls, 1971: 84). Yet it is clear enough that a system of liberal equal opportunity operating within an unequal society provides precious few people with this experience.

Additional arguments for radical egalitarianism come from reflections on the limited assumptions of liberal egalitarianism. In a curious way, liberal egalitarians seem to ignore the structured nature of inequality, the ways in which inequality is generated and sustained by dominant social institutions, and the influence of these institutions on people's attitudes, preferences and prospects. Thus when Rawls, for example, explains fair equal opportunity by saying that people's prospects "should not be affected by their social class" (1971: 73), he seems to be accepting the idea of a class divided society at the very same time as he is endorsing a principle which implies the elimination of class altogether. His work is also notorious for its neglect of gender.[15] A related problem is the liberal egalitarian emphasis on choice and personal responsibility, which plays an important role in supporting the idea of equal opportunity but tends to ignore the extent to which people's choices are influenced by their social position.

---

[15] The point about class was made as early as Macpherson's (1973) discussion and never really addressed. The classic gender-based critique of Rawls is Okin (1989). Rawls's later work (1993: xxix) briefly acknowledges the issue of gender inequality but in a way which seems to continue to ignore the depth of gender inequality.

These, then, are some of the key arguments for radical egalitarianism.[16] If they are sound, then Irish society in particular, and the
world more generally, are deeply unjust and need to be radically re-
built.

CONCLUSION

In this chapter I have tried to set out a framework for thinking about
equality, distinguishing the basic egalitarianism that is the common
assumption of all modern political thinking from what I have called
liberal and radical egalitarianism (see Table 2.1). I have outlined and
contrasted the main ideas of liberal and radical equality under six
headings, concerning basic rights, opportunities, material redistribution, social recognition, power and social structures. I have also
tried to sketch the reasons why a person who takes basic equality
seriously is obliged to move on to a belief in liberal equality, and
how the difficulties involved in holding a liberal egalitarian position
give rise to radical egalitarianism. These arguments are far from
complete, but I hope they give some sense of the case for a radical
egalitarian position.

In contemporary Ireland, basic egalitarianism is taken for granted
at the level of moral and political rhetoric. The Irish left is primarily
concerned with what I have called liberal egalitarianism. Unlike
some leftists, I do not consider "liberal" to be a term of abuse. But I
have tried to show that there is a radical alternative to liberal egalitarianism, and that this radical position is a natural extension of the
concerns and difficulties involved in the liberal outlook. If I am right
in believing that radical egalitarianism is a better outlook, this only
emphasises the scale of the tasks ahead of us. We face the challenge
not only of constructing plausible models of an egalitarian society,
but also of developing a political movement for radical change.

---

[16] For more arguments, see Nielsen (1985), Norman (1987), Baker (1987), Okin
(1989), Young (1990) and Cohen (1981; 1989; 1991; 1995; 1997; n.d.). One general
upshot of these arguments is that, contrary to appearances, it is liberal egalitarianism which is unrealistic or utopian, because its limited aims are in fact un-
realisable in a world marked by severe inequality and because it neglects the real
influence of social structures. Of course, this does not show that radical egalitarianism is any less utopian: perhaps, as many critics of equality believe, both
forms of equality are out of reach.

TABLE 2.1: BASIC, LIBERAL AND RADICAL EGALITARIANISM

	Basic egalitarianism	*Liberal egalitarianism*	*Radical egalitarianism*
Basic rights	Protection against inhuman and degrading treatment	Classic civil and personal rights Public/private distinction	Liberal rights *plus*: Restricted property rights Openness to group rights Redefined private sphere
Opportunities		Non-discrimination "Fair equal opportunity"	Radical equal opportunity
Redistribution	Provision for basic needs	Anti-poverty focus Rawls's "difference principle"	Basic needs plus equality of material condition
Recognition	Basic respect	Toleration of differences	Critical celebration of difference
Power		Liberal democracy	Equality of political and other forms of power
Social structures		Reform of current structures	Radical restructuring

REFERENCES

Arneson, Richard (1989), "Equality and Equal Opportunity for Welfare", *Philosophical Studies*, Vol. 56, pp. 77–93.

Baker, John (1987), *Arguing for Equality*, London: Verso.

Barry, Brian (1995), *Justice as Impartiality*, Oxford: Oxford University Press.

Carens, Joseph H. (1981), *Equality, Moral Incentives, and the Market*, Chicago: University of Chicago Press.

Cohen, G.A. (1981), "Illusions about Private Property and Freedom", in John Mepham and David Hillel-Rubin (eds.), *Issues in Marxist Philosophy, Volume IV: Social and Political Philosophy*, Brighton: Harvester.

Cohen, G.A. (1989), "On the Currency of Egalitarian Justice", *Ethics*, Vol. 99, pp. 906–944.

Cohen, G.A. (1991), "Incentives, Inequality, and Community", in Grethe B. Peterson (ed.), *The Tanner Lectures on Human Values*, Salt Lake City: University of Utah Press, Vol. 13, pp. 261–329.

Cohen, G.A. (1995), *Self-Ownership, Freedom and Equality*, Cambridge: Cambridge University Press.

Cohen, G.A. (1997), "Back to Socialist Basics", in Jane Franklin (ed.), *Equality*, London: IPPR, pp. 29–47.

Cohen, G.A. (n.d.), The 1996 Gifford Lectures, forthcoming, title undecided.

Dworkin, Ronald (1981a), "What is Equality? Part 1: Equality of Welfare", *Philosophy and Public Affairs*, Vol. 10, pp. 185–246.

Dworkin, Ronald (1981b), "What is Equality? Part 2: Equality of Resources", *Philosophy and Public Affairs*, Vol. 10, pp. 283–345.

Dworkin, Ronald (1987), "What is Equality? Part 4: Political Equality", *University of San Francisco Law Review*, Vol. 22, pp. 1–30.

Dworkin, Ronald (1988), "What is Equality? Part 3: The Place of Liberty", *Iowa Law Review*, Vol. 73, pp. 1–54.

Equality Studies Centre (1995), "A Framework for Equality Proofing", paper prepared for the National Economic and Social Forum, Dublin: Equality Studies Centre.

Fraser, Nancy (1989), *Unruly Practices: Power, Discourse, and Gender in Contemporary Social Theory*, Cambridge: Polity Press.

Fraser, Nancy (1997), *Justice Interruptus*, Princeton: Princeton University Press.

Macpherson, C.B. (1973), "Rawls's Models of Man and Society", *Philosophy of the Social Sciences,* Vol. 3, pp. 341–347.

Miller, David (1992), "Distributive Justice: What the People Think", *Ethics,* Vol. 102, pp. 555–593.

Nielsen, Kai (1985), *Equality and Liberty: A Defense of Radical Egalitarianism,* Totowa, NJ: Rowman & Allanheld.

Norman, Richard (1982), "Does Equality Destroy Liberty?", in Keith Graham (ed.), *Contemporary Political Philosophy,* Cambridge: Cambridge University Press.

Norman, Richard (1987), *Free and Equal,* Oxford: Oxford University Press.

Norman, Richard (1991), "Socialism, Feminism and Equality", in Peter Osborne (ed.), *Socialism and the Limits of Liberalism,* London: Verso.

Nussbaum, Martha and Jonathan Glover, (eds.) (1995), *Women, Culture and Development: A Study of Human Capabilities,* Oxford: Oxford University Press.

Nussbaum, Martha and Amartya Sen, (eds.) (1992), *The Quality of Life,* Oxford: Oxford University Press.

Okin, Susan Moller (1989), *Justice, Gender, and the Family,* New York: Basic Books.

O'Neill, Onora (1977), "How Do We Know when Opportunities are Equal?", in M. Vetterling-Braggin et al. (eds.), *Feminism and Philosophy,* Totowa, NJ: Littlefield, Adams.

Parekh, Bhikhu (1996), "Minority Practices and Principles of Toleration", *International Migration Review,* Vol. 30, pp. 251–284.

Parekh, Bhikhu (1997), "Equality in a Multi-cultural Society", in Jane Franklin (ed.), *Equality,* London: IPPR, pp. 123–155.

Rae, Douglas et al. (1981), *Equalities,* Cambridge, MA: Harvard University Press.

Rawls, John (1971), *A Theory of Justice,* Oxford: Oxford University Press.

Rawls, John (1993), *Political Liberalism*, New York: Columbia University Press.

Schaar, John H. (1967), "Equality of Opportunity, and Beyond", in J.R. Pennock and J. Chapman (eds.), *Nomos IX: Equality*, New York: Atherton Press.

Sen, Amartya (1992), *Inequality Re-examined*, Oxford: Oxford University Press.

Smith, Steven R. and Mike O'Neill (1997), "'Equality of What?' and the Disability Rights Movement", *Imprints*, Vol. 2, pp. 123–144.

Van Parijs, Philippe (1995), *Real Freedom for All*, Oxford: Oxford University Press.

Walzer, Michael (1985), *Spheres of Justice*, Oxford: Blackwell.

Weber, Max (1958), "Class, Status, Party", in H.H. Gerth and C. Wright Mills (eds. and trs.), *From Max Weber: Essays in Sociology*, New York: Oxford University Press.

Williams, Bernard (1962), "The Idea of Equality", in P. Laslett and W.G. Runciman (eds.), *Philosophy, Politics and Society: Second Series*, Oxford: Blackwell.

Young, Iris Marion (1990), *Justice and the Politics of Difference*, Princeton: Princeton University Press.

Chapter 3

THE COMMON GOOD OF
A PLURALIST SOCIETY

Patrick Riordan SJ

In recent years, Ireland has seen the publication of two Education Bills and the enactment of a *Universities Act* (1997). Despite this remarkable productivity by the legislature, there has not been much political debate about education. The fundamental question as to the ends of education, and the kind of citizenship which the educational system is designed to foster, have not received much attention. Heated political debate tends to focus on structural and institutional matters, whereby concerned groups voice their interest in having access to the processes of decision-making and the levers of power. This is indeed a legitimate item on the agenda for the political process, but it is remarkable if it becomes the whole of the agenda of public debate. A society must be concerned about its own reproduction and development, as these are achieved through the system of education. We have to debate the question of the ultimate purposes of education, and this must include a consideration of the models of the human person and citizen which are its intended products. These in turn cannot be adequately considered without an attempt to articulate the ideals of political culture and the quality of social, economic and public life which we wish to bring about.

What kind of society do we wish to construct? What kind of politics do we desire? What are the characteristics which we would wish our public life and political culture to exhibit, and which qualities would we want citizens to exemplify in their participation in public debate and political process? These are the questions guiding my reflections in this chapter. In other words, what is, or can be, the common good of a pluralist society with democratic institutions? My object in this chapter is to attempt to articulate the values that could be the object of an overlapping consensus in a society which is otherwise diverse in relation to fundamental religious and moral commitments. I begin with a consideration of issues arising in the context of education policy, and show how these can be opened up to more fundamental questions about the goals of society. In the second part I will draw from a North American debate on issues of education in order to sharpen further the issues for our political culture. In the third part I will outline the political assumptions behind my delineation of the problem, and in the final fourth part briefly sketch the values which could be part of an overlapping consensus, and which could in turn guide thinking on the ultimate purposes of education within a pluralist and democratic society.

EDUCATING CITIZENS FOR IRELAND'S FUTURE

It would be an unfair exaggeration to say that there has been no debate in Ireland on these ultimate questions. The public hearings organised by Minister Niamh Bhreathnach in preparation for her Education Bill allowed the airing of concerns about the purposes of education and its intended product. However, while many concerned parties took advantage of the opportunity, little real public debate ensued. There has also been a renewed academic interest in education among professionals in Ireland, and a number of publications have appeared. While these may have stimulated debate in academic circles, little impact has been made on the public consciousness.[1] The *Universities Act*, while radically reorganising the institutional and legal structures governing university life in Ireland, also managed to address the question of purpose. But here again it is remarkable that this section of the Act has been the least problematic, and the least discussed. And yet the question at stake here is a most important one for a society, and especially one confronted by enormous changes, such as Ireland is at the turn of the century.

---

[1] For example, see Hogan (1995), reviewed by D. O'Grady in *Studies* 85 (1996), pp. 279–284, and by Tuohy, D. in *Milltown Studies* 38 (1996) pp. 131–138. See also *The Role of the University in Society: Proceedings of the Conference held in Dublin Castle on 20–21 May 1994*, Dublin: National University of Ireland.

Section 12 of the 1997 *Universities Act* lists 11 different purposes which the University might serve. It is to be noted that the formulation does not see this list as exhaustive; rather, it asserts:

The objects of a university shall include:

(a) to advance knowledge through teaching, scholarly research and scientific investigation,

(b) to promote learning in its student body and in society generally,

(c) to promote the cultural and social life of society, while fostering and respecting the diversity of the university's traditions,

(d) to foster a capacity for independent critical thinking amongst its students,

(e) to promote the official languages of the State, with special regard to the preservation, promotion and use of the Irish language and the preservation and promotion of the distinctive cultures of Ireland,

(f) to support and contribute to the realisation of national economic and social development,

(g) to educate, train and retrain higher level professional, technical and managerial personnel,

(h) to promote the highest standards in, and quality of, teaching and research,

(i) to disseminate the outcomes of its research in the general community,

(j) to facilitate lifelong learning through the provision of adult and continuing education, and

(k) to promote gender balance and equality of opportunity among students and employees of the university.[2]

I reproduce this section in full, because as a piece of recent legislation it allows me the possibility of discussing the quality of our political reflection on fundamental questions concerning our ultimate social

---

[2] *Universities Act* (1997), p. 11.

objectives. I wish to highlight a number of issues which arise from this text, and which can open up more radical questions.

Knowledge and Education

Many traditional educators are consoled to find that the advancement of knowledge and research and the promotion of learning head the list of objects of the university, although it must be admitted that no prioritisation is intended in the ordering of the list. Fearful that the demands of the economy and the labour market's need for skilled workers has become too influential in setting the agenda for education, traditionalists will be reassured by this reaffirmation of the value of knowledge and learning. One would almost expect the phrase "... for its own sake" to be added to the last sentence. But the Act does not presume that knowledge is for its own sake. It gives no clear reason why knowledge and research are valuable for our society. Why are knowledge and learning and research to be fostered? Is it for their own sake, or for the sake of something else? In either case, what reasons can be given to make sense of this and to justify the dedication of significant social and economic resources to this purpose? The Act does not answer this question, but it is not clear that, in our political culture, there is an overlapping consensus on an answer to the question either.

Vocational Function

Alluded to in the previous paragraph is the tension between the vocational and the educational functions of the university. The training of students in the skills and expertise required in the range of professions from engineering to teaching is a recognised part of the university's role, but it is in tension with its other roles. Everyone can see easily enough the rationale behind the training of good technicians, scientists, lawyers, doctors and architects, but how do we explain the importance of educating good people and good citizens? The latter cannot be the object of certification, and yet a society which is organised politically in a democratic system must be at least as concerned about the quality of its voters as it is about the quality of its pharmacists. Yet, while reflecting this tension, the wording of the Act suggests no way of managing the tension. This remains as a task for political discourse.

Social and Cultural Roles

An innovation in the Act is the assertion of responsibility on the part of the university towards society. Against any tendency there might be for the university to become an ivory tower, comfortably isolated from the society around it, the Act imposes on the university the obligation "to promote the cultural and social life of society". Admittedly, this is qualified with a clause which allows the diversity of the university's traditions to be fostered and respected. In a further listed object, in which the promotion of the Irish language is given special place, the obligation to preserve and promote the distinctive cultures of Ireland is imposed. But which cultures are to be preserved and promoted? All which can be identified as existing in Ireland, including the culture of political violence? And is the cultural and political life of society to be understood also in a non-normative fashion? Rave concerts depending on availability of ecstasy tablets have become part of youth culture: is the university to promote this also? But if not, what criteria are available to delimit the extent of the obligation which the Act imposes on the university?

Recognition of the diversity of cultures seems impossible without at the same time facing the fact that cultures can be in conflict with one another. Different cultural and political traditions view one another as opponents and the ideals and purposes they pursue are mutually incompatible. And yet the Act speaks as if it were possible for the university to promote all cultures. How ought the university, and indeed the society in general, deal with this social and political reality of conflicted diversity? What contribution can the university make to society's handling of conflict? These are the fundamental questions which arise, and which ought to be part of a background discussion of the aims of education.

Political and Economic Roles

There is a delightful irony in the way in which the Act identifies the cultivation of independent critical thinking amongst students as a purpose of the university, while at the same time requiring the university to "support and contribute to the realisation of national economic and social development". It appears as if the university is simply to accept the goals of national economic and social development having been set by some other entity (the government perhaps) and to contribute to the national endeavour in a supportive capacity. But could its contribution be critical? Is it part of its function to provide independent critical thinking on the direction and goals of economic and social development? Should it hold up for analysis the social and economic trends which are the consequences of political decisions and apply its critical faculties? And if so, what criteria should it rely on for the critique of national development? Can it use principles of social justice other than those adopted in the national project?

This brief review of one section of the *Universities Act* has highlighted basic questions which cannot be avoided in any serious attempt to articulate the purposes of education and to delineate the kind of product of the educational system which is envisaged. I move on now to consider a debate from North America, in which similar questions were addressed.

CULTIVATING HUMANITY

Martha Nussbaum (1997) has recently published a book in an attempt to defend developments in North American College education against the kinds of criticisms made, for example, by Allan Bloom (1987). In the course of her defence, she manages to sketch out the role which education should play in training citizens who are capable of participating in a richly diverse society and political system. Her main focus is on the role of education in producing citizens. This is a classical focus, as befits a scholar of Aristotle and of Stoicism. Her title, *Cultivating Humanity*, is borrowed from Seneca. If university education produces citizens, then the most fundamental question in any attempt to specify the purpose of education is to identify what the good citizen in the present day should be and should know. Diversity of culture, background and lifestyle characterises the contemporary world. To be capable of contributing to resolving the kinds of problems which arise in this world of differences requires capacities for dialogue in search of intelligent co-operative solutions. Cultivation of these capacities is the aim of a liberal, as distinct from a technical or vocational, education.[3] Nussbaum subscribes to the Stoic ideal of the "world citizen" and the "cultivation of

---

[3] Nussbaum (1997), p. 9.

humanity" as the aim of liberal education. She lists three capacities which are essential. The first is the capacity for critical examination of oneself and one's traditions, so that one can live the "examined life", in Socrates' sense. This means the ability to subject inherited meanings and values and authorities to critical review. A second ability is the capacity to understand oneself as sharing a common humanity with all other men and women. While local identity and loyalty is easily known and expressed, it requires a deliberate process of education to inculcate the awareness of a solidarity with others of differing racial and national backgrounds, religious affiliation, and with other differences including gender and sexuality. The third ability which she emphasises is narrative imagination, namely, the ability to think and imagine oneself in the place of another, and to understand the emotions and wishes and desires of those very different from ourselves. She admits that these three abilities do not exhaust the requirements for intelligent citizenship, but they are central to the role to be played by a liberal education in preparing citizens for today's world.[4]

If people are to be capable of acting as responsible citizens in a very complex world, they must have learned to live alongside differences of many kinds. They must have learned to understand themselves and their traditions as situated in a plural and interdependent world.[5] This means that they must be capable of operating at two levels: they must be comfortable in their own tradition and be at home with their distinctive identity; on the other hand, they must be capable of meeting others from differing backgrounds in the public forum on a basis of understanding, respect and tolerance. There is a tension between these two, which is not always well managed. One tendency is to regard the public forum as a market place or bargaining table, where the differing identity and interest groups meet in order to compete for power. Nussbaum contrasts her ideal of the world-citizen and its corresponding form of politics with that of interest-group politics:

> The world-citizen view insists on the need for all citizens to understand differences with which they need to live; it sees

---

4 Ibid. pp. 9–14.

5 Ibid. pp. 298f.

> citizens as striving to deliberate and to understand across
> these divisions. It is connected with a conception of demo-
> cratic debate as deliberation about the common good.[6]

Debate and dialogue is contrasted with bargaining and deal-making.[7]

As a defence of a form of education, Nussbaum's book is somewhat anecdotal, relying on descriptions of what is being done in
various universities. She includes a number of universities which
have strong religious affiliations, including the Catholic Notre Dame,
and the Mormon Brigham Young University. She notes that colleges
and universities with religious affiliation have a dual mission: "advancing higher education in a pluralistic democracy, and perpetuat-
ing their specific traditions".[8] Her argument is that both tasks can be
fulfilled and that for both to be done well the essentials of world-
citizenship must be present. These essential qualities are: first, the
ability to reflect critically on oneself and one's own tradition; second,
the ability to understand oneself as bound by ties of recognition and
concern with all other women and men; and third, the capacity to
imagine oneself in the shoes of another.

Critics of developments in liberal education, such as Allan Bloom,
are fearful that a fostering of tolerance for a plurality of religious and
philosophical traditions will lead to relativism among young people.
Brought up to show tolerance and respect for groups and ideas with
which their own tradition is in conflict, students are likely to regard
their own inherited convictions and value-commitments as merely
one possible candidate among many, without any superior claim to
truth or validity. The resulting culture would tend to homogenisa-
tion without any representation of strong religious or moral convictions, and the consequent elimination of the very plurality which was
the favoured quality of society. Nussbaum's rejoinder is to argue that
there is no necessary link between a fostering of plurality and relativism. The cultivation of understanding and tolerance for diversity
which is essential to the education of the world-citizen is not necessarily to the detriment of local and particular identity. Rather, the

---

[6] Ibid. p. 110.

[7] I deal with this contrast in Riordan (1996) (Chapter 9, "Discourse and the Process of Politics").

[8] Nussbaum (1997), p. 258.

sense of solidarity with others based on common humanity merely means that one must accept limits, in the name of reason and humanity, to what one would do in the name of some local or particular loyalty.

> The goal of producing world citizens is profoundly opposed to the spirit of identity politics, which holds that one's primary affiliation is with one's local group, whether religious or ethnic or based on sexuality or gender.[9]

This is a frequently reiterated theme in her book:

> . . . we need not give up our special affections and identifications, whether national or ethnic or religious; but we should work to make all human beings part of our community of dialogue and concern, showing respect for the human wherever it occurs, and allowing that respect to constrain our national or local politics.[10]

THE POLITICAL CONTEXT

Nussbaum is writing about education in a society and a world which is increasingly multicultural. Ireland is not as rich in variety as the United States of America, but neither is it homogeneous. The recent presidential election campaign provided plenty of evidence of that fact. Candidates competed on the basis of various appeals. One candidate appealed to the possibility of building bridges between the different communities on the island which are in conflict with one another. Another candidate evoked the possibility of restoring in some measure the vision of a traditional, Catholic Ireland with family values firmly rooted in the public culture. A third candidate played the Europe card very strongly, reminding the electorate that the political life of the country is not to be confined to the island alone, even if issues of Northern Ireland are included on the agenda. Voluntary work on behalf of children in extreme need was the background of a further candidate, who attempted to appeal to the compassion of the electorate for those on the margins of our society. A

---

[9] Ibid. p. 109.

[10] Ibid. pp. 60f.

fifth candidate — the only male one — had previously been in the public eye in relation to issues of crime and security, and had advocated especially the interests of victims of crime. This variety in the campaign does not exhaust the complexity of Irish society, but it is a convenient reminder that our society is not homogeneous. The fact that each of the candidates received some electoral support indicates that the images and ideals they projected are well dispersed in our culture. We are different; we are complex. What then is the basis of our co-operation in political and legal institutions? What can we be said to share, in terms of beliefs and values, which can be the basis of our public life? What is our common good?

John Rawls (1993) has used the term "overlapping consensus" to name this range of agreement in an otherwise diverse situation. In a pluralist society, in which citizens are divided by reasonable though incompatible religious, philosophical and moral doctrines, what basis can there be for their co-operation in maintaining a system of law and of government? The comprehensive philosophical or religious world-view of any one group as a basis for political and legal order could not expect to evoke allegiance from adherents of other comprehensive doctrines. It would seem that an overlapping consensus in support of the basic structures of a political and legal system could only be achieved by an articulation of that order which was not tied to any one comprehensive doctrine, yet was capable of receiving the support of all.

Within pluralist societies, which are made up of groups of differing and even conflicting religious and philosophical views, there is no possibility of achieving commitment by each citizen to a civil and political system if that system is identified with only one of the competing groups. There is need for a language, accessible to all citizens equally, to express the rationale of the civil and political order. Much of the literature in the contemporary political philosophical debate is devoted to finding and clarifying the necessary language. Dr Attracta Ingram of University College Dublin states the problem well: "as citizens of modern republics, we meet as strangers without a common good except whatever we can forge together for the advancement of our diverse ends".[11] Given this complexity in our social

---

[11] Ingram (1994), pp. 3f.

situation, there is a need to find common ground which could be a foundation on which to build political and legal arrangements, capable of enjoying the support of citizens who have differing moral and religious traditions and therefore diverse substantive ideals of human flourishing. In her book, she argues for a conception of rights rooted in the good of autonomy to fill the role of an agreed starting point. Autonomy refers to the idea of self-government, and it reflects a respect for free persons as capable of ruling themselves. The rights to be accorded persons as autonomous citizens would mark out those conditions and means which anyone would have to enjoy in order to live a meaningful and independent life.[12] Her approach finds echoes in other thinkers who address similar questions as to how agreement might be constructed in a situation in which disagreement on ends and purposes prevails. For instance, a common approach is to argue that people who otherwise have independent if not conflicting goals, will nonetheless be prepared to co-operate to secure the conditions which must obtain if they are to succeed in achieving their goals. Thus John Rawls (1971) focused on primary social goods of liberties, rights and opportunities, income and wealth and the bases of self-respect, as goods which anyone would wish to have, whatever their ultimate ends turn out to be.[13] A comparable notion is that of need, defined as the conditions of life, speech and action: "such conditions include not only the conditions of physical-biological life, but also the conditions for technical and practical deliberation and the setting of goals".[14] Autonomy, need, primary social goods: these are various attempts to identify a common starting point from which agreement in an overlapping consensus could be achieved in a pluralist society. In the following section I sketch out a set of values which one could expect to belong to this overlapping consensus. It must be emphasised that the philosophical reasoning to justify these conclusions would have to be more elaborate than is attempted here.[15]

---

[12] Ibid. p. 112.

[13] Rawls (1971), sect. 15.

[14] Riordan (1991), p. 47.

[15] See Riordan (1991) and Riordan (1996) for more elaborate attempts.

SHARED VALUES

Quality of Public Debate and Political Process

What values might belong to the overlapping consensus? Since I began with a consideration of what we would desire as purpose and product of our educational system, it is useful to continue from there. My reflections allow me to list the qualities which we would wish citizens to exhibit in their participation in public debate. Since the context is the construction of agreement on shared institutions, as well as the maintenance and development of such political and legal institutions, citizens would have to possess the necessary skills of literacy and debate in order to participate. Fostering these skills would require considerable investment and co-ordination in order to ensure that everyone has access to the required levels of education and to the relevant means of communication in which public debate is conducted. However, the qualities required would have to go beyond minimal literacy skills. Citizens would have to exhibit attitudes of equal respect. They would have to be prepared to treat one another as having equal entitlement to speak. But they would also have to be prepared to listen and respond to one another, and to give an account of their own positions. The readiness to relinquish manipulative interventions, the willingness to allow others their opportunity to speak and to grant them a respectful hearing, and the submission to the discipline of accepting the better argument are acquired qualities which would tend to enable people to achieve the truth and validity which they pursue in the practice of debate.

Quality of Educational System

It is evident, however, that these qualities cannot be legislated for or commanded. Yet it must be part of the common good of such a political community that the educational system would cultivate such citizens, both by effective training and by modelling, through the example of actual practice in schools and universities, the kind of rational encounter which is desired. Accordingly, it will be part of the common good of concerned citizens in a liberal state that the practice of discourse be fostered, and that participants acquire the necessary willingness and attitudes for conducting argument. Concretely, this will mean not only a concern about the institutional means of excluding threats to open discussion, such as the protection of the freedom of speech, but more positively a concern for the quality of education of citizens in the practice of argument.

Quality of Legal Arrangements

The common good of citizens in a pluralist but liberal and democratic society will include other institutional and structural elements. Political and legal institutions are fundamental. Citizens may well pursue different ends and may disagree on what constitutes a good life; but they can have a common interest in there being a state which respects their liberties, which does not favour the interests of some over others, and which guarantees some measure of security and protection. The acknowledgement of rights, their protection in law, the rule of law and maintenance in practice of due process: these will be part of their common good.

Cultural Diversity

Part of the overlapping consensus among citizens participating in a liberal democratic system in a pluralist society would be an agreement that the diversity and plurality of the society is to be fostered, while at the same time the common conditions for public life are to be sustained. Education therefore would aim at both supporting the identity and distinctiveness of each group and sub-section of society, while at the same time inculcating the habits required for mutual understanding and tolerance and the functioning of common institutions. This would mean ensuring that all citizens and groups have access to the resources which are necessary for them to function well. So the political system, commensurate with the ideal of the world-citizen, would be designed to ensure that citizens receive the institutional, material and educational support that is required if they are to become capable of functioning well according to their own judgement and choice.

Quality of Economic Life

This is the area of social life which is liable to produce the most problems when it comes to translating agreed values into concrete policies or programmes of action. Nevertheless, it should be possible to delineate some values which could belong to the overlapping consensus. A major concern today is certainly the protection of the

physical and biological environment so that it in turn will continue to
be capable of sustaining human life and society. Another value
widely recognised today is participation: that all have the possibility
of participating according to their level of competence in society's
wealth-creating and -distributing activity. This means having access
to training, technology and markets. At this level of abstraction, it is
also possible to get agreement that work tasks be so designed and
organised that they are compatible with workers' health and welfare,
as well as dignity. An open market for goods and services ensures
competition, and therefore some element of choice for the consumer
as well as some safeguard against inefficiency. Structures and institutions which maintain open markets and which facilitate ease of
access to them would be valued in a pluralist society.

Quality of Social Welfare and Health Care

Nussbaum (1990) has elsewhere elaborated the implications of the
requirements that citizens have the material support necessary to
ensure they are capable of functioning well according to their own
judgement and choice. Focusing on what the citizen requires in order
to function well, she maintains that a state's welfare system should
not be understood primarily as residual, picking up those who have
fallen through various nets and have not been able to fend for themselves. Rather, it should be understood as aimed at facilitating all
citizens by means of a comprehensive support scheme of health care
and welfare support for their functioning in a range of areas over a
complete life. Treating citizens as free and equal means moving all of
them across a threshold into capability to choose well, should the
available resources permit this. People must be allowed scope to determine for themselves how precisely they will realise the various
aspects of their good. Therefore it cannot be the concern of government to decide people's good for them, or to make them good. However, government does need some conception of what constitutes
good human functioning in order to create and sustain the appropriate conditions which enable people to identify and pursue their
own good. A lively, shared understanding of what constitutes good
human functioning therefore is a prerequisite for this purpose and it
would be part of the overlapping consensus in a pluralist society that
this shared understanding be fostered.

CONCLUSION

Any conclusions arrived at in these reflections are very tentative. Tentative, because the argument from the role of overlapping consensus in a pluralist society to the sort of values which might be expected to make up the content of the overlapping consensus would have to be elaborated and discussed at greater length. Furthermore, the articulated values would have to be tested in attempts to translate those values into policies, and such practical attempts may reveal unwelcome implications which do not arise at the abstract level. And they are tentative, most especially because the content of overlapping consensus is not to be determined by abstract philosophical reflection, but rather through the process of political debate and public discussion. All that academic reflection can offer for this public debate is the service of clarification of both method and argument. But in the last analysis, agreement on the values which animate and guide our political and economic life must be hammered out in a process of public discussion, such as the Justice Commission of the Conference of Religious of Ireland has stimulated and facilitated through a decade of Social Policy Conferences and related publications. Seán Healy and Brigid Reynolds, through their position papers, have offered for public scrutiny and review proposals on social policy which are rooted in an articulate set of values.[16] For their arguments to succeed, this set of values must be accepted in the wider political community and achieve overlapping consensus among diverse groups. The project is precisely what is required in an evolving Ireland which is becoming more and more conscious of its diversity and of its need for a public culture. The questions about education policy highlight the need for such a project and for a more extended reflection on the values and purposes guiding social, economic and political life.

REFERENCES

Bloom, A. (1987), *The Closing of the American Mind: How Higher Education has Failed Democracy and Impoverished the Souls of Today's Students*, New York: Simon and Schuster.

---

[16] See, for example, Reynolds and Healy (1992).

Hogan, P. (1995), *The Custody and Courtship of Experience: Western Education in Philosophical Perspective*, Dublin: Columba Press.

Ingram, A. (1994), *A Political Theory of Rights*, Oxford: Oxford University Press.

Nussbaum, M. (1990), "Aristotelian Social Democracy" in R.B. Douglass, G.M. Mara and H.S. Richardson (eds.), *Liberalism and the Good*, London: Routledge, pp. 203–52.

Nussbaum, M. (1997), *Cultivating Humanity: A Classical Defense of Reform in Liberal Education*, Cambridge, MA: Harvard University Press.

Rawls, J. (1971), *A Theory of Justice*, Oxford: Oxford University Press.

Rawls, J. (1993), *Political Liberalism*, New York: Columbia University Press.

Reynolds, B. and S. Healy (1992), "Participation: A Values Perspective" in B. Reynolds and S. Healy (eds.), *Power, Participation and Exclusion*, Dublin: Justice Commission, CMRS.

Riordan, P. (1991), *The Practical Philosophy of Oswald Schwemmer*, Lanham, MD: University Press of America.

Riordan, P. (1996), *A Politics of the Common Good*, Dublin: Institute of Public Administration.

The Role of the University in Society, Proceedings of the Conference held in Dublin Castle on 20–21 May 1994, Dublin: National University of Ireland.

Universities Act (1997), Dublin: Stationery Office.

Chapter 4

THE NEW INSTITUTIONALISM AND IRISH SOCIAL POLICY

Kieran Healy[1]

INTRODUCTION

Debate about policy-making in Ireland has taken a distinctly institutional turn in recent years. Arguments about this particular change or that specific development have given way to broader questions about how policy actually gets made, and by whom. This change can be traced to the emergence of a distinctive "social partnership" approach in the late 1980s. The extended debate over what that term should mean has put the relationships, rules and assumptions of the policy-making process under close scrutiny (see, for example, NESF, 1998).

This chapter reviews and discusses contemporary work in political sociology that bears directly on this issue. Known broadly as the "new institutionalism", it focuses on the role of state and societal institutions in the creation and implementation of policy. The argument has two strands. First, research into policy conflicts shows that the strategies, bargaining power and participation of interest groups are strongly affected by their institutional context, often regardless of the power that particular groups may have. Call this the *regulatory view* of institutions. Research in this vein speaks against the claim that success in political struggles is a simple function of a group's power, strength or support. Second, it is also possible to show that

[1] Thanks to Frank Dobbin and Seán Healy for helpful comments on an earlier version of this chapter.

preferences and goals are strongly shaped by institutions. Call this
the *constitutive view*. Research here examines the role that institutions
play in limiting the range of policies we consider and legitimating
the set of policies we implement. It speaks against the claim that
policy-making is a rational, even-handed process.

Both strands describe potentially invidious tendencies within the
policy-making process, and alert policy-makers to easily missed or
taken-for-granted aspects of that process which deserve to be explicitly analysed. There are many links and overlaps between regulatory
and cultural approaches, and I separate them here simply for ease of
presentation. In the following sections, I examine the different aspects of each one in more detail, drawing on the available literature.
Where appropriate, I point to examples and applications of these
ideas in the Irish case.

INTEREST GROUPS AND INSTITUTIONS

Interest Group Explanations

How should policy-making be understood? For a long time, explanations of both the process and outcomes of policy-making focused
on classes or interest groups, playing down the role of the state and
its institutions. Despite its size and importance, sociologists and political scientists tended to see the state as a place where conflict took
place rather than as a potentially independent player in that conflict.
There are optimistic and pessimistic versions of this view. Optimisti-
cally, government policy and state action are the outcome of persistent "contestation" between a diverse body of political parties and
interest groups who participate in politics (Dahl, 1977; Lipset, 1959).
Although not everyone is equally represented, and not all interest
groups are equally powerful, politics is nevertheless a healthy competition between elites who are responsive to the needs of their supporters, within the framework of party democracy. Taken further,
politics may be seen as functionally integrated with society, acting as
a "system . . . for the authoritative allocation of values" (Easton, 1965:
56). Pessimistically, the government and the state bureaucracy are
either the instrument of the capitalist class (Miliband, 1969) or a
structure functioning to reproduce capitalism more or less automatically (Poulantzas, 1973). But both these pluralist and Marxist ac-

counts see the state as subordinate to other groups within society. The state provides an *arena* for policy conflict and a set of *mechanisms* for policy implementation.

A more sophisticated version of this view can be found in rational choice theory. This view recognises the need to explain the shape these mechanisms — these institutions — take. It does so by arguing that, in pursuit of policy goals, actors make a rational choice to enter into binding agreements that will serve their interests. Rational choice theorists argue that institutions are best understood as solutions to problems of collective action where people would be worse off in the absence of some agreement or sanction. By providing effective sanctions against unwanted behaviour and good information about the likely behaviour of others, institutions allow policial actors to solve problems efficiently.

Rational choice theory attends closely to the individual origins of collective problems and solutions, and describes ways that strategic actors can get from the former to the latter. It thereby captures an important aspect of the business of politics. However, it does so with the help of assumptions about individual choice and calculation which are unsatisfactory on both theoretical and empirical grounds (Mansbridge, 1990; Cook and Levi, 1990; Kahneman et al., 1982). Although rational choice explanations are not incapable of explaining the emergence and persistence of inefficient institutions (see, for example, North, 1982; 1990), the literature in this area tends to see institutions as relatively malleable objects which benefit all those who subscribe to them. In fact, "institution" is almost too strong a word: "convention" is more accurate.[2] This view has little to say about how some conventions are chosen over others. Chance may explain the side of the road we drive on, but "contemplating plausible examples . . . one is more inclined to point to the distribution of power" (Hollis 1994: 137).

---

[2] An analysis of convention (a particularly clear account is Lewis (1969)) shows how conventions will arise when all parties have a common interest in there being a rule to ensure co-ordination, none has a conflicting interest, and none will deviate. Examples include the convention of driving on the left. Everyone has an interest in driving on one side of the road or the other. Which side is chosen does not matter, so long as everybody chooses the same side.

The Institutionalist View

Recently, a body of theoretical and empirical work has appeared that rejects these views as incomplete. This "new institutionalism," as it has come to be called, offers a substantially different understanding of the role of the state in social policy-making. Instead of being a place where other people's problems are thrashed out, the state is seen as a potentially autonomous *actor* in these conflicts. Instead of a mechanism which simply puts policy into practice, the state bureaucracy is seen as a complex group of *institutions* with the potential to "affect individual action and collective outcomes by conditioning both the distribution of power and the definition of interests" within society (Hall and Taylor, 1994: 3). Instead of being rational solutions to common problems, policy-making institutions are seen as recalcitrant objects that benefit some players more than others. "In this perspective," says Theda Skocpol,

> states matter not simply because of the goal-oriented activities of state officials. They matter because their organizational configurations, along with their overall patterns of activity, encourage some kinds of group formation and collective political actions (but not others), and make possible the raising of certain political issues (but not others). (Skocpol, 1985: 21)

Although writers in this tradition share a commitment to understanding policy conflicts and their outcomes with reference to the active role of the state, their approach to institutions varies. I make a broad distinction between those who see institutions primarily as rules or constraints on the one hand, and those who see them as cultural products or cognitive structures on the other. The former argue that the rules of politics are themselves highly political. Rather than simply facilitating interest group or party competition, the rules of parliamentary procedure, departmental organisation or collective bargaining affect the strategies adopted by different parties, enhance or diminish their bargaining power and shape patterns of participation and exclusion. Comparative studies from this literature show how an institutional analysis can explain the differing strategies and success rates of otherwise similar interest groups. Persistent policy continuities within countries (and differences between them) also become understandable from this perspective.

Cultural approaches take a slightly different tack, probing more deeply into the long-term impact of institutions and policy-making on individual and group behaviour. The day-to-day reality of abstract rules is to be found in the taken-for-granted routines and understandings of those who work within them. Institutions therefore have an important *cognitive* component. Institutions tend to live longer than the people who make them up, which means they provide a ready-made environment within which discussion over policy takes place. As such, they tend to create cognitive commitments in the minds of policy-makers (Starr, 1987). Institutions carry the criteria which people use to assess a policy's success, or the procedures for assessing alternatives to it, or the methods for implementing decisions that flow from it. Any of these may become so taken-for-granted that they appear to be the only rational way of doing things. This in turn affects the range of alternatives that may be presented as "realistic" possibilities. Institutions provide an array of practices, categories, models and scripts which tend to be accepted as logically necessary, rational and natural, rather than historically contingent, symbolically legitimated and socially constructed (Meyer and Rowan, 1977).

INSTITUTIONS AS RULES AND CONSTRAINTS

Let us first examine the regulatory view. In recent years, a series of political scandals and legislative episodes have made "levelling the playing field" a rather hackneyed expression in Irish political life. The cliché contains a (proverbial) grain of truth, however. Ideally, in any competition both the arena and the rules should be neutral with respect to the outcome of the game. If we take this competitive metaphor seriously, then our institutions should serve to facilitate policy-making without doing anything to influence its outcome.

Political institutions do not generally attain this sort of neutrality, and it is not hard to see why. Peter Hall defines institutions as

> the formal rules, compliance procedures, and standard oper-
> ating practices that structure the relationship between indi-
> viduals in various parts of the polity and economy . . . they
> have a more formal status than cultural norms but one that
> does not necessarily derive from legal, as opposed to conven-
> tional standing. (Hall, 1986: 19)

On this definition, the institutional context includes "the rules of electoral competition, the structure of party systems, the relations amongst the various branches of government, and the structure and organization of economic actors like trade unions" (Thelen and Steinmo, 1992: 2). There are then three broad ways in which institutions tend to influence political outcomes: they affect the *strategies* adopted by players, they distribute *bargaining power* in unequal ways and they rule in advance on the criteria for *participation* in the policy-making process.

Strategies

We can assume for the moment that actors — political parties, interest groups, and so on — know what their goals are. (I return to this assumption below.) Trade unions seek wage increases for their members; employer associations want strike-free workplaces; political parties want special treatment for their supporters, and so on. The way these groups go about securing these goals will be affected by the institutional structure that they operate within.

In the simplest cases, differences in institutional design will merely shift the location of conflicts that would have happened anyway, without altering their substance or outcome. However, more interesting are those cases where the character, outcome and long-term influence of particular conflicts will vary along with their institutional expressions. For example, Linz (1994) offers a subtle analysis of the comparative strengths and weaknesses of presidential and parliamentary systems. He argues that the different systems strongly influence the character of many aspects of political life, including the tendency to political polarisation (higher in presidential systems) and the stability of cabinets (higher in parliamentary systems). Similarly, Hattam (1993) has shown how the constitutionally guaranteed power of the Supreme Court in the United States forced the American labour movement to move away from attempts to pass general labour laws and towards a more sectional strategy built around pressuring specific firms or industries. Realising the institutional problem, one union leader declared in 1894:

> You cannot pass a general eight-hour day without changing the constitution of the United States and the constitution of every state in the Union. . . . I am opposed to wasting our time

declaring for legislation being enacted for a time, possibly, after we are dead. (Adolph Strasser, quoted in Mann, 1993: 656)

In this case, the general conflict between capital and labour was significantly deflected by the power of the Supreme Court to overturn Congressional legislation. In the long run, the institutional push toward sectionalism provided by the courts impaired the ability of unions to organise collectively, form peak associations or negotiate with governments, as they more commonly do in Europe.

Bargaining Power

The strategy adopted by an organisation is tightly bound up with its relative bargaining power. This power is partly a function of the organisation's size and resources. However, similarly well-organised and resourceful pressure groups often have widely varying impacts on policy. Straightforward interest group theories are unable to explain why this happens. Immergut (1992a, 1992b) examines the efforts of doctors to influence legislation on health insurance in Sweden, France and Switzerland. She shows how the substance of the deals made by various groups in the different countries depended on the existence of "veto points" in the policy process. At different points within the executive, legislative and electoral arenas, physicians were able to intervene to affect the course of legislation. Immergut argues that "vetoes can be predicted from the partisan composition of these different arenas and from the rules transferring decision-making from one arena to the next" (Immergut, 1992b: 67). In Sweden, for example, "the political executive could count on decisions being routinely confirmed by the parliament" (ibid.). In this context, doctors found themselves at a disadvantage to employers and trade unions. In Switzerland, by contrast, the possibility existed of calling a referendum on controversial legislation. This gave interest groups room to move in the electoral arena, and doctors "found that they could use the referendum threat to gain concessions from policy-makers" (ibid: 68).

If the institutional landscape offers different leverage points where interest groups can act upon the state, the reverse is also true. Equivalent to an interest group's bargaining power is the state's *capacity* to intervene in different economic and social relations. Weir and Skocpol (1985) analyse the responses of Sweden, Britain and the United States to the Great Depression. They show how broadly similar groups — for example, left-wing governments in Sweden and Britain — developed different strategies because of the different state organisations they inherited. In Britain, the institutionalised power of the Treasury consistently foiled the Labour Government's attempts to institute new policy.

Hall (1986) illustrates this for more recent policy episodes. His argument is that

> different relationships between state, capital and labour influence policy choices in different countries, and account for the state's ability to implement some strategies rather than others. In Germany, the constitutionally guaranteed power of the Bundesbank to control monetary policy-makes it a powerful force in the German (and latterly the European) economy. Periodic bursts of annoyance in Ireland and elsewhere at the behaviour of Bundesbank officials, "mere civil servants" in the eyes of many observers, therefore have an institutional origin. German banks also have the right to hold equity in other firms, vote shares deposited with them and lend voting rights to other banks, powers which give them a direct and significant say in industrial policy. (Hall, 1986: 234–242)

Hall and others have generalised this argument about central bank independence. Central banks are generally highly inflation-averse. If they happen to be institutionally autonomous as well, they can implement their views by keeping the money supply tight (Cuikerman, 1992; Franzese, 1994). This has the effect of transferring control of an important part of economic policy out of the hands of elected representatives. Thus the range and capacity of the state is variable. An independent central bank may effectively work against the institution of which it is technically a part. Just as interest groups may be unable to intervene at the right points, states may find themselves unable to implement new policies for want of the proper institutional machinery, be it legal or administrative (Skocpol and Finegold, 1982).

Participation and Exclusion

"Were it necessary to draft a health insurance bill today, I would never come up with the insane idea of proposing our current system" says a Swiss politician in Immergut's (1992a) study. This sort of frustration is very common: much the same comment might be made about the Irish tax or social welfare systems. The name for this phenomenon is *path dependence*. Later events in the sequence of institutional development depend on earlier ones. Stephen Krasner puts the point nicely:

> once an historical choice is made it both precludes and facilitates alternative future choices. Political change follows a branching model. Once a particular fork is chosen, it is very difficult to get back on a rejected path. . . . Thus, even if there is widespread societal dissatisfaction with a particular set of institutions . . . the variable costs of maintaining the existing institutions may be less than the total costs of creating and maintaining new ones. (Krasner, 1984: 225; 235)

Institutions escape the intentions of their designers, persist over time and are used and adapted in *ad hoc* ways that may work against any tendency towards efficiency in the long run. It is usually impossible to rework arrangements from the ground up. Groups locked out of a process early on will probably find it very difficult to get involved later. Instead, actors are forced to use whatever is available in circumstances that might be very unsatisfactory.

The path-dependent nature of institutions means that they can decisively shape the conditions for political conflict and negotiation. A group's strategic options can be narrowed to nothing, or its bargaining power reduced to zero. Thelen and Steinmo (1992: 9) note that "reconfiguring institutions can save political actors the trouble of fighting the same battle again and again". Political actors are generally well aware of this: it is the reason why gerrymandering is so attractive and conflicts over constituency boundaries so hard-fought. But more is involved here than just the power to disenfranchise voters, or the outright denial of representation at a negotiating table. Manipulating the electoral system is a particularly obvious way to secure control over government, but the administrative apparatus of the state allows other institutional victories to be won in less obvious (though no less important) areas.

Policy-making institutions necessarily incorporate assumptions about who properly represents whom, who deserves to be represented and on what terms. Although these institutions come about in haphazard or even accidental ways, once in place they tend to assume a solidity and inevitability of their own. Morrissey's (1986) account of the emergence of a tripartite system of wage bargaining in Ireland during the 1960s shows that a number of alternatives were possible, given the attitudes and organisation of the State, ICTU and FUE. These actors were often unsure of what the right framework would look like, or even whether collective bargaining was a good idea at all. But despite this initial uncertainty, once in place these institutions affected both the motivation and the ability of policy-makers to question whether the needs of different groups — women, the poor or the unemployed, for example — were being adequately dealt with.

INSTITUTIONS AS CULTURE AND COGNITION

Most writers in the regulatory tradition treat interest groups as stable entities with well-defined (though often frustrated) goals. Faced with an institutional obstacle course, they do the best they can to implement their goals and pursue their interests. However, the fact that practices and assumptions become entrenched over time means that the relationship between individuals and institutions must be more complicated than this. The relatively permanent, naturalised setting provided by institutions affects how individuals think and make decisions (Douglas, 1986). Just as we do not choose our native language, we take the institutional environment as we find it, an apparently natural medium for policy-making and interest representation. This has implications for our understanding of interest groups and their preferences and goals:

> Once one opens the door . . . to historicity, power, and cross-cultural variation in the interpretation of information, it is a fairly small step from the regulatory view of institutions . . . to the constitutive one. (DiMaggio, 1994: 38)

Our own institutions of government and administration present themselves to us as rational entities, designed by individuals for the satisfaction of collective goals. Getting past this self-image can be difficult. The symbolic and ritual aspects of other societies are often obvious, but we are unaccustomed to thinking of ourselves in these terms.[3] DiMaggio (1994: 33) notes that "the more that Westerners view a country's citizens are 'different' from themselves, the more likely they are to deploy 'culture' to explain their behavior". In the following sections, I discuss three aspects of cultural approaches to policy-making: the study of *cognitive commitments*, the *construction of preferences*, and the role of ritual and symbols in the *legitimation of practices and decisions*.

Cognitive Commitments

Recent work in the sociology of culture has concentrated on the cognitive processes and practical actions of individuals and groups.[4] This is in contrast to the tendency to see culture as a set of norms or values, passively acquired through socialisation, which constrain actors in various ways. Rather than constraining otherwise rational actors, aspects of culture form the basis for judgement and analysis. This throws the nature and influence of institutions into a new light. We have already seen how institutions are resistant to change. This persistence may be explained by reference to the physical sunk costs of investment, administration or technology. However,

> these are not the only, or the most important, factors. Institutionalized arrangements are reproduced because individuals often cannot even conceive of appropriate alternatives (or because they regard as unrealistic the alternatives they can imagine). Institutions do not just constrain options: they establish the very criteria by which people discover their preferences. In other words, some of the most important sunk costs are cognitive. (DiMaggio and Powell, 1991: 11)

---

[3] This is particularly true for those institutions that explicitly deny that they have any cultural aspects: formal organisations, legal institutions, science and so on. This division into instrumental and non-instrumental action and institutions has long been replicated in sociological research. For a critique see Dobbin (1994a).

[4] "Although *cognition* sometimes refers to the full range of mental activity, we follow current usage in distinguishing between cognition, on the one hand, and affective or evaluative processes on the other. By *cognition* we refer to both reasoning and the pre-conscious grounds of reasoning: classifications, representation, scripts, schemas, production systems, and the like." (DiMaggio and Powell, 1991: 35. Emphasis in original.)

Empirical work in this tradition helps bring down to earth what might otherwise sound like rather abstract claims about the effect of institutions and systems of categorisation. For example, the essays collected in Alonso and Starr (1987) examine the development of the authoritative economic categories created by American statisticians. Perlman (1987) discusses the construction of national accounting systems in the post-war United States. He argues that the dominance of Keynesian ideas significantly influenced the way the system was put together. In particular, all government expenditure was treated as consumption and none as investment. Although the accounts were presented as an objective picture of the economy, classificatory decisions depended on *a priori* economic theory more than anything else. For this reason Simon Kuznets (one of the originators of national accounting methods) argued that instead of reporting one figure for gross national product, the US government should report a group of measures based on varying definitions. Kuznets emphasised that raw economic data required "considerable adjustment and purification" before it could be made relevant to economic concepts and therefore meaningful (quoted in Starr, 1987: 43). But this process inevitably involved philosophical and theoretical choices which were themselves not dictated by the data. Thus, he complained,

> [The 1947 estimate of US national income] recognizes families living in their houses as transactor groups, although it excludes illegal firms which are more obviously a group of transactors; it classifies retention of product by farmers as a transaction, but does not classify tax collection by government as a transaction representing charges for services rendered. One may agree with these decisions or not; there is no sign that the system of accounts affected them in any way. (Quoted in Perlman, 1987: 148)

The point here, as Starr argues (1987: 53ff), is that the arbitrariness of these decisions is quickly forgotten. They become the natural and legitimate categories for the analysis and evaluation of policy, creating cognitive commitments in the minds of individuals who use them. Commenting on a similar set of accounting decisions over the measurement of unemployment, Starr says: "We have, in effect, bound ourselves collectively to think of the social phenomenon of unemployment — its magnitude, trends, distribution — in the way that statistical agencies and commissions have settled upon."

Once institutionalised, systems of classification can feed back into the policy process in subtle ways. Starr describes how the automatic use of cost of living adjustments (COLAs) based on the consumer price index (CPI) began to be used in labour contracts in the 1950s and 1960s and then later in the calculation of social security payments. Over time, this practice of index-linking incomes to the CPI became automatic. It made wage negotiation easier. However, by the 1970s the CPI was significantly overstating inflation because it inadequately measured housing costs. Thus, the real value of any benefits arising from COLAs jumped substantially. The result was that people whose incomes were in some way linked to the CPI did much better than those who were not, thanks to the automatic process of adjustment built into the system. Starr estimates that the incomes of about half the population of the United States are directly affected by the CPI. During the late 1970s, the incomes of that half grew at the expense of the unprotected half.

Clearly, classification systems matter. It is a mistake to imagine either that they are by nature objective or that they merely describe the way the world is. Once established, classification schemes highlight some things and ignore or miss others. When put into practice, these schemes can independently affect the reality they describe. "In this case," comments Starr,

> even though it was widely known that the CPI misrepresented the inflation rate, real political consequences were felt because of the index's behavior. Not only did it redistribute income; it helped to raise inflation and panic the Carter administration into its ill-fated credit controls". (Starr 1987: 56)

Preferences and Goals

We are now in a position to examine the origin of preferences and goals, or at least one important aspect of it. It should be clear by now that interest groups are not simply "out there" waiting to be recognised or discovered. Classification by the state or other organisations can certainly hide or eliminate groups in society, but it may also create entirely new ones. Racial classifications provide a good example.

Starr (1992) describes the disappearance of mulattoes as a social category in the United States. Recognised legally and socially as a distinctive group in the early part of the nineteenth century, they became more subject to political attacks with the approach of the Civil
War. By the end of the nineteenth century, dominant whites had
ceased to make a distinction between lighter and darker skinned
black people. So had the individuals themselves, as they came to see
themselves as black. Although nothing about the pigmentation of
particular individuals changed, the reordering of their classification
was tied up with a reorganisation of their social and political interests. The process worked in both directions: Ignatiev (1995) describes
"how the Irish became white" in the US at around the same time as
mulattoes were becoming black.

Examples such as this make it clear that socially constructed categories may have enormous impacts on the outlook, interests and
life-chances of particular individuals. It is not difficult to think of
other institutional classifications that have exercised a similar force.
The condition of illegitimacy, for instance, is no longer recognised in
Irish law. At its height, however, people falling into this category
found that their social and economic opportunities and interests
were significantly influenced by it. Prior to the divorce referendum,
the same was true for those classed as legally separated. None of
these categories are in any way natural, and none of them arise from
pre-constituted interest groups. Rather, the reverse is true: institutions create categories of people who then go about defining their
interests (such as demanding the right to divorce).

As mentioned already, these phenomena are easier to grasp when
we look at others or at our past selves. There is a strong temptation
to believe that *now* we have happened upon the ideal, rational
scheme. But the evidence does not bear this out. All sorts of institutional categories have come and gone, despite their apparently en-
during — even sacred — quality at any given moment. Historians
often catch the strangeness of dead categories, though they tend not
to push the implications of this through to the present. For example,
Lee (1989: 341–365; 540–643) gives a perceptive account of policy-
making in Ireland since the foundation of the state. He is sensitive to
the hold that particular measures of progress had over the minds of
civil servants. He sardonically dissects the policy contributions of
those civil servants in the grip of "the Finance view" of the world.

The catalogue of abuse he presents from one such Department of Finance report makes sorry reading, especially given that the authors assumed they were engaged in "judicial and scientific" analysis (ibid.: 564–5).[5] Lee argues that the *Programme for Economic Expansion* was the first policy document to break out of the "strait jacket of the balance of payments", which had hitherto acted as a yardstick for the health of the Irish economy (ibid.: 346). Framing his discussion in terms of "the quality of the official mind", Lee very accurately describes the depth of cognitive and emotional commitment to particular policy formulae found within the Department of Finance in the 1940s:

> it would be quite unhistorical to call Finance officials, with James Dillon in 1950, "the 'con men' par excellence of recent times". Precisely because Finance was a seething cauldron of emotion, Finance men were *not* conscious fakirs. They passionately believed in their mission to save Ireland from profligacy. . . . The Finance mind was a repository of revealed truth. One is constantly struck by the failure of Finance memoranda to appeal to either systematic historical or systematic comparative reasoning. . . . Here were no "scientific" physicians and surgeons. Here were crusaders for truth, valiantly defending the ramparts of rectitude against the assaults of the unholy and the unclean. (Lee 1989: 572)

Lee's analysis of Irish institutions jibes nicely with the Durkheimian sociological tradition (Durkheim, 1995; Douglas, 1986), although of course he does not draw on it explicitly. He recognises the sacred quality that particular ideas and institutions may have, and grasps the violence with which they are often defended. However, Lee places this discussion of the "official mind" under the general heading of "Intelligence". This is a little unfair. There is no reason to believe that the civil servants of two generations ago were any less intelligent than the ones we have today. Their writings may seem misguided and their vocabulary outdated, but this has less to do with their native intelligence than with the categories they were

---

[5] The report Lee cites criticises its opponents for "irrational instability of judgement", "Windy polemics", "A compact of fallacies" and "The public overthrow of the seventh commandment".

thinking through. We no longer find those categories convincing, or even worthy of serious consideration. But it would be complacent to assume that whereas *they* were simply misguided, *we* face reality head on. In the next section, I discuss a branch of neo-institutionalist research that takes the scepticism we feel towards foreign or outdated institutions and applies it to our own worldview.

Ritual, Legitimation and Myth

When describing national plans and programmes, historians and political scientists will often say something like the following:

> The modifications [to the *Programme for Economic Development*] presumably partly reflect its own psychological impact, which succeeded in substituting hope for despair, at least among the policy-makers themselves. (Lee, 1989: 346)

> As an economic plan, the First Programme was fairly skeletal, its importance being primarily psychological, as "the absence of such a programme tends to deepen the all too prevalent mood of despondency about the country's future". (Morrissey, 1986: 82; quotation from *Economic Development*)

A cultural approach suggests that this "psychological" impact is in fact an aspect of the institutional production of legitimacy. Policy documents are simultaneously instrumental and symbolic. Regardless of its content, simply *having* a plan goes a long way toward securing elusive but vital "confidence" or "good faith". Legitimacy emerges from the myths and rituals that the state builds around its activities. Calling these activities "cultural" does not imply that they are without substance or carry no real effects. This charge is itself a product of the false distinction between the strictly cultural and the strictly instrumental. Planning documents and policy instruments distribute resources and so obviously have real effects on people. However, they also serve to mark symbolically the legitimacy of the state's behaviour.

The relevance of the constitutive approach to institutions is that it gives us the tools we need to analyse our present-day policy-making institutions as though they were foreign to us. The modern foundation of this approach is found in the work of Berger and Luckmann (1966) and has been systematically worked out by John Meyer and his associates. On this view, what needs to be investigated is the "process by which a given set of units and a pattern of activities come to be normatively and cognitively held in place, and practically taken for granted as lawful" (Meyer et al., 1987: 13).

Again, this very general formulation can be grasped through a number of empirical studies. Evidence can be found in cross-national and over-time analyses of policy adoption. By examining the industrial policy-making histories of France, Britain and the United States, Dobbin (1993, 1994b) shows that variation in national conceptions of economic rationality led to different constructions of economic problems and different solutions. Each country had a particular view of industrial policy which was falsified by the great depression of the 1930s. In response, countries simply reversed their policies in an attempt to reverse the downturn. In each country, groups from across the political spectrum accepted the traditional "policy paradigm" (Hall, 1993) before the depression and then came to support a new (and opposite) policy during it. In the end, traditional industrial policy was exonerated from any blame for the depression, but

> the fact that each nation came to believe in the virtue of whatever policy happened to be in effect when recovery began supports [the] argument that haphazard economic vacillations play an important role in determining which policy strategies become constructed as economically efficacious. This also tends to undermine the realist/utilitarian view, which suggests that policy improves over time as rational policymakers learn more about universal economic laws from experience, because wildly inconsistent policies won favor in different contexts. (Dobbin, 1993: 47)

It is important to note the difference between Dobbin's argument and those such as Weir and Skocpol's (1985) cited above. The latter see institutional obstacles frustrating the efforts of policy-makers. Dobbin makes the deeper claim that different countries had different causal models about what policies were effective. Thus, "shared cultural meaning, as it is institutionalised in public policies and state structures, influences the pragmatic solutions groups envision to such instrumental problems as economic growth" (Dobbin, 1993: 49). Policy-makers interpreted economic events in terms of these models.

DiMaggio and Powell (1983) argue that individual organisations will grab culturally validated practices from their environment in order to enhance their legitimacy in the eyes of their peers, competitors or the state. They call this process "institutional isomorphism". Organisations either voluntarily adopt these practices or jump on bandwagons, copying apparently successful practices in order to be seen as successful themselves. The state may also impose on organisations: those who fail to adopt the innovation risk losing their legitimacy. For example, the state might decide that it will only entertain policy proposals if they are submitted in a particular format.[6] This forces interest groups to outline their arguments under headings preferred by the state. Policy gets discussed in these terms, with everyone being forced to accept the preferred terms as a condition of continued participation.

This institutional copycat effect has been well documented. Tolbert and Zucker (1983) studied the spread of municipal civil-service reforms carried out in the United States between 1880 and 1935. These reforms were designed to rationalise government employment. The authors found that local authorities which had functional needs for improved authority were the first to adopt the reforms. However, once these reforms were generally believed to be modern and rational, all kinds of municipalities adopted the reforms, even though they had no real need for them. By adopting the package, a municipality signalled to the wider world that it deserved to be taken seriously as a modern, well-administered organisation.

A similar branch of research in this area traces the diffusion of affirmative action policies and grievance procedures across US companies since the 1960s (Edelman, 1990; Sutton et al., 1994). These studies have found that such policies became socially constructed as being necessary to firms, to the point where it was unacceptable for a large, modern company not to have one.

The production of consensus happens between states as well as within them. Political economists recognise the existence of a "Washington consensus" on policy reform for developing countries. This is a list of fiscal and monetary policies that, essentially, amounts to a recipe that states are required to follow before they are taken

---

[6] This happened with submissions to the *Partnership 2000* negotiations.

seriously by the United States, the World Bank or the IMF (Williamson, 1994). One of its proponents regards it "as embodying the common core of wisdom embraced by all serious economists" (ibid.: 18). Commenting on this, Toye (1994: 39ff) argues that the consensus functions as an "Empowering Myth", and notes that "there seems to be some conflation here of what economists believe with what is economic truth".

CONCLUSION

Concluding his analysis of the energetic state-building efforts of Irish politicians between 1919 and 1923, Tom Garvin comments that political systems are

> devices, or constitutional machines, designed by human beings for human beings to live in; they are also normally designed to suit some human beings more than others. . . . They are artificial, not natural, entities and are well or badly designed. (Garvin, 1996: 196)

Garvin is right to stress that political and legal institutions are made and not born, and that they can be made to serve some interests rather than others. In this chapter I reviewed two strands of sociological literature that pursue this insight. The regulatory approach discussed in the first part of the chapter describes the ways in which institutions influence the outcomes of policy conflicts. Both the internal organisation of the state and the structure of its relationship to other parts of society can be shown to influence decisively the strategies and bargaining power of policy-makers, and the capacity of the state to intervene in conflicts. It follows that in any policy debate, special attention should be paid to the institutional arena within which it is being fought. This involves asking questions such as: What special advantages does this arena confer on the different players? Who does it rule out from participation? To what degree are the strategies of any of the players related to the institution in question? What are the historical origins of present-day frameworks?

The cultural approach described in the second half of the chapter is more thoroughgoing in its commitment to the idea that institutions are "artificial, not natural, entities". Writers in this field reject the claim "that modern institutions are transparently purposive and that we are in the midst of an evolutionary progression toward more efficient forms" (Dobbin, 1994a: 138). Rather than taking the claims of modern institutions at face value, empirical applications of the new institutionalism have emphasised their socially constructed and historically contingent qualities. This leads us to ask deeper questions about the direction of policy and the assumptions that guide it. The history of policy-making often reveals that conflicts which seemed important at the time in fact took place within a framework of shared assumptions about the state, economy and society. When these assumptions are no longer plausible, the details of the disagreement become irrelevant to us. We see both sides relying on now defunct concepts. If we see it in the past, we should also be looking for it in the present: What does everyone agree on, despite their political differences, and why do they agree on it? What are the social origins of agreement on apparently universal, rational and objective criteria for "high and sustainable economic and employment growth" or "the constraints of international competitiveness" (*Partnership 2000*: 5)? Why have our yardsticks for progress, development and policy success turned out the way they have?

Forty years ago, the *Programme for Economic Expansion* made a broad distinction between "social" and "productive" expenditure and argued that the state should concentrate on the latter. I doubt if any such distinction would be viable today as a basis for policy-making. The body of theoretical and empirical work discussed in this chapter can help explain why that is so. While not answering all our questions about the policy process, it does raise a number of penetrating, easily missed issues that challenge makers and analysts of policy to question systematically the self-presentation of modern institutions as neutral, functional, rational and progressively evolving.

REFERENCES

Alonso, William and Paul Starr (eds.) (1987), *The Politics of Numbers*, New York: Russell Sage.

Berger, Peter and Thomas Luckmann (1966), *The Social Construction of Reality: a Treatise in the Sociology of Knowledge*, New York: Doubleday.

Brint, Steven (1990), "Rethinking the Policy Influence of Experts: From General Characterizations to Analysis of Variation", *Sociological Forum*, Vol. 5, No. 3, pp. 361–371.

Cook, Karen and Margaret Levi (eds.) (1990), *The Limits of Rationality*, Chicago: University of Chicago Press.

Cuikerman, Alex (1992), *Central Bank Strategy, Credibility and Independence: Theory and Evidence*, Cambridge, MA: MIT Press.

Dahl, Robert (1977), *Polyarchy*, New Haven, CT: Yale University Press.

DiMaggio, Paul (1994), "Culture and the Economy" in Neil Smelser and Richard Swedberg (eds.), *Handbook of Economic Sociology*, Princeton: Princeton University Press, pp. 27–57.

DiMaggio, Paul and Walter Powell (1983), "The Iron Cage Revisited: Institutional Isomorphism and Collective Rationality in Organizational Fields", *American Sociological Review*, Vol. 82, pp. 147–60.

DiMaggio, Paul and Walter Powell (eds.), (1991), *The New Institutionalism in Organizational Analysis*, Chicago: University of Chicago Press.

Dobbin, Frank (1993), "The Social Construction of the Great Depression: Industrial Policy during the 1930s in the United States, Britain and France", *Theory and Society*, Vol. 22, pp. 1–56.

Dobbin, Frank (1994a), "Organizational Models of Culture: The Social Construction of Rational Organizing Principles" in Diana Crane (ed.), *The Sociology of Culture: Emerging Theoretical Perspectives*, Oxford: Basil Blackwell, pp. 117–153.

Dobbin, Frank (1994b), *Forging Industrial Policy: The United States, Britain and France in the Railway Age*, New York: Cambridge University Press.

Dobbin, Frank, Lauren Edelman, John W. Meyer, W. Richard Scott and Ann Swidler (1988), "The Expansion of Due Process in Organizations" in Lynne Zucker (ed.), *Institutional Patterns and Organizations: Culture and Environment*, Cambridge, MA: Ballinger, pp. 71–100.

Douglas, Mary (1986), *How Institutions Think*, Syracuse, NY: Syracuse University Press.

Durkheim, Emile [1912] (1995), *The Elementary Forms of Religious Life*, translated by Karen E. Fields, New York: Free Press.

Easton, David (1965), *A Framework for Political Analysis*, Englewood Cliffs, NJ: Prentice Hall.

Edelman, Lauren (1990), "Legal Environments and Organizational Governance: The Expansion of Due Process in the American Workplace", *American Journal of Sociology*, Vol. 95: 1401–1440.

Franzese, Robert J. Jr. (1994), "Central Bank Independence, Sectoral Interest, and the Wage Bargain", Harvard University Center for European Studies, Working Paper Series No. 5.1.

Garvin, Tom (1996), *1922: The Birth of Irish Democracy*, Dublin: Gill and Macmillan.

Government of Ireland (1996), *Partnership 2000 for Inclusion, Employment and Competitiveness*, Dublin: Stationery Office.

Granovetter, Mark (1985), "Economic Action and Social Structure: The Problem of Embeddedness", *American Journal of Sociology*, Vol. 91: 481–510.

Hall, Peter A. (1986), *Governing the Economy: the Politics of State Intervention in Britain and France*, New York: Oxford University Press.

Hall, Peter A. (1993), "Policy Paradigms, Social Learning, and the State: The Case of Economic Policymaking in Britain" *Comparative Politics*, Vol. 25, No. 3, 275–296.

Hall, Peter A. and Rosemary Taylor (1994), "Political Science and the Four New Institutionalisms" Paper presented to the Annual Meeting of the American Political Science Association, New York, September.

Hattam, Victoria C. (1993), *Labor Visions and State Power: The Origins of Business Unionism in the United States*, Princeton: Princeton University Press.

Hollis, Martin (1994), *The Philosophy of Social Science*, Cambridge: Cambridge University Press.

Ignatiev, Noel (1995), *How the Irish became White*, New York: Routledge.

Immergut, Ellen (1992a), *Health Politics: Interests and Institutions in Western Europe*, New York: Cambridge University Press.

Immergut, Ellen (1992b), "The Rules of the Game: the Logic of Health Policy-making in France, Switzerland and Sweden", in Sven Steinmo, Kathleen Thelen and Frank Longstreth (eds.), *Structuring Politics: Historical Institutionalism in Comparative Analysis*, New York: Cambridge University Press, pp. 57–89.

Kahneman, Daniel, Paul Slovic and Amos Tversky (1982), *Judgement under Uncertainty: Heuristics and Biases*, New York: Cambridge University Press.

Krasner, Stephen D. (1984), "Approaches to the State: Alternative Conceptions and Historical Dynamics", *Comparative Politics*, Vol. 16, pp. 223–246.

Lee, J.J. (1989), *Ireland 1912–1985: Politics and Society*, Cambridge: Cambridge University Press.

Lewis, David (1969), *Convention: a Philosophical Study*, Cambridge, MA: Harvard University Press.

Lipset, Seymour M. (1959), *Political Man*, London: Mercury Books.

Linz, Juan J. (1994) "Presidential or Parliamentary Democracy: Does it Make a Difference?" in Juan J. Linz and Arturo Valenzuela (eds.), *The Failure of Presidential Democracy*, Baltimore: Johns Hopkins University Press, pp. 3–87.

Mann, Michael (1993), *The Sources of Social Power, Vol. 2*, New York: Cambridge University Press.

Mansbridge, Jane (ed.) (1990), *Beyond Self-interest*, Chicago: University of Chicago Press.

Meyer, John W. and Brian Rowan (1977), "Institutionalized Organizations: Formal Structure as Myth and Ceremony", *American Journal of Sociology*, Vol. 83, No. 2, pp. 340–63.

Meyer, John W. and W.R. Scott (1983), *Organizational Environments: Ritual and Rationality*, Beverly Hills: Sage.

Meyer, John W., John Boli and George Thomas (1987), "Ontology and Rationalization in the Western Cultural Account" in George M. Thomas, John W. Meyer, Francisco O. Ramirez and John Boli (eds.), *Institutional Structure: Constituting State, Society and the Individual*, Beverley Hills: Sage, pp. 12–37.

Miliband, R. (1969), *The State in Capitalist Society*, New York: Basic Books.

Morrissey, Martin (1986), "The Politics of Economic Management in Ireland, 1958–70", *Irish Political Studies*, Vol. 1, pp. 79–95.

National Economic and Social Forum (1998), "A Framework for Partnership-Enriching Strategic Consensus through Participation", Dublin: NESF Forum Report No. 16.

North, Douglass (1982), *Structure and Change in Economic History*, New York: Norton.

North, Douglass (1990), *Institutions, Institutional Change and Economic Performance*, New York: Cambridge University Press.

Perlman, Mark (1987), "Political Purpose and the National Accounts" in William Alonso and Paul Starr (eds.), *The Politics of Numbers*, New York: Russell Sage, pp. 133–152.

Poulantzas, Nicos (1973), *Political Power and Social Classes*, London: New Left Books.

Skocpol, Theda (1985), "Bringing the State Back In: Strategies of Analysis in Current Research" in Peter B. Evans, Dietrich Rueschemeyer and Theda Skocpol (eds.), *Bringing the State Back In*, New York: Cambridge University Press, pp. 3–43.

Skocpol, Theda and Kenneth Finegold (1982), "State Capacity and Economic Organization in the Early New Deal", *Political Science Quarterly*, Vol. 97, No. 2, pp. 255–278.

Starr, Paul (1987), "The Sociology of Official Statistics" in William Alonso and Paul Starr (eds.), *The Politics of Numbers*, New York: Russell Sage, pp. 7–57.

Starr, Paul (1992), "Social Categories and Claims in the Liberal State" *Social Research*, Vol. 59, No. 2, pp. 263–295.

Sutton, John, Frank Dobbin, John W. Meyer and W. Richard Scott (1994), "The Legalization of the Workplace", *American Journal of Sociology*, Vol. 99, No. 4, 944–971.

Thelen, Kathleen and Sven Steinmo (1992), "Historical Institutionalism in Comparative Politics" in Sven Steinmo, Kathleen Thelen and Frank Longstreth (eds.), *Structuring Politics: Historical Institutionalism in Comparative Analysis*, New York: Cambridge University Press, pp. 1–32.

Tolbert, Pamela S. and Lynne G. Zucker (1983), "Institutional Sources of Change in the Formal Structure of Organizations: The Diffusion of Civil Service Reforms, 1880–1935", *Administrative Science Quarterly*, Vol. 23, pp. 22–39.

Toye, John (1994), "Comment" in John Williamson (ed.), *The Political Economy of Policy Reform*, Washington, DC: Institute for International Economics, pp. 35–47.

Weir, Margaret and Theda Skocpol (1985), "State Structures and the Possibilities for Keynesian Responses to the Great Depression in Sweden, Britain, and the United States" in Peter B. Evans, Dietrich Rueschemeyer and Theda Skocpol (eds.), *Bringing the State Back In*, New York: Cambridge University Press, pp. 107–163.

Williamson, John (1994), "In Search of a Manual for Technopoles" in John Williamson (ed.), *The Political Economy of Policy Reform*, Washington, DC: Institute for International Economics, pp. 9–28.

Chapter 5

MEASUREMENT AND UNDERSTANDING IN ECONOMICS

John Healy *and* Charles M.A. Clark

INTRODUCTION

From the very beginning, economics has been partly an empirical science, partly theoretical. This is evident in the inclusion of (or at least the attempt at) empirical analysis by all the great economists (even David Ricardo was not immune to this). It is also true in the sense that it has to be both empirical and theoretical, in that no empirical analysis can exist without being based on a theoretical perspective. As Gunnar Myrdal often noted, all observation requires an observation point of view, and this is provided by theory. The historiography of economics also shows how instrumental observation of the economy (empirical analysis) is for the development of economic theory (Stark, 1994). As a discipline, economics runs into trouble, and becomes more an ideology and less a science (in the Schumpe-terian conception) when it forgets this interconnectedness and pursues one as if it were independent of the other. At one end of the spectrum, we see this in the frequent examples of what Schumpeter called the "Ricardian Vice" — the offering of economic policy advice based solely on abstract analysis. A more extreme example is the influence of mathematical formalism and the work of Gerard Debreu, where an attempt is made at a theory of equilibrium which is totally independent of any actual economy (Clark, 1992). Yet the reverse is more often the problem.

One of the greatest faults of modern economics is the pursuit of empirical analysis under the assumption that such work is theoretically neutral or independent. This atheoretical empiricism is of course anything but atheoretical, as all empirical analysis requires theoretical grounding. Yet the analysts are under the impression that their work is purely empirical. This problem has its roots in the uncritical acceptance of the neo-classical "vision" of the economy and society (itself based on the view that the economy is a natural system determined by invariants) and the delusion of "positive" (value-free) economics. Under such preconceptions, orthodox economists shift their attention to questions of measurement, and away from questions of understanding social processes. Measurement becomes the end instead of a means to an end, and the "measurements", the statistics generated by these activities, become fetishes, substitutes for the real object of social analysis — human social behaviour.

Measuring growth in output, the level of unemployment or the number of people in poverty (to give just three examples) at any given point in time can be, but is by no means necessarily, an aid to understanding economic progress, labour slack or how people become poor. Consider the last example: one can produce an estimate of the percentage of the population that falls below the poverty line(s) without having any understanding of the processes, institutions or individual actions which give rise to their level of wealth. Equally, the measuring of the number of people in poverty can be a valuable tool for highlighting that number at any given point in time and can suggest that social processes, institutions and individual actions need to be investigated to illuminate what is causing this income distribution. That is, the measuring of the number of people in poverty can be taken as one layer of reality and then the underlying causes and significance of this revealed state can be investigated.

In another instance, measuring and predicting the number of people in poverty can actually be a barrier to understanding the underlying causes of poverty, if one assumes that the revealed world is synonymous with the actual world and certain restrictive assumptions are made with regard to individuals. Then the methodology used to examine the revealed state of the number in poverty can exclude those institutions and powers which play an instrumental part in deciding any distribution of income. The root of this problem lies in the vision adopted by the analyst, as the vision supplies the methodology and the methodology determines what gets observed.

A TALE OF TWO METHODS

Methodology and social ontology are vital parts of any inquiry into social order. The extent to which measuring economic outcomes, such as the number of people in poverty, and understanding these outcomes can be complementary activities depends upon the social ontology and the methodology that one adopts.

Empirical Realism and Methodological Individualism

The positivist concept of science is based upon the idea that knowledge is based upon experience and that reality is that which we experience (for example, Hume's reduction of knowledge to impression). This perspective on reality can be classified as *empirical realism* (Lawson, 1997), a belief that one can illuminate causal laws of social behaviour by establishing regularities between events. It presupposes an atomistic view of social reality in which people react to external stimuli so that their behaviour can classified as "whenever X, then Y". Perceived events, i.e. perceived human action and movement in response to external stimuli, result in the verification or falsification of hypotheses. The consequence of trying to reduce all social action down to individual choices has the perverse effect of removing choice altogether from the actors in the model, because they could not have behaved otherwise.[1]

If one believes that explanations of social order and institutions must be couched solely in terms of individuals and that it is an enlightening process to abstract towards stable natural laws of individual human behaviour, then one will tend to see economic outcomes as a result of interaction between generally asocial individuals. The investigation will be based on certain core assumptions regarding human behaviour, and the revealed actions of individuals are used to validate or invalidate event regularities (Lawson, 1997). Individuals are seen essentially as reacting to external stimuli, usually prices. Inquiry into how any economic phenomena arise tends to take the form of "whenever X occurs then Y occurs". Methodological individualism rests on the belief that all institutions in society are the

---

[1] The work of George Shackle is most instructive here, particularly his contention that neoclassical economics eliminates individual choice. Deterministic (closed) models, such as rational economic man, have no room for free will and choice.

product of individual action and that all can be explained by their constituent parts, that is, they can be reduced down to individual self-maximising behaviour. As Veblen stated:

> The hedonistic conception of man is that of a lightening calculator of pleasures and pains, who oscillates like a homogenous globule of desire of happiness under the impulse of stimuli that shift him about the area, but leave him intact. He is neither antecedent nor consequent. He is an isolated, definitive human datum in stable equilibrium except for the buffets of the impinging forces that displace him in one direction or another. (Veblen, 1919: 73, 74)

Importantly for our purposes, as Veblen points out above, the actors in the models used by methodological individualists are asocial and generally ahistoric. That is, people react to external stimuli not because they are conditioned by their previous experiences but rather based on certain principles of self-maximising behaviour.

Neo-classical economic thought is founded upon the method of empirical realism and methodological individualism. Neo-classical economists are concerned with underlying forces only when they are revealed and only when explanations can be couched solely in terms of individuals.

> Indeed it is evident that a fundamental reason for the widespread disarray in contemporary economics is precisely a generalised neglect of ontological enquiry. This neglect is itself underpinned by the *epistemic* fallacy, by the supposition that statements about knowledge (of being) can always be reduced to epistemology. With ontology unavoidable, this error functions only to cover the generation of an implicit ontology, in which the real is collapsed onto the actual which is then anthropocentrically identified with, or in terms of, human experience, measurement or some other human attribute. (Lawson, 1997: 62)

The tools of analysis of neo-classical economists neglect those factors which are not amenable to measurement. Uncertainty, for example, can have very real consequences; however, neo-classical economists are unable to illuminate these consequences, given that their tools of analysis are unable to account for them (Knight, 1921).[2]

The use of models with asocial and ahistoric actors to gain insights into the behaviour of individuals in society in an attempt to illuminate stable laws of behaviour (i.e. natural laws) results in an over-concentration on the causal effect of price signals, rather than on the powers, habits and institutions which give rise to the status quo.

Critical Realism and Institutionalism

If, on the other hand, one believes that institutions and power shape the economic outcomes, one would see revealed economic phenomena as the results of social processes and would see human actions restricted through the ordering over time of society. Individuals are seen as complex and conditioned by the environment in which they have been brought up. That is, it is not considered helpful to view individuals as homogenous and reactionary; rather, emphasis is put on seeing individuals partly as products of their environment and background and partly as creators. People are seen as social and complex.

All knowledge is seen as fallible and society as open (that is, difficult to predict). Institutions, and in particular power structures, which can differ across societies, play a vital role in influencing the behaviour of individuals. There is a belief that social organisations are more than the sum of their parts and that institutions can in turn influence individuals significantly. The structures and institutions that influence human behaviour are seen as legitimate objects of study and emerge as structures that are irreducible to the individuals that formed them. Underlying forces are considered important, whether or not they are perceived directly in individuals' actions. That which we perceive is only one level of understanding and is often the result of a multitude of tendencies.

---

[2] This is seen clearly in what Joan Robinson (1962: 690–92) has dubbed the "Bastard Keynesian" who, in an effort to interpret Keynes in a neo-classical (Walrasian) fashion, have emptied his analysis of "Historical Time" and uncertainty. In doing this they were able to develop large macroeconometric models for measuring and predicting (the inaccuracy of which would not surprise Keynes in the least).

Implications of Methodology for the Role of Measurement

Neo-classical methods set out to illuminate causal laws of behaviour by examining the social world. Theories are deduced from axioms based on methodological individualism. Measurement for neo-classical economics is often an end in itself, which falsifies or verifies a hypothesis. The tools of analysis used (generally mathematics and econometrics) suit the reduction of societies to individuals and can accommodate the models with actors who are "lightening calculators of pleasure and pain". Measurement of the number of people in poverty over time, for example, can in turn be used to measure the statistical relationship with other phenomena, and thus it is claimed that poverty is caused by factors X, Y or Z, with proportional degrees of influence.

Questions as to the role of preconceptions and "vision" in shaping the accepted theory, or in the role of theory in shaping observations, are ignored, as the underlying premise of the whole neo-classical project is the existence of invariants and a tendency towards a general equilibrium. It is this faith that allows orthodox economists to concentrate their attention on measurement as an end, and the belief that if they can explain the measurements (that is, in the econometric definition of "explain"), they have illuminated reality.

Under a critical realist methodology, the end goal is an understanding of social processes in terms of social institutions and structures, fully cognisant of the fact that the interaction between social institutions and humans with free will causes both to evolve and change. Measurement of economic outcomes under this perspective *can only be* a tool in understanding these processes, and *can never be* an end in itself. This is so because the critical realist methodology assumes an open, and not a closed system. It rejects the assumption of invariants and a tendency towards some "general" or "natural" equilibrium (Clark, 1987–88; 1989). Thus, all measurements are necessarily tentative and inaccurate.[3] This rejection of a "natural order", towards which the economy is tending, is significant, as the factors

---

[3] One should also keep in mind the Heisenberg uncertainty principle here: that the act of observation changes the reality being observed. This is amply demonstrated in such cases as household budget surveys, where it is fairly common for those who participate in such surveys to alter their behaviour, often in line with what they think it should be.

which must be assumed away in order to hold such a tendency are exactly those that are the most important for a critical realist understanding of economic outcomes as social processes. Neo-classical economists must assume away history and society to adhere to their general equilibrium view of the economy (Clark, 1992), yet it is from history and society that we get the order-bestowing forces in the economy, not from rational maximising actions of self-interested individuals and price signals.

Furthermore, the famous *ceteris paribus* assumption shields from analysis just what is important, for, as Veblen (1946: 85–86) noted:

> the state of the industrial arts has at no time continued unchanged during the modern era; consequently other things have never remained the same; and in the long run the outcome has always been shaped by the disturbing causes.

Measurement based on a preconception of a natural order and invariants will necessarily lead to such statistics becoming fetishes. Measurement which sees itself as one tool in understanding social processes, sees the final goal of understanding economic outcomes in terms of social institutions and structures, is open to the inherent theoretical basis in all efforts to measure economic outcomes, and thus is open-minded, can do a great deal to enlighten the interested analysts.

In the next section we hope to give some examples of how an uncritical acceptance of neo-classical methodology leads to measurements which often hide as much as they expose.

PROGRESS, UNEMPLOYMENT, INEQUALITY AND POVERTY

In this section we will look at four examples of how the choice of methodology perspective and "vision" influences how the theorist investigates, and conceptualises, reality. The four examples chosen here are: the question of economic progress; unemployment (labour slack); income inequality; and poverty. In all four, we see how the methodological stance of the theorist colours the explanations offered in every way. Furthermore, it will be seen that the drive to quantify — an inherent aspect of the "physics envy" of neo-classical economics — coupled with the underlying values presupposed, have a tendency to become a barrier to a full and rich understanding of the phenomenon in question.

Progress

The conception of Gross Domestic Product, or some other measure of aggregate output or income, as the best indicator of economic well-being and progress, is based on the utilitarian view of human nature and methodological individualism, both of which are part of the hard core of neo-classical economic theory. Furthermore, the drive to quantify is also based on these preconceptions. Neo-classical economic theory, by following a hedonistic conception of human nature, a utility theory of value and a desire to create a positive economic "science" which is "value-free" and which resembles theoretical physics, necessarily leads to measures of economic and social well-being which concentrate exclusively on market transactions and exclude historical and social context and factors from their analysis.

The exclusive concentration on market transactions or income indicators to measure economic and social well-being, or more generally, progress, is reflective of the underlying values and vision of neo-classical economic theory. All social action in neo-classical economic theory is explained via the market metaphor, whether it is a market transaction or not. This started with Adam Smith's assertion of man's natural propensity to truck, barter and exchange, and culminates in Gary Becker's economic theory of the family. This perspective has caused a failure to realise that much of what is called economic growth or progress is in fact a shifting of activities from household production (home-cooked meals, parents raising their children) to market-based production (McDonalds, crèche facilities). As A.C. Pigou noted long ago, "If a man marries his house-keeper or his cook, the national dividend is diminished" (Pigou, 1944: 33). Furthermore, the growing amount of waste and pollution, caused by the high level of economic activity, also generates significant increases in market transactions, either directly (the costs of cleaning up the environment) or indirectly (the costs generated by illnesses related to pollution). In fact, pollution is a double bonus, because it adds to GDP when it is generated and when it is cleaned up, whether it be by private or public expenditure. Thus, "growth can be social decline by another name" (Cobb, Halstead and Rowe, 1995: 65).[4]

The greatest failure of this conception of economic progress is that it allows growth in statistical measures to be a substitute for more in-depth considerations of how people's lives are improving or not. As has been quite evident throughout the OECD over the past two decades, whatever economic growth there has been, its benefits have been highly concentrated in the upper-income brackets. Thus, GDP can increase by a significant amount while real incomes for many (and in some countries for the majority) fall or show little improvement. Growth in GDP, or other aggregate income statistics, becomes a fetish, well beyond its original purpose of being one tool to measure how the economy and society is progressing. In "Progress, Values and Economic Indicators", Clark and Kavanagh (1996a), after critiquing standard measures of economic well-being, constructed what they called an "Index of Social Progress" to give a broader measure of economic and social well-being. The main purpose of this effort was to show what could be done so that others would be encouraged to generate the necessary data and indexes for broader measures of progress. Yet even this approach runs the risk of being a fetish, as policy-makers could easily adopt one such index and use it as the basis of policy. Thus, policy might become skewed to influencing the index instead of the reality the index is designed to reflect (however imperfectly).

Unemployment

Unemployment is frequently cited as Europe's number one economic problem. The vision adopted plays an important role in how economists conceptualise both the problem and the solutions. For the orthodox economist, unemployment results from a malfunctioning of the labour market, with this malfunction most often being the result of some market failure caused by labour unions or government regulation and tax policy.[5] By definition, in the absence of market failures, the market produces optimal results.

---

[4] For more on the question of GDP as a measure of progress see Clark and Kavanagh (1996a).

[5] New Keynesians have developed models of market failure which are the result of individuals' rational actions and not government or unions. These insider/

Viewing the problem of unemployment as due to some failure in the labour market leads the orthodox economist to investigate unemployment by modelling the labour market through the generation of wage equations.[6] Certain variables are used to try and find which are statistically significant in preventing wages from reaching their market clearing level. The underlying assumption is that, barring such market failures (unions, government regulation and taxation to name the usual suspects), these variables will reach a "natural" level in which there will be full employment. A variation on this theme is the more macro approach in which an econometric equation is created with the level of unemployment (or employment) as the dependent variable and various other relevant and irrelevant factors as the independent variables, the purpose being to see which factors "explain" the changes in the unemployment rate, with "explain" meaning "are statistically significant" (correlates to the changes in unemployment).

The underlying preconceptions of such approaches are fairly obvious. The economy is viewed as an equilibrium system, with an underlying tendency towards a long-run equilibrium, and with temporary disturbances caused by non-market factors. The long-run equilibrium is determined by the dominant and persistent forces which are universal and invariant. This is necessarily the case, as such invariance is necessary for an adoption of the physical science approach to economics.

If we followed an institutionalist approach, we would start with the institutions which shape and form various labour markets: i.e. what are the rules of the game? Wages are here determined by the factors specific to each labour market and would not necessarily be a market phenomenon, and certainly would not be assumed to be market clearing. Wages, work time, who is included in a labour market, means for settling disputes and other important questions are addressed and determined by a combination of institutions, some

---

outsider models argue that unemployment is the result of incomplete information and information co-ordination failures (wages are set by bargaining by insiders, with the unemployed being outsiders who would like to work but do not have a mechanism to signal this information).

[6] We shall leave aside the question of whether there exists "a labour market" or if in fact there are many segmented labour markets, which are not market clearing in the neo-classical sense. For more on this, see Clark and Kavanagh (1996b).

specific to the labour market in question (union rules, corporate policies, relative power of employees and employers) and some general to society (government regulations, social norms and attitudes). Economic factors play a role (supply and demand) but they do not produce the inherent order.

The unemployment rate would here be considered as "natural" or likely any other outcome, meaning no long-run equilibrium is assumed. Furthermore, the key questions are not: "What are the invariants?" They instead deal with institutional adjustment.

The alternative visions of society have significantly different implications for the type of policies chosen to counter unemployment. If one adopts the vision of empirical realism and methodological individualism then in order to reduce unemployment, price signals need to be changed. Taxes on low paid employment and/or welfare payments to the unemployed need to be reduced. Policy emphasis will also be on reducing the costs to employers of hiring workers.

If one, however, adopts the institutionalist vision of society, the emphasis would be very different. Whilst agreeing that price signals are important, they need to be seen against the background of institutions that prevail in society. Individuals are seen as more complex and it is seen as unhelpful to model individuals as homogeneous in a single labour market, given that individuals have different talents, problems and backgrounds. Policy would tend towards questioning social institutions and providing an individualised service to address the complex problems that the unemployed face (e.g. a mediation service similar to the Local Employment Service).

Measuring Labour Slack

Much of the policy debate on unemployment in Ireland has been on determining the best measure of unemployment. Any measure of labour slack is going to reflect the values underlying the theory and theorists investigating the phenomenon, and are to a certain extent arbitrary. Fairly widespread agreement among the economics profession of the inadequacies of the Live Register as a measure of unemployment is often used to indicate that the problem is less pervasive than the official statistics indicate. As with the conception of progress, the definition of unemployment is value-laden. The neo-classical approach looks to individual attributes to explain unemployment (age, education, previous work experience, duration of unemployment) rather than social structures and institutions. For such high levels of unemployment to persist over such a long time, it must be institutionalised in some way.

A look at the most intensive investigation of the problem of unemployment, the *OECD Jobs Study* (1994) reveals the inherent basis of methodological individualism. In this vast empirical investigation of the causes of unemployment, all questions are posed with the assumption of there being a "labour market" which performs a market clearing function, and that something is preventing such market clearing. Central to this type of analysis is the attempt to understand unemployment in terms of individual characteristics. Unfortunately, but not unexpectedly, this analysis has yielded little in the way of fruitful results or conclusions. Most glaring is its exclusion of inadequate aggregate demand as an explanation of the problem, as if Keynes never existed. Yet Keynes's explanation of unemployment is in terms of institutions (money, financial institutions) and structures and is not reducible to individualistic terms.

Inequality[7]
The question of the determinants of income inequality has been extensively studied in the developed capitalist economies over the past decade. The cause of this new interest has been the rise (in some countries quite dramatic) in income inequality. Explanations of income inequality are a glaring example of this chapter's central point of the influence of method on analysis.

The neo-classical theory approach to the question of income inequality has been to change the question to one of income determination, of which earnings determination becomes the focal point of all discussions on the topic. In the neo-classical story, individual economic agents make choices, based on their preferences and endowments, which, when totalled, determine market outcomes. Any existing income distribution is merely the outcome of this market process — that is, an individual's income is determined by the price (market outcome) their particular factor service receives in a competitive market. Any long-term income inequality will be the result

---

[7] This section is adopted from Clark (1996).

of differences in productivities or initial endowments (a factor almost never brought into the analysis). Short-run inequalities might be the result of shortages or surpluses in particular factor markets, but these are alleviated when relative prices, performing the necessary role of sending market signals to individuals, adjust so that such imbalances are eliminated.

The question of income inequality is thus addressed as a problem of the determination of income differentials, which are the result of individual characteristics. The standard procedure is to investigate the relationship between some individual trait or set of traits (gender, education, race, work experience), job characteristics and earnings. This is usually done by running a regression, with income as the dependent variable and the various individual attributes as the independent variables. The coefficients for each trait or job characteristic are interpreted as prices which the market has imputed for these traits and characteristics. From the start, both the causes and effects of the change in inequality are limited by adherence to methodological individualism, to phenomena which can be depicted in terms of individuals. Even when group or collective effects (such as the influence of unions) are investigated, the mode of investigation is at the individual level, with participation in the particular group counting as the addition of one more individual trait. Changes in income distribution are thus analysed via changes in the supply and demand for the various attributes. The rise in the education differential, a frequent topic in this literature, is seen as a reflection of an increase in the demand for educated workers, usually attributed to the rise in the use of computers in the workplace, and/or changes in the supply of educated workers.

Recent work on earnings inequality has given institutional factors more of a role in explaining why different countries have different levels of earnings inequality. Here, a dichotomy is presented between market and institutional factors. Market factors include the determination of skills prices through the interaction of supply and demand, whereas institutional factors include: collective bargaining; union pay policies, and government policy. Thus institutional factors are depicted as deviations from the competitive market norm — that is, market imperfections. Implicit in this analysis is the idea that these "imperfections" produce sub-optimal outcomes, as they are non-competitive in nature.[8] Even though there is a growing literature within the neo-classical tradition dealing with institutions, the final term in their analysis is always the maximising individual. The preferred measures are individual-based, although, for the obvious reasons that many individuals receive their income outside of market relations (children, home-makers, retired), frequently the unit of analysis is the household. Little attention is placed on social class, and factors such as gender are included as another individual attribute.

An institutionalist analysis of income distribution can emphasise the inherent conflict which lies at the heart of the income distribution dynamic. It can be an exploitation theory, not only in its emphasis on structure (social, political and economic) as determining distribution, but also in its emphasis on the exploitative nature of how incomes are determined in a "market" economy. As Bill Dugger (1993: 18) has recently noted:

> The practice of class inequality is exploitation. Its original focal point in capitalism was the hierarchical workplace where owners hire workers and use them for producing commodities for profit. The owners try to enlarge the flow of income that goes to them, after all contractual costs are paid and after all costs that can be avoided are avoided (externalities). As in gender and race inequality, the practice of class inequality has become bureaucratized, far more so than in the other modes of inequality. The production and sale of commodities for a profit is now largely organized by corporate bureaucracies, some of immense size and scope. The income appropriated by the wage workers, middle managers, engineers, equity owners and by the debt owners (rentier capital) is now the subject of bureaucratic rules, state regulations, court decisions, and continual struggle between different organizations and between different hierarchical levels of the same organization. The struggle is to obtain a differential economic advantage

---

[8] Although not all neo-classical economists would view institutional factors as necessarily harmful to the operation of the economy, and some (although a minority) neo-classicals support trade unions and some labour legislation (even occasionally minimum wages), the general tone and substance of neo-classical analysis suggests that markets are superior to non-market environments.

that will allow the appropriation of more income at the expense of those who have no such advantage.

Dugger notes elsewhere (ibid.: 38) that:

> inequality is not an equilibrium state, but a circular process. Inequality either gets worse, or it gets better, but it does not reach an equilibrium. The continued practice of inequality strengthens the myths that support it and the stronger myths then lend even greater support to the practice. The resulting circular process is not characterised by offsetting forces that reach a balance but a cumulative causation that continues to move an inegalitarian society toward more inequality or that continues to move an egalitarian society towards more equality.

The changes in income distribution which took place during the 1980s can be seen as a change in the relative power of the groups struggling over the economic pie. It is a story of institutional change and of the dominance of hierarchy.

Poverty

The two visions of society outlined earlier have radically different implications for how one understands poverty. If one believes that it is helpful to abstract towards an atomistic view of society in search of stable laws of behaviour, then movements in the number of people in poverty over time will be seen as the result of movements in quantitative measurements of other causal variables. Attempts are then made to establish the extent that each single variable contributed to the change in the number of people in poverty. The vision of the methodological individualist generally perceives people entering the labour market as a voluntary exchange between employed and employer, and education as a voluntary postponement of present earnings to reap the later benefits of higher human capital. Therefore, the people who earn the most are those that work the hardest and those who are the most highly educated are those who sacrificed present earnings for higher future earnings. Institutions, and in particular structures of power, are excluded from the analysis and they therefore cannot be questioned. Since interaction in the labour market is essentially voluntary, there is no obvious justification for a redistribution of income.

If on the other hand one sees individuals in a social, historical and geographical context, one will see the likelihood of a person falling victim to poverty as dependent on their background and on the institutions which are present in society. The search for stable causal variables is no longer a priority, given that society is seen as open and complex with many different factors often emerging together to cause someone to fall victim to poverty. These causal factors are not independent of one another, nor are they stable across time and place. It is not seen as helpful to create a model in which transactions between employers and employees are part of a single labour market; rather, it is recognised that there are many different markets. Poverty is not seen primarily as the result of rational individual actions; rather it is the result of social institutions and the background and actions of individuals. This vision of society, therefore, leaves scope for questioning social institutions and justifies redistribution of income on the grounds that income distributions are not primarily the result of voluntary interaction between individuals.

CONCLUSIONS

The methodology adopted to enquire into human behaviour and institutions affects not only the scope of the analysis but also the policy prescriptions that emerge. Measurement of empirical phenomena can be a valuable tool in understanding society, but it can also hinder it if the methodology used excludes certain factors from the analysis; measuring and predicting can become ends in themselves. In this chapter, it is argued that attempts to create a value-free empirical science inevitably result in implicit value judgements being made. Methodological individualism, coupled with empirical realism, often result in institutional factors being ignored, an over-emphasis on price factors and erroneous predictions being made, with great certainty regarding the behaviour of individuals.

REFERENCES

Clark, Charles M.A. (1987–88), "Equilibrium, Market Process and Historical Time" *Journal of Post-Keynesian Economics*, Winter, Vol. 10, No. 2, pp. 270–81.

Clark, Charles M.A. (1989), "Equilibrium for What? Reflections on Social Order in Economics" *Journal of Economic Issues*, June, Vol. 23, No. 2, pp. 597–606.

Clark, Charles M.A. (1992), *Economic Theory and Natural Philosophy: The Search for the Natural Laws of the Economy*, Aldershot: Edward Elgar.

Clark, Charles M.A. (1996), "Inequality in the 1980s: An Institutionalist Perspective" in William Dugger (ed.), *Inequality: Radical Institutionalist Perspectives on Race, Gender, Class and Nation*, Westport, CT: Greenwood Press.

Clark, Charles M.A. (1998), "Unemployment in Ireland: A Post-Keynesian Perspective" in Charles M.A. Clark and Catherine Kavanagh (eds.), *Unemployment in Ireland*, Aldershot: Avebury Publishing Limited.

Clark, Charles M.A. and Catherine Kavanagh (1996a), "Progress, Values and Economic Indicators" in Brigid Reynolds and Sean Healy (eds.), *Progress, Values and Public Policy*, Dublin: CORI, pp. 60–92.

Clark, Charles M.A. and Catherine Kavanagh (1996b), "Basic Income, Inequality, and Unemployment: Rethinking the Linkages Between Work and Welfare", *Journal of Economic Issues*, June, Vol. 30, pp. 399–406.

Clark, Charles M.A. and John Healy (1997), *Pathways to a Basic Income*, Dublin: Conference of Religious of Ireland.

Cobb, Clifford, T. Halstead and J. Rowe (1995), "If the GDP is Up, Why is America Down?", *The Atlantic Monthly*, Vol. 276, October, pp. 59–78.

Dugger, William (1993), "Four Modes of Inequality", Memo, University of Tulsa.

Knight, Frank (1921), *Risk, Uncertainty and Profit*, London: Sentry Publications

Lawson, Tony (1997), *Economics and Reality*, London: Routledge.

Myrdal, Gunnar (1954), *The Political Element in the Development of Economic Theory*, New York: Simon and Schuster.

OECD (1994), *The OECD Jobs Study*, Paris: Organisation for Economic Co-operation and Development.

Pigou, Arthur (1944), *The Economics of Welfare*, London: Macmillan.

Robinson, Joan (1962), Review of *Money, Trade and Economic Growth* by Harry G. Johnson, in *The Economic Journal*, September, Vol. 72, pp. 690–92.

Stark, Werner (1994), *History and Historians of Political Economy* (edited by Charles M.A. Clark), New Brunswick: Transaction Publishers.

Veblen, Thorstein (1919), *The Place of Science in Modern Civilization*, New York: Huebsch.

Veblen, Thorstein (1946), *The Vested Interests and the Common Man*, New York: Viking.

Chapter 6

RESEARCH AND POLICY-MAKING

Sara Cantillon[1]

INTRODUCTION

This chapter is concerned with exploring the relationship between research and policy. Specifically, it explores whether such a relationship only exists on the basis of particular types of research and specific research methodologies. In such a situation, what room is there for input into the policy process from other types of research paradigms? Or do such paradigms by their nature aim for an alternative route, whereby the actual engagement process of the researcher can act as a stimulus for economic and social change by initiating a chain of grassroots reaction, collective action and influence in policy-making? The roots of these questions can be found in the concept of the role of research itself — that is, whether the purpose of research is to describe or explain the world or whether it is also to change it.

The chapter begins by showing how the concept of the role of research or knowledge and the research methodologies employed are generated from within specific philosophical frameworks. It looks at the question of the link between research and policy-making and very briefly reviews two areas that have received considerable attention in Ireland over the past 10 years, namely poverty and taxation. It considers other routes to social change raised by the employment of alternative research paradigms. It concludes by arguing the importance of engagement between the various players (researchers, researched, policy-makers), the value of inter-theoretical debate and

[1] Comments from Rory O'Donnell, Seán Healy and Kathleen Lynch were gratefully appreciated.

dialogue, and ultimately the necessity for a process of feedback from practice to theory and from theory to practice.

ROLE OF RESEARCH

Social research is generated within particular philosophical frameworks which shape the general perception of reality and social relations and the types of methods and techniques employed. Depending on the orientation of the framework, the purpose of research in social science can vary significantly.

Rothschild (1982) provides a fairly standard view of the role of research when he defines it as "the study of something [which aims] to discover and describe new facts and relationships between those facts and, if possible, to make generalisations arising from the discoveries and descriptions".

A very different view of research is offered by critical theorists, who argue that its role is to "simultaneously explain the social world, critique it and empower its audience to overthrow it" (Fay, 1987). Another view of research which has its roots in critical theory but is distinct from it, particularly in its move away from the extremely theoretical position that critical theory came to occupy, is praxis. The concept of research as praxis implies that it is explicitly committed to critiquing the status quo and building a more just society (Lather, 1991). This view seems a contradiction to the many who take objectivity as both a desirable and possible goal in social science research. The inherent presupposition in this latter view is that the researcher can be limited in their own biases, can act as a neutral observer and study what *is* rather than what *ought to be*. However, the evolving debate in the philosophy of science has demonstrated that truth varies with perspective. It is in this new space that notions of the value of "good" normative or advocacy-based research are being entertained. When one looks at what is characterised as the ideal research situation and its relationship to policy, questions as to whether there is anything inherently wrong with normative or advocacy research, and/or whether a certain level of disinterest or objectivity (even flawed) should be attempted, become more pertinent. The idea that the correct research procedure, and what the research will reveal, exist independently of any particular policy problem, and the way in which it is conceptualised, must be viewed sceptically (O'Donnell,

1992) or, as Townsend (1979) puts it, "policy prescriptions permeate the conceptualisation, measurement and formulation of theory".

Objectivity is an extremely complex question, and it seems fair to say that by far the majority of researchers — even taking on board the validity of the questions raised above — still view it as a goal in social science research.

RESEARCH METHODOLOGIES

Developments in the philosophy of science, in literature, in sociology and in science itself, have all combined both to reveal serious problems in traditional methods of social inquiry, including the limits of empirical falsification, and to emphasise the interpretative nature of the social sciences and reject the rigid, if not impossible, distinction between values and facts. Feminist theory has been at the forefront of this debate, especially the works of Sandra Harding and Dorothy Smith. The result has been an explosion in social science inquiry which goes under many names. A very brief, and somewhat simple, synopsis of the alternative approaches is attempted below.

Much of the debate between the various research paradigms revolves around the techniques employed, but this quantitative/qualitative distinction, discussed below, is a somewhat misleading way of summarising a more fundamental debate. If we feel we know what people want by looking into our own hearts — the so-called de Valera model — our research task is an easy one. If not, the research methods we employ will reflect our view of the world, our concept of knowledge and its potential for transformative action.

The most dominant paradigm in social science research has been positivism and its successor, post-positivism. There is still a tendency towards hide-bound positivism or as McCloskey says "the news of the decline of positivism has not reached all ears" (quoted in O'Donnell, 1992). This is despite Lather's claim that we live in a post-positivist age, and despite the fact that, among researchers, pure positivism (a belief that only observable, objective, provable, hard facts count) has been fading for many years. It could also be argued that the term post-positivism may be a little excessive in its implication, as in reality it constitutes a modification of the excesses of positivism rather than a fundamental break.

The four main paradigms or approaches (positivism, post-positivism, phenomenological, and critical theory) can be outlined as follows:

1. *Positivism* has its basis in traditional science. It is defined primarily by its view that reality exists: that there is an objective world from which the researcher can stand apart and observe. Research is aimed at identifying cause and effect and the conditions under which they apply in order to explain and predict.

2. *Post-positivism* attempts to resolve the problems that have arisen within positivism; namely that, while accepting the existence of reality, the idea of an independent, value-free researcher-observer is rejected. Objectivity, however, should still be aimed for in research and it is argued that this is best achieved by being upfront about assumptions and by using a much broader range of methods, techniques and sources of information.

3. *Phenomenology* (also called, with some variation in meaning and emphasis, the hermeneutic, interpretavist, relativist approach), in contrast, argues that there is no objective reality; that positivism may give facts but it does not give meaning or understanding; and that research is shaped by the interaction between the observer and the observed. The observer is part of the picture, not separate from it.

4. *Critical theory* (including feminism, neo-Marxism and some participatory approaches) shares with post-positivism the idea of an incompletely perceived, but still quite definite, reality. It differs, however, on the question of whose reality is at stake. Critical theory argues that the values of the elite, permeated through the questions selected, the methods used, the results selected and the recommendations made, are used to support their own interests and to oppress others. The purpose of research therefore is to empower people to set their own action agendas. In the emancipatory research paradigm, the issue is not so much the methodology employed to collect data but the type of research you do in the first place, who decides on it and who benefits directly from it.

The Qualitative versus Quantitative Debate

Surveys, such as the Household Budget Survey or the ESRI Living in Ireland Survey, are the technique that has dominated social science research, although they are sometimes accompanied by qualitative interviews and participant observation.

There are strengths, as well as weaknesses, in the types of information that survey data can provide. The obvious advantage is that it is conducted on a large scale and is thus able to provide a nationally representative picture. A large-scale quantitative survey also allows for sophisticated statistical analysis, and therein lies much of the debate between the quantitative and qualitative approaches to social research. This tension in social science research, which Jenkins (1994) terms a "dialogue between the deaf", arises between those who believe that a statistical analysis of nationally representative samples is essential, and those who believe that research employing qualitative or ethnographic methodologies — where a small group, community or area is intensively observed and studied — is more appropriate. While it is clear that quantitative techniques of data collection are of particular value in providing an overall picture of poverty in its societal context, it is not possible in a large-scale household survey to conduct the sort of intensive investigation of intra-household and intra-marital arrangements (financial and otherwise) which some qualitative studies have undertaken. Against this, while proponents of the quantitative tradition concede that such studies can provide valuable insights into the nature of financial management and control within households, they argue that the small and highly selective samples used in such studies do not permit reliable generalisations to national level. Thus, the fundamental problem that confronts those who do not utilise traditional statistical research methods is that their findings will be claimed to be unrepresentative and lacking in objectivity.

In relation to the interviewing process itself, it is argued that research in hidden areas requires a different approach from research in areas which do not challenge dominant norms and values. The first stage is to make visible those areas of experience which dominant norms and values tend to deny or ignore. For example, it may be taken as unproblematic, or as a given, by researchers (and interviewees) that domestic work should be unpaid. The second stage is to come to terms with the problems which arise when interviewing or asking questions in these hitherto hidden areas. Dominant norms and values not only influence the questions that researchers choose to ask, however. They also affect the way in which people respond to questions and the way that researchers interpret the answers. There may be no language available to the interviewee to describe their experience, let alone to make them meaningful to an interviewer or to themselves. Research practices which involve either pre-coded or pre-closed categories are often of limited use when trying to understand people's lives. This is because they assume that the researcher is already sufficiently familiar with the phenomenon being investigated (for example, women and poverty) as to be able to specify in advance the full range of experiences being studied and how these can be encapsulated and categorised. But of course there are aspects of women's lives that cannot be pre-known and pre-defined in such a way.

In this light, the differences between the quantitative and qualitative approaches become clearer. Complicated issues such as the distribution of power within marriage are not easily investigated by the use of structured questionnaires. If quantitative methods are used exclusively, an incomplete picture will result. A qualitative approach has many advantages in tackling sensitive subjects and can be employed to fill in the gaps. In this sense, the qualitative and quantitative traditions should be seen as complements to, rather than substitutes for, each other. This view has been expressed well by Wilson and Ramphele:

> each is periodically driven to distraction by the other, but each badly needs the other in order to avoid the Scylla of assuming that a particular case study is typical of the whole population and the Charbdis of asserting that what has been enumerated (and statistically analysed) is necessarily the whole (or even the most important part of the) truth.[2]

On the other hand, this "complementary" view has been strongly rejected (Guba and Lincoln, 1989) on the grounds that the issue is not about techniques but about the underlying assumptions which, in

---

[2] As quoted in Nolan and Callan (1994: 4)

their view, are fundamentally different. Such rigidity, in my view, can hinder the debate, as reality is more shifting than these very strong propositions seem to allow for.

All research, however, whether quantitative or qualitative, is not only influenced by the political and cultural context in which it operates; it is also influenced by the assumption of the discipline. Within each discipline there are dominant ways of defining and interpreting the world and research findings tend to be interpreted and defined according to the dominant theoretical assumptions within the discipline. This is true as much for qualitative research as for that using quantitative statistical methods (Lynch, 1993). However, the extent to which these dominant theoretical assumptions shape each piece of work is the subject of ongoing debate.

Olivier (1992) identifies a relatively new third paradigm — "emancipatory research" — which challenges the assumptions of the other approaches by arguing "that the only way to produce unalienated research is to change the social relations of research production and by confronting social oppression at whatever level it occurs". In this paradigm, analysis of any particular situation is not seen as an end in itself but as a step in understanding, which in turn promotes transformative action. This paradigm is discussed further below. The point here is to stress that what distinguishes the critical paradigm from the positivist/post-positivist or even phenomenological traditions is its emphatic normative orientation.

RESEARCH AND POLICY

What is the relationship between these different paradigms of research and social change? A continuum of least to greatest social change can be identified, extending through the forms of research which are purely descriptive to those explicitly oriented at actively making a difference to the situation.

Rowan (1981) identifies three ways in which research can change the world:

1. It makes a difference to the researcher

2. It makes a difference to those who come to know about the research and

3. It makes a difference to whatever, *or whomever*, is studied.

Under number three, research acts as an agent of change, and the researcher is involved in the process of change.

The most dominant model for research in Ireland is that coming from the positivist tradition. Evidence of an interrelationship between research findings and policy-making is difficult to establish. With the exception of the National Economic and Social Council, there are no specific policy-oriented institutions in Ireland[3] and even the NESC's role is as a central consensus builder, whose primary concern is identifying the principles which underlie economic and social policy rather than producing research findings or providing independent evaluation of policies and alternatives.

Some writers assume an identifiable and firm link between research and policy (Albaek, 1995). Others argue that there is little evidence that research findings are taken into account when policy is being drawn up: "Only a minuscule proportion, if any, of research findings affect policy" (Chambers, 1983). From a different perspective, it can be argued that such an engagement or explicit link with policy is avidly avoided by researchers, especially economists, with the "policy implications of research discussed in a perfunctory manner at the end of research papers" (O'Donnell, 1992).

The following two subsections look briefly at the relationship between research and policy in the areas of taxation and poverty, topics that have been at the forefront of political debate in Ireland over the past ten years. The evidence in relation to poverty and policy would suggest that research findings — at least in the narrow sense of specific policy implications — have been taken into account in policy-making and that the changes in poverty between 1987 and 1994 reflect policy priorities. The area of taxation proves more complicated, at two different levels. Firstly, it could be argued that, insofar as research recommendations from the NESC and from the Commission on Taxation have been taken on board, this was done belatedly, in a greatly changed, and improved, economic environment and, in some areas, under external pressure from the EU. Secondly, in the last number of years there has been a remarkable amount of consensus, among academic researchers and policy-

---

[3] Similar to, for example, the Brookings Institute in the USA. The question arises as to whether it would be advantageous to have such an explicitly policy oriented research institute in Ireland.

oriented bodies (NESC, INOU, CORI), that tax reductions should be primarily directed towards the low-paid. This has not been reflected in policy decisions most recently, at least in the general perception, in the December 1997 (1998) Budget.

Taxation and Policy

In recent years, many specific taxation reform proposals have been advanced by researchers and commentators in Ireland and there has been a remarkable level of agreement in a number of key areas. For example, it is broadly agreed that efforts should be made to reduce the tax burden on labour and, within the personal income tax system itself, that emphasis should be directed towards reducing the tax paid by those on lower incomes. Implementation of the latter implies that available resources be directed towards increases in personal allowances and/or reductions in the standard rate of tax.

Taxation policy has not, however, been overly influenced by this consensus. A significant portion of the available resources have been expended on tax reductions targeted at those on higher incomes via extensions in the width of the standard tax rate band and reductions in the higher rates of income tax.

More recently, however, the distinctions between the various proposals and their impact on taxation policy have become somewhat blurred. Recent governments have been forced to vigorously defend the distributional effects of their taxation policies, and in particular, the regressive effects of non-targeted tax reductions. When set against the two government parties' election manifestos and the programme for government, it could even be argued that Budget 1998 witnessed a bigger-than-expected increase in the personal allowance at the expense of a smaller-than-expected increase in the width of the standard rate tax band.

Poverty Research and Policy

There has been huge interest in poverty research in Ireland over the last 15 years. The increased availability of data from the various household Budget Surveys (1980, 1987 and 1994) and the review of social protection (Commission of Social Welfare, 1986) were greatly augmented by the surveys carried by the ESRI (1987, 1994) which specifically sought to establish the nature and extent of poverty and deprivation in Irish households. Numerous issues arise around the concept and measurement of poverty and on research methodologies employed in relation to these, but here the focus is on the policy implications of the research. The two ESRI studies (Survey of Income Distribution, Poverty and Use of State Services 1987 and the Living in Ireland Survey 1994) allow for a comparison in the picture of poverty presented and an assessment of the policies pursued in the intervening years. On the recommendation of the CSW and supported by the findings of the 1987 Survey, policy during this period was directed towards increasing the lowest social welfare payments — Unemployment Assistance and Supplementary Welfare Allowance. The changes since 1987 reflect those policy priorities. There was a reduction in poverty at the 40 per cent relative income line and a small increase in the overall numbers in poverty at the 50 and 60 per cent lines. This head count measure, however, takes no account of how far people fall below the income threshold. Measures that take into account the reduction in the depth of poverty at the 50 and 60 per cent lines, the poverty gap, show a consistent fall in aggregate poverty between 1987 and 1994. This anomaly arises because of the specific policies pursued: social welfare recipients were brought much closer to but not over the 50 per cent line, with the result that their poverty rate did not fall despite a substantial improvement in their relative position. The increased risk of being below the 50 and 60 percent relative income lines identified for a number of categories including the elderly also reflects the policy pursued: pensions which were set at a relatively high rate in 1987 increased more slowly than the lowest social welfare rates over the period to 1994. (See also Callan and Nolan's chapter in this volume.)

It could also, however, be argued that the poorest (i.e. those on the lowest social welfare payments) benefited at the cost of the rest of the poor, such that the total numbers in poverty remained the same over the period. By broadening the debate beyond policy-making and specific research implications, one could argue that the extensive research that has taken place on poverty over the last ten years may create a positive externality by serving to highlight the absence of research on wealth and on redistribution.

However tenuous the link between research findings from within the dominant social science research paradigms and policy-making, there is little to suggest that alternative paradigms will exert any direct influence on policy decisions, at least at the macro level. There is some evidence to suggest that findings from smaller studies employing alternative paradigms (for example, some of the studies undertaken by the Partnerships) do find their way into policy decisions at the level of individual Departments. This raises questions about both the process of mediation and timing, insofar as decisions are often made in reaction to great pressures, political or otherwise. The downside, even the danger, of relying on a "backer" to promote research findings for consideration in the policy process is the selectivity of the process.

But outcomes from research processes at the policy level are only one, even if the most emphasised, option. The question of direct action remains largely unaddressed in research discourse. Perhaps a positive by-product of the failure of different research paradigms to have a significant impact on policy is that it focuses attention on alternative loci of economic and social change.

RESEARCH AND ACTION

As the discussion on the philosophical frameworks underlying research methodologies demonstrated, there is no single way to acquire knowledge, but even this obstacle is only half of the equation. As Caputo (1987) puts it, "we are faced with the problem of not only what we can know but also of what we are to do".

Policy is not the only locus of what can be done to achieve social transformation. Economic and social change comes about in different ways and inevitably involves a disturbance of an earlier equilibrium; it occurs when people and resources are mobilised in new ways (O'Donnell, 1992). One route is empowerment at a grassroots level. Empowerment is a process one undertakes by or for oneself, not something done for someone. Critical theorists, and feminist academics in particular, have been criticised for their tendency to act (theory, empowerment, etc.) *for* instead of *with* people. A related criticism, particularly of critical theory, has been its overemphasis on theoretical problems (and again theory *for* rather than *with*), the use of which at a practical level is open to question. "The heart of the idea of empowerment involves people coming into their own power, a new relationship with their own contexts" (Fox-Keller, 1985).

This idea of research as transformative action stands in sharp contrast to the disinterested observer concept that dominates most research practices (Lynch, 1997). It specifically aims at generating radical understandings, which in turn challenge the status quo; but in seeking to free people from the domination of others, it also seeks to free them from their domination by forces which they themselves do not understand (Habermas, 1971). But keeping in mind the tendency referred to above to do "for" rather than "with", a crucial aspect of research within the critical paradigm is the process of reflexivity, as much on behalf of the researcher as of the researched. In this sense, the relationship between the two is reciprocal.

Action research however, is not, as is sometimes implied in social science research (especially economics), an excuse for the abandonment of theory. On the contrary, such engagement is central to the task of achieving useful knowledge. Figure 6.1 tries to illustrate the necessity, as well as the value, of interdependence between the different facets of research and change. It is in line with Poster's view (1989) that "we live in a world of pain, that much can be done to alleviate that pain and that theory has a crucial role to play in that process".

FIGURE 6.1: RESEARCH AS AN AGENT OF CHANGE: THEORY, METHOD, ACTION

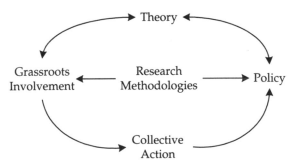

Dialogue, encounter and engagement act back on the research, just as engagement by policy-makers with researchers, and with theory, acts back on the conception of the problem faced. In this sense, praxis is the realisation of the interdependence between values, theory, method and its outcomes in terms of action, whether at policy or local level. It demonstrates the importance of non-hierarchical valuing, between method or technique on the one hand and theoretical models and the outcome of the research on the other.

REFERENCES

Albaek, E. (1995), "Between Knowledge and Power: Utilization of Social Science in Public Policy-making", *Policy Sciences*, Vol. 28.

Blackwell, J. (1986), "Social Science Research in Universities and other Institutions: Some Public Policy Issues", Working Paper No. 31, Resource and Environmental Policy Centre, UCD.

Callan, T. et al. (1996), *Poverty in the 1990s*, Dublin: Oak Tree Press.

Caputo, J. (1987), *Radical Hermeneutics: Repetition, Deconstruction and the Hermeneutic Project*, Bloomington: University of Indiana Press.

Chambers, R. (1983), *Rural Development: Putting the Last First*, Harlow: Longman.

Fay, B. (1987), *Critical Social Science*, Ithaca: Cornell University Press.

Fox-Keller, E. (1985), *Reflections on Gender and Science*, New Haven: Yale University Press.

Guba, E. and Y. Lincoln (1989), *Fourth Generation Evaluation*, Newbury Park, CA: Sage.

Habermas, J. (1971), *Theory and Practice*, Boston: Beacon Press.

Jenkins, S. (1994), "Poverty Measurement", *Journal of Social Policy*, Vol. 20, No. 4, pp. 457–83.

Lather, P. (1991), *Getting Smart*, New York: Routledge.

Lynch, K. (1993), "The Role of Research in Innovation and Change", *Nursing Review*, Vol. 12, No. 1.

Lynch, K. (1997), "Equality Studies, the Academy and the Role of Research in Social Change", Working Paper, Equality Studies Centre, UCD.

McCloskey, D. (1986), *The Rhetoric of Economics*, Brighton: Harvester.

Nolan, B. and T. Callan (1994), *Poverty and Policy in Ireland*, Dublin: Gill and Macmillan.

O'Donnell, R. (1992) "Economics and Policy: Beyond Science and Ideology", *Economic and Social Review*, Vol. 24, No. 1.

Olivier, M. (1992), "Changing the Social Relations of Research Production", *Disability, Handicap and Society*, Vol. 7, No. 2.

Poster, M. (1989), *Critical Theory and Post-structuralism*, Ithaca: Cornell University Press.

Rothschild, M. (1982), *An Enquiry into the Social Science Research Council*, London: HMSO.

Rowan, J. (1981), "A Dialectical Paradigm for Research", in P. Reason and J. Rowan (eds.), *Human Inquiry*, New York: Wiley and Sons Ltd.

Townsend, P. (1979), *Poverty in the United Kingdom*, Harmondsworth: Penguin.

Chapter 7

PARTNERSHIP AND POLICY-MAKING

Rory O'Donnell *and* Damian Thomas

1. THE LONG-TERM BACKGROUND

The relationship between the social partners and public policy-making has gone through various phases since Irish independence. For reasons summarised below, we do not dwell on the relationship between current social partnership and earlier patterns of interest group representation and mediation. Our chapter concentrates on the important developments of the past decade, the current situation and what might be done in the years ahead.

An attempt was made to establish a form of corporatism or vocationalism in the 1930s and 1940s. However, this had little discernible influence among those with political power. Also in the 1940s, Sean Lemass, while not an advocate of vocationalism, proposed a remarkable programme for the restructuring of collective bargaining and industrial relations along corporatist lines, as a means of promoting industrial development (Roche, 1997). However, in the context of the time, Lemass had little success in this project, given a lack of political support and the strong voluntarist tradition of Irish industrial relations. The opening of the economy and the emergence of growth in the 1960s was accompanied by the development of a distinct tripartism in aspects of Irish public policy. Representatives of trade unions and business were appointed to the wide range of public bodies established during those years. While some effort at national pay determination was evident in the 1960s, this approach became dominant in the 1970s, with a series of National Wage Agreements and National Understandings.

In our view it is not easy to establish the relationship between these earlier forms of tripartism and the social partnership approach which has developed since 1987. One important study by Hardiman suggested that the structures of Irish industrial relations and politics were not conducive to successful concertation (Hardiman, 1988, 1992). While that case was based on past developments, the success of social partnership since 1987 might warrant a re-examination of both the requirements for effective concertation and the patterns evident in Ireland in earlier decades. Such a re-examination might reveal previously unseen elements of continuity. Equally, however, a strong case could be made that current social partnership represents a distinctive phase in interest representation, industrial relations and public policy, so emphasising discontinuity. Since this debate cannot be resolved at present, and does not seem critical to the concerns of this volume, we say no more about the long-term background to current social partnership and public policy-making.

2. THE PAST TEN YEARS

The Social Partnership Programmes

In a context of deep despair in Irish society, the social partners — acting through the tripartite National Economic and Social Council — hammered out an agreed strategy to escape from the vicious circle of real stagnation, rising taxes and exploding debt. While the NESC is an advisory body — in which employers, trade unions, farmers and senior civil servants analyse policy issues — the NESC's *A Strategy for Development* (1986) formed the basis upon which a new government and the social partners quickly negotiated the Programme for National Recovery, which ran from 1987 to 1990. This was to be the first of four agreements that have recently brought Ireland to more than a decade of negotiated economic and social governance. Following the influence of *A Strategy for Development* (1986), the negotiation of each subsequent social partnership agreement has been preceded by an NESC Strategy report, setting out the shared perspective of the social partners on the achievements and limits of the last programme and the parameters within which a new programme should be negotiated (NESC, 1990, 1993, 1996).

The Programme for National Recovery, 1987–90 (PNR) involved agreement between employers, trade unions, farming interests and government on wage levels in both the private and public sectors for a three-year period. Moderate wage growth was seen as essential to international competitiveness and to achieving control of the public finances. However, the PNR, and its successors, involved far more than centralised wage bargaining. They involved agreement on a wide range of economic and social policies — including tax reform, the evolution of welfare payments, trends in health spending, structural adjustments and Ireland's adherence to the narrow band of the ERM. On the macroeconomic front, each partner agreed that they would not generate inflationary pressures, which would warrant devaluation, and would not seek devaluation when external problems arose. The PNR also established a new Central Review Committee (CRC) to monitor implementation of the programme and ensure ongoing dialogue between government and the social partners on key economic and social policy issues.

The PNR enlisted trade union support for a radical correction of the public finances. In return, the government accepted that the value of social welfare payments would be maintained, and that public spending cuts would not be extended to these transfer payments. In addition, it undertook to introduce reforms in income tax which were of benefit to union members. Moreover, the agreement set out the general direction of government policy in a number of areas, with the broad parameters having been agreed between the social partners.

The three subsequent agreements — the Programme for Economic and Social Progress (PESP) 1990–93; the Programme for Competitiveness and Work (PCW) 1994–96; and Partnership 2000, 1997–2000 — had a broadly similar form. Each has covered a three-year period, and has set out agreed pay increases for that period. They also contained agreements on a variety of policy areas, including commitments to social equality and tax reform. While the macroeconomic strategy has been adhered to consistently since 1987, subsequent agreements contained policy initiatives which are worthy of note.

The PESP (1990–93) contained a "local bargaining" clause which allowed bargaining to take place at plant level for up to an additional three per cent wage increase. That agreement also initiated an experimental new approach to long-term unemployment. Partnership companies were established, on a pilot basis, in 12 areas of particular disadvantage in order to design and implement a more coordinated, multi-dimensional approach to social exclusion. These were complemented by the Community's LEADER programme, which involves a partnership approach to rural development. This approach has been examined and strongly supported by the social partners, through the NESC (see NESC, 1995). Indeed, a recent OECD evaluation of Ireland's local economic development policies considered that the partnership approach constituted an experiment in economic regeneration and participative democracy which is, potentially, of international significance (Sabel, 1996). This pilot initiative was subsequently extended to a larger number of areas. The PCW (1994–96) extended the focus on increasing the number of people at work and reducing the level of unemployment. Although we cannot be sure, it seems that the existence of national-level social partnership was a condition for the emergence of new, experimental, approaches at local level. There continues to be a complex relationship between the national-level arrangements — including both social partnership and the national civil service — and the important local development initiatives of recent years.

The Partnership 2000 agreement also marks some progress in addressing what was seen by many as a weakness in the PNR, PESP and PCW. It had been argued that the high level of partnership at national level was not adequately reflected at enterprise level. In addition to weakening the perceived benefits of social partnership, from a trade union perspective, this might also limit the economic benefits to the macroeconomic and public finance areas. It was argued that the high degree of consensus could also be used to address Ireland's deeper developmental challenge in product development, innovation, training and the introduction of new work and organisational patterns. Reflecting recommendations in the 1996 NESC Strategy report, Partnership 2000 made provision for a National Centre for Partnership to develop partnership at enterprise level and to provide encouragement, training, information and support to employers' and employees' representatives.

The current programme also contains a significant measure of agreement on action to modernise the public service enlisting the social partners in support of the Strategic Management Initiative which has been developing in the past two years. This is potentially an important aspect of the most recent agreement, since it was felt by many that the pay moderation and improved performance delivered by the private sector since 1987 was not matched in the public sector.

Widening Inclusion in the Partnership Process: the NESF

An important feature of social partnership in the past ten years has been the widening of partnership. In 1993, the government established a new partnership body, the National Economic and Social Forum (NESF). Its membership encompassed what are sometimes referred to as the "traditional social partners" — trade unions, employer associations and farm organisations — and representatives of the community and voluntary sectors and of the main political parties in the Oireachtas, which had previously been outside the partnership arrangements. The changing participation in social partnership was also marked by a widening of the NESC's membership, to include a representative from the Irish National Organisation of the Unemployed (INOU) among the Government nominees.

The role of the NESF is to develop economic and social policy initiatives, particularly initiatives to combat unemployment, and to contribute to the formation of a national consensus on social and economic matters. Since its establishment, the Forum has published 16 Reports and eight Opinions. Its Report Number 4, *Ending Long-term Unemployment* (1994b), played an important strategic role in the development of active labour market policy. This is widely seen as having prompted the development of the Local Employment Service, which aims to assist actively the transition from welfare to work.

The Forum re-appointed in 1995 finished its work with an overview of Irish social partnership, *A Framework for Partnership — Enriching Strategic Consensus through Participation* (1997). That study analysed the strengths and weaknesses of social partnership arrangements, and proposed new arrangements for a more inclusive and effective partnership approach. We draw on that report in the Section 4, when we discuss possible changes in partnership and the policy process.

The recently negotiated agreement, Partnership 2000, continued this process of widening inclusion. The negotiation of the programme was undertaken in a new manner, with a wider range of social and economic interests involved. These included the INOU, and other groups addressing problems of social exclusion. The new "four-pillar" structure for negotiation is discussed in Section 3. Following the recommendations of NESC and NESF, Partnership 2000 includes an action programme for greater social inclusion. In

addition to the general pay and tax provisions of the programme —
which are designed to promote employment — this includes the National Anti-Poverty Strategy; reforms of tax and welfare designed to
improve the incentives for and reward from work; an expansion of
targeted employment measures; further measures to address educational disadvantage; and consolidation of the local partnership approach to both economic and social development. The impact of
some of these elements of Partnership 2000 on government policy is
considered in Section 3.

Characterising the Emerging Partnership System

The development of social partnership since 1987 has involved a
wide range of economic and political actors in a complex process of
negotiation and interaction. Detailed, shared analysis of economic
and social problems and policies has been a key aspect of this process. Indeed, that analysis has, for a variety of reasons, focused on the
partnership system itself. In order to assess the applicability of the
partnership approach in the new economic context of EMU, it was
necessary to assess thoroughly the effects of the centralised partnership system of wage bargaining and the consensual approach to
management of the public finances (NESC, 1996). In order to develop
the overall approach and make it more inclusive, it was necessary to
characterise the nature, purpose and goals of partnership. In its 1996
report, *Strategy into the 21st Century*, the NESC offered the following
characterisation of social partnership, as it has developed in the past
decade.

1. The partnership process involves a combination of *consultation,
    negotiation* and *bargaining*

2. The partnership process is heavily dependent on a *shared under-
    standing* of the key mechanisms and relationships in any given
    policy area

3. The *government* has a unique role in the partnership process. It
    provides the arena within which the process operates. It shares
    some of its authority with social partners. In some parts of the
    wider policy process, it actively supports formation of interest
    organisations

4. The process reflects *interdependence* between the partners. The partnership is necessary because no party can achieve its goals without a significant degree of support from others

5. Partnership is characterised by a *problem-solving* approach designed to produce consensus, in which various interest groups address joint problems

6. Partnership involves *trade-offs* both between and within interest groups

7. The partnership process involves different participants on various agenda items, ranging from national macroeconomic policy to local development (NESC, 1996: 66).

Careful examination of a process with these characteristics shows that it involves a tension between two different conceptions, or dimensions, of partnership:

• Functional interdependence, bargaining and deal-making and

• Solidarity, inclusiveness and participation.

While effective partnership involves both of these, it cannot be based entirely on either. Indeed, there is a third dimension that transcends these two:

• Deliberation, interaction, problem-solving and shared understanding.

The relationship between these three, and the preconditions for effective partnership, are examined in the recent NESF report *A Framework for Partnership — Enriching Strategic Consensus through Participation* (1997), upon which we draw in Section 4.

Economic Performance under Social Partnership

The social partnership approach produced the much-needed recovery from the disastrous early and mid-1980s and has underpinned a sustained period of growth since then. In the decade 1986–96, Irish GDP has grown by an average of 4.9 per cent a year, compared to an OECD average of 2.4 per cent. Employment has grown by 1.8 per cent per year, compared to an OECD average of 1.0 per cent and an

EU average of 0.3 per cent. More recently, growth of output and employment has reached unprecedented levels. From 1993 to 1996, Irish
national output has risen by 7.5 per cent a year, and employment by
a remarkable 4.0 per year. The debt/GDP ratio, which reached 117
per cent in 1986, has fallen steadily, to 76 per cent in 1996. Inflation
has remained significantly below the EU average and, having reduced inflation in the 1980s, Ireland did not need a second bite of the
cherry (and a second deep recession), as the UK did. Low and predictable inflation has underpinned the three-year wage agreements
which have, in turn, freed both management and trade union energies
for issues such as corporate strategy, technical change, training in the
workplace, working practices and other important influences on international competitiveness. However, the performance on unemployment has been much less satisfactory. Indeed, unemployment actually
increased in the early 1990s, and has only begun to fall significantly in
recent years. Despite the recent fall in unemployment, the single greatest problem facing Irish society remains the high proportion of long-
term unemployment and the associated poverty and social exclusion.

Consensus and Opposition

While the evolution of Irish economic policy in the past decade has
been marked by a high level of consensus — both between the social
partners and across the political spectrum — some economists have
stood outside the consensus. Some have objected to the politicisation
of industrial relations, because it "adds to the bargaining power of
trade unionism on an ongoing basis" (Durkan, 1992; though see
Durkan and Harmon, 1996). Others have argued that the social partners are "insiders", whose pay and conditions have been protected at
the expense of "outsiders who would work for less", and that social
partnership has had the effect of "raising the level of unemployment
and emigration" (Walsh and Leddin, 1992). In its 1996 assessment of
the achievements and limits of the social partnership approach, the
NESC argued that these arguments require careful consideration. It
suggests that at least two qualifications are warranted.

First, the proposition that centralised agreements have prevented
the unemployed undercutting the wages of existing workers, and
have thereby increased unemployment, is both conceptually and
empirically questionable. In *The Labour Market as a Social Institution*,

Nobel prize-winning economist Robert Solow (1990) identifies the absence of wage undercutting by unemployed workers as one of the fundamental features of labour markets, observed almost everywhere. He develops a conceptual framework which explains why wage undercutting is no more in the interests of firms than it is in the interest of workers and unions. Thus, he shows that in normal labour markets, there are norms which prevent wage undercutting. Consequently, it seems inaccurate, on the part of the opponents of Irish social partnership, to attribute the absence of wage undercutting to the centralised agreements of the past decade (NESC, 1996: 111–12).

Second, in arguing that social partnership arrangements are maintaining a high level of unemployment, these economists ignore the fact that, without national agreements, income determination will remain a non-competitive, highly collectivised process, with tendencies to monopoly power on both sides of industry. Ireland is unlikely to move to atomistic bargaining, which would seem to underpin the analytical argument and the preference for decentralised bargaining. It remains to be explained how, in a world of decentralised, sectional and non-political bargaining, agents acting in their own self-interest will take *greater* account of the problems of the unemployed and other marginalised groups.

3. THE CURRENT CONTEXT

Social Partners and Policy Process

Through the negotiation of three successive Programmes, the social partners have aligned themselves to a consistent and coherent consensus-based strategic framework, focused on macroeconomic policy, income distribution and structural adjustment (O'Donnell, 1993; NESC, 1996). However, this emerging type of "neo-corporatist" governance extends beyond the (re)negotiation of multi-annual agreements, as the social partners have been effectively co-opted into the public policy-making domain. Whilst interest groups in Ireland — particularly peak associations representing business, agriculture and labour[1] — have traditionally enjoyed a relatively high degree of

---

[1] During the 1980s, the trade union leadership experienced increased "political isolation" due to a combination of Fitzgerald's disavowal of Social Partnership arrangements and relatively poor personal relationships with the Taoiseach, and

access to the political arena (see Collins, 1995; Girvin, 1989; Regan and Wilson, 1986; McCann, 1993; Weinz, 1986), the social partnership has resulted in a more institutionalised, structured and regularised mode of participation, and in particular, increased involvement in policy formulation, monitoring and, to a lesser degree, implementation.

> [The social partners] are now a more powerful influence in the policy process, to the extent that some politicians feel that trade unionists, for example, have more power than backbenchers. It would be unthinkable to set up a task force or policy committee of any seriousness or weight without social partner representation (Senior civil servant, Department of Tánaiste).[2]

Informal, highly personalised interaction between the principal participants remains an integral feature of this emerging corporatist governance, with the trade union leadership, in particular, forging close working relationships with senior civil servants within the Department of the Taoiseach.

Deeper and Wider Participation in the Social Partnership

Prior to the negotiation of Partnership 2000, this conferral of "public status" (Offe, 1985) was confined primarily to the peak level economic actors, namely ICTU, IBEC, the IFA and ICMSA.[3] Whilst the National Economic and Social Forum (NESF) was, in a comparative context, an important innovation in public consultation through partnership (Davis, 1997) and the Council had exerted some influence on policy design, it was recognised that participation in the so-

---

as such a primary incentive for ICTU in seeking a return to centralised concertation was that it offered them an opportunity to regain political voice and influence at the national level (Hardiman, 1992; NESC, 1990; Roche, 1997; Sheehan, 1996).

[2] In interview with Damian Thomas, May 1997.

[3] National farming organisations in Ireland had, from the mid 1960s, enjoyed a close working relationship with the Department of Agriculture (Dooney, 1988; Murphy, 1997), forming what some commentators have referred to as a policy network (Collins, 1995) or "closed policy community" (Adshead, 1996). Consequently the social partnership merely paralleled the *meso* or sectoral corporatist relationship that prevailed with regards to agricultural policy.

cial partnership process remained unevenly developed (NESC, 1996; NESF, 1994, 1996). More specifically, constituent groups such as INOU, The Community Workers Co-operative and the Conference of Religious of Ireland (CORI) articulated the view that the "third strand's" involvement, through NESF and ad hoc task forces, was effectively "participation without power". Also, they felt that their relative inability to exert any discernible influence on the direction of public policy was institutionalised and perpetuated by the lack of full social partner status and their continued exclusion from the formal negotiation process for the national agreements.[4]

In this context, the decision to fully incorporate the "third strand" into the process of negotiating and ratifying Partnership 2000, and to accord full social partnership status to the social pillar, represented a potentially innovative and significant development in the evolution of economic and social governance within the state.[5] The decision to reconfigure the social partnership on the basis of four pillars (see Table 7.1), in addition to the government, reflected to an extent the considerable momentum and pressure that had been generated regarding the necessity of widening and extending the degree of participation in policy deliberation and implementation within the framework of the social partnership (NESF, 1996; NESC, 1996). This development was certainly encouraged by the growth in stature and standing of some third-pillar groups as a result of their performance both within NESF and in local-level partnership initiatives. They had, moreover, garnered considerable support for national level inclusion amongst the key players, including the leadership of ICTU, the senior civil servants in the Departments of the Taoiseach and Tanaiste and also critically from across the political spectrum, as all of the party leaders had articulated the need to develop a broader-based national consensus. As such, the INOU, who had vigorously campaigned for full social partner status for their organisation, argued that by this stage they were effectively "pushing at an open door".[6]

---

[4] This analysis of issues relating to the Third Strand or Social Pillar draws on interviews conducted by Damian Thomas with representatives from the INOU, CWC, Community Platform, National Youth Council, National Women's Council of Ireland and the NESF Secretariat in 1994 and 1997.

[5] This perception was confirmed by many participants from the social pillar.

[6] Mike Allen (INOU).

TABLE 7.1: THE FOUR PILLARS OF THE SOCIAL PARTNERSHIP

I.	Farming Organisations	IFA: Irish Farming Association ICMSA: Irish Creamery and Milk Suppliers Association Macra na Feirme ICOS: Irish Co-operative Society
II.	Trade Unions	ICTU: Irish Congress of Trade Unions

III.	Community and
	Voluntary Organisations
		INOU: Irish National Organisation of the
		   Unemployed
		NWCI: National Women's Council of
		   Ireland
		NYCI: National Youth Council of Ireland
		CORI: Committee of Religious Superiors
		Centres for the Unemployed
		Society of St. Vincent de Paul
		Protestant Aid
		Community Platform[7]

IV.	Employer and Business Organisations	IBEC: Irish Business and Employers Confederation CIF: Construction Industry Federation CCI: Chambers of Commerce of Ireland ITIC: Irish Tourist Industry Confederation IEA: Irish Exporters Association SFA: Small Firms Association

---

[7] The Community Platform was set up by the Community Workers Co-operative, the INOU, the NWCI, Irish Rural Link, Irish Traveller Movement, Focus on Children, Gay and Lesbian Equality Network, One Parent Exchange Network, CORI, Forum for People with Disabilities, Pavee Point, Community Action Network, European Anti-Poverty Network and Irish Commission for Prisoners Overseas as a mechanism to organise the future participation of this sector in the Partnership. Whilst established to facilitate more effective and extensive participation in Social partnership, the decision to involve the Social Pillar in the negotiations on non-pay issues may have come too quickly for the network as they suddenly found themselves thrust into the national political arena. Moreover, the fact that certain constituent groups within Community Platform have also been awarded individual social partner status, which they will be loathe to relinquish, generates a number of issues regarding how the Platform will co-ordinate third-strand participation with regards to the monitoring function.

Even in the context of this momentum for inclusion, the rationale for affording social partner status to such a disparate and diverse range of groups was not fully articulated — and may not have conformed to the principles set out by NESC (1996). Indeed, a prevailing perception amongst the participants from all four pillars was that the consequences of extending participation and the mechanisms by which this was to achieved were "not fully thought through" and that having decided to allow some groups in, the process effectively "snowballed".[8] This perception was given further credence by the decision to broaden the business pillar beyond those organisations, IBEC and CIF, who were to have responsibility for negotiating the private-sector pay elements of the deal. Although formally a part of the widened "business pillar", in reality they formed a distinctive entity, as IBEC were determined to retain their status as the voice of business at the national level on all issues, not solely pay.[9]

The Political and Economic Context

As with its predecessors, the political and economic conjuncture within which Partnership 2000 was negotiated invariably impinged

---

[8] This is particularly evident in the case of the religious organisations who were invited to participate in the negotiations. Whilst CORI are a well-established pluralist pressure group on issues of social justice and equity who have participated, for example, in NESF, The St Vincent De Paul Society are effectively a charitable organisation. Having allowed these groups into the process, it was thought necessary to include Protestant Aid, lest it appeared that that process favoured Catholic organisations only. As such, two groups who had not voiced any desire to be social partners were thrust into the negotiations process. The speed with which this decision was taken was also evident, as it was only in August 1996, two months before negotiations were to open on Partnership 2000, that NESF had stipulated that the issue of extending full negotiation status to third-strand bodies on non-pay issues remained unresolved (NESF, 1996).

[9] There was undoubtedly a degree of interaction and informal tic-tacking between IBEC and the other business groups. Indeed, the SFA are an affiliate of the former and as such held extensive pre-negotiation meetings in order to finalise their respective agenda. Leading representatives from IBEC indicated that the other business groups, aside from the SFA, were mainly single-issue groups whose agenda was broadly compatible with their own. Nevertheless IBEC displayed no enthusiasm for negotiating as part of a broader business grouping, even on non-pay issues. There was some concern on the trade union side that IBEC utilised the other business group in the negotiations to push a more overt business agenda, so that IBEC would appear to be settling for less than this constituency.

on and shaped the nature of the agreement. The fact that Fine Gael
and Democratic Left formed part of the incumbent government ensured that all five of the main political parties had now engaged in
and concluded a neo-corporatist type of agreement. This demonstrated that the social partnership has been institutionalised within
party political landscape to the extent that there was now an identifiable cross-party consensus that this represented a viable and appropriate approach to economic and social policy formulation.[10] John
Bruton's endorsement of the social partnership was particularly significant, as he was a prominent advocate of Fine Gael's orientation
away from "tripartism" in the 1980s (Redmond, 1985), and more significantly, he had again been a stern critic of such arrangements since
1987, arguing that they undermined the Dáil by ceding political
power to unelected interest groups. As Taoiseach, however, he publicly stated his conversion, no more symbolically than in his address
to the 1995 ICTU Biennial Conference[11]. The political climate was also
coloured by the fact that this would be the last agreement before a
general election and, consequently, the Rainbow Coalition were ea-
ger to ensure an agreement was concluded as they did not want to be
labelled as the administration that could not deliver the social partners, given its presumed association with national economic success.

The economic context in which Partnership 2000 was negotiated
was also different, for whilst the social partnership era had been associated with improved economic performance, lower inflation and
the correction of public finances, the PCW years (1994–96) had witnessed unparalleled success across a whole range of economic indicators (NESC, 1996). Economic growth had not only accelerated in
the period 1994–96, with GNP growth averaging 7.5 per cent but,
more significantly, some 145,000 jobs had been generated (Table 7.2),
which represented a remarkable turnaround in what had been one of
the less impressive aspects of economic and social concertation.

---

[10] See Denis Coghlan, "Social Partners in the Bag", *Irish Times*, January 1997.

[11] "You are quite accurate in saying that my experience of social partnership
started out as one of scepticism. I would have to say however that the results of
social partnership are such that anybody who has intelligence has to support the
concept because it has worked for the benefit of everybody." John Bruton's
Opening Address to the ICTU Biennial Delegate Conference, Tralee 1995; Report
of the Proceedings of the Biennial Delegate Conference, p. 2.

Similarly, unemployment, which had remained unacceptably high, was now showing a discernible downward trend and on both accounts this impressive performance continued into 1997. Consequently, as NESC emphasised, the context had shifted from one of "managing crisis" to "managing growth" and, whilst welcomed, this generated attendant pressures in terms of maintaining the necessary coherent and consistent strategy at a time of rising expectations. Certainly, there was recognition amongst the trade union leadership regarding the need to "reward" workers for their pay restraint in the face of the seemingly inexorable rise in company profits (OECD, 1997; Sweeney, 1997). Equally, the social pillar were of the view that the economic boom had equipped the state with the resources to make a substantive attack on social exclusion.

TABLE 7.2: NUMBERS AT WORK AND UNEMPLOYMENT RATE, 1987–97

Year	Total at Work	Change	Unemployment Rate
1987	1,090,000	9,000	18.8
1988	1,090,000	0	16.4
1989	1,088,000	–2,000	15.1
1990	1,134,000	46,000	13.0
1991	1,134,000	0	14.7
1992	1,145,000	11,000	15.3
1993	1,152,000	7,000	15.7
1994	1,188,000	36,000	14.7
1995	1,248,000	60,000	12.2
1996	1,297,000	49,000	11.9
1997	1,338,000	41,000	9.7

Source: Sweeney (1997: 55).

The Negotiation Process for Partnership 2000

Figure 7.1 illustrates the model that was adopted for the negotiation of Partnership 2000; apart from an initial multilateral session,[12] discussions were conducted bilaterally between the "rooms" and the government's negotiating team[13]. IBEC and ICTU were thus conceptualised as constituting one room, given their joint responsibility for the negotiation of the pay and tax elements of the agreement.[14]. Whilst the social pillar were critical of the fact that this precluded any substantive three-way negotiation of the distribution of resources between pay, tax and social exclusion measures, from the perspective of the trade unions and employers it was indicative of the fact that pay is the "glue" of the national agreements and that consequently this rationale must permeate the deliberative process.

FIGURE 7.1: THE FOUR-ROOM NEGOTIATING MODEL

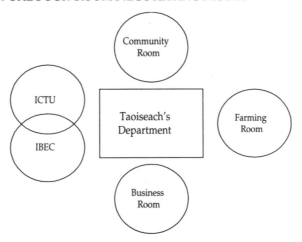

---

[12] At this session all of the participants were given the opportunity to present position papers in the context of the NESF document *Post PCW Negotiations — A New Deal?* and the NESC Report *Strategy into the 21st Century*.

[13] Top ranking officials from the Department of the Taoiseach constituted the core of this team and they were supplemented by ministers and senior civil servants from various departments, depending on the issues which were being addressed.

[14] For this reason representatives from the INOU were of the opinion that NESC was the forum in which the real negotiations effectively took place with regards to the tax/wage trade-off for the subsequent national agreement.

The discourse, bargaining and trade-offs which were channelled through this formal mode of negotiation were both reinforced and at times paralleled by extensive informal interaction between the participants. The consensus among the participants was that the skill and acumen of the negotiators from the Department of the Taoiseach were ultimately critical to the success of this often "bewildering" discursive process,[15] as it was they who had the pivotal role of formulating the views, concerns and objectives of all the "rooms" into a final document whose content the participants could live with.

Partnership 2000

In Section 2, we summarised the main provisions of Partnership 2000. Here our interest is in its emphasis on the use of budgetary mechanisms to deliver on income distribution and social inclusion, to the extent that there was a stipulated figure for tax reductions. This inevitably focused attention on the Rainbow Coalition's Budget introduced in the wake of the social partnership agreement. The budget was actually referred to by the Finance Minister, Ruairí Quinn, as the Social Partners' Budget, thus demonstratively highlighting both the role of the social partners in policy formulation and the degree to which pay bargaining and budgetary policy had been incorporated within a broader economic and social concertation. Commenting on the emergence of such a "linkage" in the 1970s, O'Brien (1981) suggested that it was creating profound changes in the nature, functions and prerogatives of democratic government. In the current era, however, the integration of the social partners into the formal political and administrative machinery of the state was perceived as a positive development, both in terms of "good policy-making" and also with regards to actually enhancing democracy within the state.

Despite Consensus, Politics Still Matters

It was suggested by some that the relationship between budgetary policy and the social partner agreements, in an election year,

---

[15] The participants interviewed highlighted, in particular, the cycle of drafts and reworked sections which were circulated between the rooms and the fact that, at times, changes could be made and one would not have a clear view who was responsible for them.

introduced an unfortunate layer of ambiguity into the relationship between parliamentary and interest group democracy. Whoever was victorious at the polls was bound by policy commitments entered into by the previous administration and the "unelected" social partners (Lee, 1997a). Whilst Lee acknowledges that macroeconomic policy was conditioned by the requirements of the Maastricht Treaty, he may overestimate the direct influence which national agreements have on policy formulation. The political institutionalisation of the social partnership since 1987 has ensured that, rather than operating as an alternative to the Dáil,[16] it has effectively evolved into a symbiotic and functional sub-polity of the formal representative system.[17] The emphasis within Partnership 2000 on establishing broad strategic or theoretical policy guidelines ensures that it can be envisaged as a dynamic process of bargained co-operation[18] in which there is considerable scope for shaping or orienting policies in a certain direction.[19] Thus, Partnership 2000 was a considerable influence on, but

---

[16] P. Yeates, "The Fifth Estate", *Irish Times*, 5 January 1991. The argument that there was an emerging corporatist threat to the power of the Dáil and the parliamentary representative system has tended to ignore the perennial weakness of the Dáil as a legislature (Chubb, 1992; Farrell, 1993; Gallagher and Komito, 1993) which ensured that policy-making power resided with the Executive (Arkins, 1990).

[17] This is how Lehmbruch (1979) describes the relationship between corporatist institutions and parliament within Austria, generally considered to be the prime example of a "corporatist state". It is important to consider that the social partnership emerged in the context of a "governance" crisis regarding the capacity of the formal administrative and political machinery to develop appropriate policies to address the nation's economic and fiscal problems (Honohan, 1988; O'Donnell, 1993; Sheehan, 1996). Thus, whilst social partnership arrangements may have been perceived initially as a threat, in reality they have supported and contributed to the development of formal representative democracy. One interviewee noted that social partnership, rather than replacing the traditional political parties, had in effect saved them.

[18] Archer (1991) argues that Australian Wage Accords of the 1980s should be considered not as policies *per se*, but as a process through which government, trade unions and employers co-operated on bi- and tripartite bases in policy consultation, formulation and implementation.

[19] The Central Review Committee was considered, by the unions in particular, as a key institutional arrangement through which they could seek to influence economic and social policy within the context of the social partnership. Whilst the efficacy of the monitoring arrangements for Partnership 2000 have still to be

did not necessarily determine, the agenda of the new administration elected in June 1997.

> Incorporated into these policies is the commitment to fulfil the engagements entered into with the social partners in Partnership 2000 which runs until 1999. (Fianna Fáil and Progressive Democrats Action Programme for the Millennium, 1997: Foreword, p. 1)

The nature of this relationship between national agreements and government policy was clearly demonstrated by the Fianna Fáil/PD government's decision to honour the Partnership 2000 tax commitments, primarily through a reduction in the rate of personal income tax rather than by reforming the bands or increasing personal allowances.[20] This approach ensured that the benefits of the £519 million tax cuts were captured primarily by middle to higher income earners, leading to considerable criticism from the social pillar and ICTU,[21] who as one of the architects of the tax-wage trade-off, accused the government of contravening the spirit, if not the letter of Partnership 2000.[22] The Programme had stipulated that "action on personal taxation will be implemented in an integrated manner with measures to promote social inclusion". The Fianna Fáil/PD government had clearly not ignored Partnership 2000,[23] but rather had shaped the "commitments" to reflect its own policy preferences[24] and, indeed, it

---

determined, there is a perception amongst the social pillar that it represents a potential mechanism for seeking to shape the development of social partnership.

[20] The NESC Report, *Strategy into the 21st Century*, suggested that increasing personal allowances was the preferred policy option for meeting the strategic priority of reducing the tax burden on lower to middle income earners (p. 240–41).

[21] Sheehan (1997) notes that there was a discernible hardening of ICTU's stance on the budget due to the influence of SIPTU who, given their high proportion of members in lower pay categories, adopted a hostile stance to McCreevy's budget from the outset.

[22] Sheehan, ibid.

[23] As already noted, it is directly referred to in the coalition's Programme for Government, whilst McCreevy's Budget speech stated that the measures introduced were designed to deliver the resources to meet the tax and social inclusion commitments agreed upon in Partnership 2000.

[24] Whilst a predominant theme of the political commentary during the election was the "consensus" or lack of difference between the two coalition options, it

defended this decision by claiming that it was the government's prerogative to do so.[25] Thus within the space of less than 12 months,
there was a shift from the social partners' budget to the party political budget.

An Evolving Model of Economic and Social Governance

Although a defining feature of the social partnership has been its capacity to align the social partners with a coherent and consistent
policy framework, it is evident that within this broad consensus,
there is still space for real "political" choices. The structured co-
option of the social partners into the public policy domain has fostered the emergence of a neo-corporatist mode of economic and social governance, which has been primarily tripartite in character.
However, the emergence of a "social pillar" with full social partner
status represents a systematic attempt to extend the process of concertation beyond functionally interdependent economic actors.
Whilst the social pillar were clearly the "junior partners" within
Partnership 2000, they did partake in substantive negotiations and
have been afforded an equal role in monitoring the development of
the social partnership.[26] Whilst the inter-associational relationships
within corporatist institutions are invariably influenced by the distribution of power in the wider society, there is not a direct linear

---

was generally recognised that there was a discernible difference in their proposed tax reforms. Whilst the unions and social pillar pointed to the fact that the
Government's approach deviated from the NESC strategy, which was champi-
oned by the Rainbow Coalition, it was clearly based on the stance with which
they had approached the electorate.

[25] SIPTU claimed that the government had effectively reneged on commitments
given to the unions during the negotiations for Partnership 2000. Mr McCreevy,
however, countered this arguing that SIPTU were referring to "options", not
firm commitments, and that it was the Government's prerogative to finalise the
precise details of budgetary policy within the overall commitment to deliver
£900 million in tax reductions over three years. Indeed, the McCreevy Budget, in
conjunction with its predecessor, ensured that these commitments were met
within two years.

[26] NESF (1996) had postulated three options for third-strand involvement in the
social partnership — consultation, participation and negotiation — and the view
from the social pillar was that their role in Partnership 2000 went beyond the
first two options and was closest to full negotiative status (Community Platform,
1996: interviews with social pillar representatives).

transfer of power and resources into these "forums", and they then create an opportunity for less empowered organisations to exert an "unexpected" influence within the political domain (Cohen and Rogers 1992; Mansbridge, 1992; Regini, 1984, 1995).[27]

This more "inclusive" structure suggests that the conceptualisation of social partnership concertation as a model of tripartite functional economic interdependence is increasingly insufficient. There is a nascent "corporate pluralism" emerging in which there is regularised, compartmentalised and structured co-option into the public policy process for a diverse network of interest groups (Amin and Thomas, 1996; Jordan, 1984). These developments at the centre, in conjunction with partnership initiatives at the local and regional level, represent innovative attempts to reconfigure the relationships between representative and participative democracy which are fostering a new forums of deliberative democracy. This emerging corporatist governance, in its tripartite or more heterogeneous forms, has not replaced but coexists and overlaps with pluralist modes of policy in a shifting and dynamic relationship (Crouch, 1983; Martin, 1983), thus effectively generating hybrid forms of governance, both within and between policy spheres.[28]

---

[27] Commentators such as Cohen and Rogers and Mansbridge highlight the democratic potential of neo-corporatist relationships by stressing the fact that there is a more equitable distribution of power between interest groups than in the free market and that their interaction is imbued with a sense of national interest. Regini (1984, 1995) indicates that the stimulus for trade unions to enter into tripartite political exchange is that this can actually compensate for their relative lack of power in the labour market. Whilst it would be generally accepted that IBEC are the most powerful of the social partners in terms of their influence over the agenda, there is a perception amongst employers that the social partnership had enabled the union movement to actually "punch above their weight". Given the nature of interest group politics in Ireland, it is obvious that national employers' associations would continue to exercise considerable influence without corporatist-style agreements, and thus it is arguable that the social partnership, if not wholly attenuating their power, certainly shapes how they seek to articulate their interests.

[28] Pontussen (1992), referring to Sweden, states that no state is "corporatist *in toto*" and highlights that the role of the corporatist social partners in public policy-making varied according to the policy sphere in question. Moreover, it is evident that the range of areas in which they are involved and the degree of authority afforded to them varies over time (Lehmbruch, 1982) What is interesting from the Irish example is that these hybrid forms of governance emerge within the same policy sphere.

4. WHAT NEEDS TO BE DONE?

The achievements and limits of social partnership have been analysed in numerous studies of economic performance, industrial relations, unemployment and poverty. Indeed, its achievements in
addressing, and failing to address, social needs are reflected in the
substantive chapters on these issues included in this volume. Our
concern here is with ways in which social partnership might be made
more effective in reflecting social needs, analysing and, most of all,
solving problems. Our discussion suggests that there is a complex
relationship between social partnership and government policy. The
impact of partnership on policy is variable and contingent. While this
leads some to seek ways of strengthening the *direct* influence of partnership on policy, we do not see that as a feasible or wise *general*
strategy. It may, of course, be possible to achieve that in certain policy spheres at certain times. Given the complexity and contingency of
the relationship between partnership and policy, we suggest that it is
best to focus on developing *partnership itself*. By this we mean: improvement of its internal procedures and relationships; greater inclusiveness (not just of organisations, but also of their members); the
refinement of the national partnership bodies (NESC, NESF and the
National Centre for Partnership); and, most of all, the development
of the partnership organisations themselves. Since government and
public agencies are themselves partners, we envisage this kind of development leading, indirectly, to an improved relationship between
partnership and policy.

In outlining this line of development, we draw on the recent NESF
(1997) report, *A Framework for Partnership — Enriching Strategic Consensus through Participation*. In that report, the Forum examined the
development and current tasks of social partnership, and asked
whether the existing partnership arrangements are equal to the tasks.
It concluded that there is a widespread sense that the arrangements
are not adequate. It identified seven problems, which it summarised
as follows:

1. The limits of consensus

2. The limited terms of inclusion

3. The difficulty of linking national representation and/or policy formation to local action

4. Effectiveness in achieving real change

5. The proliferation of partnership bodies

6. Problems of monitoring

7. The relationship between social partnership and representative democracy.

An important argument in the NESF report is that many of these problems — particularly the problems of linking to the local level, limited effectiveness and proliferation — are experienced by all social partners. Furthermore, these problems are serious enough and diverse enough to warrant significant change in national partnership arrangements. Indeed, the Forum reports the comment of one contributor with wide experience of national partnership: "The status quo will collapse under the weight of paper, procedure, meetings and repetitive discussion" (NESF, 1997: 51).

The Forum identifies three trends which throw light on these problems, and allow a renewed vision of social partnership:

- The nature and role of social partners is changing, in ways which accentuate mobilisation, information and action

- The roles of national government are changing, in ways that weaken traditional policy-making and administration, and accentuate its role as policy entrepreneur and facilitator of information-pooling and deliberation

- The relationship between policy-making, implementation and monitoring is changing, in ways which place monitoring of a new sort at the centre of policy development, and require a new combination of all three.

The Forum argues that these trends describe a challenging new context for social partnership. Exploration of these trends, and reflection on the experience of social partnership, leads the Forum to a number of principles which inform its proposals for change.

Emerging Collaboration between Social Partners as a Model

Various social partner organisations have begun to get together to solve problems. Examples include work between ICTU and Women's Aid on domestic violence, between INOU and ICTU on long-term unemployment, between IBEC and ICTU on training, and between ICTU, IBEC and the Community Platform against racism in the workplace. This emerging collaboration between social partners is a significant model for what might be achieved with a renewed framework for partnership.

The Policy Process as a Circle

The policy process should be seen as a continuous circle, involving policy-making, implementation and monitoring. There should be no sense of hierarchy in approaching these three. Indeed, if anything, implementation and monitoring are more important, since they are not adequately handled at present.

We Require Both Strategic Focus and Self-transformative Participation

Strategic focus is necessary because different parties must work from a shared understanding of the priority areas of action and of the main policy approaches to be adopted in those priority areas. Where there is a "failure" to act on or adopt a particular idea, this can usually be traced to one of two things: the system has insufficient strategic focus; or there is, in fact, no real agreement on what that focus should be. Consequently, the development of the partnership system requires:

- That more parts of the system acquire the ability to set strategic priorities

- That we deepen and widen the shared understanding (particularly on social exclusion) that informs a strategic focus.

All of this could be achieved, but still leaves us with poor results on many fronts, such as social exclusion, training and enterprise-level partnership. The reason is that even a strategic focus, based on a shared understanding between the social partners at national level, is not enough in policy areas characterised by complexity and diversity. There is agreement that something additional is required: new levels of participation which enable the recipients of policy to judge what works, and new policy systems which feed that back into the shared understanding and the strategic focus.

The Co-evolution of Partnership Bodies and Partnership Organisations

In considering a new framework for partnership, there is a tendency to oscillate between a discussion of the partnership institutions or *bodies* (NESC, NESF, etc.) and the partnership *organisations* (IBEC, INOU, NWCI, etc.). All are agreed that the two are mutually determining. Consequently, there is no purpose in seeking the perfect design of national partnership institutions and arrangements. The only way to proceed is to adopt some provisional re-design of the partnership institutions, and to choose projects which will both develop the partners and throw light on how the institutions might then be changed further.

Consequently, the Forum says that the task is to find institutional arrangements which do two things:

- Assist each organisation individually, and all organisations collectively, to address their common problems

- Move the overall system in the direction of the three trends summarised above.

The challenge is to feel our way to a new pattern of organisation in which central action and central co-ordination are linked, in ways which feed experiments into the wider system, and in which national policies are reshaped in the light of local or sectoral experiments. To this end, the Forum proposes the following changes in national partnership arrangements:

- Further widening of the membership of NESC

- Close institutional relations between NESC and NESF

- NESF projects to be undertaken by teams

- Closer and more continuous involvement of civil servants in the NESF

- Involvement of both NESF and NESC in monitoring

- Involvement of both NESC and NESF in the SMI and the NAPS.

It sees a further widening of the membership of NESC as desirable, both to achieve more inclusion and to clear the way for improved effectiveness in both NESC and NESF. Perhaps the most important proposed change is the achievement of a new balance between policy-making, implementation and monitoring. To achieve this, once agendas and work programmes have been discussed and agreed, NESF would undertake its projects mainly through teams. These teams would be drawn from the social partner organisations in NESF, and would be put together and resourced to undertake what the Forum calls "policy-design" in specific policy areas, and possibly in specific local areas. "Policy design" involves a combination of implementation, monitoring and revision of policy goals and methods. The national-level organisations would reach into their organisations to identify the people most suited for an in-depth exploration of policy implementation and monitoring in a particular policy or geographic area. This proposal is designed to address the seven problems identified by the Forum, and to move with the trends summarised above. Movement of the partnership system in the direction outlined in the recent Forum report is a significant challenge in the years ahead.

REFERENCES

Adshead, A. (1996), "Beyond Clientelism: Agricultural Networks in Ireland and the EU", *West European Politics*, Vol. 19, No. 3, pp. 583–608.

Amin, A. and D. Thomas (1996), "The Negotiated Economy: State and Civic Institutions in Denmark", *Economy and Society*, Vol. 25, No. 2, pp. 255–281.

Archer, A. (1991), "The Unexpected Emergence of Australian Corporatism" in J. Pekkarinen, M. Pohjola and B. Rowthorn (eds.), *Social Corporatism and Economic Performance*, Oxford: Oxford University Press.

Arkins, A. (1990), "Legislative and Executive Relations in the Republic of Ireland", *West European Politics*, Vol. 12, No. 1, pp. 90–102.

Chubb, B. (1992), *The Government and Politics of Ireland*, Harlow: Longman.

Coghlan, D. (1997), "The Social Partners are Safely in the Bag", *Irish Times*, 14 January.

Cohen, J. and J. Rogers (1992), "Secondary Associations and Democratic Governance", *Politics and Society*, Vol. 20, No. 4, pp. 393–472.

Collins, N. (1995), "Agricultural Policy Networks: the Republic of Ireland and Northern Ireland", *Political Studies*, Vol. 43, pp. 664–682.

Community Platform (1997), *Achieving Social Partnership: The Strategy and Proposals of the Community Platform at the Partnership 2000 Negotiations*, Dublin: Community Platform.

Crouch, C. (1983), "Pluralism and the New Corporatism: A Rejoinder", *Political Studies*, Vol. 31, pp. 452–60.

Davis, G. (1997), "Rethinking Policy-making: A New Role for Consultation", *Administration*, Vol. 45, No. 3, pp. 26–48.

Dooney, S. (1988), *Irish Agriculture: An Organisational Profile*, Dublin: Institute of Public Administration.

Durkan, J. (1992), "Social Consensus and Incomes Policy", *Economic and Social Review*, Vol. 23, No. 3, pp. 347–363.

Durkan, J. and C. Harmon (1996), "Social Consensus, Incomes Policy and Unemployment", UCD, Centre for Economic Research, Working Paper 96/11.

Farrell, B. (1993), "The Government" in J. Coakley and M. Gallagher (eds.), *Politics in the Republic of Ireland*, Limerick: PSAI Press.

Gallagher, M. and L. Komito, (1993) "Dáil Deputies and their Constituency Work" in J. Coakley and M. Gallagher (eds.), *Politics in the Republic of Ireland*, Limerick: PSAI Press.

Girvin, B. (1989), *Between Two Worlds: Politics and Economy in Independent Ireland*, Dublin: Gill and Macmillan.

Girvin, B. (1997), "Political Culture, Political Independence and Economic Success in Ireland", *Political Studies*, Vol. 12, pp. 48–78.

Hardiman, N. (1988), *Pay, Politics and Economic Performance in Ireland 1970–1987*, Oxford: Clarendon Press.

Hardiman, N. (1992), "The State and Economic Interests: Ireland in a Comparative Perspective" in J. Goldthorpe and C.T. Whelan (eds.), *The Development of Industrial Society in Ireland*, Oxford: Oxford University Press.

Honohan, P. (1988), "The Role of the Adviser and the Evolution of the Public Service" in M. Hedermann (ed.), *The Clash of Ideas: Essays in honour of Patrick Lynch*, Dublin: Gill and Macmillan.

ICTU (1995), "Report of the Proceedings of the Biennial Delegate Conference", Dublin: ICTU.

Jordan, G. (1984), "Pluralistic Corporatisms and Corporate Pluralism", *Scandinavian Political Studies*, Vol. 7, No. 3, pp. 137–153.

Lee, J. (1997a), "Partnership 2000 and its Hold on the Next Government", *Sunday Tribune*, 19 January.

Lee, J. (1997b), "Budget Process Reveals the Emasculation of the Dáil", *Sunday Tribune*, 26 January.

Lehmbruch, G. (1979), "Liberal Corporatism and Party Government", in P. Schmitter and G. Lehmbruch (eds.), *Trends Towards Corporatist Intermediation*, London: Sage.

Lehmbruch, G. (1982), "Neo-Corporatism in a Comparative Perspective" in G. Lehmbruch and P. Schmitter (eds.), *Patterns of Corporatist Policy-Making*, Beverly Hills: Sage.

Mansbridge, J. (1992), "A Deliberative Perspective on Neo-corporatism", *Politics and Society*, Vol. 20, No. 4, pp. 493–505.

Martin, R. (1983), "Pluralism and the New Corporatism", *Political Studies*, Vol. 31, No. 1, pp. 86–102.

McCann, D. (1993), Business Power and Collective Action: The State and the Confederation of Irish Industry 1970–1990", *Irish Political Studies*, No. 8, pp. 37–53.

Murphy, G. (1997), "Towards a Corporate State? Sean Lemass and the Realignment of Interest Groups in the Policy Process 1948–64", Dublin City University Business School Research Paper No. 23.

NESC (1986), *A Strategy for Development, 1986–1990*, Report No. 83, Dublin: NESC.

NESC (1990), *A Strategy for the Nineties*, Report No. 89, Dublin: NESC.

NESC (1993), *A Strategy for Competitiveness, Growth and Employment*, Report No. 96, Dublin: NESC.

NESC (1995), *New Approaches to Rural Development*, Report No. 97, Dublin: NESC.

NESC (1996), *Strategy into the 21st Century*, Report No. 99, Dublin: NESC.

NESF (1994a), *Negotiations on a Successor Agreement to PESP*, Forum Report No. 1, Dublin: NESF.

NESF (1994b), *Ending Long Term Unemployment*, Forum Report No. 4, Dublin: NESF.

NESF (1996) *Post PCW-Negotiations – A New Deal?* Opinion No. 4, Dublin: NESF.

NESF (1997), *A Framework for Partnership — Enriching Strategic Consensus through Participation*, Forum Report No. 16, Dublin: NESF.

O'Brien, J.F. (1981), "A Study of the National Wage Agreements in Ireland", Dublin: Economic and Social Research Institute.

O'Donnell, R. (1993), *Ireland and Europe: Challenges for a New Century*, Dublin: Economic and Social Research Institute.

O'Donnell R. and C. O'Reardon (1997), "Ireland's Experiment in Social Partnership 1987–96", in G. Fajertag and P. Pochet (eds.), *Social Pacts in Europe*, Brussels: European Trade Union Institute.

OECD (1997), *Economic Surveys: Ireland 1997*, Paris: OECD.

Offe, C. (1985), *Disorganised Capitalism*, Cambridge: Polity Press.

O'Halpin, E. (1993), "Policy-making" in J. Coakley and M. Gallagher (eds.), *Politics in the Republic of Ireland*, Limerick: PSAI Press.

Pontussen, J. (1992), *The Limits of Social Democracy*, Ithaca: Cornell University Press.

Redmond, V. (1985), "An Analysis of the Breakdown of National Agreements and Understandings", Unpublished M. Comm. Thesis, Dublin: UCD.

Regini, M. (1984), "The Conditions for Political Exchange: How Corporatist Concertation Emerged and Collapsed in Great Britain and Italy" in J. Goldthorpe (ed.), *Order and Conflict in Contemporary Capitalism*, Oxford: Clarendon Press.

Regini, M. (1995), *Uncertain Boundaries: The Social and Political Construction of European Economies*, Cambridge: Cambridge University Press.

Regan, M.C. and F.L. Wilson (1986), "Interest-Group Politics in France and Ireland: Comparative Perspectives on Neo-Corporatism" *West European Politics*, Vol. 9, No. 3, pp. 393–413.

Roche, W.K. (1997), "Pay Determination, the State and the Politics of Industrial Relations" in T.V. Murphy and W.K. Roche (eds.), *Irish Industrial Relations in Practice*, Dublin: Oak Tree Press.

Sabel, C. (1996), *Ireland: Local Partnerships and Social Innovation*, Paris: OECD.

Sheehan, B. (1996), "Crisis, Strategic Re-evaluation and the Re-emergence of Tripartism in Ireland", Unpublished M. Comm. Thesis, Dublin: UCD.

Sheehan, B. (1997), "McCreevy Cites Government Prerogative in Post-Budget Row with SIPTU", *Industrial Relations News*, No. 47, pp. 12–13.

Solow, R. (1990), *The Labour Market as a Social Institution*, London: Gill and Macmillan.

Sweeney, P. (1997), *The Celtic Tiger: Ireland's Economic Miracle Explained*, Dublin: Oak Tree Press.

Walsh, B. and A. Leddin (1992), *The Macroeconomy of Ireland*, Dublin: Gill and Macmillan.

Weinz, W. (1986), "Economic Development and Interest Groups" in B. Girvin, and R. Sturm (eds.), *Politics and Society in Contemporary Ireland*, Aldershot: Gower Publishing Company Ltd.

Chapter 8

POVERTY AND POLICY

Tim Callan *and* Brian Nolan

INTRODUCTION

Tackling poverty and social exclusion is widely recognised as one of the major challenges facing Irish society, as evidenced by its inclusion as an integral part and strategic objective of the national agreement between the social partners, Partnership 2000, and by the recent adoption by government of a National Anti-Poverty Strategy. This challenge will only be successfully met if there is a shared understanding of the scale and nature of the problem, if policies are developed in that light, and if these policies are implemented. Here we summarise very briefly the main results of a broad programme of research on poverty measurement, dealing with the period from 1973 to 1994, which has been pursued at the ESRI; outline the response of social welfare and other policies in tackling the poverty problem; and highlight what we see as the key issues in looking to the future.

MEASURING POVERTY

No single measure of poverty commands universal acceptance or is appropriate for all purposes. Measuring poverty in terms of some common absolute standard across countries is valuable from a global perspective — for example, the World Bank (1990) uses poverty lines of $275 and $370 per annum (in 1985 purchasing power parity terms) — but has little relevance to identifying those considered poor in a country like Ireland. Most people would agree with Piachaud that "close to subsistence level there is indeed some absolute minimum necessary for survival but apart from this, any poverty standard must reflect prevailing social standards: it must be a relative standard" (1987: 148). Such a relative standard is incorporated in the definition of poverty recently officially adopted in Ireland by the Government's National Anti-Poverty Strategy:

> People are living in poverty if their income and resources (material, cultural and social) are so inadequate as to preclude them from having a standard of living which is regarded as acceptable by Irish society generally. As a result of inadequate income and resources people may be excluded and marginalised from participating in activities which are considered the norm for other people in society. (1997: 3)

In actually implementing such a definition to measure the extent of poverty, the most common approach has been to define a poverty line in terms of income, and regard those with incomes below the line as poor. Many different ways of establishing an income cut-off have been proposed, but none can avoid an arbitrary element of judgement, and life will not be very different for those with incomes just above or just below any such line. One straightforward method is the relative income poverty line approach, which derives poverty line incomes as fixed proportions of average incomes, adjusted for family size and composition. A cut-off of half average income is most commonly used, but alternatives such as 40 per cent and 60 per cent of average income can also be examined, and help to identify conclusions which are robust with respect to the level of the poverty cut-off. As well as measuring the numbers below such lines, it is very important to also take into account how far people are falling below them.

The information on income and household composition required to apply this method to Ireland is available for large household samples for each of the years 1973, 1980, 1987 and 1994. With relative income poverty lines, the poverty standard rises over time in line with average incomes. Standards constructed to represent a particular standard of living in real terms are also of value — for example, in establishing whether or not the poor have benefited from a period of economic growth — although over any prolonged period where real incomes are rising, they will lose contact with the reality of life and what it means to be poor in that society.

Low income on its own may not be an entirely satisfactory measure of *exclusion* arising from lack of resources. This is not primarily because of the (real) difficulties in measuring income accurately, but more because a household's command over resources is affected by much more than its current income. Long-term factors, relating most importantly to the way resources have been accumulated or eroded over time, as well as current income, play a crucial role in influencing the likelihood of current deprivation and exclusion. An approach which combines information on income and on indicators of deprivation to provide an alternative identification of those who are poor has therefore also been developed at the ESRI (described in detail in Nolan and Whelan, 1996; and Callan et al., 1996). This has been applied to data for 1987 and 1994, and as we will discuss, it provides the measure of poverty which underlies the global poverty reduction target adopted in the National Anti-Poverty Strategy.

THE EXTENT OF POVERTY IN IRELAND

In 1994, about 22 per cent of persons were in households with incomes below half the average; about 7 per cent had incomes below 40 per cent of the average; and close to 35 per cent had incomes below the 60 per cent relative income cut-off. Since there is no strong *a priori* reason to choose any one of these lines as "the" indicator of poverty, it is useful to put the income levels corresponding to these lines into perspective. In 1994, the 40 per cent cut-off fell below the minimum social welfare payment (from the Supplementary Welfare Allowance scheme), the 50 per cent cut-off was somewhat above that minimum, and the 60 per cent cut-off was above the highest social welfare payment, the Old Age Contributory Pension rate.

Figure 8.1 shows that, over the full 1973 to 1994 period, there was little change in the numbers below the 40 per cent line but a substantial increase in the percentage below half or 60 per cent of average income. Over the more recent sub-period, between 1987 and 1994, there was a modest increase in the percentage below the 50 per cent line but a more pronounced rise, of 3–4 percentage points, with the highest, 60 per cent line. However, simply counting the number of persons below an income threshold takes no account of how far below it they fall. As Figure 8.2 shows, a measure which takes into account both the number of people falling below the line and the depth of their poverty tells a rather different story. Over the full

FIGURE 8.1: PROPORTION OF INDIVIDUALS BELOW RELATIVE INCOME
POVERTY LINES, 1973–1994

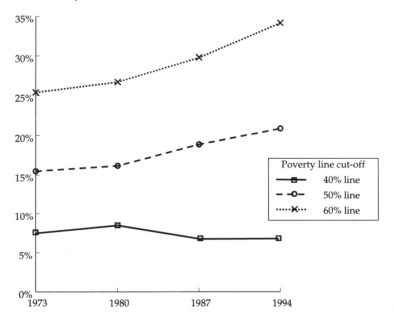

FIGURE 8.2: PER CAPITA INCOME GAPS AT ALTERNATIVE RELATIVE
INCOME POVERTY LINES, 1973–1994

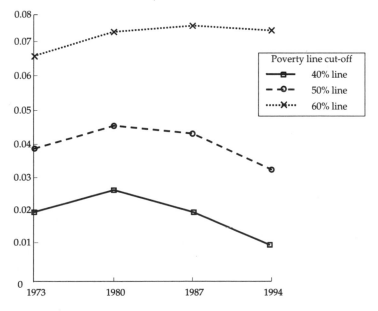

period, this measure shows a fall in poverty at the 40 per cent and 50 per cent relative income lines, and a small increase at the 60 per cent line. Over the most recent period from 1987 to 1994, we see that this measure fell sharply with the 40 per cent and 50 per cent lines and marginally with the 60 per cent line.

Comparisons of the extent of poverty in Ireland versus other European Union countries are available only in terms of the numbers below relative income (or expenditure) poverty lines. These suggest that the percentage below half average income in Ireland (about one person in five) is a good deal higher than in Denmark, the Netherlands or Belgium, but lower than in Portugal or Greece. In terms of trends over time among EU members, the increase in numbers below such poverty lines in the UK has been striking: in the late 1970s/early 1980s the UK had a much lower rate than Ireland, but by the mid-1990s the rates had converged.

Current income alone may not accurately reflect a household's living standards, which as already noted will be influenced by resources over a much longer period. Measures combining information on income and indicators of deprivation are available for 1987 and 1994 only. A set of eight items or activities was identified from a more extensive list as representing basic deprivation and suitable to serve as an indicator of underlying generalised deprivation. (For example, being able to afford new rather than second-hand clothes or a warm overcoat). In 1987, 16 per cent of households were experiencing such deprivation, stating that this was because of lack of resources, with income falling below the 60 per cent relative income poverty line. Ten per cent were below half average income and experiencing such "enforced" deprivation. By 1994, the corresponding figures had fallen marginally, to 15 per cent and 9 per cent respectively. This may provide a better indicator of the scale of generalised deprivation or exclusion due to lack of resources than do numbers, taken in isolation, for those below income lines.

Between 1987 and 1994, average household income rose by about 50 per cent. With consumer prices rising by about 21 per cent over the same period, this represents a substantial increase in real terms. This did benefit those on low incomes, with a substantial decline in the numbers below income thresholds held constant in real terms. While poverty must in our view be seen primarily in relative terms, concentrating entirely on relative income poverty lines will miss the

difference between this and a period when average incomes stag-
nated, as they did for much of the 1980s. It will also fail to highlight
the seriousness of a situation where the real incomes of the poor actually fall, as apparently occurred in the UK during the 1980s.

Because of the nature of poverty itself and of the evidence available, it is in our view unrealistic at this point to hope for firm conclusions along the lines of "X per cent of the Irish population is in
poverty", "Poverty has risen in Ireland by Y per cent over the last
decade", or "Poverty in Ireland is Z per cent above the EU average".
(The complexities are brought out, for example, in Atkinson's (1997)
discussion of the Irish evidence in comparative perspective.) What
one can conclude is that substantial numbers experience deprivation
and exclusion as a result of inadequate financial resources; that this
did not change markedly between 1987 and 1994; and that Ireland
fares worse in this regard than some of our EU partners such as
Denmark and the Netherlands, but better than others such as Greece
and Portugal. These modest but robust conclusions have important
implications for policy, as do results on who is affected by poverty,
to which we now turn.

WHO IS POOR?

From a policy perspective, knowing the types of individuals and
households affected by poverty is of central importance, and key
conclusions about the types of household most affected by poverty
do not depend on precisely how poverty is measured. Looking at
those below relative income poverty lines, Table 8.1 shows that the
key developments between 1973 and 1987 were a sharp rise in the
proportion of poor households headed by an unemployed person,
and a marked fall in the proportion of those headed by an elderly
person. The fall in the risk of relative poverty attached to the elderly
was partly due to improvement in occupational pensions, and partly
to improved coverage and increased rates of payments for the relevant social welfare schemes (to which we return shortly). The growing importance of unemployment reflected the general rise in
unemployment over the period, and also brought with it an increased risk of poverty for families with children.

TABLE 8.1: COMPOSITION OF HOUSEHOLDS BELOW HALF AVERAGE
INCOME BY LABOUR FORCE STATUS OF HOUSEHOLD HEAD

Labour force status of household head	% of households below line				% of all households in sample			
	1973	1980	1987	1994	1973	1980	1987	1994
Employee	9.0	10.3	8.2	6.2	42.4	47.1	38.6	37.5
Self-employed	3.6	3.5	4.8	6.7	6.5	6.8	7.5	8.5
Farmer	26.0	25.9	23.7	8.9	22.4	16.1	11.7	8.1
Unemployed	9.6	14.7	37.4	32.6	2.9	3.9	10.6	10.2
Ill/Disabled	10.2	9.3	11.1	9.5	4.5	3.3	6.0	4.0
Retired	17.0	18.9	8.1	10.5	10.6	13.7	14.5	18.3
Home Duties	24.6	17.4	6.7	25.5	10.7	9.1	11.1	13.5
Total	100	100	100	100	100	100	100	100

Developments in the 1987 to 1994 period have been somewhat different, as the table also shows. By 1994, the unemployment rate had only begun to fall, but unemployment remained the single most important cause of poverty. The risk of income poverty for the retired was still well below average, but for households headed by women conventionally categorised as "in home duties" — mostly elderly and/or widowed — that risk rose sharply (though this was less pronounced within the 60 per cent line). Farm households made up a much smaller proportion of those below the poverty line in 1994 than in 1987. (The combined income and deprivation measure of poverty, available for 1987 and 1994, identifies rather fewer farmers and self-employed as "poor" than the income-based measures.)

POLICY RESPONSES TO POVERTY

Policy towards poverty for many years could be characterised as based on the twin notions that "a rising tide lifts all boats" — implying that economic growth was the key — and that residual poverty among particular groups was primarily an issue for the social welfare system — to be tackled by increased payment rates, or new schemes to cover groups with a high risk of poverty, such as lone parents. With poverty particularly severe for the elderly, increases in social welfare pensions were seen as providing a way of targeting resources to those in need without reducing financial incentives to work. During the late 1970s and early 1980s, rates of payment for Old Age Contributory and Non-Contributory Pensions increased quite rapidly. By 1987, payment rates varied considerably between contributory and non-contributory schemes, and between the elderly, widows and the unemployed. The lowest rates of payment were close to the 40 per cent relative income line, while the highest rates were close to the 60 per cent relative income standard.

Social welfare policy between 1987 and 1994 was heavily influenced by the findings of the Commission on Social Welfare (1986), which focused particular attention on the inadequacy of the lowest payment rates and set an adequacy standard approximating the higher rates of payment. (For a recent review of the issues raised by the Commission's findings, see Callan, Nolan and Whelan, 1996.) Thus the rates of payment for the lowest paid schemes — Unemployment Assistance and the safety net of Supplementary Welfare Allowance — were increased a good deal more rapidly than average incomes, and this sufficed to bring recipients of those schemes much closer to (but not quite up to) half average income by 1994. At the same time, support rates for other groups, notably the elderly and widows, rose by a good deal less than mean incomes (though still ahead of inflation). As a result, by 1994 many of those relying on old age or widow's pensions were on incomes at or about the 50 per cent line and below the 60 per cent one, whereas in 1987 they had been comfortably above half average income. Together with a rapid rise in farm incomes, this helps to explain the fact that those measures of poverty which take into account the extent to which people fall below the 50 and 60 per cent relative income lines were stable or fell, while the headcount of numbers below those lines rose between 1987 and 1994. They also underlie the marginal decline in the numbers of people living below relative income lines and experiencing basic deprivation.

While social welfare policy remains central, the emergence and persistence of high rates of unemployment has meant that anti-poverty policy has come to be viewed in much wider terms, as explicitly recognised in the National Anti-Poverty Strategy (NAPS) developed in 1995–96 and adopted in 1997. The main areas of policy seen by that Strategy as contributing to the fight against poverty include:

- General economic policy, aimed at maximising the growth in employment

- Labour market programmes aimed at ensuring that the long-term unemployed and other disadvantaged groups can break the cycle of deprivation by obtaining a job

- Education and training programs which are aimed at preventing additions to the stock of long-term unemployed, or improving the skills of those who are long-term unemployed

- Community development initiatives aimed at improving the economy and/or quality of life in particular areas and

- A number of initiatives in the areas of health and housing.

The Strategy sets out a global target for reducing poverty over the next decade, and also contains a number of supplementary targets for what it identifies as key areas. The overall or global target is:

> Over the period, 1997–2007, the National Anti-Poverty Strategy will aim at considerably reducing the numbers of those who are "consistently poor" from 9 to 15 per cent to less than 5 to 10 per cent, as measured by the ESRI. (1997: 9)

This target thus relates to the numbers both below relative income poverty lines and experiencing basic deprivation, as measured by the non-monetary indicators we have described earlier. While some might see this as an unduly restricted measure, it has the great merit of focusing attention firmly on those who are most in need of sustained and targeted intervention. If the global target is to be attained, it is likely that other measures such as the numbers in relative income poverty will also have to come down substantially. The fact that Ireland now has such an official poverty target itself represents a major step forward.

The NAPS also identifies five key areas requiring particular attention, and sets out targets for each:

- *Educational Disadvantage*: To eliminate early school-leaving before the Junior Certificate, have 90 per cent completing the senior cycle by the year 2000 and 98 per cent by 2007, and ensure that there are no students with serious literacy and numeracy problems in early primary education within five years.

- *Unemployment*: To reduce the rate of unemployment (as measured in the Labour Force Survey) from 11.9 per cent in April 1996 to 6 per cent by 2007, and reduce the rate of long-term unemployment from 7 per cent to 3.5 per cent, with a particular focus on the very long-term unemployed.

- *Income Adequacy*: To contribute to reducing the percentage of the population whom the ESRI have identified as "consistently poor" from 9 to 15 per cent to less than 5 to 10 per cent by 2007; all social welfare payments to reach the minimum of the lower range recommended by the Commission on Social Welfare.

- *Disadvantaged Urban Areas*: To reduce the numbers suffering the greatest deprivation in disadvantaged urban areas by increasing their standard of living and providing opportunities for participation, thus reducing the measured indicators of disadvantage in the area, especially the rate of unemployment and particularly long-term unemployment by 2007.

- *Rural Poverty*: To ensure that strategies are developed with regard to the provision of services in rural areas, especially those concerned with educational disadvantage, unemployment and income adequacy, so that the overall targets of the NAPS are achieved in rural areas.

These specific targets are rather a mixed bag. Those in the areas of educational disadvantage and unemployment are concrete and, for the most part, meet what should be two central criteria for targets in this context. Success in meeting them can be readily monitored over time, and would manifestly make a substantial contribution to attaining the overall anti-poverty target. A good deal of progress has already been made in cutting the numbers leaving school early, but the remaining core leaving before the Junior Certificate is likely to prove more difficult to tackle. The value as a target of eliminating serious literacy and numeracy problems in early primary education will depend on transparent mechanisms being set up to monitor progress.

Reducing unemployment on the scale envisaged is not as ambitious as it might appear at first sight, in the light of the very favourable macroeconomic prospects for Ireland over the next decade. The number in employment has grown rapidly since 1994, and the recently-published ESRI Medium Term Review (1997) in fact forecasts that economic growth will be sufficient to bring the unemployment rate down to the NAPS target level of 6 per cent in ten years' time. This forecast is highly contingent, depending especially on continued wage moderation, and the target reduction in long-term unemployment may be more challenging. In addition the forecast, like the Labour Force Survey, counts those currently on schemes such as Community Employment as employed rather than unemployed, and assumes no fall in the numbers involved: meeting the NAPS target by maintaining or expanding these schemes in the medium term would hardly be satisfactory.

The targets in the other three areas are much less concrete and contribute little to the strategy. On income adequacy, the target amounts to restating the overall NAPS target and a short-term commitment on social welfare rates already included in Partnership 2000. The crucial issue of what happens to rates over the next decade is left open. On urban and rural disadvantage, the targets are so non-specific and anodyne as to scarcely merit the name.

As well as the adoption of the National Anti-Poverty Strategy, the latest agreement between the government and social partners, "Partnership 2000 for Inclusion, Employment and Competitiveness", contains a set of other measures aimed at "promoting greater social inclusion". These include:

- An expansion of targeted employment and training measures, and further development of public employment services

- An expansion of targeted programmes aimed at breaking the cycle of educational disadvantage

- Real increases in social welfare payments sufficient to reach — in real, though not in relative terms — the standards identified by the Commission on Social Welfare, and

- A number of specific commitments regarding anti-poverty actions at local level, including both urban and rural areas.

The programme contains an overall commitment to expenditure of £525 million on social exclusion measures during the period of the Partnership, including increases in social welfare payments. It also has a commitment to introduce personal tax reductions to a cumulative value of £900 million over the three years. While no major changes in the structure of the social welfare or personal tax systems were agreed, the Programme undertook to examine both the issue of standard rating of allowances and a tax credit system, and the concept and implications of introducing a basic income payment for all citizens.

The two Budgets in 1997 have already committed amounts exceeding the Programme's £525 million figure to expenditure labelled "social exclusion". However, the levels of payment under short-term Unemployment Assistance and Supplementary Welfare Allowance have not yet reached the target of the minimum recommended by the Commission on Social Welfare (indexed to prices). The December 1997 Budget increased social welfare pensions more than other payments, reversing the trend seen for much of the previous decade. The income tax measures implemented in that Budget gave much more emphasis to cutting tax rates than to increasing personal allowances, thus missing an exceptional opportunity to make substantial progress in the direction recommended by the Expert Group on the Integration of the Income Tax and Social Welfare Systems (which reported in 1996).

FUTURE PROSPECTS AND PRIORITIES

Ireland has seen remarkably high levels of economic growth in the 1990s, with employment growing strongly in the past three years, and the medium-term macroeconomic prospects for the Irish economy appear bright. Although unemployment has been falling significantly, it remains a substantial problem — particularly long-term unemployment, with its associated high risk of poverty. Other factors such as disability and changing family structures will continue to place significant numbers at risk of poverty. Increases in national income will not percolate automatically to people whose living standards depend on the level of social welfare payments.

Against this background, there are no "quick fixes". Tackling poverty and social exclusion is now widely recognised as one of the major challenges facing Irish society, as evidenced by both Partnership 2000 and the National Anti-Poverty Strategy: this is a necessary but hardly a sufficient condition for success. We made the point at the outset that this challenge will only be successfully met if there is a shared understanding of the scale and nature of the problem, if policies are developed in that light, and if these policies are implemented. While progress has been made on all these fronts, there remains much cause for concern at the strategic level. In conclusion, we highlight what we see as major concerns about three core elements of the anti-poverty strategy.

It is now widely recognised that success in reducing long-term unemployment will be crucial to combating poverty, and a variety of programmes are being implemented with that end in view. The danger is that such a plethora of programmes will generate confusion among both the employers and the unemployed at whom they are targeted, and among policy analysts and policy-makers as to what is working and what is not. There is also the danger that if unemployment does indeed continue to fall and the view that "there are plenty of jobs for those willing to work" becomes more widespread, the support for such programmes will be undermined. (The level of income support to the unemployed and the basis on which it is provided could also be called increasingly into question.) This makes it all the more important that the disparate elements are implemented in such a way as to facilitate rigorous evaluation and honing down as early as possible into a tighter and more coherent package of measures aimed at the long-term unemployed.

The second issue of concern is the role which area-based measures are expected to play in a national anti-poverty strategy. Area-based approaches can clearly make a significant contribution in harnessing the energies of local communities and combating powerlessness and exclusion, and certain areas have very particular needs. However, the limitations of such strategies must also be recognised: it is not realistic to expect local area-based initiatives to deal with a national unemployment or poverty problem, and they have to be seen as only one element in a strategic response. In any case, although particular areas with very high unemployment and poverty rates clearly face very special challenges, most of the unemployed and most poor people are not concentrated in those areas (Nolan, Whelan and Williams, 1998). Where "black spots" of pronounced urban disadvantage do exist, they are for the most part in public housing, and housing and other policies at both local and national level must be reoriented to address the special needs of such areas (see, for example, Fahey and Watson, 1995 and the chapter on housing by Fahey in this volume). There is, however, the real danger that recognition of this need could inadvertently promote a distorted view of the generality of those experiencing poverty.

The final area we highlight is tax and social welfare policy. While there is widespread consensus about the importance of reducing poverty and improving incentives, and about how alternative tax and benefit reform packages affect different income groups, recent experience amply illustrates that such consensus does not in itself guarantee implementation of policies most likely to reduce poverty. In the run-up to the December 1997 Budget, it seemed to be widely accepted (at the level of rhetoric) that income tax reforms should give priority to reducing the burden on the low paid and increasing their work incentives, and that increasing personal tax allowances was the best way to do so. But the policies actually implemented had a different emphasis. Nonetheless, agreeing on how best to achieve such an aim is an important step in the right direction.

No such consensus has yet emerged about the direction which the social welfare system should take. (Significant progress should be made in the near future in evaluating one option: the basic income proposal advanced by CORI (see for example Clark and Healy, 1997), with a government commitment to preparing a Green Paper on the topic.) Stepping back from how best to structure the system, we would highlight the issue which is, if anything, more important: how are the levels of support to social welfare recipients to change over time as incomes generally rise? To the extent that there has been a coherent policy stance about social welfare levels in recent years, it has been framed in terms of reaching the targets set by the Commission on Social Welfare. These will soon be reached, and simply maintaining those levels in real terms would require indexation to consumer prices. If average incomes continue to grow ahead of inflation, this would be a modest target indeed, with those relying on social welfare falling further and further behind the rest of society over time. Past experience does not suggest that such a modest goal is likely to be adopted, nor does it inspire confidence that anything other than a rather haphazard policy of determining increases from year to year will be followed. With the minima recommended by the Commission on Social Welfare nearing irrelevance, the case for explicitly linking changes in the social welfare support rates to general living standards in society from here on needs to be urgently and openly debated. In the absence of such a link, it is difficult to see how the NAPS global poverty reduction target over the next decade will be met.

In Ireland today, substantial numbers remain below what most people would see as a minimum acceptable standard of living. While neither sustained economic growth nor increasing employment would be enough on their own to bring everyone up to that level, they would make it a realistic possibility — if the opportunity is grasped.

ACKNOWLEDGEMENTS

This paper draws on the 1994 wave of the *Living in Ireland Survey*, the Irish element of the European Community Household Panel. Brendan Whelan and James Williams of the ESRI's Survey Unit were responsible for the survey design, data collection and database creation. Christopher Whelan has collaborated in the programme of research on poverty measurement summarised here and has provided valuable comments on this chapter.

REFERENCES

Atkinson, A.B. (1997), "Poverty in Ireland and Anti-Poverty Strategy: A European Perspective", in A. Gray (ed.), *International Perspectives on the Irish Economy*, Dublin: Indecon.

Callan, T., B. Nolan, B.J. Whelan, C.T. Whelan and J. Williams (1996), *Poverty in the 1990s: Evidence from the Living in Ireland Survey*, Dublin: Oak Tree Press.

Callan, T., B. Nolan and C.T. Whelan (1996), *A Review of the Commission on Social Welfare's Minimum Adequate Income*, Policy Research Series Number 29, Dublin: The Economic and Social Research Institute.

Clark, C. and J. Healy, (1997), *Pathways to a Basic Income*, Dublin: CORI.

Commission on Social Welfare (1985), *Report of the Commission on Social Welfare*, Dublin: Stationery Office.

Duffy, D., J. Fitz Gerald, I. Kearney and F. Shortall (1997), *Medium-Term Review: 1997–2003*, Dublin: The Economic and Social Research Institute.

Expert Group on the Integration of the Income Tax and Social Welfare Systems (1996), *Integrating Tax and Social Welfare*, Dublin: Stationery Office.

Fahey, T. and D. Watson, (1995), *An Analysis of Social Housing Needs*, General Research Series Paper 168, Dublin: The Economic and Social Research Institute.

Government of Ireland (1996), *Partnership 2000 for Inclusion, Employment and Competitiveness*, Dublin: Stationery Office.

Government of Ireland (1997), *Sharing in Progress: National Anti-Poverty Strategy*, Dublin: Stationery Office.

Nolan, B. and T. Callan (1994), *Poverty and Policy in Ireland*, Dublin: Gill and Macmillan.

Nolan, B. and C.T. Whelan (1996), *Resources, Deprivation and Poverty*, Oxford: Clarendon Press.

Nolan, B., C.T. Whelan and J. Williams (1998), *Where are Poor Households?*, Dublin: Oak Tree Press/Combat Poverty Agency.

Piachaud, D. (1987), "Problems in the Definition and Measurement of Poverty", *Journal of Social Policy*, Vol. 16, No. 2, 147–164.

Chapter 9

FOR RICHER, FOR POORER: THE CHANGING DISTRIBUTION OF HOUSEHOLD INCOME IN IRELAND, 1973–94

Micheal L. Collins *and* Catherine Kavanagh

INTRODUCTION

No assessment of the well-being of a society can have much credibility unless it takes some account of the distribution of income as well as its aggregate level. The distribution of income in the economy, whether among persons or households, is an important issue, since it affects consumption, saving, growth, inflation, and taxation. Additionally, it is reasonable to suppose that most advanced societies have some regard to the "fair" and "equitable" distribution of income and wealth (however defined).

In a free market, the distribution of income may be highly unequal. Moreover, market imperfections will tend to make inequality greater. The initial distribution of income in society is determined by the market value placed on the services rendered by different individuals and households in the production of national output, and on the distribution of skills, talents and wealth within the community. Because this initial distribution of income may not be deemed "fair" by society, the government, by intervening — via the tax and benefit system, for example — can change the pattern of distribution to produce a more "equitable" distribution. Indeed, many taxation and benefit spending programmes are often explicitly directed at addressing issues of inequality and redistribution. Hence, society is also concerned with the extent to which the distribution is changed by government policies.

Whether the distribution of income in society is desirable or not is a normative question. The political right argues that a certain amount of inequality is the inevitable price paid for an efficient and growing economy. Inequality has an important economic function related to the operation of factor price differences. Factor prices are the price signals that encourage resources to move to sectors of the economy where demand is growing, and away from sectors where demand is declining. The political right argues that government intervention with this process may discourage people from acquiring greater human capital and distort the mobility of workers. The undermining of incentives may in turn reduce growth and efficiency. The political left however, sees fewer dangers in reducing incentives and stresses the moral and social importance of redistribution from rich to poor. They argue that growth and employment are best encouraged by direct state support for investment.

Economists cannot settle the normative debate over how much the government should redistribute incomes from the rich to the poor. They can however, identify the extent of inequality and analyse how it has changed over time. This is precisely the purpose of this chapter. We investigate how the distribution of household income in Ireland has changed over the period 1973–94. Confining the analysis to the distribution of direct and disposable income allows us to comment on the redistributive efforts of the tax and social welfare systems. We also estimate total household inequality using three different indexes: the Gini coefficient; the coefficient of variation; and the Theil index.

The chapter is structured as follows. In the next section, we provide a brief overview of the changes in the macroeconomic environment for the period 1973–94. This sets the context for the third section, which examines the changing distribution of household income by decile groups over the period. Although this analysis is partial, it allows us to comment on the extent to which certain categories of income recipients have fared over the past 20 years. The fourth section expands on the analysis by presenting total measures of inequality which relate to the whole distribution of household income. The final section concludes with a summary of the main points.

THE MACROECONOMIC ENVIRONMENT

The changing nature of the macroeconomic environment has been well documented (Leddin and Walsh, 1995; O'Hagan, 1995). The purpose of this section is not to provide an all-inclusive summary of these changes. Rather, we briefly summarise the main developments that have occurred in three important areas: output; employment; and unemployment. Although there are many factors that determine the pattern and depth of inequality, each of these is likely to have had a significant impact on the distribution of income.[1]

Output

The pattern of growth has been irregular over the period (see Figure 9.1). Following the oil crises of 1973 and 1979, growth slowed significantly. The early and mid-1980s was a period of prolonged recession, with negative growth rates in some years.

Since 1991, Ireland has been the fastest growing economy in the European Union (OECD, 1995). While economic growth was negative in the EU in 1993, Ireland's GNP increased by approximately 3.5 per cent. This buoyant performance has continued into the mid-1990s.[2]

FIGURE 9.1: GROWTH RATE OF REAL GNP, 1973–1995

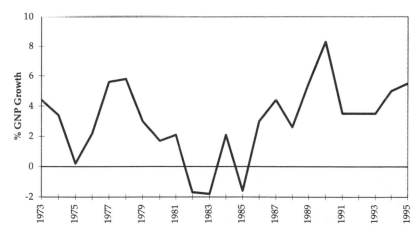

Source: Adapted from Leddin and Walsh (1995: 16).

---

[1] All data used in this section are provided in Appendix A.

[2] For an interpretation of the recent growth experience in Ireland, see Bradley et al (1997).

Employment

After falling significantly in the first half of the 1980s, employment began to increase again in 1986 (see Figure 9.2). In contrast to most other OECD countries, employment growth has been rapid since 1993, expanding at an annual rate of almost four per cent despite the continued secular decline in the number of jobs in agriculture (OECD, 1997).

A significant proportion of the new jobs have been on a part-time basis, boosting the share of such employees from five per cent of total employment in 1983 to ten per cent in 1995 (OECD, 1997). Part-time employment is concentrated among women, who account for 70 per cent of the part-time workforce, and it is most prevalent in service industries such as distribution and finance.

FIGURE 9.2: THE GROWTH IN THE NUMBERS AT WORK, 1977–95 ('000S)

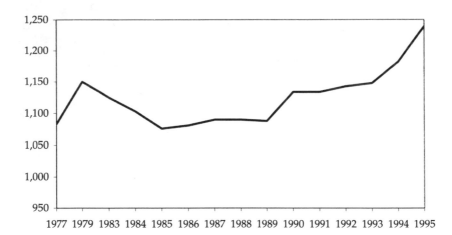

Source: Labour Force Surveys, various issues.

The structure of employment has changed significantly over the last 20 years. The share of the labour force in agriculture fell from 17 per cent in 1981 to 11 per cent in 1996, which is still double the EU average. This trend is expected to continue (OECD, 1997). The decline in agriculture has been offset by increased employment in the services sector.

The share of the labour force in manufacturing has also fallen over the past 20 years, as a result of the absolute decline in employment in the traditional sector.

There have been significant changes in the occupational structure of the labour force in line with the growth of the services sector and the increased level of educational attainment (O'Connell and Sexton, 1994). In particular, the number of managerial and professional jobs requiring advanced skills has grown rapidly. At the same time, there has been a corresponding decline in the number of agricultural and unskilled workers.

The share of temporary workers has increased from five per cent in 1983 to seven per cent in 1995 (OECD, 1997).

The proportion of self-employed persons in the workforce has remained relatively stable at about 20 per cent, despite the significant fall in the number of such workers in the agricultural sector. Self-employed persons and part-time and/or temporary employees represent about a third of the labour force.

Unemployment

Since the early 1970s, the unemployment rate has increased faster in Ireland than in other countries (OECD, 1995), rising from just over five per cent in 1973 to over 15 per cent in 1994 (see Figure 9.3).

FIGURE 9.3: UNEMPLOYMENT RATE, 1973–1995

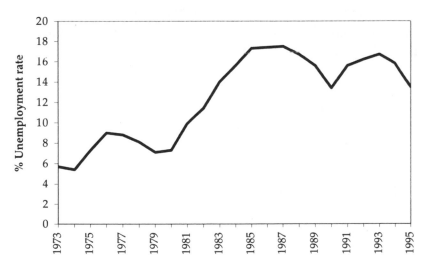

Source: Adapted from Leddin and Walsh, (1995: 13).

Unemployment in Ireland has tended to be more long-term in nature than in other countries, and is associated with low levels of human capital (OECD, 1995).

Despite rapid employment gains in recent years, the 11.25 per cent unemployment rate in Ireland in 1996 is still the third highest in the OECD area and is substantially higher than the OECD average of 7.8 per cent (OECD, 1997).

High unemployment has been concentrated amongst those with the lowest level of education, including young people who do not complete the minimum secondary education and older people who did not benefit from free secondary education (O'Connell and Sexton, 1994). By contrast, people with higher levels of human capital have benefited from growth, experiencing unemployment rates at or below those found in the rest of the OECD area (OECD, 1995). These factors suggest that ensuring an improvement in the quality of education for all will be essential in preventing the unemployment problem from worsening. Indeed, recent governments have focused on reform of the education and training systems to improve employment opportunities.[3]

In 1996, the unemployment rate for persons in the 15–24 age group was close to 20 per cent compared with an average of 15.6 per cent in the OECD area. About 30 per cent of the unemployed fall into this category. As a result, single persons account for a disproportionate share of unemployment.

The interaction of the tax and social welfare systems has weakened work incentives for many persons, particularly the unemployed with low educational qualifications (OECD, 1997).

Against this changing macroeconomic environment, how has the distribution of household income fared? It is to this issue that we now turn.

INCOME DISTRIBUTION

The distribution of income can be examined at a number of levels. These include:

---

[3] For a review of the role and effectiveness of recent active labour market policies in Ireland, see Kavanagh (1998).

1. The size distribution of income (looking at how evenly incomes are distributed)

2. The functional distribution of income (analysing income according to the source of that income) and

3. The distribution of income by recipient (examining income by classifications of people, e.g. women, men, age group, etc.).

Each seeks to highlight a different aspect of inequality. In this chapter, we focus on the first category and examine the extent of inequality among Irish households.[4]

The Data

We use the Household Budget Survey (HBS) as our primary data source. The HBS is conducted every seven years by the Central Statistics Office (CSO) and is a random sample of over 7,000 urban and rural households throughout the country. The purpose of the survey is primarily to determine in detail the current pattern of household expenditure in order to update the weighting basis of the Consumer Price Index, but other information, including household income etc., is also collected.

The first HBS was carried out in 1973, with subsequent surveys in 1980, 1987, and 1994. We employ all four HBSs. We stress that, while it is impossible to summarise the trends over two decades by picking four isolated years, the analysis does give an indication of the changes in the distribution of income over the period.

The income unit used in the HBS is the household. It is defined as "a single person or group of people who regularly reside together in the same accommodation and who share the same catering arrangements", (CSO, 1989: 213). The HBS distinguishes four different household income concepts. *Direct household income* is defined by the

---

[4] The following analysis implicitly assumes income as a measure of household welfare. Despite the widespread use of income as a proxy, it has been argued that consumption expenditure may better reflect expected lifetime resources (Poterba, 1989; Cutler and Katz, 1992; and Slesnick, 1993). The choice of any measure of living standards will inevitably exclude perspectives which could be gained from the choice of other measures. See Blundell and Preston (1995) for a discussion of measures of household welfare.

CSO as "all money receipts of a recurring nature which accrue to the households at annual or more frequent intervals, together with the value of any free goods regularly received by the household, and the retail value of own farm or garden produce produced by the household" (CSO, 1989: 208). Direct income is composed of earned income, employee's wages and salaries, self-employed farming and non-farming income, property income, investment income, retirement pensions, own garden or farm produce, and "other" direct income, which includes income-in-kind, trade union sick or strike pay, and income from securities, trusts and covenants. *Gross income* is defined as direct income plus state transfer payments (that is, unemployment benefits, children's allowances, old age pensions, etc.). *Disposable income* is defined as gross income less direct taxes (that is, income tax and employee share of social insurance contributions). Finally, *final income* is defined as disposable income plus estimated value of non-cash state benefits less indirect taxes (that is, licences, motor tax, estimated VAT and duty content of household expenditure).

We confine our analysis to direct and disposable income for two reasons. First, at the time of writing, the calculation of 1994/95 final income has not yet appeared for the 1994 HBS. This leaves three measures. Second, direct income is analogous to the initial income allocation, and is determined by the returns in the market to the factors of production of national output. Disposable income corresponds to how much each household has to spend each week and as such, is probably the most important income concept. It includes the redistributive efforts of the government. By comparing the distribution of direct income to that of disposable income, we can comment on the effectiveness of the tax and benefit system.

Two further issues warrant a mention. First, it should be emphasised that we are examining four cross-sectional surveys, and the households in each survey differ. Hence, caution should be exercised in interpreting our results. Second, all household incomes in the analysis are *unequivalised*. This means that differences in household size and composition have not been accounted for. While changes in the family size and composition are unlikely to be significant in the short run, they are likely to change in the longer run. In order to provide a common basis for comparison between households of varying composition and income level, household income is usually adjusted by weighting household incomes using an appropriate equivalence scale. Equivalence scales are attempts to control for relative consumption needs of households with differing composition, and represent the proportionate change in income necessary to maintain a constant standard of living as household composition changes. The choice of an appropriate equivalence scale is a matter of some debate.[5] However, as we did not have access to the raw data of all four HBSs, we are unable to adjust the distribution of income for household size and composition. Although the use of equivalised income would perhaps produce more reliable results, we nevertheless feel that an examination of the four HBSs by unequivalised income allows us to draw some important conclusions regarding the distribution of income in Ireland.

Problems with the HBS

There are a number of problems with the reliability of the HBS income data. These include:

1. Capital gains and rent from home owner-occupation are excluded, which understates the overall total income as well as the degree of concentration of incomes

2. As noted by Atkinson (1974: 44), the adoption of a household basis assumes that income sharing takes place within the household, and to the extent that it does not, inequality will be underestimated

3. Problems of under-reporting (income is generally understated in surveys of this type) and sampling error are present.[6]

---

[5] For example, Madden (1996) uses the square root of family size as the equivalence scale (an approach that does not distinguish between adults and children), while in the UK, by convention, the incomes of all households are standardised to the situation of a married couple without dependants (e.g., Goodman and Webb, 1995). Indeed, in the UK, the Royal Commission on the Distribution of Income and Wealth (1978) tested the sensitivity of income statistics to the choice of equivalence scales and concluded that the variation produced by different equivalence scale was less than the difference between any one of them and the unadjusted distribution.

[6] For a discussion of these problems and their impact on the income statistics, see Nolan (1978) and O'Connell (1982).

These problems do not mean that one should not use household data for distribution purposes; rather, such data should be used with care. Hence, the HBS remains an important source of income data.

Distribution of Income by Decile, 1973–94

Tables 9.1 and 9.2 illustrate the changing distribution of income by decile across all four HBSs.

The structure of the distribution of direct income is such that the bottom two deciles received less than 1.5 per cent of the total earned income during the entire period, while if we take the bottom three deciles, we find their share of income has actually declined over the period, from 4.97 per cent to 2.48 per cent. Taken together, the bottom five deciles received just over 18 per cent of total income in 1973, and by 1994, this had declined significantly to 11.5 per cent. At the other end of the distribution, the top two deciles have steadily increased their share of income, from 46.7 per cent in 1973 to almost 52.5 per cent in 1994. By itself, the top decile received 29 per cent of total income in 1973 and increased its share to over 32 per cent by 1994. This portrayal of the distribution of direct income indicates an exceptionally high degree of concentration of incomes among the top tenth or top fifth of households. More importantly, there has been a marked increase in the level of inequality over the past 20 years.

State transfer payments and direct taxes necessarily reduced the level of inequality in direct income in each year, but the net effect of state redistribution measures is limited. The distribution of disposable income, which reflects the relative spending power of households, shows that on the one hand, the bottom two deciles received 5.7 per cent of income in 1973, and although this share rose slightly to approximately 6 per cent in 1980 and 1987, it declined again to 5.7 per cent in 1994. In 1973, the bottom three deciles received 10.8 per cent of income and by 1994, this had fallen slightly to 10.5 per cent. On the other hand, redistribution efforts have reduced the share of the top 20 per cent in each year. The net effect of taxes and transfers has left this group with just over 40 per cent of total income throughout the entire period and at 41 per cent in 1994. Similarly, redistribution has reduced the top 10 per cent's share; over the period, they have also witnessed a slight decline in their share of disposable income from 26 per cent in 1973 to 24.7 per cent in 1994.

TABLE 9.1: DISTRIBUTION OF DIRECT INCOME, 1973–94/95 (%)

Decile	1973	1980	1987	1994/95
Bottom	0.01	0.00	0.38	0.29
2nd	1.18	0.54	1.00	0.92
3rd	3.78	2.84	1.39	1.27
4th	6.06	5.70	3.26	3.10
5th	7.65	7.68	6.05	5.92
6th	9.25	9.46	8.73	8.80
7th	11.27	11.49	11.55	11.76
8th	13.82	14.24	15.09	15.43
9th	17.73	18.34	20.08	19.90
Top	29.24	29.72	32.46	32.61
Totals	100.00	100.00	100.00	100.00

Source: Household Budget Survey, various issues.

TABLE 9.2: DISTRIBUTION OF DISPOSABLE INCOME, 1973–94/95 (%)

Decile	1973	1980	1987	1994/95
Bottom	2.67	3.15	2.28	2.23
2nd	3.03	3.20	3.74	3.49
3rd	5.11	4.62	5.11	4.75
4th	6.56	6.38	6.41	6.16
5th	7.79	7.68	7.71	7.63
6th	9.07	9.03	9.24	9.37
7th	10.83	13.17	11.16	11.41
8th	12.86	12.64	13.39	13.64
9th	16.06	15.55	16.48	16.67
Top	26.03	24.58	24.48	24.67
Totals	100.00	100.00	100.00	100.00

Source: Household Budget Survey, various issues.

Table 9.3, which shows the percentage differences between decile disposable income and mean income, supports these trends. It highlights that the bottom six deciles continued to receive incomes below the mean income, while incomes of the top four deciles were substantially higher than the mean.

TABLE 9.3: PERCENTAGE DIFFERENCES BETWEEN DECILE DISPOSABLE INCOME AND MEAN "STATE" INCOME, 1973–1994/95

Decile	1973	1980	1987	1994/95
Bottom	–73.35	–68.49	–77.17	–77.74
2nd	–69.72	–67.96	–62.60	–65.15
3rd	–48.87	–53.76	–48.88	–52.52
4th	–34.45	–36.23	–35.93	–38.38
5th	–22.12	–23.22	–22.92	–23.68
6th	–9.25	–9.65	–7.59	–6.34
7th	+8.31	+31.68	+11.57	+14.08
8th	+28.59	+26.36	+33.87	+36.36
9th	+60.58	+55.46	+64.83	+66.70
Top	+160.27	+145.82	+144.82	+146.65
Mean (£)	36.28	109.44	200.98	281.90

Note: Mean state income is calculated by the CSO from all the income data collected in the HBS. The value of £281.90 in 1994/95 suggests this was the mean weekly income of households.
Source: Household Budget Survey, various issues.

Two conclusions emerge from the analysis. First, it is clear that even after government redistribution efforts, the distribution of disposable income remained highly concentrated at the top of the income distribution. Second, inequality in direct income is more pronounced than inequality in disposable income, suggesting that redistributive efforts have succeeded in stemming the growth in income inequality to some extent. However, in comparing the degree of inequality across income distributions, it is generally more informative to adopt summary measures of inequality, which we do below.

INEQUALITY

Several different methods exist for measuring the extent of inequality. One widely used method is the Lorenz curve, a device that
plots cumulative proportions of the population from the poorest to
the richest against the proportions of total income that they hold. The
Lorenz curve proves a useful tool, since it gives a pictorial representation of the degree of income inequality. In the case of perfect
equality, the Lorenz curve is a 45-degree line, but otherwise, it will be
bowed out below the 45-degree line. The degree to which the Lorenz
curve lies below the 45-degree line gives an impression of the sever-
ity of the inequality in the income distribution. If one distribution has
a Lorenz curve everywhere above that of a second and the same total
income, then there is good reason to think of inequality as being
lower in the first than in the second, because this will occur if and
only if the former distribution could be obtained from the latter by a
series of income transfers from richer to poorer individuals. Figure
9.4 illustrates the Lorenz curve.

FIGURE 9.4: THE LORENZ CURVE

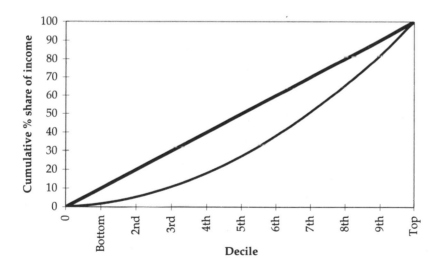

Although the Lorenz curve is useful for showing the change in income distribution over time, the problem with simply comparing

Lorenz curves by eye is that it is imprecise.[7] This problem is overcome by using the Gini coefficient, manifested by the Lorenz curves. The Gini coefficient summarises inequality in terms of an index and is calculated as the lens-shaped area between the Lorenz curve and the diagonal, expressed as a proportion of the complete triangle below the diagonal. The higher the Gini coefficient, the greater the degree of inequality. We discuss the Gini measure in more detail below.

Another measure quite commonly used is the ratio of the bottom 40 per cent's share of income to the top 20 per cent's share. Although this is a very simple method of measuring income distribution, it is useful for tracking changes in any one country over time. Table 9.4 gives an example of this method for Ireland. The lower the ratio, the greater the degree of inequality.

TABLE 9.4: THE RATIO OF THE BOTTOM 40 PER CENT'S SHARE OF HOUSEHOLD INCOME TO THE TOP 20 PER CENT'S SHARE, 1973–1994

Year	Share of Highest 20%	Share of Lowest 40%	Ratio of the Bottom 40% to Top 20%
1973 Direct	46.97	11.04	0.23
1980 Direct	48.06	9.08	0.19
1987 Direct	52.54	6.04	0.11
1994/95 Direct	52.51	5.59	0.11
1973 Disposable	42.09	17.36	0.41
1980 Disposable	40.13	17.36	0.43
1987 Disposable	40.97	17.54	0.43
1994/95 Disposable	41.34	16.62	0.40

Source: Household Budget Survey, various issues.

The ratio supports the earlier conclusion that the growth in inequality in direct income has been pronounced (the value of the ratio declined from 0.23 to 0.11). Further, inequality in disposable income appears to have remained relatively unchanged.

---

[7] We do no present the Lorenz curves here for the four distributions in question; as they lie so close together, it is impossible to distinguish between them.

Although useful, this measure is incomplete, as it does not take account of the middle deciles. Other all-inclusive measures such as the Gini coefficient, the coefficient of variation and the Theil index are more informative measures of inequality. Condensing changes in inequality into movements in a single statistic such as the Gini co-efficient inevitably obscures much of what is going on, but do make quantitative comparison possible. Although they provide a clear way of comparing income distribution in the same country at different times, there are several drawbacks associated with such summary measures. First, a single measure cannot take into account all the features of inequality. Second, there is the question of what statistics to use in calculation — whether to employ pre- or post-tax income, to include benefits, and to use households or individuals as the unit of investigation. Third, it is important to recognise, as noted by Atkinson, that when examining these indexes, "there is no reason to believe that they correspond to any values that we should like to hold regarding equity" (Atkinson, 1974: 51) — they are statistical not moral measures.

Indexes of inequality are often divided into two main categories: descriptive and normative. The Gini coefficient, the coefficient of variation and the Theil index are examples of the former and are derived from the statistical examination of dispersion. Normative measures are grounded upon an explicit formulation of social welfare; the value of such an index is generally interpreted as the loss in welfare due to an unequal distribution of income (for example, Dalton's (1920) measure of inequality). There is no rigorous division between the two types of measures (Sen, 1973).

The performance of any index is frequently gauged by the extent to which it satisfies a set of axioms, which are general enough to be accepted by most economists. The first axiom is the principle of transfers, also known as the Pigou-Dalton condition. It states that "if a transfer of income occurs from a poorer person to a richer one, *ceteris paribus*, then the measure of inequality should increase" (McGregor and Borooah, 1991: 84). Sen (1973: 27) proposed this condition's name based on the work at the beginning of the century by both Pigou and Dalton. The second axiom demands that the index be symmetric. This implies that if the same incomes are redistributed between individuals, the index would be unchanged. The third axiom is the population principle, which maintains that in comparing two income distributions where the second replicated the first, then the inequality index will be unaltered. Finally, the homogeneity principle requires that the index be homogeneous of degree zero in incomes, thereby satisfying the fourth axiom. This implies that, were the income levels expressed in different units, the measure would remain unchanged.

The Gini Coefficient[8]

The Gini coefficient is one of the most widely used summary measures of inequality. It satisfies all of the above four axioms, and has the advantage of being relatively simple to understand and use. This measure rises with rising inequality and varies between zero (everyone has the same income) and one (one person has all the income).

In recent decades, criticisms have been directed at the Gini measure which have undermined its once principal position as the main inequality measure (Osberg, 1984: 18–22). Osberg (1984) and Atkinson (1970) challenge its ability to reflect changes in income distributions. They both maintain that the Gini measure is more sensitive to income changes which occur in the middle ranges of income distributions. This implies that a transfer of £100 from one rich individual to another rich individual will have little effect on the Gini coefficient, whereas the same £100 if transferred to a lower decile household would have a larger effect on the Gini. This occurs as such changes broaden the differences between income shares, thereby decreasing the variance and changing the Gini.

A further critique of the Gini coefficient is that, via its calculation, it assumes equality exists within distributions, implying that within each decile, income is distributed evenly. Such an assumption is basically untenable, and undermines the Gini's reliability. Despite these criticisms, the Gini coefficient stands as the central index of inequality.

Coefficient of Variation

The coefficient of variation ranges from zero — implying perfect equality — to a maximum of $\sqrt{n-1}$ (with n equal to the number of

---

[8] See Appendix B for a detailed description of each index together with its mathematical formula.

income groups) where complete inequality exists. Though not as popular as the Gini, the coefficient of variation has an established record as a measure of inequality. It satisfies the Pigou-Dalton condition, as well as being sensitive to income transfers at all income levels. Both Sen (1973: 28) and Atkinson (1972: 255) highlight that the coefficient of variation is characterised by attaching equal weights to transfers of income at different income levels. Neither conclude whether such "neutrality" is a desirable phenomenon, though both contemplate whether an equal transfer at a lower level of income should impact on inequality more than at a higher level.

Theil "Entropy" Index

Theil's "entropy" index (1967) derives from the notion of entropy in statistical information theory (Osberg, 1984: 22). The index spans from zero, where perfect equality exists, to a maximum of *log n* (where *n* represents the number of income groups), implying complete inequality.

Similar to the Gini index, the Theil index satisfies the established axioms by meeting the Pigou-Dalton condition, symmetry, the population principle and homogeneity. Theil notes that the index could be aggregated in a simple manner over groups, and numerous economists have found that the index "naturally" decomposes into inter- and intra-group components of inequality (Theil, 1967: 4–96; Murphy, 1984: 22).[9]

The Theil index has also been the source of some criticism. It has been suggested that the Theil proves more sensitive to movements in the middle part of the income distribution, thereby implying a bias in its assessment of changes in inequality (Osberg, 1984: 23–31). Further, it has been argued that the index relies on relative rather than absolute income changes, which once again undermine its reliability (Jenkins, 1991: 18). However, the Theil remains a popular inequality measure (Osberg, 1984: 32).

---

[9] The decomposability of an index is a useful attribute, as it helps in our understanding of the pattern of inequality. In Ireland, advances in decomposing the Theil index have been made by Murphy (1984) and for the Gini coefficient, by Madden (1996). See also Cowell (1995: 66) and Osberg (1984: 22) for a discussion of the decomposition advantages of the Theil.

Hence, each of these three measures provides a useful indicator of the extent of inequality. None of the problems associated with each index causes major difficulties in the analysis of Irish household incomes. We now turn to the estimation of these three measures.

Estimated Measures of Inequality

The results for the three measures of inequality are presented in Table 9.5. It should be noted that the measures presented here consistently underestimate the extent of inequality to some degree, because the within-decile income inequality is not taken into account.

TABLE 9.5: CHANGES IN THE MEASURES OF INEQUALITY OF DIRECT AND DISPOSABLE INCOME, 1973–94/95

Year	Gini Coefficient	Coefficient of Variation	Theil Index
1973 Direct	0.45	0.83	0.35
1980 Direct	0.47	0.86	0.39
1987 Direct	0.52	0.97	0.46
1994/95 Direct	0.52	0.98	0.47
1973 Disposable	0.35	0.67	0.20
1980 Disposable	0.34	0.63	0.19
1987 Disposable	0.35	0.64	0.19
1994/95 Disposable	0.36	0.65	0.20

In the case of direct income, all three measures exhibit a similar pattern. The most striking feature of the measures is that, since 1973, they have been continually rising, indicating rising inequality. From 1973 to 1994, the Gini coefficient has risen from 0.45 to 0.52, the coefficient of variation from 0.83 to 0.98, and the Theil index from 0.35 to 0.47. These changes represent a significant rise in direct income inequality. Over the entire period, the Gini coefficient has increased by 15.5 per cent, the coefficient of variation increased by over 18 per cent increase, and the Theil index rose by a substantial 34 per cent. The most notable increase in inequality occurred during the period 1980–87, a period of prolonged recession. However, the coefficient of variation and the Theil index also suggest that inequality has increased since 1987.

The table highlights that the growth in inequality in disposable income has been less pronounced. The Gini coefficient increased from 0.35 to 0.36 over the entire period, approximately a 2 per cent increase. The coefficient of variation suggests that while inequality in disposable income has declined slightly since 1973, it has been increasing since 1980. Similarly, the Theil index indicates a slight rise since 1987. Hence, examination of the measures confirms the less formal decile analysis: rising inequality in market incomes was counteracted by the redistributive effort, but disposable income remains highly concentrated.

In order to further examine the extent of inequality over the period 1987–94, and identify the impact of redistribution on inequality, we attempt to illustrate the progressivity[10] of the tax system. There is a considerable literature on methods measuring the progessivity of the tax system, including measures of the divergence from proportionality of the tax system. A straightforward numerical approach is to examine the proportion of tax paid by each decile over the period (Giles and Johnson, 1994).[11] Table 9.6 provides such a disaggregation. Redistribution efforts can also be examined by comparing pre-tax and pre-transfer Gini coefficients to disposable income coefficients (Giles and Johnson, 1994). The results of this analysis are presented in Table 9.7.

The progressive nature of the direct tax system is evident from Table 9.6. The proportion of income taken rises by decile in both years, with the exception of the bottom decile in 1994/95. Perhaps the most striking feature of Table 9.6 is the increased contribution of the bottom three deciles to direct taxation while the other seven deciles witnessed a declining contribution. More importantly, the rise in the bottom decile's contribution from 3.14 per cent in 1987 to 11 per cent in 1994 is pronounced. Hence, although successive governments attempted to reform the tax system during the period, the

---

[10] A progressive tax is one which levies a greater proportion of income from high incomes than from lower incomes, while a regressive tax levies a greater proportion from low incomes than high incomes.

[11] See also Morris and Preston (1986) and Lambert (1989) for surveys of the measurement of progressivity.

extent to which the bottom deciles benefited from these tax changes (exclusive of benefit changes) is questionable.

TABLE 9.6: PER CENT OF DIRECT INCOME PAID BY EACH DECILE IN DIRECT TAXATION, 1987 AND 1994/95

Decile	1987	1994/95	% Change
Bottom	3.14	11.00	+7.86
2nd	3.36	4.87	+1.51
3rd	4.52	7.53	+3.01
4th	9.34	7.78	−1.56
5th	14.33	12.49	−1.84
6th	18.19	16.28	−1.92
7th	19.96	18.26	−1.70
8th	22.25	20.33	−1.92
9th	25.60	22.83	−2.77
Top	28.62	27.66	−0.95
Average	22.96	20.15	−2.81

Source: Household Budget Survey, various issues.

TABLE 9.7: GINI COEFFICIENT AND PRE-TAX AND PRE-TRANSFERS GINI COEFFICIENTS

	1987	1994–95
Pre-Tax Gini*	0.2628	0.2815
Pre-Transfers Gini	0.4879	0.4956
Disposable Gini	0.3462	0.3562

Notes: *We use disposable income to calculate both pre-tax and pre-transfers Gini coefficients, and subtract both tax and transfers separately. The Gini coefficient for the pre-tax concept corresponds to direct income plus transfers. Similarly, for the pre-transfers Gini coefficient, we use disposable income minus transfers, or direct income plus taxes.

Table 9.7 supports the hypothesis that inequality has risen over the 1987–94 period. All measures of the Gini increased. While the pre-

transfers and pre-tax Gini coefficients indicate that both systems necessarily reduced income inequality in both years, inequality has continued to grow. Nevertheless, transfers play an important role in
reducing inequality. The pre-transfers Gini fell from approximately
0.49 to a disposable Gini of 0.34 in 1987 and from 0.49 to 0.35 in
1994/95.

To investigate the possible sources of income inequality, we show,
in Table 9.8, the composition of average household income in each of
the years, 1973–94/95.

TABLE 9.8: SOURCES OF AVERAGE HOUSEHOLD INCOME (%), 1973–
94/95

Income Source	1973	1980	1987	1994/95
Earnings	58.595	66.015	62.071	61.486
Self-employed (Farming & non-farming)	22.632	15.229	12.257	12.617
Retirement Pensions	1.964	2.239	3.270	3.876
Investment Income	1.038	1.420	1.075	0.819
Transfers (total)	10.475	11.373	17.639	16.770
Others	5.295	3.723	3.688	4.433
Total	100.00	100.00	100.00	100.00

Source: Household Budget Survey, various issues

The pattern of earnings growth is of interest. Having increased
sharply from 58.5 per cent in 1973 to over 66 per cent in 1980, the
trend since then has been one of decline. This may in part reflect the
decline in the percentage of the labour force at work — in particular,
the fall in the percentage of males at work — and the rise in lower-
paid part-time female employment. A significant proportion of the
declining contribution of self-employment to household income reflects the decline in the numbers employed in agriculture. Investment
income has declined slightly throughout the whole period, while income from pensions has increased from almost 2 per cent to 3.9 per
cent. The source of income which has shown significant growth is
clearly transfers, rising from 10.5 per cent to almost 17 per cent over

the period. The rise in unemployment during the 1980s is an obvious contributor to the increase, together with changes in benefit levels.

TABLE 9.9: MADDEN'S (1996) SOURCES OF INCOME INEQUALITY USING EQUIVALISED INCOME, 1987*

Income Source	Decomposition Coefficients
Positive Effects on Inequality:	
Wages and salaries	+0.679
Self-employed income (non-farm)	+0.042
Self-employed income (farm)	+0.026
Negative Effects on Inequality:	
Income tax	−0.212
Old age pensions	−0.171
Unemployment benefit and assistance	−0.120
Other long-term social welfare	−0.062
Widows' pensions	−0.053
Social insurance	−0.034
Other transfers	−0.033
Retirement pensions	−0.028
Other disposable income	−0.016
Children's allowance	−0.012
Farm produce	−0.011
Scholarships etc.	−0.002
Investment income	−0.001
Property income	0.000

Notes: *The results are presented here by size and divided into positive and negative effects.
Source: Madden, (1996: 15).

Madden (1996) has advanced this debate by examining the sources of income inequality in 1987, using a decomposition of the Gini coefficient based on the 1987 HBS. Disaggregating disposable income into 17 components, he calculated the contribution to inequality of each of them at the margin (see Table 9.9). His results indicate that wages and salaries are the largest influence on inequality. Additionally, the income tax coefficient of –0.212 suggests income tax has the potential to reduce inequality. However, as Madden (1996: 8) recognises, his results should be interpreted with caution, as the impact on inequality of an income tax change could be very considerable depending on its size and focus.

CONCLUSION

This chapter has tracked the level of inequality over the past two decades by examining the four HBSs from 1973–94/95. Our analysis of various inequality indexes yields the same conclusion: taking direct income as a measure of income, the gap between the rich and the poor has increased significantly since 1973. Although redistribution through the combination of the tax and benefit systems has stemmed the growth in inequality, disposable income remains highly concentrated at the top of the income distribution. An analysis of the sources of inequality indicated that the changing contribution of earnings is likely to have impacted significantly on the initial distribution of income. In an environment where the demand for high-level skills has risen and where poorly qualified school-leavers quickly become unemployed (Barry and Hannan, 1998), it is not surprising that the income gap between those with a good education and those with poor qualifications has increased (OECD, 1995). For these reasons, the OECD argues that one important aspect to improving inequality in Ireland is education. This is because "the accumulation of human capital through education, improves a person's 'market value' and hence income" (OECD, 1995: 75). In other words, the accumulation of human capital enables countries to move from a low to a high level of income. Hence, they suggest that education and training policies will have a crucial role to play in the fight against poverty and unemployment among poorly educated people.

However, the sources of inequality are many. The problem has many dimensions and there are many factors that determine the pattern and depth of inequality. Other possible contributors to the growth in inequality include: differences in ability; differences in attitudes; differences in hours worked; inequality of wealth; and of course, unemployment. Additionally, the changes to household size and composition are likely to have affected inequality. An examination of these issues should be the source of future research.

Redistribution is not costless. Whether it takes place through taxes or benefits or both, it is possible that there will be a problem of disincentives. The disincentive problem in Ireland was pronounced during the 1980s. The lack of co-ordination between tax and welfare policies reduced the gap between the level of income support available to the unemployed and net income from work, thus making the transition from unemployment to work less attractive and lessening the incentives for low-paid workers to remain in employment (OECD, 1997: 75). Initiatives designed to increase the incentive to work have been features of recent Budgets. In addition, priority has been given to closer co-ordination of changes in the tax and benefit systems to reduce disincentives. However, the size of the disincentive problem varies from one tax to another and from one benefit to another. It is therefore important to estimate the particular effects of each type of proposal, not only on income distribution itself, but also on economic efficiency. Further, supply-side arguments for reforms to reduce disincentives should not ignore the demand-side. It is imperative that the increased supply of labour as a result of improved incentives is accompanied by greater opportunities for employment in the labour market.

Ultimately, the questions of how much income should be redistributed and whether the costs are worth bearing are normative questions, and ones that we do not address in this chapter. Yet decisions have to be made. While it is of interest to know if overall inequality is increasing or decreasing, the real centre of interest is in understanding why it is occurring. A better understanding of the reasons for inequality should facilitate the drawing-up and implementation of better policies that aid in its alleviation.

REFERENCES

Atkinson, A.B. (1970), "On the Measurement of Inequality", *Journal of Economic Theory*, Vol. 2, pp. 244–63.

Atkinson, A.B. (1974), "Poverty and Income Inequality in Britain", in D. Wedderman (ed.), *Poverty, Inequality and Class Structure*, London: Cambridge University Press.

Barry, F. and A. Hannan (1998), "Education, Deprivation, Hysteresis, Unemployment", in C. Clark and C. Kavanagh (eds.), *Unemployment in Ireland: Alternative Perspectives*, Aldershot: Avebury.

Blundell, R. and I. Preston (1995), "Income Expenditure and the Living Standards of UK Households", *Fiscal Studies*, Vol. 6., No. 3, pp. 40–54.

Bradley, J., J. Fitz Gerald, P. Honohan and I. Kearney (1997), "Interpreting the Recent Irish Growth Experience", in *Medium-term Review*, Dublin: The Economic and Social Research Institute.

Butler, R.J. and J.B. McDonald (1986), "Income Inequality in the United States, 1948–1980" in R.G. Ehrenberg (ed.), *Research in Labour Economics*, Vol. 8, Part A, Connecticut: JAI Press Inc.

Central Statistics Office, *Household Budget Survey*, Various Issues, Dublin: Stationery Office.

Central Statistics Office (1989), *Effects of State Taxes and Benefits on Household Incomes in 1987*, Dublin: Stationery Office.

Cowell, F.A. (1995), *Measuring Inequality: London School of Economics Handbooks in Economics Series*, Second Edition, London: Prentice Hall/Harvester Wheatsheaf.

Cutler, D. and L. Katz (1992), "Rising Inequality? Changes in the Distribution of Income and Consumption in the 1980s", *American Economic Review*, Vol. 82, pp. 546–51.

Dalton, H. (1920), "The Measurement of Inequality of Incomes", *Economic Journal*, Vol. 30, pp. 348–361.

Giles, C. and P. Johnson (1994), "Tax Reform in the UK and Changes in the Progressivity of the Tax System, 1985–95", *Fiscal Studies*, Vol. 15, No. 3, pp. 64–86.

Goodman, A. and S. Webb (1995), "The Distribution of UK Household Expenditure, 1979–92", *Fiscal Studies*, Vol. 16, No. 3, pp. 55–80.

Jenkins, S. (1991), "The Measurement of Income Inequality", in L. Osberg (ed.), *Economic Inequality and Poverty, International Perspectives*, New York: M.E. Sharpe, Inc.

Kavanagh, C. (1998), "A Review of the Role of Active Labour Market Policies in Ireland", in C. Clark and C. Kavanagh (eds.), *Unemployment in Ireland: Alternative Perspectives*, Aldershot: Avebury.

Lambert, P. (1989), *The Distribution and Redistribution of Income*, Oxford: Basil Blackwell.

Leddin, A. and B. Walsh (1995), *The Macroeconomy of Ireland*, Third Edition, Dublin: Gill and Macmillan.

Madden, D. (1996), "Sources of Income Inequality in Ireland", Working Paper Series, Centre for Economic Research, University College Dublin.

Morris, C.N. and I. Preston (1986), "Inequality, Poverty and the Redistribution of Income", *Bulletin of Economic Research*, Vol. 38, pp. 277–344.

Murphy, D.C. (1984), "The Impact of State Taxes and Benefits on Irish Household Incomes", *Journal of the Statistical and Social Inquiry of Society of Ireland*, Vol. 25, Part 1, pp. 55–120.

McGregor, P.P.L. and Borooah, V.K. (1991), "Poverty and the Distribution of Income in Northern Ireland", *The Economic and Social Review*, Vol. 22, No. 2, pp. 81–100.

Nolan, B. (1978), "The Personal Distribution of Income in the Republic of Ireland", *Journal of the Statistical and Social Inquiry Society of Ireland*, Vol. 23, Part 5, pp. 91–161.

O'Connell, P.J. (1982), "The Distribution and Redistribution of Income in the Republic of Ireland", *The Economic and Social Review*, Vol. 13, No. 4, pp. 251–278.

O'Connell, P.J. and J.J. Sexton (1994), "Labour Market Developments in Ireland, 1971–1993", in S. Cantillon, J. Curtin and J. Fitz Gerald (eds.), *Economic Perspectives for the Medium Term*, Dublin: The Economic and Social Research Institute.

OECD (1995), *OECD Economic Surveys, 1994–1995: Ireland*, Paris: OECD.

OECD (1997), *OECD Economic Surveys, 1996–1997: Ireland*, Paris: OECD.

O'Hagan, J. (1995), *The Economy of Ireland: Policy and Performance of a Small European Country*, Dublin: Gill and Macmillan.

Osberg, L. (1984), *Economic Inequality in the United States*, New York/London: M.E. Sharpe Inc., Armonk.

Poterba, J. (1989), "Lifetime Incidence and the Distributional Burden of Excise Taxes", *American Economic Review*, Vol. 79, pp. 325–30.

Royal Commission on the Distribution of Wealth and Income (1978), *Lower Incomes*, London: HMSO.

Sen, A.K. (1973), *On Economic Inequality*, Oxford: Oxford University Press.

Slesnick, D. (1993), "Gaining Ground: Poverty in the Post-war United States", *Journal of Political Economy*, Vol. 101, pp. 1–38.

Theil, H. (1967), *Economics and Information Theory*, Amsterdam: North Holland.

APPENDIX A: DATA APPENDIX

TABLE 9A.1: GROWTH RATE OF REAL GNP, 1973–1994/95

Year	GNP Growth Rate (%)	Year	GNP Growth Rate (%)
1973	4.4	1985	–1.6
1974	3.4	1986	3.0
1975	0.2	1987	4.4
1976	2.2	1988	2.6
1977	5.6	1989	5.5
1978	5.8	1990	8.3
1979	3.0	1991	3.5
1980	1.7	1992	3.5
1981	2.1	1993	3.5
1982	–1.7	1994	5.0*
1983	–1.8	1995	5.5*
1984	2.1		

Notes: *indicates an estimate or forecast.
Source: Leddin and Walsh, (1995: 16).

TABLE 9A.2: NUMBERS AT WORK, THE LABOUR FORCE AND THE
PROPORTION OF THE LABOUR FORCE AT WORK, 1977–1995

Year	No. at Work ('000s)	Labour Force (15+)	% of LF at work
1977	1,083	1,172	92.41
1979	1,150	1,235	93.12
1983	1,125	1,309	85.94
1984	1,103	1,307	84.39
1985	1,076	1,302	82.64
1986	1,081	1,308	82.65
1987	1,090	1,323	82.39
1988	1,090	1,308	83.33
1989	1,088	1,289	84.41
1990	1,134	1,310	86.56
1991	1,134	1,342	84.50
1992	1,143	1,360	84.04
1993	1,148	1,378	83.31
1994	1,182	1,400	84.43
1995	1,239	1,430	86.64

Source: Labour Force Survey, various issues.

TABLE 9A.3: UNEMPLOYMENT RATE, 1973–1995

Year	Unemployment Rate	Year	Unemployment Rate
1973	5.7	1984	15.6
1974	5.4	1985	17.3
1975	7.3	1986	17.4
1976	9.0	1987	17.5
1977	8.8	1988	16.7
1978	8.1	1989	15.6
1979	7.1	1990	13.4
1980	7.3	1991	15.6
1981	9.9	1992	16.2
1982	11.4	1993	16.7
1983	14.0	1994	15.8*
1984	15.6	1995	13.5*

Notes: *indicates an estimate or forecast.
Source: Leddin and Walsh, (1995: 16).

APPENDIX B: INDEX DEFINITIONS AND FORMULAS

Gini Coefficient

A variety of equivalent methods of defining the Gini exist, all of which present a result between zero, implying perfect equality, and one, implying complete inequality (see Sen, 1973; and Cowell, 1995, for examples of these various methods to achieve the same result). Sen presented a Gini formula (G) where n represented the number of income groups, μ stood for the mean income and $|yi - yj|$ was the difference between each pair of income shares (Sen, 1973: 31). The formula is given by:

$$G = \left[1/\left(2n^2\mu\right)\right] \sum_{I=1}^{n} \sum_{J=1}^{n} |yi - yj| \qquad \text{(Equation 1)}$$

Jenkins (1991: 16) later proposed an equivalent yet "more easily estimated form" of Sen's formula which is used in calculating the Gini coefficients throughout this paper. His formula took yi to represent the lowest income level and was derived as:

$$G = 1 + \left(1/n\right) - \left[2/\left(n^2\mu\right)\right] \sum_{i=1}^{n} \left(n - i + 1\right)yi, \qquad \text{(Equation 2)}$$

Further and more complex methods of derivation exist which allow the Gini to be decomposed between its component parts (see Butler and McDonald, 1986 and Madden, 1996). However, such methods of disaggregation are not required in this analysis.

Coefficient of Variation

Calculating the variance, v, is the most commonly used measure of dispersion within distributions among statisticians. However, such a method proves unsatisfactory as a measure of inequality (Osberg, 1984: 21). The variance is neither mean independent nor scale-free. Thus, if the variance was used as a measure and all households' incomes doubled, the result would be a quadrupled variance. This would seem to indicate that inequality had changed, when in fact percentage income shares remained constant (see Cowell, 1995: 24; and Osberg, 1984: 21, for a more complete discussion of the variance's weaknesses). Dividing the square root of the variance by the mean income, $\bar{y}$, normalises the variance and produces a more reliable inequality measure known as the coefficient of variation (Cowell, 1995: 24).

The coefficient of variation is calculated using the formula:

$$C = \frac{\sqrt{v}}{\bar{y}} \qquad \text{(Equation 3)}$$

where $\bar{y}$ represents the mean level of income and v stands for the variance. Initially the variance is derived as:

$$v = \frac{1}{n} \sum_{i=1}^{n} \left(yi - \bar{y} \right)^2 \qquad \text{(Equation 4)}$$

Hence, the coefficient of variation may be directly calculated as:

$$C = \frac{\sqrt{\dfrac{1}{n} \sum_{i=1}^{n} \left(\bar{y} - yi \right)^2}}{\bar{y}} \qquad \text{(Equation 5)}$$

with n corresponding to the number of income groups and yi representing the income level attributed to each of those groups.

Theil "Entropy" Index

Entropy, or the expected information content of a situation, evolved from the aggregation of a set of n probabilities relating to each of n events. The entropy aggregates to one if the events are sure to occur and to zero if the events are unlikely to happen. Theil saw the feasibility of replacing the probabilities with income shares, thereby turning the entropy measure into a measure of inequality. The Theil index is calculated using the formula:

$$T = \frac{1}{n} \sum_{i=1}^{k} ni \; \frac{yi}{n\bar{y}} \; \log_{10} \left(\frac{yi}{\bar{y}} \right) \qquad \text{(Equation 6)}$$

where n represents the number of income groups, yi stands for the income of group i and $\bar{y}$ represents the mean income. Equivalent expressions for calculating the Theil can also be found in Cowell (1995: 49), Osberg (1984: 31) and Sen (1973: 35).

Chapter 10

THE WELFARE STATE IN IRELAND: A EUROPEAN PERSPECTIVE

Brendan Kennelly *and* Eamon O'Shea[*]

INTRODUCTION

This chapter analyses recent developments in the welfare state in Ireland and sets out desirable pathways for its evolution during the next decade. The paper is comparative in its analysis of recent developments, with particular emphasis on trends in the welfare states of the European Union (EU). There are a number of reasons why it is important to analyse the Irish welfare state in a comparative European context. First, social policy analysis is becoming more comparative in its outlook as researchers discover that the challenges facing one particular country may be similar to challenges facing other countries. This is increasingly true in a highly integrated economic area such as the EU. Second, while much has been written about the success of the Irish economy during the last ten years, less has been written about the progress Ireland has made in social policy. Third, much work has been done at exploring the practicality of a European social policy. We attempt to develop this concept, with particular emphasis on recent efforts to encourage the development of a standard measure of social quality across Europe.

The chapter is organised as follows. The first section introduces the basic societal process, a framework which is used to organise our analysis. While social policy analysis has traditionally focused on the

---

[*] This work was completed while Brendan Kennelly was a visiting researcher at the Work and Organisation Research Centre (WORC) at Tilburg University, The Netherlands.

link between the welfare state and social protection, we argue that more attention should be placed on the relationship between the welfare state and social participation. The second section provides an empirical overview of the main developments in the Irish welfare state over the past ten years. This is followed in the third section by an attempt to locate Ireland within conventional classifications of European welfare states. The fourth section examines what we believe have been the most important policy changes in Ireland in recent years. In the final section, we argue for the re-orientation of the Irish welfare state towards social participation, through the promotion of social citizenship as the means of enhancing social quality among excluded populations.

CONCEPTUAL FRAMEWORK

The welfare state covers such a broad range of activities that it is essential to choose a framework to organise our analysis. It is useful to begin with what Berghman (1997) terms the basic societal process. The first stage in this process is that people are educated and (re)trained in order to ensure that they are adequately integrated into the (paid) labour force (Figure 10.1). This gives them the opportunity to earn a primary income. This income in turn gives them the resources to guarantee their social participation.

FIGURE 10.1: BASIC SOCIETAL PROCESS

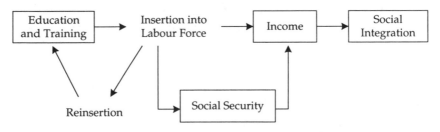

Source: Berghman, 1997.

Traditional social security systems have concentrated on the protection and assistance stages of this process: safeguarding the acquired standard of living through earnings-related income maintenance and guaranteeing minimum income protection. While both of these are an integral part of the welfare process, it is now recognised that the welfare state can also make an important contribution towards the reintegration of unemployed workers through various support structures such as retraining, work mediation, and rehabilitation schemes. In this context, social integration is the process whereby citizens' participation in the social, economic and democratic life of society is "experienced", while the outcome of that process, the actual degree of participation that results from it, is the level of social quality in society, incorporating elements of income security, social cohesion and solidarity (Berghman, 1997: 230).

Defining the basic societal process in this way provides a framework for much of what follows in this paper. Most discussion of the welfare state is confined to social protection elements. Social participation, if mentioned at all, is characterised in terms of enforced workfare for a workforce which is seen at best as work-shy, and at worst as morally degenerate. In this paper, participation is characterised in more positive, inclusive terms, with the emphasis on the strong link between education, training and employment, and between education and earnings in market economies.

AN EMPIRICAL OVERVIEW OF THE WELFARE STATE

While many definitions of the welfare state exist, the term is generally used to refer to the "public mechanisms of support (in cash, in kind, or through public services) against a catalogue of standard social risks: old-age, death of a supporting spouse, invalidity, sickness, maternity, and unemployment" (Ferrera, 1997: 119). In addition to this core, a number of other programmes have evolved, such as transfers and direct care for children and other persons in special need, minimum income schemes, labour market policies, and measures aimed at social integration. The EU has compiled a database that compares social protection expenditure[1] (SPE) across all of the member states. In this section we use this database to briefly outline the most important aspects of the nature of the welfare state in Ireland and other EU countries.

---

[1] Social protection expenditure is any expenditure involved in meeting costs incurred by individuals or households as a result of the materialisation or the existence of certain risks, contingencies or needs, in so far as this expenditure gives rise to the intervention of a "third party", without there being any simultaneous equivalent counterpart by the beneficiary (Eurostat, 1996a: 132).

Table 10.1 shows the ratio of SPE to GDP in EU countries for selected years between 1970 and 1994 (the most recent year for which data are available). In 1994, SPE averaged 29 per cent of GDP in the 12 countries of the EU (before the accession of Finland, Sweden and Austria). SPE/GDP varied from 34 per cent in Denmark to 16 per cent in Greece. The 1970s saw a dramatic increase in the SPE/GDP ratio in Ireland and it reached a peak at 23.9 per cent in 1983. The upward trend was reversed between 1986 and 1990 when SPE/GDP fell from 23.1 per cent to 19.4 per cent. Between 1991 and 1994 the ratio has remained relatively stable, averaging 21.2 per cent for the

TABLE 10.1: SOCIAL PROTECTION EXPENDITURE IN THE EU MEMBER STATES AS % OF GDP

	1970	*1980*	*1985*	*1990*	*1994*
Belgium	18.7	28.0	29.3	27.0	27.0
Denmark	19.6	28.7	27.8	29.8	33.7
Germany	21.5	28.8	28.4	26.9	30.8
Greece	–	9.7	15.4	16.1	16.0
Spain	–	18.2	20.0	20.6	23.6
France	19.2	25.4	28.8	27.7	30.5
Ireland	13.2	20.6	23.6	19.5	21.1
Italy	17.4	19.4	22.6	24.1	25.3
Luxemboug	15.9	26.5	23.4	22.1	24.9
Netherlands	20.8	30.1	31.7	32.2	32.3
Portugal	–	12.9	14.2	15.0	19.5
UK	15.9	20.5	23.8	22.1	28.1
EU12	19/0	24.1	25.9	25.2	28.6
Austria	–	–	–	–	30.2
Finland	–	–	–	26.0	34.8

Note: The figures for the EC in 1970 refer to the 9 Member States for which data are available. The figure for Germany in 1994 includes the new Lander, other figures for Germany exclude new Lander.

Sources: Eurostat, 1996b.

FIGURE 10.2: SPE PER HEAD AND GDP* PER HEAD, 1994

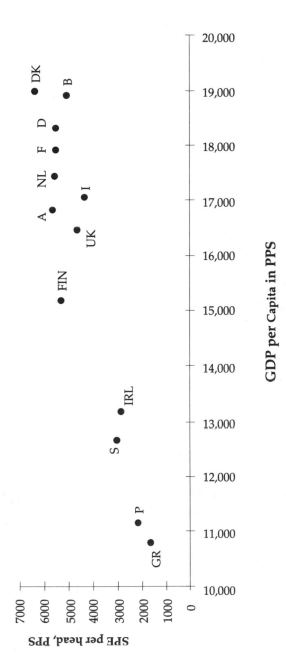

GDP per Capita in PPS

SPE per head, PPS

* *Note:* For Ireland, GNP per head has been used

Source: Eurostat, 1996b; 1997.

period. Of course, the usual caveat about GNP being a more appropriate measure of the amount of resources that are available for distribution in Ireland should be remembered here, although the trend
in the ratio of social expenditure to GNP has followed a similar path
to the SPE/GDP ratio. The ratio of social welfare expenditure[2] to
GNP fell from 13.7 per cent in 1987 to 11.6 per cent in 1990. Since then
this ratio has averaged 12.4 per cent for the period 1991 to 1996.

SPE has grown in all EU countries between 1980 and 1994. The
rate of increase has been highest in relatively poor countries such as
Portugal and Spain. The percentage increase in Ireland over this period was about 55 per cent, which was slightly higher than the increase in the EU12 as a whole (European Commission, 1995: 59).
When per capita SPE is expressed in PPS[3] we find that there are considerable differences between expenditure per capita across the EU.
These differences are not just a function of differences in national income as Figure 10.2 shows.[4] While Callan and Nolan (1992a: 202)
concluded that "the Irish welfare effort is rather higher than might be
expected on the basis of level of income per head", the large increases
in per capita income over the last ten years means that this conclusion is no longer valid. The data in Figure 10.2 is for 1994 and therefore the 20 per cent increase in GNP over the past three years is not

---

[2] Social welfare expenditure excludes several expenditures such as health
spending that are included in social protection expenditure.

[3] PPS refers to Purchasing Power Standard, which is a measure reflecting the real
purchasing power of a currency within the country concerned, providing a better indication than the exchange rate of the volume and structure of goods and
services and the relative level of GDP (European Commission, 1995).

[4] It is important to note that these measures are not perfect measures of the extent
of social protection in any country. For example, they do not take into account
the amount of expenditure that may be reclaimed by the state through taxation
of benefits; they don't take into account the extent of tax expenditures which
subsidises various private expenditure on pensions, housing and private health
care; and they don't account for differences in the extent of welfare provided by
families and by voluntary organisations. The OECD has recently calculated net
public social expenditure for five countries. They found that much of the difference in SPE/GDP between countries was reduced when taxes on benefits and tax
expenditures were taken into account. For example, while social expenditure in
the Netherlands in 1993 was 30.6 per cent of GDP, net social expenditure was
24.9 per cent (the difference being mainly due to the fact that taxes on benefits in
the Netherlands amounts to about 5 per cent of GDP). Unfortunately, Ireland
was not included in the OECD exercise.

included. A recent classification of welfare states by Bonoli places Ireland in the low-spending category (Bonoli, 1997).

The composition of SPE varies across countries. Ireland is something of an outlier in that in 1994, expenditure on pensions took up just 28 per cent of total SPE (as compared to an average of 44 per cent in the EU12), while expenditure on family benefits and payments to the unemployed took up a significantly higher share of SPE in Ireland than the EU average. A major question underlying these figures is: are changes in expenditure due solely to changes in the number of beneficiaries or are they due to higher levels of payment? The European Commission has addressed this question by decomposing expenditure on different categories (European Commission, 1995: 68–81). In Ireland, the small decline in the share of GDP accounted for by old-age pensions between 1980 and 1990 was the result of two factors working in opposite directions. There was quite a significant increase in the number of people claiming pensions (from 10.8 per cent of the population to 12.4 per cent), but this was offset by the fact that the pension relative to GDP per head declined significantly. If we examine expenditure on unemployment benefits, we see that the increase in spending on this category in Ireland between 1980 and 1993 was due entirely to the increase in the unemployment rate during this period. In fact, the average benefit paid to claimants declined relative to GDP per head.

Finally, a major issue in all EU countries is the source of funding for the welfare state. On average in the EU, about two-thirds of receipts come from contributions by employers and protected persons. Ireland and Denmark are the only countries which rely on general contributions from government for the majority of social protection receipts.

TYPOLOGIES OF WELFARE STATES

The most useful way of understanding the long-term background to the welfare state in Ireland is by reference to the well-established analysis of welfare state regimes[5]. One advantage of Berghman's

---

[5] Cousins (1997) is critical of the development of typologies of welfare states, arguing that they conceal more than they reveal, especially for post-colonial countries such as Ireland.

framework is that it allows us to locate the different welfare state regimes[6] as concentrating on different stages of the basic societal process. Following Esping-Andersen (1990), Leibfried (1992) and Ferrera
(1996), four regimes of welfare state provision have been identified as
follows:

1. The Scandinavian, or Social Democratic, model has a high degree
    of universality and institutionalisation, and is financed to varying
    degrees by general taxation and social insurance contributions.
    The emphasis is on social rights, with the state the primary
    agency for ensuring citizenship. The welfare state is inclusive,
    covering workers in both market and non-market activities. The
    de-commodification of social goods is, by and large, complete in
    this model. The labour market continues to be the primary focus
    for participation. The state ensures participation through an em-
    phasis on training and education and significant public interven-
    tion in the labour market. The state has been the employer of first
    resort, especially for women. In Berghman's framework, the
    Scandinavian examples emphasise the first stage of the basic
    societal process.

2. The Continental, or "social capitalism" model is a selective wel-
    fare state which is financed mainly by the contributions of em-
    ployers and employees through work-based social insurance
    schemes. Entitlement to social rights is based on an attachment to
    the paid labour force. People outside the labour market are left to
    depend on support from families, local governments, voluntary
    organisations and the Church (Jarre, 1991). The principle of sub-
    sidiarity underpins the selectivity implicit in this system. Because
    social protection is tied to employment status, the redistributive
    impact of the welfare state is weak. The preservation of status dif-
    ferentials is a fundamental aim of the selective welfare state.
    Germany and Austria are examples of countries with strong con-
    servative and selective traditions in welfare state provision. In
    Berghman's framework, the Continental examples emphasise the
    second stage of the basic societal process. The key relationship is
    between the labour market and pay-related social protection.

---

[6] For a more detailed discussion of theoretical developments in welfare regime
theory, see O'Shea and Kennelly (1997).

3. The liberal, Anglo-Saxon, model combines modest universal schemes and extensive means-tested assistance. The welfare state is a compensator of last resort. Need is the principle on which the state intervenes on a discretionary basis. Intervention is necessary in order to support people unable to insure themselves, either because they are not attached to the labour market, or because they belong to a high-risk group. This model has been most associated with the United Kingdom. Ireland is often regarded as being another, albeit weaker, example of this model. Benefits paid by the state are usually flat rate and are financed out of general taxation. While social assistance expenditure accounts for over one-third of social security expenditure in both Ireland and the UK, it accounts for less than 12 per cent in every other EU country[7] (Gough et al., 1997: 24). Most emphasis is placed on the last stage of the basic societal process, whereby flat-rate social assistance is supposed to guarantee a minimum level of social participation.

4. In the "Latin Rim" countries (Greece, Portugal, Spain, Italy), the state does little to regulate employment or redistribute income (Ferrera, 1996). The solution to traditional welfare state problems has been located primarily in civil society. The emphasis is on family, the Church, and private charity. Leibfried (1992) describes the Southern Europe welfare state as rudimentary, but in the process of catching up, since many of these countries have made promises towards a modern welfare state in their constitutions. In all of these countries, social expenditure has been increasing in recent years (see Table 10.1). Notwithstanding these changes, social protection in Southern Europe continues to be categorical and work-focused.

The search for general and universal welfare state classification systems has mainly focused on social protection and social transfer payments. However, for many people, the welfare state is synonymous with social care and its interaction with family care and voluntary provision. The care of children and of old people is mediated

---

[7] Data is not available for Greece. Gough et al. use an OECD definition of social security expenditure which is slightly different from what the EU defines as social protection expenditure.

outside of, as well as within, the market-state nexus (Alber, 1995). Problems are resolved within families, between families and the voluntary sector, and between the market, state, family and voluntary sectors. There is, therefore, a much richer set of possibilities associated with social care provision than is covered by a simple comparative analysis of aggregate expenditure on social protection.

The diversity of social care provision and the complexity of organisation make it difficult to develop typologies of care, as has been done with respect to social security. There are no comprehensive international data sets on social services provision. In addition, countries tend to be idiosyncratic in the way social care services are described, making comparisons difficult. Anttonen and Sipila (1996) have examined social care provision for two categories of social care consumers — children and older people — across Europe. Their data suggests that Denmark and Portugal represent the two ends of the social care continuum in Europe — Denmark representing the highest level of provision, Portugal the lowest. There is some correspondence between the groupings of social care provision and Leibfried's (1993) classification of income support systems. In particular, it is possible to identify both a Scandinavian universalist model and a Latin Rim family care model. Beyond these groupings, classification becomes more problematic. Subsidiarity plays an important role in care of the elderly in Central Europe, particularly in Germany, but it is stretching credibility to talk in terms of a generalised Continental model of elderly provision. Differences are even more pronounced in the area of services for children across the countries of Continental Europe. Countries may also fall into more than one regime. It is possible to identify both a residualist and family care orientation in the Irish social services mix. The welfare mix of social services provision may also change over time, as witnessed by the movement from a universalist provision to a residual system in the UK in the past two decades.

CURRENT POLICY INTERVENTIONS

Recent OECD reports have singled out Ireland, the Netherlands and the UK as having achieved significantly higher rates of employment growth than other EU countries in the past ten years (OECD, 1997a: 12–13). The OECD claims that much of this growth is due to these countries having introduced policy changes recommended by the OECD, particularly in labour market reforms. However, closer analysis of these countries indicates significant differences in policy evolution over the last ten years. Indeed, what is striking about Ireland is how little large-scale welfare reform there has been compared to Britain and the Netherlands.

Over the past 15 years, the real value of benefits in the UK have fallen as a percentage of the average wage, while there has been an increased emphasis on means-tested benefits (Clarke and Langan, 1993: 58–9). However, the number of people dependent on the welfare state has continued to grow, so the proportion of GDP accounted for by social protection expenditure has not changed very much (see Table 10.1). Le Grand (1997) claims that recent policy changes in the UK can be characterised as the substitution of fiscal welfare by legal welfare. Legal welfare involves the use of regulation, or legislation, to intervene in market outcomes. It covers redistributive mechanisms whereby specific groups of individuals are identified as having responsibility for redistributing to another group, and are coerced by legal means to make the appropriate transfers. Examples of legal welfare include the minimum wage, legal limits on the working week, the child support agency, making divorce more difficult, and the *obligation alimentaire*. The other significant change has been the development of quasi-markets, especially in the health sector. Thus, welfare reform in the UK has been institutional in nature (this explains why Pierson (1996) concludes that, with the notable exception of housing and pensions policy, the welfare state in the UK did not experience much change between 1980 and 1994). Current debates in the UK concentrate on the cost of the welfare state, and focus on particular groups where the number of beneficiaries has increased significantly (lone parents and disability claimants for example).

The Netherlands has introduced wide-ranging reforms to its welfare state over the same period, involving (a) a reduction in some benefit levels (either directly or through non-indexation of benefits), (b) measures to reduce the number of beneficiaries on particular programmes (especially the disability and sickness programmes) and (c) attempts to re-insert people into the paid labour force. The latter incorporates a renewed emphasis on the obligation of people on social assistance to be available for work. This obligation is matched by the responsibility of local authorities to devise and fund re-insertion plans which covers training and work experience. In some cities this has been organised by the establishment of Centres for Work and Income. Clients who fail to fulfil their obligations under these plans may suffer financial penalties (these involve reductions in, rather than suspension of, benefits). Concern about dependency ratios has led to a new provision that makes the indexation of benefit levels dependent on the ratio of the active population to the inactive population. While the welfare state in the Netherlands remains extensive, these changes have been characterised by some commentators as a movement towards a more selective welfare state (van Oakschott, 1997).

The Netherlands has also made various attempts to directly increase the demand for labour, particularly for low-skilled workers. "Labour-pools" were established in 1990 which grant minimum wage jobs in the public sector to long-term unemployed people. The Youth Work Guarantee Programme was established in 1992 and offers a combination of training and work experience to school-leavers up to the age of 23 who have not been able to find a job within six months, and have less than one year's previous work experience. A series of fiscal incentives have also been offered to employers who hire long-term unemployed. An employer hiring somebody who has been long-term unemployed at a wage less than 130 per cent of the minimum wage does not have to pay social security contributions for four years. The marginal tax rate facing the long-term unemployed has been reduced by increasing the amount of income they can earn from part-time work without losing their benefits (Visser and Hemerijck, 1997).

In Ireland, by contrast, there has been a relative absence of both a wide-ranging debate about the nature of the welfare state and significant changes in the structure of the welfare state. The major fiscal adjustment between 1986 and 1990 did not involve a large-scale assault on social welfare spending (Cousins, 1995: 24). While cutbacks in particular areas of social spending such as public housing and primary education may ultimately have a long-term negative impact on those at the bottom of the income distribution, the real incomes of those reliant on the lowest social welfare rates increased substantially between 1986 and 1990 (Callan and Nolan, 1992b: 338).

Over the last ten years, policy in Ireland has evolved towards placing more emphasis on the first stage of the basic societal process.

Expenditure in Ireland on active labour market policies is 1.8 per cent of GDP, a proportion exceeded only by Denmark and Sweden in the OECD countries (OECD, 1997b: 96). Many of the programmes under this heading appear to have a strong local or community base. In his review of local partnerships in 1996, Sabel praised the quality of organisational development in many of these projects (OECD, 1996). Similarly, many of the people employed under the Community Employment programme, the part-time jobs initiative, or the Back-to-Work Allowance scheme are engaged in the local economy, where the activities are geared towards improving the local economic and social infrastructure of particular communities rather than satisfying market demand. However, less than 5 per cent of activity in this area is in the social services sector. Even though the gap between client need and statutory social care provision in the community has been well documented (see Ruddle et al., 1997, for the problems encountered by dependent elderly people), little attention has been paid to developing the social economy to deal with problems in the social services. By and large, families are left to care for dependent kin, with the state only intervening when family care breaks down, or is absent entirely.

As in the UK, there has been a significant increase in Ireland in the proportion of social welfare spending accounted for by social assistance expenditure. In 1986, expenditure on social assistance was about 40 per cent of combined expenditure on social insurance and social assistance, whereas in 1996 it was about 52 per cent. The increase in real terms in unemployment assistance, which contributed to the reduction of the depth of poverty (but not its incidence) between 1987 and 1994, maintains the emphasis in Ireland on the last stage of the basic process. Even in the late 1980s, almost 80 per cent of the pre-transfer poverty gap was eliminated by social security provision. Apart from the number of people on the Live Register, the only group of social welfare recipients that has increased significantly in Ireland has been the number of unmarried people claiming the lone parent's allowance, which has increased from 12,039 in 1986 to 37,506 in 1996. Unlike many EU countries, Ireland does not have a significant demographic problem regarding the number of elderly dependants (Fahey and Fitzgerald, 1997).

In recent years, no attempt has been made to increase the share of GNP accounted for by social protection. There have been some positive developments, however, such as the increase in the number of people covered by the social insurance system from 1,343,200 in 1987/88 to 1,844,950 in 1995/96 (Department of Social Welfare, 1997: Table A13).[8] There was also a significant increase in child benefit between 1993 and 1996. This increase was based, in part, on the finding that poverty tended to be associated with large families. The relatively higher increase in the latest Budget in pension levels may also have been influenced by the most recent findings that showed an increase in poverty incidence among old people (Callan et al., 1989; 1996).

Significant changes have occurred in the institutional framework of the basic social process in Ireland. While the revival of national wage agreements in 1987 was based on the traditional partners of government, the unions and the employers, recent agreements have evolved into a more inclusive framework, based on social partnership. This has been facilitated by the development of the National Economic and Social Forum (NESF) as a significant contributor to policy debate in Ireland. The NESF provides an opportunity for groups outside of the traditional institutional process to make a contribution to economic and social planning. The participation of these groups is likely to become even more formalised in the years to come.

One of the notable differences between the Netherlands and either the UK or the US is that the recent growth in employment there has not been accompanied by a significant increase in earnings inequality (Visser and Hemerijck, 1997: 40–41). Data is not yet available for Ireland which would allow us to analyse whether the large increase in employment over the last four years has been accompanied by changes in earnings inequality. However, Barrett et al. (1997) found that there was a large increase in earnings inequality in Ireland between 1987 and 1994. While there may be important differences in definition and coverage of earnings, the data shows that the ratio of the top decile to the bottom decile is higher for Ireland than any other OECD country, including the US (Barrett et al., 1997: 6). Furthermore, the increase in earnings dispersion was higher in Ireland between 1987 and 1994 than in the other OECD countries for which data is

---

[8] In contrast, the phasing out of pay-related unemployment benefit in 1994 was a move away from Continental-style social capitalism.

available for both years[9]. Given the already high incidence of low pay in Ireland (24 per cent of the labour force earned less than two-thirds of median earnings in 1994, one of the highest rates in the OECD), the question of adequate social participation by many working people is likely to become a more important issue in the near future.

FUTURE DIRECTIONS

The Berghman framework makes it clear that the social participation system involves a myriad of policies and institutions depending on the abilities and (in)capacities of different individuals. The key question is whether the welfare state is enhancing the social quality of recipients and claimants. While the concept of social quality is new in Europe, it is already attracting interest, particularly since it allows social and economic objectives to be dealt with on equal terms (Beck et al., 1997: 291). We do not attempt a definition of social quality for Ireland in this short chapter, but we are anxious to provide a framework for thinking about the relationship between the future development of the welfare state and social progress. The key elements for an increase in social quality are social participation, political participation, social entrepreneurship and income support.

Social Participation

Marshall (1950) argued that citizenship should be understood as a set of rights enjoyed equally by every member of society. Perhaps it is now appropriate to revise the concept of social citizenship as entailing a right to lifelong learning and training, leading to meaningful participation in society (Esping-Andersen, 1996). This approach can be justified on several grounds, but it is primarily an equity-enhancing measure. Given the increasing divisions between households where one or more members have secure well-paying jobs and households subject to income insecurity, or having to rely on non-market income, the inclusion of training and education in the social welfare "package" is an attempt to equalise individual choice sets (Le Grand, 1991; Cohen, 1993).

---

[9] The Gini coefficient on household income in Ireland remained stable between 1987 and 1994 (Atkinson et al., 1997), indicating that the link between low pay and household poverty has not become closer.

Downward wage pressure in the labour market is mainly directed at the unskilled, who are also less likely to be well educated and, therefore, more likely to be unemployed. In Ireland, the unemployment rate among people with primary or lower secondary education was 18 per cent in 1995, while the rate for those with university education was only 4 per cent. Furthermore, there is a strong association between the risk of being or becoming a member of the long-term unemployed and one's education. While those with low education levels constitute two-thirds of the unemployed they account for three-quarters of the long-term unemployed in Ireland (OECD, 1997: 66). The problem of poverty and poor employment prospects being passed on from one generation to another has been recently analysed as a hysteresis phenomenon (Barry and Hannan, 1997). Lifelong learning and social investment strategies offer a positive-sum solution to the trade-off between jobs and equality. A dynamic life-chances commitment to equality implies a social policy more explicitly designed to optimise the self-reliant capacities of individuals. The key to progress is the replacement of the guarantee of social protection with a new guarantee of social participation, which is linked to the introduction of a basic income guarantee for all people.

Political Participation

Several commentators have noted how changes in economic and social conditions have affected the evolution of the welfare state. It is reasonable to expect that these changes will also affect the attitudes that citizens will adopt towards the welfare state, which, in turn, affects the potential of the welfare state to meet its objectives. Le Grand has analysed the changes in welfare state policies in Britain as being based in part on a shift in beliefs about human nature (Le Grand, 1997). Recent policies are based on rational self-interested behaviour as being the norm, whereas earlier policies were based on altruism among taxpayers and passive acceptance by recipients. By contrast, other Western and Northern European countries are more likely to place emphasis on developing and maintaining values and norms of solidarity. Sometimes there is a presumption among commentators and policy-makers in Ireland that the only country we need to look at in this regard is the UK. This, in part, reveals why economic objectives generally take precedence over social objectives in this country.

An important goal of comparative social research should, however, be to evaluate critically these presumptions.

One of the critical issues facing policy-makers is whether political support for comprehensive social participation structures is waning. While detailed survey evidence for Ireland on this question is unavailable (although the value of such evidence has been questioned), the recent emphasis by various governments in Ireland on tax reductions suggests that social expenditure has fallen behind private expenditure in importance. For example, a poll in April 1997 (MRBI/4510/97) found a large majority in favour of cutting taxes even if this meant a reduction in government spending. What this suggest to us is that many people in Ireland are quite happy to see government expenditure cut, as long as they themselves do not benefit from the programmes being curtailed or withdrawn. A renewed emphasis on education as the key to social participation might, however, receive wide support from the electorate, because the benefits from publicly-funded education are universal, and, if anything, favour the better-off in society, particularly those in third-level education.

While reference is sometimes made in Ireland to the development of a two-tier society, it is probably more useful to think in terms of three groups. We have already noted that earnings inequality has increased in Ireland between 1987 and 1994, and that Ireland has now one of the most unequal earnings distributions in the OECD. Furthermore, the wage share in the economy has steadily declined from 73 per cent in 1987 to 63 per cent in 1996 (Sweeney, 1998: 160). High wage-earners and those whose income mainly comes from profits, or rent, could be regarded as one group. The second group contains the rest of the working population. The third group contains people who are likely to be dependent on social welfare payments for all, or most, of their income. The key question is whether it is possible, given these constituent groups, to envisage the emergence of a broad-based coalition supporting a reorientation of the welfare state towards more inclusive participation. This would involve a continued commitment to publicly funded education, increased support for low-paid households through an expansion of in-work benefits, and higher benefit levels for those with little capacity, or opportunity, for earning income from work.

Given the apparent all-party agreement in Ireland on tax reductions, one would have to be pessimistic about the possibility of achieving all of these objectives. An increasing emphasis on the values of justice and solidarity will be necessary to effect change, but these values are difficult to nurture in an economy increasingly dedicated to achieving ever higher growth rates within a values framework which is based more on individualism than on community. Paradoxically, self-interest may also have a role in developing support for an enhanced welfare state. Many recent studies in comparative growth theory have found "a puzzling positive association between the size of transfer programs and the growth rate of the economy" (Sali-Martin, 1997: 82). Sali-Martin proceeds to provide an economic model that explains this relationship based on the idea that social transfers are a means to buy social peace and reduce social unrest (which in turn have positive effects on the productive efficiency of an economy).

Social Entrepreneurship

The gap between the social needs of people and the public and private resources available to meet those needs has focused attention on the possibilities of bridging that gap through the development of the social economy. The social economy is most relevant where market failure exists, but the state cannot, or will not, intervene. In such circumstances, needs and demands arising from the market failure are met through community, voluntary, or co-operative forms of organisation, rather than through conventional public sources. Latent needs are transformed into effective demand through innovative community-based supply-side responses to the problem of provision.

There have been many references to the social economy in recent policy documents at both national and European Union levels (NESF, 1995; European Commission, 1993; 1994). So far, however, the emphasis has mainly focused on the local employment potential of the social economy. While employment is important, it is largely derivative, and the social economy should be seen primarily as a means of bridging the gap between need and existing provision for dependent and vulnerable people living in the community. For old people in particular, need exists in relation to home help services, community nursing services, respite facilities, sitting services, day care, transport, housing, security, and a range of repair and refurbishment opportunities. But it is not just old people who have unmet social needs. People with physical and mental handicap are not being properly served by the public system of care; neither are community psychiatric patients. Currently, families are bearing the brunt of the special care needs of each of these categories, often at great personal cost in terms of opportunities foregone in their own lives. Another area of neglect is public transport provision, which is poorly developed in many areas of the country, particularly in rural areas. Pre-school facilities for young children are also poorly provided in some places. The social economy has the potential to respond to need in all of these important areas.

The critical question is how to transform social care needs into demands that can be met within the social economy. To some extent, this depends on people's willingness to pay for the services provided in the new social economy, since this will determine the level of state support required for any new initiatives. Willingness to pay is, of course, influenced by the amount of income available to people. For social care recipients, the income received from state transfers may not be sufficient to enable them to participate in the social economy, even with nominal charges for services. If consumer resistance to charges and personal payment is high, demand may have to be stimulated through the use of state-sponsored, provider-specific, vouchers for social services, thereby offsetting some of the cost for clients.

While there is some evidence of experiments in social economy provision in Ireland (Keane et al., 1996; Keane, 1997), there is a dearth of information on why some communities are better than others in developing innovative projects within the social economy field. Civic leadership may play an important role in developing the social economy. There are also indications that the previous involvement of community groups in training and education projects may provide a fertile ground for the subsequent identification and development of innovative social projects. Many of the social economy experiments have so far concentrated on work for females within the social care sector. In the future, seed funding may be required to encourage social entrepreneurship within a broader range of activities and people. This funding could take the form of capital grants, start-up grants, loan/credit facilities, and help with information gathering and training supports. Training and managerial programmes for providers will be especially necessary if opportunities are to be realised and exploited. A legal framework will also have to be developed if organisations working in the social economy are to become fully integrated with existing providers of social services.

The task, therefore, is to develop models for social entrepreneurship which will provide the catalyst for local groups to address their own problems, with the support of statutory agencies. Funding issues should be addressed at the same time, with particular attention given to new ways of financing consumption. The nurturing of both sides of the social economy within the framework of a more complex and integrated welfare state, is an important element of social quality. In the transformation of the economy away from the production of goods towards the production of services, it is important to focus attention on the type of services being produced. Meeting basic human need is an important indicator of our humanity, and production which serves to enhance social quality should be encouraged, in the same way as industrial production is currently supported through grant aid and financial concessions.

Income Support

The final element of social quality concerns the adequacy of social welfare payments. Even within a new framework which emphasises social participation rather than income maintenance, many people will continue to depend on social welfare for their income. Improvements in the level and flexibility of social welfare payments are important in providing a secure base for unemployed people seeking to (re-)enter the labour market. Inadequate payments constrain the ability of some unemployed people to manipulate potential economic opportunities, where taking up these opportunities leads to a withdrawal, or a reduction, in welfare payments in return for an uncertain future. Many unemployed people operate within very tight budgets, to such an extent that any shock to the stability of income sources may have catastrophic and immediate consequences for their standards of living. Even a short time period without adequate income may be too much for low-income families to bear, resulting in a decision not to take up the job in the first place.

The real value of transfer payments to social welfare recipients has been maintained by successive governments in the past decade, even in years when the social welfare expenditure/GNP ratio declined. While this trend shows a positive disposition towards social welfare recipients, the income inadequacy problem for the vast majority of recipients has not yet been solved. Despite promises in both the PESP and PCW agreements, a significant number of social welfare dependants remain below the adequacy standards set by the Commission on Social Welfare in 1986 (Callan et al., 1996). In 1985 the Commission estimated income adequacy for a single adult living independently to lie within the range £51 to £59 per week. In 1996, money terms, an adequate income, based on the Commission's calculations, lay between £68 and £81 for a single person. In 1996, only the contributory old-age pension and the widow's/widower's pension exceeded the bottom of the Commission's recommended range.

In response to criticisms in this regard, political parties are likely to point out that the priority rates recommended by the Commission have now been achieved for all long-term social welfare payments. However, the priority rates were viewed by the Commission as merely interim targets for the lowest level of payments and were set at levels between 10 and 25 per cent below the minimally adequate rates referred to earlier. If one accepts the adequacy guidelines specified by the Commission, then quite clearly the government is failing in its responsibilities towards those people in the community who are currently receiving welfare. On the other hand, if one is concerned more with labour market efficiency than with equity, or does not accept the legitimacy of the given rates of adequacy, then judgement of the government's performance in this area is likely to be very different. In terms of social quality, however, the most pressing need is to link the concept of adequacy in social protection to changes in net earnings, disposable income, and consumption patterns in the economy. There is a necessity for a much more explicit process for setting social welfare rates, one that allows comparison to be made with the overall rate of progress in the economy, and the capacity of different groups to benefit from economic growth.

Concern about incentives, adequacy and passivity have led to calls in recent years for a more radical overhaul of the welfare state in the form of a basic income scheme to replace both social insurance and social assistance (Parker, 1989; Callan et al., 1994; Ward, 1994;

Healy and Reynolds, 1995). The attraction of basic income is the freedom it would give to individuals to take up whatever work is available consistent with their own preferences and lifestyle. The safety-net income provides a base on which to build, while eliminating both "poverty traps" and "unemployment traps". The basic income scheme would be consistent with the development of the economy away from a situation where the norm is full-time work for an entire working life. It would facilitate atypical work patterns such as people working for part of each week and people leaving the paid labour force for part of their lives (Atkinson, 1992).

The main problem with basic income schemes concerns the cost of introducing schemes that would provide an adequate income for recipients. Callan et al. (1994) estimate that a tax rate of the order of 62 per cent would be required to finance a basic income scheme for Ireland, at a level close to the lowest welfare payments. The Conference of Religious of Ireland has been the strongest advocate of a basic income scheme in this country. A full basic income under their scheme would mean that every adult would have a basic income of £70 a week in 1997 (Healy and Reynolds, 1997). The tax rate necessary to finance this scheme would be close to 50 per cent on all income over the basic level. The response in official circles, up until recently, has been to prevaricate on the introduction of a basic income (Department of Enterprise and Employment, 1996; Report of the Expert Working Group on the Integration of the Tax and Social Welfare Systems, 1996).

For all the concern about costs, basic income schemes remain the best means of facilitating the genuine work-choices of individuals, providing they are backed up by public support for life-long education and training for all citizens. Basic income would also solve the income adequacy problem, providing rates were set at a high enough level. In that respect, a basic income approach would facilitate an openness with respect to the setting of payments which could be linked explicitly to changes in economic activity in the economy. This would in turn facilitate a more equal distribution of the benefits of economic progress, as well as contributing to a sense of shared citizenship — but perhaps this is what people are really against when they oppose basic income.

CONCLUSION

In this chapter, we have argued that the welfare state should be evaluated as part of the basic societal process whereby citizens are trained in order to develop their earnings capacity, receive income from paid work, and achieve social participation through this process, thereby maximising their overall human potential. The concept of social quality has been developed in response to concerns about the priority given to economic objectives over social ones. Social quality recognises that both social and economic objectives are important, and that progress in one sphere does not necessarily imply progress in the other. One of the dangers of the current economic boom in Ireland is that a kind of Panglossian approach to policy analysis is adopted — if the economy is doing so well, why confuse matters by suggesting alternative goals? If the only objective is to maximise economic growth, it is indeed difficult to propose alternative policies.

The reason we think social quality is so important is that it emphasises the importance of a broader set of issues rather than concentrating solely on economic progress. It allows us to raise questions about the extent of social participation in a country where three-quarters of the long-term unemployed have very low educational attainment; where almost a quarter of the labour force receive low pay; where earnings inequality has increased; where the share of wage income in national income has declined; and where the social needs of many individuals are not being satisfied adequately. Economic growth has delivered substantial gains to this economy in the areas of employment and increased economic and social opportunities for many people. The simple message of this chapter is that now is the time to allocate significant additional resources to resolving remaining social problems.

REFERENCES

Alber, J. (1995), "A Framework for the Comparative Study of Social Services", *Journal of European Social Policy*, Vol. 5, No. 2, pp. 131–149.

Anttonen, A. and J. Sipila (1996), "European Social Care Services: Is it Possible to Identify Models?", *Journal of European Social Policy*, Vol. 6, No. 2, pp. 87–100.

Atkinson, A.B. (1992), "Social Policy, Economic Organisation and the Search for a Third Way" in Z. Ferge and J.E. Kolberg (eds.), *Social Policy in a Changing Europe*, Frankfurt am Main: Campus Verlag, pp. 225–236.

Atkinson, A.B. et al. (1997), "Measurement of Trends in Poverty and the Income Distribution", Department of Applied Economics, University of Cambridge, Working Paper, No. 9712.

Barrett, A. et al. (1997), "The Earnings Distribution and Returns to Education in Ireland, 1987–94", Centre for Economic Policy Research, Discussion Paper, No. 1679.

Barry, F. and A. Hannan (1997), "Education, Deprivation, Hysteresis, Unemployment", Department of Economics, University College Dublin, Working Paper, WP 97/24.

Beck, W. et al. (1997), "Social Quality: From Issue to Concept" in W. Beck et al. (eds.), *The Social Quality of Europe*, The Hague: Kluwer Law International, pp. 263–296.

Berghman, J. (1997), "Social Protection and Social Quality in Europe" in W. Beck et al. (eds.), *The Social Quality of Europe*, The Hague: Kluwer Law International, pp. 221–236.

Bonoli, G. (1997), "Classifying Welfare States: a Two-dimension Approach", *Journal of Social Policy*, Vol. 26, No. 3, pp. 351–372.

Callan, T. et al. (1989), *Poverty, Income, and Welfare in Ireland*, Dublin: The Economic and Social Research Institute.

Callan, T. and B. Nolan (1992a), "Income Distribution and Redistribution: Ireland in Comparative Perspective", in J.H. Goldthorpe and C.T. Whelan (eds.), *The Development of Industrial Society in Ireland*, Oxford: Oxford University Press, pp. 205–239.

Callan, T. and B. Nolan (1992b), "Distributional Aspects of Ireland's Fiscal Adjustment", *Economic and Social Review*, Vol. 23, No 2.

Callan, T. et al. (1994), *An Analysis of Basic Income Schemes for Ireland*, Dublin: The Economic and Social Research Institute.

Callan, T. et al. (1996), *Poverty in the 1990s: Evidence from the 1994 Living in Ireland Survey*, Dublin: Oak Tree Press.

Clarke, J. and M. Langan (1993), "Restructuring Welfare: The British Welfare Regime in the 1980s" in A. Cochrane and J. Clarke (eds.), *Comparing Welfare States: Britain in International Context*, London: Sage, pp. 49–76.

Cohen, G.A. (1993), "Equality of What? On Welfare, Goods and Capabilities" in M. Nussbaum and A. Sen (eds.), *The Quality of Life*, Oxford: Clarendon Press, pp. 9–29.

Commission on Social Welfare (1986), *Report of the Commission on Social Welfare*, Dublin: Stationery Office.

Cousins, M. (1995), *The Irish Social Welfare System*, Dublin: Round Hall Press.

Cousins, M. (1997), "Ireland's Place in the Worlds of Welfare Capitalism", *Journal of European Social Policy*, Vol. 7, No. 3, pp. 223–235.

Department of Enterprise and Employment (1996), *Growing and Sharing our Employment: Strategy Paper on the Labour Market*, Dublin: Stationery Office.

Department of Social Welfare (1997), *Statistical Information on Social Welfare Services 1996*, Dublin: Stationery Office.

Esping-Andersen, G. (1990), *The Three Worlds of Welfare Capitalism*, Cambridge: Polity Press.

Esping-Andersen, G. (1996), "Positive-Sum Solutions in a World of Trade-Offs?" in G. Esping-Andersen (ed.), *Welfare States in Transition: National Adaptations in Global Economies*, London: Sage Publications, pp. 256–267.

European Commission (1993), *Growth, Competitiveness, Employment: The Challenges and Ways Forward into the 21st Century*, Luxembourg: Office for Official Publications of the European Communities.

European Commission (1994), *European Social Policy: A Way Forward for the Union*, Luxembourg: Directorate General for Employment, Industrial Relations and Social Affairs.

European Commission (1995), *Europe: Social Protection*, Luxembourg: Directorate General for Employment, Industrial Relations and Social Affairs.

Eurostat (1996a), *Social Portrait of Europe*, Luxembourg: Office for Official Publications of the European Communities.

Eurostat (1996b), *Social Protection Expenditure and Receipts, 1980–1994*, Luxembourg: Office for Official Publications of the European Communities.

Eurostat (1997), "Gross Domestic Product and its Components: First Values for 1996", *Statistics in Focus, Economy and Finance*, 1996 (1).

Fahey, T. and J. Fitz Gerald (1997), *Welfare Implications of Demographic Trends*, Dublin: Oak Tree Press.

Ferrera, M. (1996), "The Southern Model of Welfare in Social Europe", *Journal of European Social Policy*, Vol. 6, No. 1, pp. 17–37.

Ferrera, M. (1997), "New Problems, Old Solutions? Recasting Social Protection for the Future of Europe" in *European Social Policy Forum: A Summary*, Luxembourg: European Commission, pp. 119–128.

Gough, I. et al, (1997), "Social Assistance in OECD Countries", *Journal of European Social Policy*, Vol. 7, No. 1, pp. 17–43.

Healy, S. and B. Reynolds (1995), "An Adequate Income Guarantee For All" in B. Reynolds and S. Healy (eds.), *An Adequate Income For All: Desirability, Viability Impact*, Dublin: Conference of Religious of Ireland, pp. 10–63.

Healy, S. and B. Reynolds (1997), *Surfing the Income Net*, Dublin: Conference of Religious of Ireland.

Jarre, D. (1991), "Subsidiarity in Social Services Provision in Germany", *Social Policy and Administration*, Vol. 25, No. 3, pp. 211–217.

Keane, M. et al (1996), *Pilot Projects for the Benefit of the Long-term Unemployed* (Western Regional Authority, Ireland, Report on Stages 1 and 2), Brussels: European Commission.

Keane, M. (1997), "New Fields of Employment: Problems and Possibilities in Local and Community Economic Development", Department of Economics, University College Galway, Working Paper No. 18.

Le Grand, J. (1991), *Equity and Choice*, London: Harper-Collins.

Le Grand, J. (1997), "Knights, Knaves or Pawns? Human Behaviour and Social Policy", *Journal of Social Policy*, Vol. 26, No. 2, pp. 149–169.

Leibfried, S. (1992), "Towards a European Welfare State? On Integrating Poverty Regimes into the European Community" in Z. Ferge and J.E. Kolberg (eds.), *Social Policy in a Changing Europe*, Bolder, Colorado: Westview Press, pp. 245–280.

Leibfried, S. (1993), "Towards a European Welfare State?" in C. Jones (ed.), *New Perspectives on the Welfare State in Europe*, London: Routledge, pp. 133–156.

Marshall, T.H. (1950), *Citizenship and Social Class*, Cambridge: Cambridge University Press.

National Economic and Social Forum (1995), *Jobs Potential of the Services Sector*, Report No. 7, Dublin: National Economic and Social Forum.

OECD (1996), *Ireland: Local Partnerships and Social Innovation*, Paris: OECD.

OECD (1997a), *Implementing the OECD Jobs Strategy: Member Countries' Experience*, Paris: OECD.

OECD (1997b), *Economic Surveys: Ireland*, Paris: OECD.

O'Shea, E. and B. Kennelly (1997), "The Welfare State in Ireland: Challenges and Opportunities", Department of Economics, University College, Galway, mimeo.

Parker, H. (1989), *Instead of the Dole: An Enquiry into the Integration of the Tax and Benefit Systems*, London: Routledge.

Pierson, P. (1996), "The New Politics of the Welfare State", *World Politics*, Vol. 48, pp. 143–179.

Report of the Expert Working Group on the Integration of the Tax and Social Welfare Systems (1996), *Integrating Tax and Social Welfare*, Dublin: Stationery Office.

Ruddle, H., F. Donoghue and R. Mulvihill (1997), *The Years Ahead Report: A Review of the Implementation of Its Recommendations*, Dublin: National Council on Ageing and Older People.

Sali-Martin, X. (1997), "Transfers, Social Safety Nets, and Economic Growth", *IMF Staff Papers*, Vol. 44, No. 1, pp. 81–102.

Sweeney, P. (1998), *The Celtic Tiger: Ireland's Economic Miracle Explained*, Dublin: Oak Tree Press.

Tanzi, V. and L. Schuknecht (1997), "Reforming Government: An Overview of Recent Experience", *European Journal of Political Economy*, Vol. 13, pp. 395–417.

Van Kesbergen, K. (1995), *Social Capitalism: A Study of Christian Democracy and the Welfare State*, London: Routledge.

Van Oakschott, W. (1997), "The Reconstruction of the Dutch Social Security System, 1980–2000", Tilburg Institute for Social Security Research, mimeo.

Visser, J. and A. Hemerijck (1997), *"A Dutch Miracle": Job Growth, Welfare Reform and Corporatism in the Netherlands*, Amsterdam: University Press.

Ward, S. (1994), "A Basic Income System for Ireland" in B. Reynolds and S. Healy (eds.), *Towards an Adequate Income for All*, Dublin: Conference of Religious of Ireland, pp. 74–109.

Chapter 11

TAXATION POLICY

Noel Cahill *and* Francis O'Toole

INTRODUCTION

This chapter explores elements of taxation policy in Ireland, concentrating on the period since 1987. The first section places taxation policy in its international context and highlights the need for explicit policy choices regarding the future development of the composition of tax revenue in Ireland. The next section focuses on the area of income tax and social insurance, where the scope for, and importance of, domestic policy-making is greatest. The final section attempts to identify, and comment upon, certain important medium-term taxation policy themes. The links among taxation, social consensus and economic performance, progressivity within the taxation and social insurance system and the potential role for sources other than labour income for revenue-raising purposes provide these themes.

TAXATION: THE INTERNATIONAL CONTEXT

This section addresses two international aspects of taxation: the relationship between economic performance and the level of taxation across countries, and the composition of taxation revenue.

The Total Tax Burden

A striking feature is the stability in the level of the tax burden — taxation as a percentage of GNP — in Ireland over the past decade. While over shorter periods the tax burden has increased and declined, it is noteworthy that in 1997 the overall tax burden remained essentially unchanged from 1987, at approximately 40 per cent of GNP. Given the significant correction of the public finances in the late 1980s, it may seem surprising that the tax burden has not fallen. However, the correction of the public finances involved a large reduction in the share of public expenditure in GNP rather than in taxation. Because the initial position of the public finances in 1987 was one of an unsustainable deficit, a reduction in the share of public expenditure as a percentage of GNP did not allow for a corresponding reduction in the tax burden. The fact that there has been a remarkable improvement in economic performance over the past decade — the rate of economic growth has been higher than any other OECD country and the rate of employment growth has been stronger than in any period since 1926 — while at the same time the overall tax burden has been relatively stable indicates that reductions in the tax burden are not essential for improved economic performance.

In addition to the Irish experience, the evidence from other OECD countries does not appear to support a strong link between the overall tax burden and economic performance. One way of considering this is to look at the relationship between unemployment and the overall tax burden. The tax burden as a percentage of GDP and unemployment for 1994 for a number of OECD countries are shown in Figure 11.1.

FIGURE 11.1: UNEMPLOYMENT AND THE TAX/GDP RATIO 1994

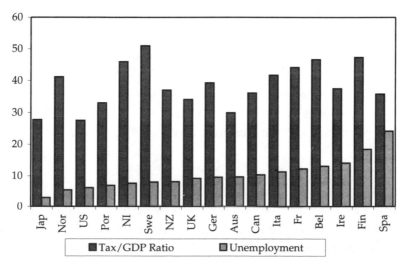

Source: OECD (1996), *Revenue Statistics 1965–1995* and OECD (1996), Economic Outlook, No. 60.

As the OECD (1995: 14) notes, "there is no evidence of any simple linkage between the tax burden and unemployment". Sweden had the highest tax burden for the countries surveyed in 1994, but its rate of unemployment was well below the OECD average, whereas Spain had the highest rate of unemployment in 1994, but its tax burden was below the OECD average. While the evidence does not support a simple link between the overall tax burden and economic perform-ance, this does not imply that the tax system is irrelevant to such per-formance. In the remainder of this chapter a more disaggregated approach will be used to examine the impact of the tax system.

Composition of Taxation Revenue

Ireland has become more European in terms of the composition of its tax revenue, as evidenced by the data in Table 11.1. This is not surpris-ing, as membership of the EU represents, at least to some extent, a willingness to co-ordinate and harmonise fiscal policies across member states. This desire has been reinforced by the difficulties associated with attempting to be different from major trading partners; it is not possible for a small country to impose significantly higher tax rates than other countries on mobile goods, services or factors of production within a free trade area. For example, Ireland has become less reliant on excise taxes since joining the European Community in 1973. It is, of course, possible, and perhaps beneficial, for a single country to impose signifi-cantly lower tax rates than other countries on mobile goods, services or factors of production within a free-trade area. For example, Ireland has benefited from a relatively low tax regime in the manufacturing sector. This has, however, been a cause for concern in other EU countries.

These data suggest that there is little scope for dramatic change in the present composition of taxes and social insurance contributions in Ireland. Indirect expenditure taxes remain relatively high and it could be argued that the revenue from the taxation of personal (la-bour) income, taken together with social insurance contributions, is being held at a low level by the larger-than-expected revenue from corporation tax. Indeed, it is likely that Ireland will have to confront serious taxation policy choices in the near future. Revenue buoyancy at recent record levels is unsustainable and policy choices regarding the identity of the beneficiaries of tax reductions are likely to be

TABLE 11.1: COMPOSITION (%) OF TAX REVENUE IN IRELAND AND
THE EUROPEAN UNION, 1975 AND 1995

	Ireland 1975	EU 1975	Ireland 1995	EU 1995
Taxes on personal income	25.2	28.5	30.7	26.4
Employee social security contributions	5.5	8.6	4.8	10.4
Taxes on payroll and workforce	—	1.4	1.2	0.9
Employer social security contributions	8.2	18.4	8.9	16.3
Taxes on goods and services	46.5	31.3	40.7	31.0
of which:				
• *value-added taxes*	*14.7*	*15.2*	*21.2*	*17.7*
• *taxes on specific goods and services*	*29.7*	*14.5*	*17.5*	*11.8*
Corporation tax	4.8	6.0	8.5	6.9
Taxes on property	9.7	4.9	4.5	4.2
Total tax as percentage of GDP	31.3	34.8	33.8	41.8

Source: OECD, OECD Revenue Statistics of Member States 1965–1996, Paris 1997.

replaced by somewhat more painful policy decisions. Ireland will to some extent also become a victim of its own success, for two separate reasons: (i) structural funds will decrease in magnitude and (ii) Ireland's rather unique corporate tax policy will come under increasing scrutiny from the EU.

INCOME TAX AND SOCIAL INSURANCE

This section addresses two facets of personal income taxation policy: the recent changes in the levels of tax, as they would be paid by (hypothetical) individuals with incomes set equal to various proportions of average industrial earnings; and the distribution of taxpayers across tax bands.

Distributional Effects of Taxation Policy: 1987–98

Table 11.2 attempts to show the effects of the income tax and social insurance system on taxation progressivity by focusing on the average tax rate — the total tax, levies and social insurance contributions paid as a percentage of gross income — confronting individuals at different income levels in Ireland over the period 1987 to 1998. All income classifications are with respect to various proportions of average industrial earnings so as to facilitate a comparison across time. Average industrial earnings were approximately £10,070 in 1987 and £14,060 in 1996 and are assumed to be £14,500 for 1997 and £15,000 for 1998. For the purposes of the construction of these data, it is also assumed that the individual avails of no discretionary tax allowances. Comparing 1987 with 1998, it is clear that the Irish tax and social insurance system has become less "burdensome". Individuals on 50 per cent of average earnings have seen their tax burden fall from 22 per cent to 12.7 per cent, those on average earnings have seen their tax burden fall from 35.2 per cent to 24.4 per cent and those on two-and-a-half times average earnings have seen their tax burden fall from 50.8 per cent to 39.8 per cent.

TABLE 11.2: AVERAGE TAX RATE (%) FOR IRISH EMPLOYEES 1987/88 TO 1998/99

Year	50%	75%	100%	125%	150%	175%	200%	225%	250%
1987/88	22.0	28.9	35.4	41.2	45.3	47.4	48.8	49.9	50.8
1988/89	21.9	28.9	34.5	39.8	44.1	46.3	47.9	49.2	50.1
1989/90	21.5	27.6	33.1	38.5	42.6	44.8	46.3	47.5	48.4
1990/91	20.6	26.7	32.3	37.5	41.3	43.2	44.6	45.6	46.4
1991/92	21.2	26.4	32.3	37.4	41.1	43.0	44.4	45.5	46.4
1992/93	20.8	25.5	30.7	35.7	39.1	40.8	41.9	42.9	43.6
1993/94	21.2	26.7	32.4	37.3	40.5	42.1	43.3	44.2	44.9
1994/95	18.7	25.5	30.6	35.6	39.0	40.8	42.0	42.9	43.6
1995/96	16.9	24.3	29.0	35.2	37.9	39.9	41.2	42.2	43.0
1996/97	16.0	23.7	28.3	33.8	37.5	39.6	40.9	41.9	42.8
1997/98	14.6	22.2	26.2	31.9	35.7	38.0	39.6	40.8	41.7
1998/99	12.7	20.2	24.4	30.1	33.9	36.2	37.7	38.9	39.8

Source: Authors' calculations

There has been an approximately 49 per cent increase in average
(pre-tax and social insurance) industrial earnings between 1987 and
1998 and Table 11.3 charts the interactions between this increase and
changes (almost inevitably reductions) in the tax and social insurance
system.

TABLE 11.3: POST-TAX AND SOCIAL INSURANCE INCREASES IN
EARNINGS 1987/88 TO 1998/99

Proportion of Average Industrial Wage	Increase
50%	66.6%
75%	67.1%
100%	74.4%
125%	77.1%
150%	80.0%
175%	80.5%
200%	81.2%
225%	81.9%
250%	82.4%

Increases in post-tax and social insurance earnings differ according
to pre-tax and social insurance earnings. Those on 50 per cent of average earnings have seen their incomes increase by approximately 67
per cent, whereas the figures for those on average earnings and two-
and-a-half times average earnings are approximately 74 per cent and
82 per cent respectively. Changes in the tax and social insurance
system have reduced everyone's tax "burden", but these reductions
have benefited those with the highest incomes most; reductions in
tax and social insurance contributions are almost inevitably biased
towards those on higher pre-tax incomes.

Distribution of Taxpayers across Income Tax Bands

There were 1,409,000 units who were eligible to pay tax on file in the
1997/98 tax year.[1] Of this total, 335,883 units were exempt (i.e. faced
a marginal tax rate of 0 per cent), 124,335 units were on marginal re-

---

[1] Units include single males, single females, married couples (both earning), married couples (one earning), widowers and widows.

lief (i.e. faced a marginal tax rate of 40 per cent), 551,759 units were on the standard rate (faced a marginal rate of 26 per cent) and 397,023 units were on the higher rate (faced a marginal rate of 48 per cent). Consequently, tax units were distributed between the tax bands in the following way: exempt (24 per cent); marginal relief (9 per cent); standard rate (39 per cent) and higher rate (28 per cent). The marginal relief system reduces the tax burden on low-income tax units but suffers from the side effect of increasing marginal tax and benefit withdrawal rates and, as such, contributes to poverty traps. Therefore, from a low-income perspective, the relatively small number of tax units currently on marginal relief represents significant progress. There were 153,300, 159,600 and 174,200 marginal relief tax units in the tax years 1994/95, 1995/96 and 1996/97, respectively. Significant increases in the personal tax allowances combined with modest increases in exemption limits were responsible for this change. Budget 1998 continued this process by increasing personal allowances by £250 and the (general) exemption limit by £100.

Table 11.4 charts the proportion of taxpayers paying income tax at a rate in excess of the standard rate over the period 1987 to 1998. Over 44 per cent of taxpayers paid tax at the higher rate of income tax in 1987/88 and approximately 37 per cent of taxpayers will pay tax at the higher rate in 1998/99. Tax units who face a marginal rate of 0 per cent (i.e. who are exempt) are not included in these data, however, and the data are potentially misleading in the context of the commitment of the present government to widen the standard rate tax band so as to leave at most 20 per cent of taxpayers paying the higher rate of income tax. Measures which increase the number of exempt tax units (such as increases in personal allowances) actually increase the proportion of taxpayers paying tax at the higher rate. Conversely, measures which decrease the number of exempt tax units (e.g. decreases in personal allowances) decrease that proportion. Budget 1998, for example, by increasing the standard personal allowance by £250 and widening the standard rate tax band by "only" £100 will increase (slightly) the proportion paying tax at the higher rate in 1998/99.

TABLE 11.4: PROPORTION OF TAXPAYERS PAYING TAX AT HIGHER
RATE 1987/88 TO 1998/99

Year	Proportion
1987/88	44.1%
1988/89	35.9%
1989/90	37.4%
1990/91	38.0%
1991/92	40.9%
1992/93	38.7%
1993/94	39.7%
1994/95	38.4%
1995/96	36.6%
1996/97	37.8%
1997/98	37.0%
1998/99	>37.0%

In the context of this commitment, it would seem sensible to define
taxpayers more broadly.

POLICY THEMES

The links between taxation, social consensus and economic performance; progressivity within the tax and social insurance system; and
the potential role for sources other than income for revenue-raising
purposes provide three important medium-term policy themes.

Taxation, Social Consensus and Economic Performance

The most significant change in the Irish taxation system since 1987
has been the reduction in personal taxation. This reduction has been
examined in some detail above. The concern here is the impact of this
change on the economy. The most direct influence is through the
wage bargaining system. Taxation has been an important element of
the National Agreements that have been negotiated since 1987. Personal tax reductions have facilitated moderate gross pay increases
and industrial peace, which in turn have helped the development of
the economy. There was an increase in real average industrial earnings of 10.5 per cent between 1987 and 1997. However, due to tax
reductions, the real increase in take-home pay for a (single) average

industrial worker was 22.6 per cent. Hence, over the past decade, over half of the increase in real take-home pay was provided through tax reductions. The reduction in marginal tax rates may also have encouraged people to be more enterprising. A caveat to this is that, despite schedule rate reductions, many taxpayers have not had a reduction in their marginal tax rate since 1987. Nonetheless, there have been large reductions in the higher marginal tax rates, and it is possible that this has had positive incentive effects on some of the beneficiaries.

Base-widening measures such as reductions in mortgage interest and private health insurance contributions relief, as well as the widening of the corporation tax base have provided some of the revenue for income tax reductions. However, the primary source of revenue has been the buoyancy associated with strong economic growth. The underlying revenue buoyancy has been such that it has been possible to achieve income tax reductions without significant reductions in the overall tax burden. Due to strong employment growth since 1987, the broadly unchanged tax burden has become less "burdensome", because it is shared by more people. To an extent, there has been a virtuous circle: wage moderation has contributed to employment growth and revenue buoyancy; revenue buoyancy has facilitated personal tax reductions, which in turn have helped to consolidate wage moderation (at least to date).

Social consensus also facilitates the low corporation tax strategy pursued by successive Irish governments and, in turn, the low corporation tax strategy has contributed to the development of the Irish economy. There has been significant reform of corporation tax over the past decade. In the past, the Irish tax system provided very large subsidies to capital income. A study by the OECD (McKee, 1986) estimated marginal tax rates for labour and capital in different OECD countries in 1983. This study showed that the marginal tax rate on labour in Ireland was one of the highest in the OECD, while a range of marginal tax rates on capital income for Ireland were negative and far lower than any other OECD country. Since then, reform of the corporation tax system, including the phasing out of accelerated capital depreciation, has eliminated these large negative tax rates on capital income. Base-widening measures in corporation tax have facilitated a reduction in the standard nominal rate of corporation tax from 50 per cent in 1988 to 32 per cent following the 1998 Budget. An indication of the positive effect of the reduction in the bias in favour of capital in the tax system is that there has been a decline in the rate at which capital is substituted for labour. The annual average rate of substitution of capital for labour in Ireland has declined from 1.4 per cent per annum for 1974–85 to 0.4 per cent in the second half of the 1980s to 0.1 per cent in the first half of the 1990s (European Commission, 1997). This reduction in the tax bias in favour of capital has been a positive development in an economy with a rapidly growing labour force.

Taxation Reform Priorities

In recent years there have been many specific proposals for reform of personal taxation. Rather than making another specific proposal, it may be more useful to focus on the key points that have emerged from the previous reform proposals. A notable feature of this debate is the extent of agreement on key issues. A common feature of proposals by many commentators in recent years, including the Report of the Expert Working Group on Integrating Tax and Social Welfare, NESC, the Combat Poverty Agency, the INOU and the Quarterly Economic Commentary of the ESRI is that the primary emphasis should be placed on increasing personal allowances or tax credits. Either of these measures is oriented towards the lower paid.

There are a number of reasons why a focus on the lower paid is particularly appropriate. In terms of equity, reducing taxes on the low paid can make a direct, if modest, contribution to the incomes of those at the lower end of the income distribution. However, there are also efficiency considerations. When account is taken of the inter-action with the social welfare system, the highest effective combined tax and benefit withdrawal rates tend to be for those on low incomes. In the current circumstances of buoyant labour demand, addressing the ability, or incentive, to take up employment is of primary significance. Tax cuts aimed at the lower paid can make some contribution to addressing these problems, although reform of social welfare, particularly child income support, is also necessary. Both the European Commission White Paper (1994), *Growth, Competitiveness, Employment*, and the OECD's (1995) *Jobs Study* considered that reductions in the tax wedge aimed at the lower paid could contribute to reducing unemployment.[2] Ten years ago, the same consensus on the need to focus on the lower paid did not exist. At that time, there were high tax rates, at least in nominal terms, over most of the income distribution spectrum. Since then, however, there have been large tax reductions for those on higher incomes and the higher nominal rates have fallen dramatically. A focus on measures oriented more towards the lower paid is now timely. There are a number of ways in which changes in personal taxation can be made; here we provide a check-list of the principal instruments.

Personal Allowances

The personal allowance is essentially the "zero rate tax band" for each taxpayer. The Expert Working Group Report (1996) recommended increasing the level of the personal allowance up to the exemption limit in order to eliminate the marginal relief system. Considerable progress has been made in this respect and the numbers taxed under marginal relief have fallen substantially, as noted earlier. However, for a one-earner married couple taxed under PAYE, there is still a gap of £1,100 between the personal allowance and the exemption limit, so a further significant increase is required in order to address this issue. An increase in the personal allowance would also contribute to reducing replacement ratios. It should be noted that in money terms, an increase in personal allowances is of more benefit to higher rate taxpayers, but the lower paid still gain substantially.

Tax Credits

If the personal allowance system were replaced by a tax credit system and the tax credits were then increased, this increase would be of equal value to lower and higher rate taxpayers. The advantage of tax credits lies in their transparency and simplicity. Once tax credits have been introduced, a proposal to increase tax credits by, say, £100, would simply mean a reduction in most taxpayers' liability of £100.

---

[2] Assisting the transition from long-term unemployment to employment also depends on a range of other policy measures, including employment services and appropriate training.

Standard Rate Band

Many commentators, including trade unions, have proposed widening the standard rate band. This would not be of any benefit to the lower paid since around 63 per cent of taxpayers are already on the standard rate. However, some single taxpayers, if they do not have any discretionary allowances, are liable for the higher tax rate at approximately average industrial earnings. An increase in the standard rate band would achieve a large reduction in the marginal tax rate for this group. However, an equivalent increase in the threshold for the higher tax rate can also be achieved by increasing personal allowances.[3]

Tax Rates

A reduction in the standard rate of tax would be of considerable benefit to some lower paid workers, and the benefit of such a reduction increases as one moves along the standard rate band. A single taxpayer with an income of £10,000 derives more benefit from a reduction in the standard rate than a cost-equivalent reduction in the personal allowance. However, a reduction in the higher tax rate is of no benefit to most taxpayers and even many higher rate taxpayers (on comparatively modest incomes) would derive considerably more benefit from an increase in personal allowances or a reduction in the standard rate.

Discretionary Reliefs

A notable feature of the Irish tax system is the wide range of discretionary reliefs which erode the tax base. There has been significant reform in relation to mortgage interest relief and relief for private health insurance payments. At the same time, however, a range of new reliefs have been introduced and those on higher incomes derive most benefit from discretionary reliefs. These reliefs can have a dramatic impact on the tax liability of those on very high incomes. A recent survey by the Revenue Commissioners (as reported by Mark O'Connell in the *Sunday Business Post*, 14 December 1997) found that

---

[3] Removing some taxpayers on quite modest incomes from the higher rate could have indirect benefits for the lower paid as it could reduce the political constraints on focusing tax reform on lower income levels (O'Connor, 1997).

only eight per cent of those earning over £250,000 actually paid tax at the highest effective rate of between 45 and 48 per cent. Almost 20 per cent of this group paid an effective tax rate of 20 per cent or less.[4]

Alternative Sources of Revenue

Given the stated desire to continue the process of reducing tax rates on personal income from labour, it will be necessary to increase the tax take from alternative sources. A number of possibilities exist.

Environmental Taxes

A number of studies, including the EU White Paper (1994), *Growth, Competitiveness, Employment* and the OECD (1995) *Jobs Study* have explored the potential benefits of switching some of the tax burden from labour to energy. Up to now, Irish policy-makers do not appear to have looked favourably on this possibility. However, for environmental reasons, this issue is likely to become more prominent on the policy agenda. There is now widespread concern about the threat posed to the environment by the problem of global warming. Global warming refers to the growth of the average earth temperature, stemming from the concentration of "greenhouse gases" in the atmosphere.[5]

The problem of global warming requires a co-ordinated global strategy and the object of a major conference held at the end of 1997 in Kyoto was to develop such a strategy. The EU's proposal to this conference was to cut its emissions of greenhouse gases by 15 per cent from their 1990 level by 2010. Ireland's contribution to this offer was a proposal to restrict the increase in its emissions to 15 per cent above its 1990 level by 2010; this increase was in recognition of Ireland's developmental status. The outcome from this conference was that the EU agreed to cut its greenhouse emissions by 8 per cent. The implications of this outcome for member states will have to be worked out at EU Council level.

---

[4] Restrictions on the value of relief that can be claimed under certain capital allowances introduced in the 1998 Budget could prove significant in this context.

[5] Greenhouse gases included carbon dioxide, methane and nitrous oxide. The major source of greenhouse gases is energy consumption, but agriculture and deforestation also contribute to the problem.

A recent ESRI report has examined the potential policy mechanisms for achieving a reduction in greenhouse gas emissions at EU and national level. At EU and national level, the preferred option is a tax on greenhouse gases, levied on all sectors. If this is not acceptable, the next preferred option would be the auctioning of quota rights for emissions. The key advantage of either a tax or the auctioning of quota rights over alternatives is that these methods would generate revenue which could be used to reduce taxes on labour. This would help offset the costs of achieving the required reduction in pollution. There are significant uncertainties in this area concerning the extent of the action required, including the inevitable uncertainty with respect to long-term projections of energy consumption. However, assuming corrective action is required, then there is a compelling case to adopt the options of a tax or the use of auctioned quotas: whatever method is used, costs will be incurred, but the adoption of these methods would at least provide partial compensation in the form of a reduction in labour taxes.

Property Tax

The efficiency and equity arguments in favour of a comprehensive residential property tax, with the proceeds applied to a reduction in income tax, have been stated many times. The efficiency argument is essentially that property is the least mobile resource, so the distortionary costs associated with taxation are minimised. The revenue from a property tax would make a contribution to reducing the burden of taxation on labour — the more mobile factor. As European integration proceeds and the mobility of factors increase, this issue will become of even greater relevance. The equity argument in favour of a residential property tax is that the owner-occupier derives an imputed income from occupation of the house. In practical terms, this is equivalent to the money saved by not having to rent an equivalent property. A flat-rate property tax serves as a proxy for the taxation of imputed income. In the past in Ireland, there was both taxation of imputed income and a property tax in the form of domestic rates. Many other countries have one or both of these taxes.[6]

---

[6] For a precise statement of this analysis, see NESC (1988: 15–18). See also the Commission on Taxation (1982) and Callan (1991).

The introduction of a small tax allowance for private renters makes some contribution to reducing the inequitable treatment of private renters, but at the cost of further narrowing the tax base.

Whatever the efficiency and equity arguments in favour of a property tax, it is clear that the (voting) public does not accept the case for such a tax. In this context, however, there is a case for re-examining the operation of mortgage interest relief. If there were a comprehensive residential property tax, there would be a clear efficiency and equity rationale for mortgage interest relief. When a commercial investment is undertaken, the interest costs are tax deductible while the profits (net of interest and other costs) are normally subject to tax. In the same way, were the return on investment in owner-occupied housing to be subject to tax, it would be appropriate to provide tax relief on the interest cost of making this investment. In the absence of a property tax, however, there is no obvious rationale for allowing mortgage interest relief.

The imminent move to EMU could provide a timely opportunity to further reform mortgage interest relief. Assuming an economic downturn does not emerge in the next couple of years, the move to EMU with the associated reduction in interest rates will provide a further stimulus to the housing market; it is likely that the anticipated reduction in interest rates is already being capitalised in house prices. It may be desirable to offset this interest rate reduction by further restricting or eliminating mortgage interest relief. Such a reform would contribute to long-term structural reform of the tax system.

Capital Income and Transfer Taxes

Revenue from the taxation of individuals' capital gains make a very modest contribution to taxation revenue in Ireland; less than one-half of one per cent in 1994. The 1998 Budget's major contribution in this area was to halve the tax rate imposed on capital gains from 40 per cent to 20 per cent. The likely surge in realisations (and tax revenue) may cloud the regressive effects of this change for some time.

Until a certain limit or threshold is reached, no tax is paid by the donee on the transfer of capital between individuals in Ireland. This threshold is cumulative in that the value of all previous acquisitions is aggregated. Once the threshold has been exceeded the donee pays tax at the appropriate marginal rate which increases from 20 per cent to 40 per cent. The initial threshold beyond which tax is paid in Ireland depends on the relationship between donor and donee. The threshold (indexed) for an immediate member of one's family, for example, is close to £200,000.[7]

One striking feature of data from all EU member states is the consistently low revenue yield arising from taxes on capital transfers; the annual tax yield from such taxes has never surpassed two per cent of total tax revenue for any country. The revenue yield from estate, inheritance and gift taxes in Ireland for 1994 was £59.14 million; less than one-half of one per cent of the total tax yield for 1994. Ireland's tax yield is also below average when compared to the EU. A second significant feature of the data is the decreasing importance of taxes based on capital transfers. The low revenue yield does not, however, imply acceptance of the argument for the elimination of such taxes, it merely reinforces arguments for the introduction of a more effective tax on capital transfers.

CONCLUSION

Over ten years ago it was argued by the NESC that, "tax reform may now be the most powerful instrument to promote faster growth in output and employment in the short to medium term" (NESC, 1986: 228). Since then, there has been a significant improvement in economic performance. This chapter examined key aspects of the role that future tax policy can play in sustaining that improved economic performance. In particular, this chapter highlighted the need to target tax reductions at the low paid and to develop sources of taxation revenue other than labour income.

REFERENCES

Callan, T. (1991), "Property Tax: Principles and Policy Options", Dublin: ESRI Policy Research Series, Paper No. 12.

---

[7] Although Ireland's tax base for capital acquisitions is, as its name suggests, a tax based on the receipts of the donee rather than on the size of the original estate, the 1993 Budget introduced a probate tax which imposed a two per cent tax on the transfer of all estates valued in excess of £10,000.

Commission on Taxation (1982), *First Report: Direct Taxation*, Dublin: Stationery Office.

European Commission (1994), *Growth, Competitiveness, Employment: The Challenges and Ways Forward into the 21st Century*, Brussels: European Commission.

European Commission (1997), "Annual Economic Report for 1997", *European Economy*, No. 63.

Expert Working Group Report (1996), *Integrating Tax and Social Welfare*, Dublin: Stationery Office.

McKee, M.J. (1986), "Marginal Tax Rates on the Use of Labour and Capital in OECD Countries", *OECD Economic Studies*, No. 7.

NESC (1986), *A Strategy for Development 1986–1990*, Report No. 83, Dublin: National Economic and Social Council.

NESC (1988), *A Review of Housing Policy*, Report No. 87, Dublin: National Economic and Social Council.

O'Connor, J.S. (1997), Response to O'Toole, F. (1997), "Tax and PRSI Reform from a Low Income Perspective", Dublin: Combat Poverty Agency, Poverty and Policy Discussion Paper No. 3.

OECD (1997), *Revenue Statistics of OECD Member Countries 1965–1996*, Paris: Organisation for Economic Co-operation and Development.

OECD (1995), *Jobs Study: Taxation, Employment and Unemployment*, Paris: Organisation for Economic Co-operation and Development.

Chapter 12

BASIC INCOME

Sean Ward

BACKGROUND

What is Basic Income?

Basic income is usually defined as an income paid unconditionally to everyone on an individual basis, without any means test or work requirement. Under basic income, every person receives a weekly tax-free payment from the Exchequer and all other personal income is taxed, usually at a single rate. For someone who is unemployed, the basic income payment replaces income from social welfare; for someone who is working, the basic income payment replaces the tax-free allowances of the income tax system.

Why Basic Income?

Basic income has been advocated using the widest range of arguments. Liberty and equality, efficiency and community, common ownership of the earth and equal sharing in the benefits of technical progress, the flexibility of the labour market and the dignity of the poor, the fight against unemployment and inhumane working conditions, against the desertification of the countryside and interregional inequalities, the viability of co-operatives and the promotion of adult education, autonomy from bosses, husbands and bureaucrats — all have been invoked in favour of basic income (Van Parijs, 1992).

Arguments for basic income from the perspective of *liberty* can be traced back to Thomas Paine. In his view, everyone has an equal right to the value of the earth. Proprietors who cultivate land have the right to retain only the value of the improvements which they make to the land; however, they must compensate all other persons, rich and poor, for the loss of their natural inheritance. Compensation would be received as a lump sum at the age of 21 and as annual amounts from the age of 50. However, libertarian arguments, while they may support a low basic income, are inadequate to support a substantial basic income (Van Parijs 1992).

An *egalitarian* case for basic income has been put forward by John Baker (Baker, 1992). According to Baker, an affluent society should be unconditionally committed to meeting the basic needs of all of its members. He envisaged a system of "compensating differentials", whereby people are entitled to adequate (and unequal) compensation for their work and, beyond that, to a share of what is left over, as an unconditional income. This unconditional income must be sufficient to satisfy basic needs and, in a highly productive economy, it would exceed this level.

The *communitarian* case for basic income is that it is an essential instrument for the achievement of the common good. Jordan's view is that libertarian theories of justice are insufficient in themselves to deal with the claims of sharing, co-operation and democracy (Jordan, 1992). His case for basic income is that there is a substantial underclass who do not have access to jobs: by giving everyone a share of resources on the ground of citizenship, basic income would be a mechanism for including all in the common good.

Arguments based on *efficiency* have been put forward by Parker (1989) and Brittan (1996). According to Parker, the maze of laws and regulations that passes for an income redistribution system produces the following perverse effects:

- It locks people into claimant roles

- Its adds to unemployment

- It penalises marriage and weakens the family

- It leaves much poverty unattended to.

In her view, basic income can address all of these perverse effects. In particular, it can increase the effective demand for unskilled and semi-skilled labour by lowering unit labour costs, without reducing the living standards of the unemployed.

Most of the arguments for basic income have been contested. The main concern has been the unconditional nature of basic income payments. It has been argued that this would reinforce inequality by institutionalising the distinction between those in work and those depending on basic income (Barry, 1992). This distinction would also be incompatible with full membership by the poor in society (Gorz, 1992). In response to these criticisms, Atkinson has proposed that basic income be made conditional on participation (widely defined) in society (Atkinson, 1995).

Early Empirical Work in Ireland

In the late 1970s, the National Economic and Social Council commissioned Brendan Dowling to report on how personal income tax and transfers might be integrated. This report (Dowling, 1977) examined three broad options, one of which was basic income. This option was summarised as follows:

TABLE 12.1: INDIVIDUAL TAX AND GRANT SCHEME (BASIC INCOME)

• Tax free allowances	Abolished. Replaced by a non-taxable cash grant
• Expenditure on mortgage, consumer debt interest, superannuation, etc	Not allowed as deduction for income tax purposes
• Social welfare payments	All social welfare and social assistance payments replaced by individual grant with supplements for old age, widows and employees
• Social insurance contributions	Employee contributions absorbed into general tax structure. Employers' contributions replaced by general 9 per cent payroll tax
• Tax rates	Tax on employee income at 34 per cent. Tax from self-employment 37 per cent
• Tax base	All incomes including farm incomes. Transitional arrangements for farm incomes through notional multiplier
• Net cost to the Exchequer of proposal	£83.4 million

Dowling's paper initiated little debate about basic income (Callender 1989). However, a wide-ranging debate about tax reform ensued which culminated in the establishment of the Commission on Taxation. The First Report of the Commission on Taxation (1982) contained a cursory examination of basic income which it rejected, mainly on cost grounds. Similarly the Commission on Social Welfare (1986), quoting the Report of the Commission on Taxation, rejected basic income on cost grounds, but also because basic income might represent a detour from the priority objective, according to the Commission, of increasing social welfare rates to adequate levels.

THE LAST TEN YEARS

Two approaches to basic income have been developed in Ireland over the last decade. The first approach (Honohan, 1987; and Callan et al., 1994) preserved key elements of the existing tax and spending systems. The second approach (Ward, 1994; CORI, 1994, 1995 and 1996; Healy and Reynolds 1995; Clark and Kavanagh, 1995; Clark and Healy, 1997a and 1997b) substituted basic income for the existing tax and welfare systems, and some other government spending.

Honohan and Callan Approach

The models developed by Honohan and Callan were quite similar. Each adult of working age would receive an untaxed payment equivalent to that paid as unemployment assistance: this is a "full basic income". Elderly people would receive somewhat higher payments and children would receive smaller amounts. All social welfare payments would be discontinued. Existing "discretionary" tax reliefs (such as mortgage interest, employee pension contributions, etc.) would be retained. All government spending programmes would also be retained.

Both authors found that a very high tax rate would be required to fund this type of proposal. Tax rates in excess of 65 pence in the pound would be required on all personal incomes. It was mooted that such a high tax rate could act as a disincentive to work. In addition, Callan found that the income distribution effect of this proposal was not advantageous for significant numbers of low-income households. Honohan and Callan concluded that these models of basic income should be rejected.

Some official reports in 1996 reviewed the findings of Callan, notably the Department of Enterprise, Trade and Employment (1996), Forfás (1996) and the Expert Group on the Integration of the Tax and Social Welfare Systems (1996). These reports endorsed Callan's conclusion that this model of basic income was not viable.

The CORI Approach

The approach suggested by Ward (1994) sought to achieve the main benefits of basic income, while reducing the cost, so that the tax rate required would be no more than 50 pence in the pound.

The main changes were the following:

- While "full" basic income would be paid to the elderly and children, adults of working age would receive a substantial "partial" basic income instead; this would, however, be topped up to the level of unemployment assistance for the unemployed

- All discretionary tax reliefs would be abolished

- A range of public expenditures (e.g. headage payments, community employment payments, etc.) would no longer be required

- Employers' PRSI would be abolished and government support to industry would be reduced.[1]

Ward found that this model would bring benefits to many low and middle-income households in terms of net income and work incentives. He cited the following advantages of his proposal over the current systems:

- More equity, both horizontal and vertical

- Improved incentives to recruit labour and seek work

- Greater simplicity and certainty.

He found that a tax rate of 50 pence in the pound would leave a modest Exchequer shortfall in 1994 compared with the existing systems. He suggested that this might be bridged by a small general

---

[1] In addition, Ward and Callan used different methods for estimating tax receipts. Callan used the ESRI tax-benefit model, SWITCH, and Ward used adjusted National Income accounts.

cut in government spending; alternatively, strong economic growth would eliminate the Exchequer deficit within one year. Ward concluded that this basic income model or variants thereof provided a better approach to tackling the problems of poverty, work incentives and exclusion than the existing tax and welfare systems.

CORI adapted and developed this approach (CORI, 1994, 1995, 1996; Healy and Reynolds, 1995). These changes brought the proposal more into line with the principles for any tax and welfare systems that had already been proposed by CORI (Healy and Reynolds, 1994). CORI's revisions also took account of the observations of many individuals and organisations. The main changes were:

- Increase the minimum income that would be available to every adult from the rate of long-term unemployment assistance (proposed by Ward) to the minimum rate recommended by the Commission on Social Welfare (1986)

- Restore Employers' PRSI, but at a reduced rate of 8 per cent and also restore support for industry

- Introduce additional anti-poverty payments.

Healy and Reynolds (1995) evaluated their proposal against the principles which they had previously developed. Following is a summary of the results:

TABLE 12.2: RATING OF EXISTING SYSTEMS AND CORI PROPOSAL

Principles	Existing systems	Proposed system
• Nature and resources for the benefit of all	fair	good
• Adequacy	poor for adults, fair for children	good
• Adequate income guaranteed	poor for adults, fair for children	good
• Penalty-free	poor	good
• Equity	poor	good
• Efficiency	poor	good
• Simplicity	poor	good
• Freedom	poor	good

Clark and Healy (1997a and 1997b) further developed the CORI proposal for the period covered by Partnership 2000, i.e. 1997–2000, using the additional revenue resources which it was then agreed would be available to the existing systems under the Partnership. Given these additional resources, Clark and Healy developed three variants of the CORI proposal for the year 2000 as follows:

- Variant A: Full basic income of £70 per week (in 1997 prices) to adults of working age. Tax rate required: 47 pence in the pound.

- Variant B: Full basic income, while retaining existing farm supports, such as headage payments. Tax rate required: 48 pence in the pound.

- Variant C: Full basic income, while retaining existing discretionary tax reliefs, such as mortgage interest. Tax rate required: 49 pence in the pound.

These are described in Table 12.3.

The net revenue generated by each of these variants for the Exchequer was close to the net revenue projected for the existing tax and welfare systems in 1997; hence each of these options was "revenue neutral".

Official evaluations of the CORI proposal have been sparse. Neither the Department of Enterprise, Trade and Employment (1996) nor Forfás (1996) gave the proposal any consideration. However, the Expert Working Group on the Integration of the Tax and Social Welfare Systems (1996) considered the CORI proposal. They reported that:

- The tax rate required to finance the proposal in 1994/95 would be 53 per cent, not 50 per cent

- Ninety-six per cent of single people earning over £8,000 per annum would lose out

- They were opposed to the elimination of the Social Insurance Fund and tax relief on employee pension contributions.

TABLE 12.3: THREE VARIANTS OF THE CORI PROPOSAL FOR THE YEAR
2000 (IN 1997 PRICES)

Costs	Annual cost (£ million)		
Weekly payment schedule	*Variant A*	*Variant B*	*Variant C*
Age 80: £82	399	399	399
Age 65–79: £77	1,291	1,291	1,291
Age 21–64: £60	6,067	6,067	6,067
Age 20: £45	153	153	153
Age 19: £35	119	119	119
Age 18: £25	85	85	85
Age 0–17: £21	1,173	1,173	1,173
Total BI payments	10,298	10,298	10,298
Social Solidarity payments			
Elderly	163	163	163
Optical, dental, aural	28	28	28
Mortgages	25	25	–
Useful work	100	100	100
Savings on interim welfare	(41)	(41)	(41)
Total social solidarity payments	275	275	250
Exchequer savings			
Community employment	267	267	267
Third level and ESF	23	23	23
Farm incomes	197	–	197
FÁS employment and training grants	52	52	52
Administrative savings in DSCFA	91	91	91
Total savings	630	433	630
Total cost	9,943	10,140	9,918
Revenue	Annual revenue (£ million)		
	Tax rate 47p	*Tax rate 48p*	*Tax rate 49p*
Income tax	11,529	11,755	11,981
Less tax reliefs	–	–	550
Social responsibility tax	1,054	1,054	1,054
Total revenue	12,583	12,809	12,485
Net revenue	2,640	2,669	2,567

The Group concluded that the high tax rate made the effect of the scheme on employment uncertain and they did not recommend it.

The Expert Group analysis was criticised by Healy (1996). Among the criticisms made were:

- The assumptions and calculations underlying the reported findings were not set out

- The marginal tax rate[2] in the CORI proposal was not "high" compared with the marginal tax cum benefit withdrawal rates faced by many households under the existing systems; also, the effective tax rates[3] for households under the CORI proposal compared favourably with the current systems

- The Group's analysis was focused on 1994 and ignored revenue buoyancy for succeeding years which made the system increasingly affordable.

The last criticism was borne out subsequently by Clark and Healy (1997a).

THE PRESENT SITUATION

Analysis Available

Analysis of the CORI proposal that is to hand includes:

- The Exchequer cost of the proposal

- The income distribution effect

- The effect on work incentives

- Implementation options.

---

[2] Marginal tax cum benefit withdrawal rate: Additional income tax plus employee PRSI and levies plus loss of social welfare benefit or assistance if gross pay increases by £1.

[3] Effective tax rate: (Income tax plus employee PRSI and levies less transfer income such as child benefit or basic income) divided by gross pay at work.

Exchequer Cost

Ward (1994) and O'Toole (1995) analysed the Exchequer cost of the
Ward proposal for 1994 and the CORI proposal for 1995 respectively.
Ward used adjusted National Income accounts data and O'Toole
used imputed Revenue data. Both authors found small Exchequer
deficits, which would be eliminated within a short period. Clark and
Healy (1997a) used Revenue data and found that the CORI proposal
for 1997 would generate a greater surplus for the Exchequer than the
existing tax and welfare systems. Additional "Partnership 2000" resources could be used to enhance the CORI proposal by the year
2000, as described earlier.

   These analyses of Exchequer cost have confirmed the affordability
of the CORI proposal. While further analysis of Exchequer cost is desirable, it is likely to be marginal for the decision to introduce basic
income.

Income Distribution Effect

This was analysed by Clark and Kavanagh (1995) using CSO Household Budget Survey data. The out-turn for 1994 is shown in Figure
12.1.

FIGURE 12.1: INCOME DISTRIBUTION EFFECT OF THE CORI PROPOSAL IN
1994

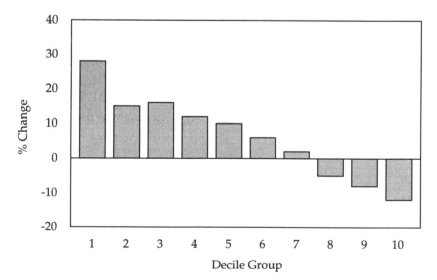

This pattern of income gains and losses is positive from the perspectives of equity and the alleviation of poverty. Analysis is not available, however, regarding the gains and losses at individual household level within each decile.

Effect on Work Incentives

This was also analysed by Clark and Kavanagh (1995). They concluded that the CORI proposal:

- Would not adversely affect the efficiency of the Irish economy or reduce the level of output

- Would reduce the female, youth and elderly components of the labour force by between 20,000 and 40,000

- Would generate a small increase in employment in the short run

- Would reduce the unemployment rate (Labour Force Survey) by over 2 per cent

- Could increase employment in the long run

- Would not lead to a downward adjustment in wages

- Would not address the issue of low pay directly

- Would be a first step in the move towards a post-industrial definition of work and labour.

Clark and Kavanagh acknowledged that their analysis was not definitive and that further analysis of this complex issue was required.

Implementation Options

Clark and Healy (1997a) examined the following implementation options

1. One year, all at once

2. By groups, over a four-year period

3. Gradually, over three years.

They concluded that option 3, which could be implemented over any chosen time period, was superior to the other two options. Over a three-year period, option 3 would involve implementing one-third of the CORI proposal in year one, two-thirds in year two and three-thirds in year three (for example, the basic payment for an adult would be £23 in year one, £47 in year two and £70 in year three). Simultaneously, one-third of the existing tax and welfare systems would be dismantled in year one, two-thirds in year two and the balance in year three (for example, the top tax rate would be reduced to 32 per cent in year one, 16 per cent in year two and 0 per cent in year three).

This implementation option is very clever. When associated with increasing revenue buoyancy, it would allow minimum "pain" to be experienced by some, mainly better-off, taxpayers during the transition period. These taxpayers would gain more from a continuation of conventional government tax strategies than from the introduction of basic income. However, the gradual implementation of basic income would minimise or eliminate their losses with respect to their *present* circumstances and channel the benefits of revenue buoyancy mainly towards the less well-off. In addition, the pace of implementation could be adjusted to minimise any perceived risk to the economy or the Exchequer.

Current Policy Interventions

Clark and Healy (1997a) modelled three "conventional" government strategies which could be followed in the period 1998–2000, using the tools currently available to policy-makers and availing of the additional Exchequer resources which it was agreed would be available under Partnership 2000.

The first conventional strategy showed what the government could do if it was concerned with cutting the tax rates and not primarily concerned with raising the incomes of the lower paid. The second strategy assumed that the government would continue the approach of Budget 1997. The third conventional strategy showed what the government might do if it was primarily concerned with increasing the incomes of the low paid, i.e. increase allowances and child benefit.

It was found that the third government strategy was better than the other two from a distributional point of view. However, even this "best" conventional strategy suffered from the following weaknesses:

- Those on very low incomes did not benefit at all, since they did not pay tax or PRSI

- Those on low incomes who were covered by the marginal exemption system (around one in six workers) did not gain from increases in personal tax allowances

- The strategy did not address significantly poverty and unemployment traps

- Those on unemployment assistance only gained from child benefit increases

- Those at the bottom of the income scale gained less than those at the top.

Clark and Healy went on to compare the "best" conventional strategy with variants B and C of the CORI proposal. (Variant B would retain farm income supports and Variant C would retain discretionary tax allowances.) The results were as follows:

TABLE 12.4: DISPOSABLE INCOME SHARES BY DECILE, 1994, CORI (VARIANT B) AND CORI (VARIANT C) AND THE "BEST" GOVERNMENT STRATEGY

Decile	1994 %	CORI, Variant B %	CORI, Variant C %	"Best" conventional government strategy %
Bottom	2.22	2.72	2.76	2.17
2	3.49	3.90	3.93	3.42
3	4.75	5.21	5.31	4.68
4	6.16	6.58	6.67	6.12
5	7.63	8.27	8.19	7.34
6	9.37	9.75	9.83	9.36
7	11.41	11.55	11.61	11.42
8	13.64	13.38	13.42	13.67
9	16.67	15.92	15.90	16.79
Top	24.67	22.73	22.39	25.03
Top/ Bottom	11.11	8.36	8.11	11.53

Clark and Healy concluded that the conventional government strategies were very ineffective for helping those in the lower deciles, for the simple reason that tax reductions or manipulating the tax bands, exemption limits, etc., hardly reach the bottom 40 per cent of households.

Competing Proposals

In 1996, several proposals for changes to the tax and welfare systems were suggested. Those that are considered here were put forward by the Department of Enterprise, Trade and Employment, Forfás and the Expert Working Group on the Integration of the Tax and Social Welfare Systems.[4]

The main suggestion by the Department of Enterprise, Trade and Employment (1996) was to increase tax allowances and exemption limits and widen the standard tax band. This kind of approach may be considered as a hybrid of government strategies two and three that were evaluated by Clark and Healy (1997a). From an income distribution point of view these strategies would "worsen" income distribution (see Table 12.4) and would be inferior to basic income. In addition, this suggestion would suffer from the disadvantages of the third conventional government strategy noted by Clark and Healy (1997a, see above).

Forfás (1996) proposed to reduce the standard and top tax rates. This approach was evaluated by Clark and Healy as government strategy one. From an income distribution perspective, this strategy performed very badly.

The Expert Working Group on the Integration of the Tax and Social Welfare Systems (1996) did not reach a consensus about how the tax and welfare systems should be developed. However, the Group put forward for discussion three policy options which they called Integrated Child Benefit, In Work Benefit and Means-tested Child Benefit Supplement. All of these options were accompanied by large increases in tax allowances.

---

[4] In addition, NESC (1996) and O'Toole (1997) suggested that there would be merit in the introduction of tax credits in the medium term. This topic is being studied by a committee established under the aegis of Partnership 2000.

According to the Group's analysis (which assumed that an additional £1,000 million of Exchequer resources would be available to fund these policy options), the income distribution results of these options would be very weak. Whereas on average the net incomes of households would rise by 6–7 per cent under each policy option, the net incomes of the bottom three deciles would rise by less than 1 per cent.

A conclusion which may be drawn from the above is that, to date, *no concrete proposal for tax and welfare reform is available which can compete on income distribution with the CORI basic income proposal.*

Summary of Merits, Demerits and Unknowns

Table 12.5 attempts to summarise the state of knowledge about basic income in Ireland. The reader should be aware that the classifications used are subjective. In particular, what may be counted as a "merit" or "demerit" by some may be classified differently by others.

WHAT NEEDS TO BE DONE

It is worthwhile to reflect on what is involved in basic income. At its core, it involves a redistribution of earned income by a different mechanism than the existing systems. All of the benefits of basic income vis-à-vis existing systems (such as greater equity, elimination of financial barriers to work and simplicity) derive from this redistributive mechanism.

"No Reform" Option

However, it might be objected: "Why bother evaluating basic income? Indeed, why bother with tax reform at all?" Such an argument might run as follows: "The best antidote for inequity, unemployment and exclusion is employment growth. From 1990–1997, employment in Ireland grew by 17.4 per cent (Gray, 1997). Surely this employment growth (and earnings growth) is more important than tax reform? Surely the existing tax and welfare systems are more conducive to employment growth than basic income?"

TABLE 12.5: SUMMARY OF MERITS, DEMERITS AND UNKNOWNS OF BASIC
INCOME VS EXISTING SYSTEMS

Merits	Demerits
Would provide financial incentives to work for those currently without much incentive	Would increase the marginal tax rate for those now below the exemption limit or paying tax at the standard rate
Would facilitate some to withdraw from the labour force to pursue other ends	(In some versions) loss of discretionary tax reliefs in the existing system would make some people on middle/high incomes worse off
Would ensure that no household's income fell below the basic income level	(In some versions) loss of existing farm income supports
Would promote retraining and further education, with greater freedom of choice	For those aged under 21 and at work, many would be worse off
Would promote vertical and horizontal equity	*Unknowns*
Would facilitate self-employment, atypical and part-time working	Would labour force participation rise or fall? Would this be good or bad?
As a policy tool would facilitate direct implementation of chosen trade-offs between the level of basic income and the tax rate	Would employment increase or decrease?
Would promote financial independence of women	Would people save more or less?
Would promote dignity	Would wages rise or fall?
Would eliminate take-up problems	Would there be increased tax evasion or better tax compliance?
Would promote living in rural Ireland	Would there be increased immigration from other EU states?
Would be simpler and cheaper to administer	Would overall competitiveness improve or disimprove?

Several points may be made in response to this objection:

- Recent impressive employment growth may not endure. For example, in the period 1980–1989, employment *fell* by 0.4 per cent (Gray, 1997). A tax/welfare system should promote equity and inclusion at all stages of the economic cycle.

- Most employment growth is accounted for by labour force growth. Even in a buoyant job market, those with poor education and low skill levels find it difficult to escape from long-term unemployment and into a job (Duffy et al, 1997). A tax/welfare system should cater for these people.

- While unemployment is a very important cause of poverty, many poor households do not have an unemployed household head. In 1994, one-third of poor households had an unemployed head; the remainder were self-employed, farmers, employees, retired, ill or on home duties (Callan et al., 1996). A tax/welfare system should include these people also.

- Trends in earnings can exacerbate inequity. From 1987 to 1994, the ratio of the hourly earnings of the top decile to the bottom decile grew from 4.2 to 4.9 (Gray, 1997). A tax/welfare system should promote equity in the presence of widening wage dispersion.

- The employment effect of basic income is not certain. Basic income should not be simply *assumed* to have a negative effect on employment. Indeed, the only analysis available (Clark and Kavanagh, 1995) suggests that it would have a small positive effect. Neither should basic income be introduced without the employment effect being thoroughly analysed.

Basic income deserves serious consideration on the grounds of equity, efficiency and freedom to participate in work and society. Notwithstanding the analysis of the CORI proposal which is to hand, much more in-depth analysis needs to be done to assess how basic income would measure up to these principles in order to justify its introduction.

Research Agendas

It was agreed in Partnership 2000 to carry out a comprehensive evaluation of basic income. The Programme for Government includes a commitment to publish a government Green Paper on basic income by mid-1999.

At a seminar in September 1997, three "research agendas" were proposed by Clark and Healy (1997b). The main headings were the following:

Workers' and Citizens' Research Agenda

- Labour market

- Human capital

- Demography

- Income distribution and poverty.

Business and Macro-economy Research Agenda

- Economic stabilisation

- Industry

- Balance of trade

- Payment level

- Alternative sources of funds.

Legal and Implementation Research Agenda

- Legal

- Implementation.

These topics should be evaluated against pre-defined principles.

CONCLUSIONS

The existing tax and social welfare systems suffer from many disadvantages, which have been widely recognised, including:

- *Unemployment traps*: where net income when unemployed is higher or almost as high as net household income in work

- *Poverty traps*: where an individual at work receives a pay increase, net household income either declines or rises by only a small amount

- *Complexity*: where citizens are unsure of the effects on household income of decisions regarding work, marriage, family size, etc.

- *Policy inflexibility*: it is difficult to modify the existing systems to increase the incomes of the poorest households (who do not have "proper" jobs), without simultaneously decreasing work incentives.

These disadvantages are unintended consequences of the current tax and welfare systems, which were designed for a different era (Parker, 1989).

Today, society is less homogenous. We experience rapid technology change, increasing self-employment, atypical work and fluctuating incomes. There is increasing complexity in household responsibilities and relationships. These need to be catered for by our system of taxation and income distribution.

Several changes were introduced over the years with a view to addressing particular difficulties. Frequently the outcomes have been unsatisfactory, in that new anomalies have arisen and old problems have remained largely unresolved[5].

Basic income is a simple idea designed to overcome the disadvantages of the current systems. In recent years, a considerable amount of analysis has been carried out of the basic income proposal developed by CORI. This analysis has confirmed the proposal as a serious contender for implementation. Further comprehensive and rigorous analysis is now required before deciding whether the system should be introduced.

The gradual approach to implementation developed by Clark and Healy (1997a) would be a simple and flexible way of implementing the system. However, all aspects of implementation, including

---

[5] For example, Family Income Supplement (FIS) was introduced so that families would be better off if a parent on unemployment assistance or benefit took up low-paid employment. However, FIS suffers from low take-up and if the employee on FIS achieves a wage increase he or she may be no better off as a result, due to tax and the withdrawal of FIS.

change management and ongoing management, need to be investigated thoroughly.

REFERENCES

Atkinson, Anthony (1995), *Incomes and the Welfare State*, Cambridge: Cambridge University Press.

Baker, John (1992), "An Egalitarian Case for Basic Income" in P. Van Parijs (ed.), *Arguing for Basic Income*, London: Versó.

Barry, Brian (1992), "Equality Yes, Basic Income No" in P. Van Parijs (ed.), *Arguing for Basic Income*, London: Verso.

Brittan, Samuel (1996), *Capitalism with a Human Face*, Fontana.

Callan, Tim, Cathal O'Donoghue and Ciarán O'Neill (1994), *Analysis of Basic Income Schemes for Ireland*, Dublin: ESRI.

Callan, Tim, B. Nolan, B.J. Whelan, C.T. Whelan and J. Williams (1996), *Poverty in the 1990s: Evidence from the 1994 Living in Ireland Survey*, Dublin: Oak Tree Press.

Callender, Rosheen (1989), "Down to Basics", *Making Sense*, May/June.

Clark, Charles M.A. and Catherine Kavanagh (1995), "Basic Income and the Irish Worker" in Brigid Reynolds and Seán Healy (eds.), *An Adequate Income Guarantee for All*, Dublin: CORI.

Clark, Charles M.A. and John Healy (1997a), *Pathways to a Basic Income*, Dublin: CORI.

Clark, Charles M.A. and John Healy (1997b), Presentation to a seminar on Basic Income in Dublin Castle, September.

CORI (1994), *Tackling Poverty, Unemployment and Exclusion: A Moment of Great Opportunity*, Dublin: CORI.

CORI (1995), *Ireland for All*, Dublin: CORI.

CORI (1996), *Planning for Progress*, Dublin: CORI.

Department of Enterprise, Trade and Employment (1996), *Growing and Sharing our Employment: Strategy Paper on the Labour Market*, Dublin: Stationery Office.

Dowling, Brendan (1977), *Integrated Approaches to Personal Income Taxes and Transfers*, Dublin: NESC.

Duffy, D., J. Fitz Gerald, I. Kearney and F. Shortall (1997), *Medium-Term Review: 1997–2003*, Dublin: ESRI.

First Report of the Commission on Taxation (1982), Dublin: Stationery Office.

Forfás (1996), *Shaping our Future*, Dublin: Forfás.

Gorz, André (1992), "On the Difference between Society and Community, and Why Basic Income Cannot by Itself Confer Full Membership of Either" in P. Van Parijs (ed.), *Arguing for Basic Income*, London: Verso.

Gray, Alan (1997), "Foreword: Irish Economic Challenges and International Perspectives" in Alan Gray, *International Perspectives on the Irish Economy*, Dublin: Indecon.

Healy, Seán (1996), "Response to the Report of the Expert Group on the Integration of the Tax and Social Welfare Systems", Presentation to the Foundation for Fiscal Studies seminar, July.

Healy, Seán and Brigid Reynolds (1994), "Arguing for an Adequate Income Guarantee" in Brigid Reynolds and Seán Healy (eds.), *Towards an Adequate Income for All*, Dublin: CORI.

Healy, Seán and Brigid Reynolds (1995), "An Adequate Income Guarantee for All" in Brigid Reynolds and Seán Healy (eds.), *An Adequate Income Guarantee for All*, Dublin: CORI.

Honohan, Patrick (1987), "A Radical Reform of Social Welfare and Income Tax Evaluated", *Administration*, Vol. 35, No. 1.

Jordan, Bill (1992), "Basic Income and the Common Good" in P. Van Parijs, *Arguing for Basic Income*, London: Verso.

National Economic and Social Council (1996), *Strategy into the 21st Century*, Dublin: NESC.

O'Toole, Francis (1995), "The Costing of a Basic Income Scheme" in Brigid Reynolds and Seán Healy (eds.), *An Adequate Income Guarantee for All*, Dublin: CORI.

O'Toole, Francis (1997), *Tax and PRSI Reform from a Low Income Perspective*, Dublin: Combat Poverty Agency.

Parker, Hermione (1989), *Instead of the Dole: An Enquiry into Integration of the Tax-benefit systems*, London: Routledge.

Partnership 2000 for Inclusion, Employment and Competitiveness (1996), Dublin: Stationery Office.

Report of the Commission on Social Welfare (1986), Dublin: Stationery Office.

Report of the Working Group on the Integration of the Tax and Social Welfare Systems (1996), Dublin: Stationery Office.

Van Parijs, Philippe (1992), "Competing Justifications of Basic Income" in *Arguing for Basic Income*, London: Verso.

Ward, Seán (1994), "A Basic Income System for Ireland" in Brigid Reynolds and Seán Healy (eds.), *Towards an Adequate Income for All*, Dublin: CORI.

Chapter 13

RURAL DEVELOPMENT: TOWARDS THE NEW CENTURY

Patricia O'Hara *and* Patrick Commins

INTRODUCTION

In a previous paper, we argued that from 1960 to 1990 rural development policy in Ireland was characterised by "starts and stops" (O'Hara and Commins, 1991). Integrated rural development and regional development were prominent themes in policy statements of the 1960s, but were eclipsed in the 1970s by the emphasis given to the Common Agricultural Policy (CAP). As successive governments sought to maximise the CAP financial transfers from Brussels, there was an implicit assumption that the benefits accruing to agriculture would solve the problems of the rural economy. However, the reality was that the undoubted economic performance of the agricultural sector in general deflected attention from the widening disparities among different categories of farmer and from other issues of rural disadvantage and development.

By the mid-1980s, two circumstances revived rural and regional development as policy themes. One was the growing urgency to reform the CAP because of its unsustainable high price supports, its skewed distribution of financial benefits, the build-up of production surpluses, and concerns about the environmental consequences of intensive farming. The second was an acknowledgement that the Single European Market carried risks for peripheral regions, which should be offset by a greater commitment to European economic and social cohesion. Within this context, EU policy moved in a number of new directions. CAP reforms aimed to reduce farm price supports and provide funding for "non-market" farm activities and for rural development. The volume of EU Structural Funds was doubled, and to draw down this funding, member states were required to prepare multi-annual national plans and "operational programmes" for different sectors. The principles of partnership and participation were promoted: stronger vertical linkages were envisaged between the EU, state and national entities, while horizontal partnerships were advocated to link up agencies and other players across sectors at various levels.

In Ireland, the response to these EU orientations was quite marked, as evident in the vocabulary and intensity of public debate, in proposals for actions, and in policies and programmes themselves. Rural development — though interpreted somewhat narrowly — was included in two Operational Programmes for agriculture (for 1991–93 and 1994–99), which also included for non-market agricultural support measures. A Pilot Programme for Integrated Rural Development (IRD) in 1988–90 was a testing ground for the "bottom-up" approach and was followed by the implementation of the EU LEADER Initiative in 1991–94. An evaluation of LEADER I was published (Kearney et al., 1994), and LEADER II is now underway. The IRD and LEADER programmes gave expression to the principles of partnership, and to the relevance of local area-based actions. So also did the establishment of 12 local partnership companies, under the 1991 Programme for Economic and Social Progress (PESP), to deal with the problems of social exclusion. Four of these companies were in rural areas and the programme has been expanded under the Operational Programme for Local Urban and Rural Development 1994–99. Spatially, the focus of rural development measures has moved country-wide from a traditional concentration on the more deprived western region. However, the establishment of the Western Development Commission in 1996 represents an attempt to continue "special problem" status for the region.

In 1994, the National Economic and Social Council issued its report, *New Approaches to Rural Development* (NESC, 1994). In late 1996, a major European Conference in Cork culminated in the "Cork Declaration" — a set of principles to promote sustainable rural development. In the same year, the Minister of State at the Department of Agriculture, Food and Forestry established a Rural Development Advisory Group which reported in 1997 (Government of Ireland, 1997). By 1995 the Irish experience with locally based development had gained the attention of the OECD which published an analysis of our progress (Sabel, 1996).

Accompanying these policy activities were changes both in the rural development agenda and in the institutional arrangements for its implementation. The need to foster social inclusion (or counter social exclusion) came to be seen as integral to the meaning of "development", especially in publications of the Combat Poverty Agency (Curtin et al., 1996) and of the National Economic and Social Forum (NESF, 1997). In this context, new alliances between various interests have formed and new participatory and consultative mechanisms have been instituted which bring together community interests and the established social partners. These include the National Economic and Social Forum, the National Anti-Poverty Strategy consultations, and the involvement of the Community Platform in negotiations for the most recent national agreement — Partnership 2000. County Strategy Groups have been set up to co-ordinate actions at county level.

A period of unprecedented activity in agricultural policy reform and rural development is now drawing to a close. Further CAP reforms and a reorganisation of EU Structural Funds will take place in 1999 in the context of the EU's Agenda 2000. It is opportune, therefore, to take stock of the activities of the past decade. What kind of development model has emerged? Has Ireland merely been reacting to initiatives coming from Brussels or has a coherent rationale been formed for a specifically Irish approach to rural development? What have been the outcomes of efforts expended? How have the benefits been distributed; have they reduced the incidence of disadvantage and social exclusion? How adequate is the current institutional framework for implementing rural development strategies?

These questions are the starting point for this chapter. In the first part, we analyse the main CAP reform policies that bear on rural development and conclude that, in large part, these measures have the effect of replicating the imbalance of benefits that characterised pre-reform policies. In the second part, trends in rural development policy and practice and their effects are reviewed. In the final part, we consider the implications of the analyses for rural development policy and practice in the context of likely changes at EU and national level.

FARM POLICIES IN 1990s

The Post-productivist Transition

Economic trends in Irish farming reflect the dynamics of agricultural restructuring in developed market economies since the 1950s. Two major phases in the patterns of change have been identified (Ilberry et al., 1997). The first was a "productivist" phase, from the 1950s to the mid-1980s, characterised by technological developments in agriculture, the modernisation of farming structures, and the expansion of output in a policy regime dominated by commodity price supports. Since the mid-1980s, a second or "post-productivist" period has emerged, in which the emphasis has been on stabilising or reducing farm output and integrating agricultural practices with broader rural economic, social or environmental objectives.

The central features of agricultural restructuring in the productivist phase have been described for Ireland (Commins and Keane, 1994; Commins, 1996). Farms became larger and more specialised; production became more concentrated in a minority of farms, so that by the late 1980s, the top 20 per cent of the country's farms — in terms of income — produced 60 per cent of farm output, on 40 per cent of the country's land. Farm incomes showed increasing differentiation by farm size and farming system. Generally, the policy of supporting commodity prices favoured the larger-scale dairy farmers more than others. Considerable numbers of farmers, especially in small-scale and non-dairying systems, found it increasingly difficult to remain above the critical thresholds of economic viability for their holdings. There was significant disengagement from full-time farming by farm operators who took up other gainful employment or moved into semi-retirement or total retirement. The more recent phase of agricultural restructuring in modern economies has been labelled "the post-productivist transition" (PPT) (Shucksmith, 1993; Ilberry et al., 1997). Elements of the productivist phase are carried forward to the PPT, but the latter is also characterised by the reform of price support policies and the supplementation of farm incomes in other ways.

What then are the implications of PPT policies for different categories of farm and farming household and for the rural development agenda? We may approach this question under a number of headings, suggesting that the reform measures have done little to alter the longer-term economic and social polarisation within the farming sector.

Reducing Farm Output

When milk quotas were introduced in 1984, it was expected that the quota system would rigidify the structure of production. Fingleton (1995) has shown how dairy herd numbers declined dramatically since the application of quotas. Between 1983 and 1993, there was a total loss of 40,000 herds, mainly from smaller farms (under 30 cows).[1] Of particular interest in the present context is that, despite quota rules which targeted smaller milk producers for preferential allocation of milk quotas unused or becoming available, these smaller herds showed an increased rate of decline in the latter years of the 1983–93 decade.

It is now expected that milk quotas will be retained until 2006. Furthermore, EU proposals in Agenda 2000 (CEC, 1997) envisage a reduction in milk price supports, and a greater reliance on direct payments as a means of compensating producers for price reductions. Fingleton (1995) has projected that by 2005 there will be fewer than 30,000 dairy herds in Ireland (compared to 43,000 in 1993), with the small herds accounting for most of the decline and the numbers of larger herds remaining virtually unchanged. Despite the fact that milk prices under the quota system were maintained at levels higher than they would otherwise have been, the reduced prospects for expansion and rising production costs, as well as the ageing of many farm operators, have resulted in a marked exit of smaller producers from milk production.

Reducing Price Supports and Increasing Direct Payments

A major feature of the 1992 reforms of the CAP was the reduction of support for commodity prices and the increase in the scale of payments made directly to farmers. Such payments, which are made on the basis of eligibility criteria, are of three main kinds:

---

[1] This is an annual decline rate of 6.4 per cent. Excluding very small herds of 1–2 cows gives an annual decline of 4.6 per cent, or a total of 25,000 herds for the period 1983–93.

1. Livestock "headage" allowances paid to farmers in disadvantaged areas

2. "Premia" payments for eligible livestock and crops, mainly to compensate producers for lower price support since 1992

3. Payments to induce farmers to change farming practices by diversifying production (e.g., tree farming), to adopt environmental management practices, or to retire from farming.

Two aspects of the direct payments system are of relevance here. One is their increasing significance as a percentage of aggregate farm income, doubling to 44 per cent during 1992–96. (The absolute amounts more than doubled to £911 million.) The second is that increasing proportions of this rising volume of payments have been taken up by higher-income farms. In 1996, 41 percent of direct payments accrued to farms with family farm incomes over £15,000 (one quarter of all farms), compared to 22 per cent in 1992 (Frawley, 1997). This redistribution is a consequence of the dominance of premia — to offset price reductions — and the linking of payments to the scale of production. In a study in County Mayo, Frawley (1997) estimated that, for 1995, the more commercially oriented farms received over £8,000 in direct payments, compared to £2,600 for part-time farmers, £3,500 for young operators on small farms, and £2,100 for older operators also on small farms.

The levels of direct payments also vary considerably by farming system. Farm incomes on cattle and sheep farms — over 60 per cent of all farms — are now almost entirely based on these supports. Specialist dairy farms receive less than one-quarter of their incomes from direct payments, though the absolute amounts differ little from those obtained by other farmers.

Clearly, in the 1990s direct payments have become a most important source of income for farmers, and vital to the survival of many farming households. Whereas the pre-1992 payments were redistributive in favour of less-favoured areas and smaller farms, the post-1992 payments, by compensating for price reductions, have favoured the larger volume, higher income farmers. However, present policies are unlikely to be sustained, and current thinking (for example, in the European Commission) points to the "decoupling" of direct payments from production, their "coupling" with the maintenance of environmentally friendly farming, and the "capping" of amounts payable to individual recipients.

Diversification from Conventional Production

Incentives to encourage farmers to diversify production long pre-dated CAP reform, but were increased significantly in the context of controlling surplus production in conventional commodities. A new impetus was given to such activities as agri-tourism, forestry, organic farming, deer farming, mushroom growing, free-range poultry, and speciality foods.

Information on the responses of farmers is limited. Apart from agri-tourism (and related activities) and forestry, the adoption rate appears to be slow, localised, and selective, in that it is the more successful units in conventional farming that take up these new enterprises (Cawley et al., 1995). Afforestation currently accounts for the major shift in land use and most private afforestation is now undertaken by farmers. In the early 1990s, commercial farmers in the south and east were shown to have made a greater response to afforestation incentives than the smaller-scale farmers in the west and north — where forestry companies were more prominent (Hannan and Commins, 1993). More recent data indicate that this pattern appears to have modified somewhat, although forestry is still more attractive to the commercial farming counties.

The promotion of farm forestry will continue to be an important element in future policy and as traditional attitudes change there will likely be a greater rate of adoption than hitherto in the small farm counties.

Managing the Environment

The 1992 CAP reform provided financial incentives to encourage farmers to adopt production methods which conserve landscape features, and protect wildlife habitats and endangered species of flora and fauna. These have been delivered in Ireland since 1994 under the Rural Environment Protection Scheme (REPS). By the end of 1997, some 32,000 of the country's 155,000 farmers (21 per cent) had subscribed to REPS. The grants payable are an important source of income for many of the participants; one estimate suggests that, on 40 per cent of farms, they account for over half of the total farm income (Leavy, 1997). The rates of participation in REPS vary considerably across farm sizes, being highest in the 30–50 ha category (37 per cent) and moderately high in the two other medium-to-large farm size groups (23 per cent in the 20–30 ha group and 24 per cent in the 50–100 ha group). According to Leavy, low-income farmers are inhibited by the high capital costs of compliance with the scheme, while the intensive (mainly dairy) farmers do not find the incentives attractive or consider the eligibility conditions too restrictive.

It is likely that more low-income farmers will be included in environmental management schemes, as over 200 Special Areas of Conservation have been designated. These are mainly high priority areas of wildlife and environmental value along the western seaboard. Also, the European Commission's proposals in Agenda 2000 (CEC, 1997) indicate that measures aimed at maintaining and enhancing the quality of the environment shall be reinforced and extended, especially for areas of high landscape and nature value.

Promoting Retirement among Farmers

The 1992 CAP reform enabled EU member states to institute a scheme promoting early retirement among farmers. By the end of 1997, some 7,000 farmers had opted for the scheme. However, the rate of acceptance has been much higher in the larger farm counties of the east and south (Commins, 1997). Cultural and attitudinal factors may help to explain this variation, but the differences are also related to the eligibility conditions. Prospective retirees must be main occupation farmers for 10 years and there are minimal requirements for the size of holding to be transferred, and for the size to which the holding must be enlarged.

Farmer retirement policies are likely to be maintained but may be reviewed in respect of their suitability for small-farm areas.

Generating Alternative Employment to Farming

The capacity to absorb labour displaced from farming is critical to the development of the rural economy. The Operational Programme (1994–99) for Industrial Development states that policy is aimed at achieving a regional balance in economic development and establishing clusters/sectors of industry most appropriate to the locational characteristics of each sub-region. County Enterprise Boards were set up to stimulate economic activity at local level, especially through the development of smaller-scale enterprises with the support of the Operational Programme (1994–99) for Local Urban and Rural Development.

It is clear that employment policy is now achieving unprecedented success, but there has been some concern about the extent to which recent employment growth has been shared by the more rural regions. The answer depends on the reference base used. When county *growth rates* are calculated for 1990–96, a number of western counties (Galway, Mayo, Roscommon and Sligo) show rates of increase exceeding the national average. Others (Cavan and Leitrim) have declined. However, reference to changes in *absolute numbers* reveals that, during 1990–96, seven counties (Dublin, Kildare, Meath, Wicklow, together with Cork, Limerick and Galway) accounted for almost 80 per cent of the net increase in employment.[2] The problem with the rural counties is not so much that their rates of growth are low (allowing for exceptions) but that their job growth is from a low base. Nevertheless, the percentage contribution of non-farm employment to Gross Household Income on farms has almost doubled (to 36 per cent) over the past two decades. In 1994/95 it varied from 45.5 per cent on farms under 30 acres to 19.9 per cent in the over 100-acre group (CSO, 1997). For the period 1987 to 1994/95 the rate of increase in non-farm employment income was faster on farms between 30 and 100 acres than in the other farm categories. By contrast, old age and retirement pensions, as well as unemployment payments, increased at a faster rate on farms under 30 acres. This suggests that non-farm employment earnings are becoming more important on middle size farms, while State transfers are increasingly of greater significance in households on small farms.

Given this pattern of farm policy outcomes, and that farming occupations account for less than one-third of the rural workforce, what has been the role of other rural policy initiatives in dealing with the problems of rural communities? This question is taken up in the next section.

---

[2] Authors' analysis of data supplied by Forfás and relating to job creation in enterprises supported by employment promotion agencies.

RURAL DEVELOPMENT POLICY AND PRACTICE:
FROM NATIONAL TO LOCAL

Locally Based Rural Development: The LEADER Experience

The LEADER Initiative in 1991 was the EU's first attempt to give significant support to locally based development in rural areas by establishing a network of local rural development action groups to "find innovative solutions which will serve as a model for all rural areas and ensure maximum integration between sectoral measures". Funding involved an unprecedented transfer of global grants by the EU Commission directly to designated groups via an "intermediary body" — the Department of Agriculture, Food and Forestry. Half the monies came from the EU and the national government and the remainder from the groups themselves. LEADER was essentially a testing ground for the bottom-up strategy and for the capacity of local groups in rural areas to deliver on a development programme. Seventeen Irish groups were accepted in the programme for 1992–94. Its successor (LEADER II) runs until 1999 and includes 34 groups in Ireland.

Although some LEADER groups evolved from existing local development organisations, the majority were formed specifically to participate in the programme. The driving forces in the formation of groups have included the private sector, local authorities and state bodies. LEADER boards typically consist of partnerships between a range of public, private and community interests, with state agencies prominent on almost all. In the initial years of LEADER I, the activities of groups where the private sector was the leading partner were oriented towards encouraging new enterprises and businesses, with little emphasis on social or community objectives. Groups which were community-driven, on the other hand, emphasised training and capacity-building, but private sector representatives had little interest in such activities. The participation of the statutory sector tended to be inflexible, paternalistic and "top-down" in orientation and resistant to the partnership idea. Statutory representatives saw themselves as custodians of public resources, which they could make available in whatever manner they considered appropriate (Kearney, Boyle and Walsh, 1994).

Because of the short duration of LEADER I, and the fact that much of the support went to private entrepreneurs, it is generally under the operation of LEADER II (1994–99) that locally based projects are becoming well-established and reaching maturity. There is considerable variation in the operation and activities of groups but there is, as yet, no evaluation of LEADER II. Nevertheless, drawing on experiences reported at a 1997 European Seminar involving the groups across Europe, and from examples of practice in Ireland, it is possible to discern a number of key aspects of the programme which have had a substantial impact on rural areas here.

Firstly, by providing resources directly to local groups and proposing an institutional framework for their operation, LEADER has enabled and facilitated rural residents to become involved in development activity in an unprecedented way. LEADER groups have initiated and sponsored a wide range of economic and social actions and have built on a tradition of community and local involvement which in the past had received little public recognition or support. This is a significant reversal of the situation when local projects operated with virtually no state support (indeed almost in spite of the state), to one where there is now a widespread acceptance and appreciation of the value of voluntarism in local development. The availability of technical assistance to produce an integrated, multi-sectoral plan, and the challenge of implementing it by drawing on relatively generous and predictable funds, have facilitated the emergence of development ideas, leadership and new alliances at local level. They have also acknowledged and further stimulated voluntary effort.

Secondly, the promotion of the partnership structure involving the public, private and "community" sectors has facilitated a range of actors, who would otherwise operate in separate spheres (local business and the public sector, for example), to promote and engage in joint "integrated actions". While LEADER groups might have started out by supporting mainly private enterprise, as they have evolved, and in the context of LEADER II, they are increasingly broadening the scope and range of their activities. The more progressive groups are now involved in a very wide range of initiatives and they are combining their sectoral activities with animation (stimulating and encouraging involvement in development) and capacity-building (training and support) activities.

Thirdly, for many groups LEADER I provided the opportunity to consolidate an embryonic local development organisation or establish new structures. Many of these have since managed to access significant additional funding (often from other EU budget lines, or the Local Development Programme, as we shall see below) and put in place a range of complementary actions, thus creating a "critical mass" of development activity in their local areas. The kinds of projects which groups may be engaged in or support typically fall under one of three headings.

1. Economic enterprise is the most common and is aimed at income generation and employment creation. Examples include: business and enterprise support through advice, grant schemes and mentoring; small enterprise centres; support for new commercial exploitation of local resources such as fish farming, alternative farm enterprises or tourism development; and the provision of services, otherwise not available locally, on a commercial basis.

2. Culture and heritage activities are aimed at the promotion and revival of local identity. Examples include: local cultural festivals, community arts, revival of traditional crafts, development of archaeological and historical sites.

3. Community service and social economy activities are aimed at addressing local needs and are often targeted at social exclusion. Examples include: the establishment of resource centres providing facilities, information and advice; training; the development and co-ordination of new social economy services such as child care and community care for older people or those with disabilities, and the provision of community transport.

In LEADER II, there is an emphasis on innovation and this has stimulated some exceptionally imaginative local development strategies often based on new ways of utilising local resources.

Fourthly, LEADER has highlighted the issue of gender imbalance in rural development. For instance, in the LEADER I Programme, only about 10 per cent of all board directors were women and almost two-thirds of boards had none or only one female director. The average group had twice as many male as female project promoters. In the light of these imbalances, the evaluators of LEADER I (Kearney,

Boyle and Walsh, 1994) recommended that LEADER II boards should consider ways of increasing the number of female members and make greater efforts to encourage women to come forward with project proposals. As a result, and in line with the commitment to gender equality, LEADER II groups are required to incorporate gender awareness and gender balance in the operation of their programmes. A specific target for groups is to ensure that, by the conclusion of the programme, at least 40 per cent of board directors are women. This has led some groups to actively encourage women's involvement in LEADER activities so that for the first time women are being publicly acknowledged and encouraged as key actors in local rural development. Indeed, many of the activities of local development groups are heavily dependent on the unpaid work of women, particularly initiatives associated with local service provision and the social economy.

From Social Provision to Enterprise

The LEADER Programme has been part of a general shift in the orientation of rural development activity to economic enterprise. Pre-LEADER locally based rural development was (with some notable exceptions) concerned primarily with social provision (for example, the building of community centres, care of the elderly, local history and cultural expression, provision of youth facilities, tidy towns competitions). Many groups were not necessarily tackling economic decline in any systematic way. While the quality of rural life may have been enhanced by collective action to provide or improve community facilities and amenities, it was not easy to connect this to any alleviation of the economic problems of rural decline.

By contrast, support for "integrated development" and the provisions of LEADER I encouraged a recognition at local level that tackling rural development problems from the "bottom-up" necessitated targeting job creation and economic development. The emphasis on enterprise development, evident also in the establishment of County Enterprise Boards in 1993, was reflected in support to individual entrepreneurs, rather than to a collectivity, and in an associated emphasis on the importance of business skills and practices in the running of projects. Around two-thirds of the expenditure under LEADER I, for instance, went to projects promoted by individuals.

This shift in emphasis from community and social development to enterprise and business development diverted attention from the more intractable problems of rural disadvantage. However, the targeting of social exclusion in the Operational Programme for Local Urban and Rural Development (OPLURD) has provided a counterbalance to the promotion of individual enterprise in rural development. It has led many rural development groups to adopt a broader development agenda, combining economic and social actions.

Local Development and Social Exclusion

The Local Development Programme of the OPLURD provides support for area-based partnerships and community groups. There are now 38 partnership companies in 35 Designated Areas, 18 of which are rural, as well as 33 Rural Community Groups in Non-Designated Areas (ADM, 1997). Local development in this context is defined as a collective effort to tackle unemployment and social exclusion. Many LEADER groups are operating as Rural Community Groups or are involved closely with Partnerships.

The emphasis on disadvantage and social exclusion in the Local Development Programme has facilitated and challenged groups with a strong economic development agenda to retain or acquire a significant social and community focus as well. The provision of technical assistance, the necessity to produce a strategic development plan through a consultative process, and the requirement to target social exclusion have all been important in influencing the way in which the social agenda is addressed by groups. More enterprise-minded groups have been introduced to a whole range of issues and concerns (such as long-term unemployment, the problems of rural women, problems of access to services) that may otherwise have been overlooked. Although they vary a great deal, the overall achievements of the partnerships and community groups in tackling social exclusion are quite considerable (ADM, 1997) and some of the rural partnerships and groups have been among the most successful. However, there are distinct and formidable challenges involved in addressing social exclusion problems in a rural context. They include the cost of covering a wide geographical area, a heavy reliance on a corps of committed volunteers, and the associated real limitations on human and physical resources.

Combining an economic enterprise and community development focus is not without its tensions. Groups often create separate organisational structures or delivery mechanisms for enterprise development and social exclusion. A "local development" sub-board or group may find itself operating relatively autonomously in addressing social exclusion problems while the main board or other economic/business-oriented committees promote and support more prominent economic enterprise projects. It is important that members of the business community — those whom Sabel (1996) refers to as "managers with a heart" — buy into the social agenda; otherwise, community development and social exclusion actions can become isolated from the economic activities of development groups. It is not unknown for such a separation to be associated with gender divisions, with women predominating in measures associated with social exclusion. It remains to be seen whether the momentum for a social agenda can be sustained in a rural context.

Institutional Issues

Among the biggest challenges facing local development partnerships are their representativeness and accountability — what Sabel (1996) refers to as their "fragile democratic legitimacy". The very elements which give the current phase of local development its dynamism and community dimension are also potentially the most problematic. Local development structures do not have very well-developed mechanisms of accountability to a local constituency and exist in parallel to local government structures. The latter do not as yet have the institutional flexibility (or mandate) to initiate such comprehensive local development actions as those already described. Local authorities are, of course, often prominent on local development partnerships and boards, and on LEADER groups.

Some of these concerns were reflected in the government document, *Better Local Government — A Programme for Change* (Department of the Environment, 1996), adopted at the end of 1996. This proposed the integration of local government and local development from 2000 onwards, but stressed continued commitment to the principles of partnership and local area action planning. Strategic Policy Committees and Community and Enterprise Development Groups are proposed at county level to oversee integration between local government and local development. These would replace the existing County Strategy Groups which have a co-ordinating role at present. Although the need for better integration is incontrovertible, many of those involved in local development express considerable foreboding about closer links with local authority structures, because these are perceived to be conservative, bureaucratic and unlikely to mobilise the kind of dynamism associated with the current phase of local development activity. The Rural Development Policy Advisory Group advocated the creation of sub-county and local level structures as a basis for the delivery of local-level programmes, which would also be mechanisms for linking the voluntary and community sector, business, social partners, local authorities and the public sector (Government of Ireland, 1997).

TOWARDS THE NEW CENTURY

Ideals and Pragmatism: the Cork Declaration and Agenda 2000

Two policy statements provide the broad context for rural development as we move into the next century. The Cork Declaration was the outcome of a conference organised by the European Commission which brought together a broad range of rural interests from the EU and other European countries. It sets out a ten-point rural development programme for the EU which includes principles of integrated development, economic diversification, sustainability and subsidiarity (that is, devolution of responsibility). The Declaration states that "sustainable rural development must be put at the top of the agenda of the EU", that rural development policy should be "multi-disciplinary in concept, and multi-sectoral in application, with a clear territorial dimension". It must be as "decentralised as possible and based on partnership and co-operation between all levels" with an emphasis on "participation and a 'bottom-up' approach, which harnesses the creativity and solidarity of rural communities". Such principles have not been enthusiastically or universally welcomed across the spectrum of political and sectoral interests in Europe, where there are radically different views on further CAP reform (Lowe, Rutherford and Baldock, 1996). The ideals set out in the Cork Declaration are likely to be tempered by pragmatism as various interests seek to influence policy over the next few years.

This is evident in the Agenda 2000 proposals (CEC, 1997). This document (also known as the "Santer Package") contains proposals for EU policy in the context of global trade liberalisation, the need for increased competitiveness, and the prospect of EU enlargement. It is envisaged that Ireland will no longer qualify for Objective 1 status (to which two-thirds of Structural Funds are to be directed) or Cohesion funding from 2000. This will significantly reduce the amount of structural funding available, but there is to be a phasing-out period. The number of Structural Fund Objectives is to be reduced from seven to three, but Ireland may be able to access Structural Funds through the new Objectives, which include measures to support local development and social exclusion. The proportion of funding to be spent on Community Initiatives (such as LEADER) is to be cut back and the number of Initiatives reduced from 14 to three. One of these is for rural development, presumably a form of LEADER III. The other two, dealing with human resources and cross-border development, may offer some possibilities for special project funding at local level. Funding under the CAP is expected to rise but to be oriented towards compensatory payments to farmers and to farm-related supports such as agri-environmental measures, farm improvement and diversification. These and other non-price supports to agriculture will be co-financed for the first time from the market support section of the CAP, thus clearly linking them to agricultural restructuring rather than to a broader rural development agenda.

It appears then that some of the principles contained in the Cork Declaration are given effect in Agenda 2000 by rationalisation of the various supports to rural development at European level, but that the bulk of the monies will come through the CAP. This arrangement will locate rural development primarily within the ambit of agriculture, rather than treating it as a coherent complex of actions across several sectors. This is combined with facilitating member states to tailor rural development programmes to their own particular circumstances through a specific rural development Initiative, possibly along the lines of LEADER, but with less overall funding. However, there is no coherent model of rural development in Agenda 2000, nor any clear attempt to flesh out the ideal of a comprehensive, integrated multi-sectoral approach as promised in the Cork Declaration. Agenda 2000 represents a rather more confined "agri-model" of rural development which will not meet the wide range of needs of rural areas in the next century (see Commins 1997, for a detailed discussion).

Key Issues, Post-2000

Our analysis of recent agricultural restructuring in Ireland has shown that the different measures to control farm production, while maintaining farm incomes, have had some clear outcomes. Restrictions on production in the form of milk quotas have accelerated the exodus of small-scale farmers from the most profitable farming enterprise — dairying. While increased non-market payments have been critical to the survival of many farm households, their link to some types of production — drystock mainly — has meant that larger-scale farmers benefit disproportionately. The conditions governing future direct payments are likely to link them to agri-environmental objectives. So far, however, payments for environmental functions go to larger than average farms of lower production intensity. Measures to encourage diversification from conventional production have mainly attracted those already successful in conventional farming. Retirement policies have appealed more to those on larger farms. While non-farm employment contributes proportionately more to the smaller-farm households, the geographical distribution of new employment has not favoured the small farming counties. Farmers at the bottom of the size scale are increasingly reliant on state income transfers, as well as on non-farm employment.

Unprecedented locally based rural development activity has been characterised by partnership structures and integrated local area plans. The most recent phase of rural development activity has involved a shift from mainly social provision to enterprise development, but this emphasis in LEADER has been counterbalanced to a considerable extent by the targeting of social exclusion in the Local Development Programme. Many rural areas have experienced a new development dynamic and local groups have delivered a wide range of supports to individuals and communities. Development "from below", largely marginalised in the past, has found a new and long-awaited legitimacy, which has allowed local people to participate in the development process and has elicited considerable commitment and enthusiasm from rural communities.

A number of key issues arise from our analysis, which we examine briefly below.

The Need for a Clear and Coherent Irish Rural Development Policy

Two models of rural development are currently in operation in Ireland, each of which is associated with a set of EU support measures. The first has a narrow agricultural focus and is associated with the CAP. It is articulated in Sub-Programme 1 of the Operational Programme for Agriculture, Rural Development and Forestry 1994–99. A set of measures, which account for most of the EU transfers to the rural sector, are directed to farmers and linked primarily to farm development, diversification and supporting farm incomes. Direct income support has become an increasingly significant part of the CAP; both these and other measures associated with CAP reform have tended to be most attractive and beneficial to medium to larger landholders. For the majority of landholders, farm production has ceased to be a primary source of earned income; they have become recipients of payments requiring their acquiescence to an essentially dependent and passive role in agriculture and rural development. A minority of commercial producers, who are generally better resourced, are benefiting from some of the adjustments occurring (access to extra milk quota, for instance) as well as from a range of supports for farm diversification, environmental protection and farm retirement.

Parallel to this is a second model which is an area-based approach and emanates from a series of measures and supports to rural development which, although originating in Brussels and supported by Structural Funds, have been adapted and shaped by the Irish state. This model of rural development is locally based, often referred to as "bottom-up" and associated with LEADER and the Local Development Programme. It is multidimensional, involves partnership and participation and encompasses a much wider constituency than farming. Most importantly, it is active and empowering in orientation. Although largely conceived and guided from "the top", programmes and initiatives in this model have generated sufficient local autonomy to raise concerns about representation and accountability.

The EU context for rural development is changing and the broad parameters of policy after 2000 have been set out but are as yet subject to political negotiation. The scale and scope of structural funding to Ireland will decrease rapidly and enlargement will divert attention and support to the large rural sectors in the new member states. While there is an undoubted commitment to the principles of the Cork Declaration on the part of Commissioner Fischler (see Fischler, 1997) the provision of funding and measures for rural development must yet be steered through the political process in which other interests will loom large.

These conditions present a challenge to the Irish State in the new century: to set out a clear national agenda for rural development policy and its articulation with other sectoral policies. While Ireland's success in obtaining and utilising Structural Funds in a creative manner has to be acknowledged, the sum of the efforts in relation to rural development has not as yet amounted to a coherent or comprehensive national policy for the development of rural areas. This has been repeatedly pointed out in the various reports. Significantly, it is acknowledged in the recently announced decision (early 1998) to prepare a White Paper on Rural Development (Department of Agriculture and Food, 1998). Such a Paper will provide a clear opportunity to construct a new model of Irish rural development policy based on the lessons of the past decade or so, and incorporating the widely agreed (and already tried and tested) principles of multidimensionality, participation, partnership and inclusiveness. It will need to take account of the pervasive role of the state in supplying public services to rural areas (e.g. health, education, housing, policing) and how this can be most effectively linked to locally-based actions.

Moreover, although regional disparities are obvious and freely acknowledged, policies and programmes to date have not yet responded adequately to the problems of the more disadvantaged rural regions. There is enormous diversity in local conditions and in the stage of development of rural groups. In situations of scarce resources, such as is likely to obtain from 2000, the most marginalised and underdeveloped regions or groups might well lose out unless they are specifically targeted. In short, it is important that rural development policy be articulated within the context of a more deliberate regional framework which takes account of the diversity of situations "on the ground".

The current wave of locally based development is built to a very considerable extent on voluntary effort — in participation on boards and committees and involvement in projects, but also in terms of the enthusiasm and sense of citizen involvement which is at the heart of many groups' efforts. There is universal agreement on the need to rationalise and reform the structures of policy delivery and address the "democratic deficit". But any attempt to do this will need to ensure that such effort is encouraged and validated rather than stifled. "Mainstreaming" of successful projects should not sideline voluntary effort but should aim at inclusiveness, both in targeting and delivery. Here, surely, is an opportunity to construct an "Irish solution to an Irish problem" and provide a model for rural development in the rest of Europe.

REFERENCES

ADM (Area Development Management Limited) (1997), *Partnerships: Making a Difference in People's Lives*, Dublin: ADM.

Cawley, M., D. Gilmor, T. Leavy and P. McDonagh (1995), *Farm Diversification: Studies Relating to the West of Ireland*, Dublin: Teagasc.

CEC (Commission of the European Communities) (1997), *Agenda 2000: For A Stronger and Wider Union*, Brussels: CEC.

Commins, P. (1996), "Agricultural Production and the Future of Small-Scale Farming" in C. Curtin, T. Haase and H. Tovey (1996), *Poverty in Rural Ireland: A Political Economy Perspective*, Dublin: Oak Tree Press, pp. 87–125.

Commins, P. (1997), "Rural Areas in the Next Century: Prospects and Policy Issues", Proceedings of Agri-Food Economics Conference, Dublin, 9 December, pp. 19–35.

Commins, P. and M. Keane (1994), "Developing the Rural Economy: Problems, Programmes and Prospects" in *New Approaches to Rural Development*, Dublin: National and Economic and Social Council, Part II, pp. 1–263.

Curtin, C., T. Haase and H. Tovey (1996), *Poverty in Rural Ireland: A Political Economy Perspective*, Dublin: Oak Tree Press.

CSO (Central Statistics Office) (1997), *Household Budget Survey 1994–95*, Dublin: Stationery Office.

Department of Agriculture and Food (1998), Press Release announcing White Paper on Rural Development, 28 January.

Department of the Environment (1996), *Better Local Government: A Programme for Change*, Dublin: Stationery Office.

Fingleton, W.A. (1995), "Structural Change in Dairying in Ireland and the EU: Actual and Projected", Paper presented at Conference on Dairy and Beef Industries, Dublin, Teagasc, December.

Fischler, F. (1997), "LEADER: Ideas and Initiatives for Development", Opening address to the LEADER Symposium, Brussels, 10 November.

Frawley, J. (1997), "Impact of Direct Payments on Farm Incomes and Viability", Proceedings of Agri-Food Economics Conference, Dublin, 9 December, pp. 1–18.

Government of Ireland (1997), *Report of the Rural Development Advisory Group*, Dublin: Stationery Office.

Hannan, D.F. and P. Commins (1993), *Factors Affecting Land Availability for Afforestation*, Dublin: ESRI.

Ilberry, B., Q. Chiotti, and T. Rickard (1997), "Introduction" in B. Ilberry, Q. Chiotti and T. Rickard (eds.), *Agricultural Restructuring and Sustainability*, New York: CAB International.

Kearney, B., G.E. Boyle and J.A. Walsh (1994), *EU LEADER I Initiative in Ireland*, Dublin: Department of Agriculture, Food and Forestry.

Leavy, A. (1997), "The Rural Environment Protection Scheme (REPS)", *Farm and Food*, Vol. 7, No. 1, pp. 12–15.

Lowe, P., A. Rutherford and D. Baldock (1996), "Implications of the Cork Declaration", *ECOS*, Vol. 17, No. 3/4, pp. 43–45.

NESC (National Economic and Social Council) (1994), *New Approaches to Rural Development*, Dublin: NESC.

NESF (National Economic and Social Forum) (1997), *Rural Renewal —
Combating Social Exclusion,* Forum Report No. 12, Dublin: NESF.

O'Hara, P. and P. Commins (1991), "Starts and Stops in Rural Development: An Overview of Problems and Policies" in B. Reynolds
and S. Healy (eds.), *Rural Development Policy: What Future for Rural
Ireland?,* Dublin: CORI.

Sabel, C. (1996), *Ireland: Local Partnerships and Social Innovation,* Paris:
OECD.

Shucksmith, M. (1993), "Farm Household Behaviour and the Transition to Post-productivism", *Journal of Agricultural Economics,* Vol.
44, pp. 466–478.

Chapter 14

HOUSING AND SOCIAL EXCLUSION

Tony Fahey

INTRODUCTION

The purpose of the present chapter is to examine housing in Ireland as an aspect of poverty and social exclusion and to consider some of the policy issues which arise in that context. Housing has not been central to policy debate or academic research on poverty issues in Ireland in recent years. However, few would dispute that it is an important influence on the day-to-day quality of people's lives and that it should be brought closer to the centre of the debate about social inclusion in Ireland.

Three aspects of this question will be taken up here. The first and most obvious is that, considered in narrow material terms, housing is a major component of living standards. Bad housing or lack of housing are important forms of material deprivation and their elimination must be central to any programme of poverty eradication.

Secondly, a house is an address as well as a dwelling — it locates a household in a neighbourhood and draws much of its character from its social and physical surrounds. It thus has a significance for social integration and social exclusion that may not be fully captured by the material characteristics of the house itself. This is particularly so in urban areas, where the poor tend to be sectioned off into lower class housing areas. For many of the urban poor, it is the public space surrounding the house rather than the house itself which is the main form of housing impoverishment they experience. On the other hand, such impoverishment of public space or community life is by no means a universal feature of poorer housing areas. Some poor neighbourhoods have a good quality of community life (in some cases remarkably so in view of the poverty and high unemployment which exist at household level) while other ostensibly similar areas suffer from severe problems. For some lower class housing areas, the stigma attached to their neighbourhoods by outsiders is as much of a problem as the real internal difficulties they experience. In any event, the spatial and community-level aspects of the housing system are important as second-order sources of social exclusion, over and above those which operate at the level of the individual household. These need to be given greater attention in efforts to understand how social exclusion operates and to overcome its effects.

A third distinctive interest of housing, from a social policy point of view, is the large role of the local authorities in the area, especially in connection with the housing of the poor. Social housing[1] is one of the main areas of responsibility of the local authorities and is the only major field of social provision in which local government plays such a large part. Policy development in this area, therefore, raises challenges for the reform of the local government system and gives rise to institutional questions of a kind not found in the same form in other areas of social policy.

Before examining these aspects of the present housing situation, it may be helpful to outline some of the distinctive features of the evolution of the housing system in Ireland, with particular reference to the role of the state in shaping how housing resources are distributed. A long-term perspective on this question is useful, not only for filling in historical background but also because housing is a capital asset with a long lifespan. The distributional effects of state intervention in housing take a similarly long time to unfold. While it is extremely difficult to measure these long-term distributional effects, we at least need to be aware that a focus on the immediate or short-term effects of housing policy fail to capture the full story.

---

[1] The term "social housing" has come into widespread currency in Ireland since the introduction of the Department of the Environment's *Plan for Social Housing* (1991). In some usages, it is applied as a generic label to encompass traditional local authority housing plus the newer forms of public housing provided by voluntary housing agencies, while in other usages it is applied to voluntary housing alone. The generic usage is the one adopted here.

THE HOUSING SYSTEM IN IRELAND:
SOME DISTINCTIVE FEATURES

The housing system in Ireland is marked by a number of distinctive features. Among these are the long-standing and extensive nature of the state's interventionist role, the prominence of home-ownership as a persistent goal of state housing policy and the role of local authority housing as an alternative avenue to home ownership. These features together have given the housing system in Ireland a distributional character which is unique in European terms, though it is difficult to assess how equitable or otherwise that distributional character is. The most recent comprehensive effort to assess the impact of housing subsidies on equity and income distribution is contained in Blackwell (1988).

The strong interventionist role of the state in the Irish housing system originated in the land reform programme which began in the late nineteenth century. That programme, which was heavily subsidised by the state, transformed the farming population from tenants into owner-occupiers. In the process, it made home-owners of the farming population — farm housing came with farm land as part of the land purchase package. In addition, the improvement or provision of housing was often incorporated into land reform activities, first through the work of the Congested Districts Board and later through the Land Commission (the legacy of these activities is still widely visible in the Land Commission houses which dot the eastern half of the country and the Congested Districts Board houses which are found along the western seaboard counties).

Agitation for land reform in Ireland also resulted in an ambitious programme of public housing for agricultural labourers. In the period between the 1890s and the First World War, a quarter of a million rural dwellers were re-housed under the Labourers' Acts, the most important of which was passed in 1906 (Bourke, 1993, p. 209). This was one of the earliest public housing programmes in Europe; in relative terms it was one of the largest, if not the largest, of its time; it was highly successful in achieving its aim of reducing the housing deprivation in rural Ireland; and, as Fraser points out in his excellent study of housing policy in Ireland in this period, its popularity and success generated "virtually unanimous support for state-subsidised housing" in Ireland (Fraser, 1996: 43). It also created the

basic model of social housing provision which subsequently came to
dominate British as well as Irish housing policy, involving large subsidies by the central state, implementation through the local authorities and the adoption of standardised housing designs (Fraser, 1996).

In urban areas in Ireland, despite some early initiatives (such as
the 1908 Housing Act), state housing policy was slower to develop
than in rural areas. Large-scale urban public housing got underway
only in the 1930s, in the form of the slum clearance programmes initiated by de Valera's early governments. By then also, the practice of
providing state subsidies for private house-building had become established, initially in the form of direct grants, subsequently in the
form of a wide, complex and ever-shifting array of direct and indirect
supports. In the post-war years, the net effect was to make the state's
role in the financing of housing exceptionally large by European
standards. A study carried out by the Economic Commission for
Europe in the 1950s estimated that three-quarters of the capital funds
invested in housing in Ireland at the time came from public funds
whereas a half or less was the rule in the majority of countries
(quoted in Ó hUiginn, 1959–60: 49). In the mid-1960s, Pfretzschner
estimated that "98 per cent of all housing constructed in the past 15
years had benefited by some form of public subsidy" (Pfretzschner
1965: 37).

State supports for public and private housing have persisted side
by side until today. It is often difficult to quantify their value, partly
because they often take the form of revenue foregone rather than
cash expenditures. Examples of such difficult-to-measure supports
include various forms of preferential tax treatment for housing[2] and
the subsidisation of local authority rents.[3] Because these are so perva-

---

[2] Prior to 1969, owner-occupation of houses was deemed to give rise to income-
in-kind and this "imputed income", which was estimated on a notional basis,
was subject to income tax (similar in principal to the taxation of actual income
derived by landlords from rents). This practice was abolished in the 1969 Finance
Act, though the taxation of landlords' rental income was continued (and is still
with us today, thus preserving a fiscal bias against private rental accommodation). In 1978, rates on domestic dwellings were abolished, a measure which
benefited all residential accommodation.

[3] The differential rents scheme by which local authority rents are set relates rents
to the household's ability to pay and these are usually well below economic
rents. However, since the local authorities have no obligation to determine what

sive in their application, one could argue that *all* housing receives some form of indirect support from the state, apart from more direct subsidies to particular categories of housing or householders (such as first-time house buyers' grants or rent supplements for low-income households in the private rented sector).

While all forms of housing could be said to benefit financially in some way or other from this long tradition of state intervention, some categories have benefited more than others. This leads us to the second distinguishing feature of Irish housing policy — the long-standing bias in favour of home ownership as a housing tenure. Because of the land reforms already mentioned, owner-occupation was already the dominant tenure in rural areas by the early decades of the present century. It was very much a minority tenure in urban areas at that time, where private renting was the norm, but it had become the majority tenure even in urban areas by the 1970s. Eight out of ten dwellings in Ireland are now owner-occupied, the highest rate of home ownership in Europe (and indeed, alongside New Zealand, one of the highest in the developed world). The balance is accounted for by private renting and social housing (Table 14.1), along with a small component of other tenures (such as accommodation provided free or as a benefit of employment).

TABLE 14.1: DWELLINGS BY TYPE OF TENURE IN IRELAND, 1946–1991 (%)

	1946	1961	1971	1981	1991
Owner-occupied	52.6	59.8	68.8	74.4	79.3
Social housing		18.4	15.5	12.5	9.7
	42.7				
Private rented		17.2	13.3	10.1	8.0

Note: The figure for 1946 makes no distinction between social housing and private rented dwellings.
Source: Censuses of Population 1981, 1991.

In addition to direct subsidies for private house-building, another important plank in support of home ownership has been the long tradition of sales of local authority housing to tenants. This is the third of the distinctive features of the Irish housing system I wish to

---

economic rents would be, it is difficult to know what level of rental subsidy is being provided to tenant households under the differential rents scheme.

highlight here. Following the precedents set by the land purchase Acts, tenant purchase was extended to public housing in a piece-meal way in the 1920s. In 1936, a more widespread and effective scheme was introduced to enable tenants in cottages built under the Labourers' Acts to acquire ownership. Provisions for the purchase of urban local authority housing at that time were relatively ungener-ous and there was little take-up (Pfretzschner, 1965: 33–34). Never-theless, by 1961, about a quarter of the houses which had been built by local authorities, urban and rural, had transferred to private own-ership (Kaim-Caudle, 1965: 2).

Tenant purchase was stepped up in the 1970s, and some of the tenant purchase schemes which have been implemented since then have been remarkably generous. As a result, some two-thirds of all the housing built by local authorities has been purchased by tenants, amounting to in excess of 200,000 dwellings out of a total of some 320,000 built. This pattern continues up to the present, as the supply of newly provided local authority housing is heavily counter-balanced by sales of existing housing to tenants, thus limiting the overall growth of the local authority rental sector.[4] Local authority dwellings purchased by tenants account for a quarter of all the owner-occupied housing in the country, and are a major part of the reason why owner-occupation in Ireland is so high by the standards of other countries.

The cumulative effect of this tradition of tenant purchase over the past 70 years is that, for the majority of local authority tenants, rent-ing from the local authority has assumed the character of a staging post on the route to heavily subsidised home ownership rather than a life-time alternative tenure. While this is beneficial for those who succeed in making the transition, it is less healthy for those who are left behind. Local authority housing which is still in rental tenure ac-

---

[4] In 1996, local authorities helped some 3,450 households into owner-occupation, made up of 2,284 tenant purchases and 1,166 shared ownership completions (that is, where the householder and the local authority jointly purchase a dwell-ing, with the householder paying a mortgage on his or her share and paying a rent to the local authority on the remainder). This compares to a total of some 3,500 units added to the local authority rental stock (2,615 new build units and 892 acquisitions). Only if we add in the 917 new units provided by the voluntary housing agencies does expansion of the social rental sector come out in front of increased owner-occupation as an outcome of local authority housing activity.

counts for less than 10 per cent of the total housing stock, the lowest share for social housing in Europe,[5] and caters overwhelmingly for the economically weak and marginalised. This residualisation and marginalisation of those in local authority housing is an important issue for social exclusion in Ireland and we will return to it further below.

The policy bias in favour of owner-occupation reflects a view, cultivated by both Catholic and nationalist social thought in the formative years of state-building in Ireland, that ownership was a more "natural" and socially more healthy tenure than any other. This view has since been elevated into one of the most consistently held principles of social policy in twentieth-century Ireland. While policy researchers have periodically queried the supposed social and economic benefits of strong state support for home ownership (see, for example, Pfretzschner, 1965; Blackwell, 1988; O'Connell, 1994), the overwhelming political consensus at present is to accept it as a given and to consider only the means by which it should be applied and the extent to which it should be promoted.

HOUSING, LIVING STANDARDS AND MATERIAL POVERTY

However one may question the level or nature of the state's role in the financing of housing, there is little doubt that it has contributed to the enormous improvement in the material standards of housing that has been made over the past hundred years in Ireland, much of which has been concentrated into the last three decades or so. NESC (1988: 13) judged that "among countries of roughly similar GNP per capita, Ireland has close to the best overall standard of housing". The incidence of overcrowding, defined as two or more persons per room in a dwelling, has fallen from 11.5 per cent of the population in 1961 to 0.9 per cent in 1991 (Census of Population 1991, Vol. 10). In 1961, less than six out of ten houses had piped water or a flush toilet, while

---

[5] In the UK, the "right to buy" schemes for council tenants promoted by the Thatcher governments in the 1980s sharply depleted the council housing stock, but it still remains very large (at 18 per cent of the total stock) by the standards of this country (*Social Trends 1997*). In Northern Ireland, housing rented from the Northern Ireland Housing Executive (the Northern Ireland equivalent of council housing) accounted for 28 per cent of the housing stock in 1994, down from 39 per cent in 1983 (Northern Ireland Abstract of Statistics, 1995).

today over 97 per cent of dwellings have both these amenities (ibid.). Certain categories of the population still experience severe housing deprivation. This is particularly so in the case of the homeless and Travellers living on the roadside, while questions have often also been raised about accommodation standards at the lower end of the private rental sector. But the improvement in housing standards has been widespread and has been sufficient to raise the vast majority of the population above the threshold of absolute housing deprivation.

It is more difficult to draw conclusions about trends in housing inequality and relative deprivation. Poverty research in Ireland has made some reference to examination of relative housing deprivation, but there is no regular comprehensive quantification of housing standards in the population or of the numbers who fall below what might be considered a minimum housing threshold. It is also difficult to incorporate the benefits-in-kind which arise from various kinds of state subsidies to housing into measures of household income, so that existing measures of poverty and low incomes generally do not take housing costs and benefits into account (for an interesting exception, see Callan et al., 1989: 134–5).

In the absence of systematic information on this question, all we can do is look at some indirect indicators. Local authority housebuilding, the category of housing most relevant to the less-well-off, has gone through some periods of poor design and poor build quality (particularly in the 1960s and early 1970s), and the stock of older local authority flat dwellings in the cities has often shown physical decline through poor maintenance. On the other hand, while systematic comparisons are hard to make, more recent local authority housebuilding standards compare well with those for much private housebuilding, and indeed local authorities often claim that their building specifications often exceed those of the private sector.

The periodic assessments of housing need which local authorities are obliged to carry out under the 1988 Housing Act contain useful information on housing need. However, housing need in this sense is limited to those who meet somewhat stringent criteria for eligibility for various kinds of social housing support, along with separate counts of the homeless. The 1996 assessment counted 27,427 households as being in housing need in this restricted sense, or less than 3 per cent of all households. A further 2,501 persons were counted as being homeless (Department of the Environment, 1996). Nolan and

Whelan, taking a broader measure of housing deprivation, which focused on the enforced lack of individual housing qualities or amenities which survey respondents deemed as necessities, found that a quarter of households lacked at least one item (Nolan and Whelan, 1996, especially Chapter 4). They also concluded that housing deprivation in this sense correlated rather weakly with poverty measured in purely income terms. However, their study did not examine housing deprivation in depth, either empirically or conceptually. A recent pioneering study by Threshold (1997) attempted to estimate the extent of housing debt, as indicated by rent and mortgage arrears, but this relates to income inadequacy rather than to problems with the material conditions of housing.

SOCIAL SEGREGATION AND SOCIAL EXCLUSION

Over and above the material standards of the individual dwelling, housing quality is also affected by the neighbourhood in which it is located, an issue which especially arises in urban areas. This is reflected in the well-worn estate agents' adage that there are three things which determine the value of a house — location, location, location. In some instances, housing locations may be desirable or undesirable for underlying physical reasons, such as closeness to attractive amenities (the sea, the mountains, good transport connections) or, in the case of unattractive locations, to ugly features such as unsightly industrial zones, dumps or noisy motorways. Frequently, however the key influence on the attractiveness of an area is the social composition of the households that live in it. Physical features may be consequent on social composition rather than antecedent to it — collective architectural standards, building quality and local environmental characteristics (such as landscaping and amenities) are shaped by the economic resources of resident households, and perhaps also by their ability to influence planning decisions and the provision of public services.

This points to a form of housing deprivation which has increasingly been identified in Ireland in recent years and which is increasingly disconnected from questions of the underlying material quality of housing. It consists in the social marginalisation of the housing areas in which poorer households are clustered, leading to a range of problems which are essentially social rather than architectural in character. In addition to the disadvantage which an individual household may experience because of poverty, unemployment or lone parenthood, additional or second-order layers of disadvantage may be created by clustering such households together and segregating them off from the wider society. Such second-order or community-level disadvantage can amount to a form of housing deprivation which is not caused by traditional housing problems such as overcrowding or dilapidated buildings but by social consequences arising from the way lower class housing is marginalised spatially and socially.

The local authority housing estate — in the shape either of the pre-1970s corporation flat complex in city areas[6] or the post-1970s greenfield council housing estate in the suburban fringes — is often pointed to as the stereotype of this housing problem in Ireland. Poorer households in either owner-occupied or private rented accommodation are less likely to be found in large clusters and thus generally are not prone to the same kind of spatial segregation. This is the type of housing which, because of the narrow, economically marginalised clientele on which local authority rental accommodation in Ireland is focused, is subject to the negative selection and residualisation mentioned earlier. In the popular imagination, these areas are associated with crime, drug addiction, vandalism, alienation and disaffection, and a poor physical and social environment for personal wellbeing and family life. They are the "estates on the edge", as the title of a recent international study of marginalised housing put it (Power, 1997). They cause concern in wider society, partly out of sympathy for those forced to live in them but also because of an uneasy fear that they threaten social order — that, in the words of a recent *Irish Times* feature article, unless the social exclusion they give rise to is combated, "social chaos will be a foregone conclusion" (*Irish Times*, 12 January 1998, p. 8).

---

[6] Unlike older house-type local authority dwellings, tenant purchase options are rarely taken up in the case of corporation flats, most of which date from the pre-1970s period, mainly because of difficulties in combining ownership tenure with rental tenure in multi-dwelling buildings with extensive common spaces. Estates of flats therefore remain in the local authority rental sector long after house-type estates built at the same time have been bought out by tenants.

While these images of social exclusion in local authority estates are widespread, the reality has been little explored and is open to much distortion. There is no doubt that those in local authority housing have a high risk of poverty, unemployment and lone parenthood (for recent data on this issue, see Nolan et al., 1998). It is true too that, partly in consequence of this concentration of economically marginalised households in particular areas, some individual estates are desolate places with extensive social order problems. It should also be recognised, however, that the quality of community life found in clusters of poor households varies greatly and is by no means always negative. There are many urban local authority housing areas, some of them quite large, where crime and vandalism are relatively limited, where there is no drugs problem, where social integration and social stability are reasonably strong, where there is a waiting list for housing applicants to get in, where residents have a strong attachment to the area and have no desire to move out, and where many of the households are likely eventually to purchase their dwellings from the local authority, if and when their means allow. In the pecking order of status and prestige in the national housing system as a whole, these areas might not rank as highly as most owner-occupied housing, but, in the residents' eyes at least, neither do they fall outside the rankings altogether, nor do they warrant the extreme imagery that is often used to characterise social conditions in local authority housing.

We can therefore say that, on the one hand, household-level social exclusion arising from such things as low incomes and unemployment is widespread in local authority housing and thus is widely dispersed around the country. On the other hand, the second-order forms of social exclusion, which might be expected to arise at the neighbourhood or community level from such factors as widespread drug abuse, low-level social disorder or external stigma, are disproportionately present in a number of localities in Dublin, and to a lesser extent in other urban centres such as Cork and Limerick. Even in Dublin city, where the worst such blackspots are found, the problems are by no means evenly distributed — some local authority housing areas are much worse off than others.

Concentrations of disadvantage in certain housing areas thus have quite variable implications for the quality of community life. Household-level marginalisation sometimes feeds through into various community-level problems, some of them quite severe. A number of multiply-disadvantaged communities have been created as a result, mainly housed in the local authority sector. However, these connections are not universal or consistent — many local authority housing estates with the stereotypical patterns of household disadvantage (unemployment, low incomes, low educational attainment, etc.) do not suffer from the stereotypical neighbourhood problems just mentioned, or do not do so to the same extent.

We know relatively little about this variability — how great it is, what might account for it or what implications it might have for policy on social exclusion. In particular, we know little about the community resources (such as neighbourliness, extended family networks and informal social controls) which seem to be present in many poorer neighbourhoods and which preserve their communities from the worst effects of the material deprivations they suffer. Even in cases where symptoms of community disruption are present (such as high levels of drug abuse or vandalism, or a high incidence of difficult-to-let dwellings), we have little information on exactly how pervasive the effects are on the households in the neighbourhood or what mechanisms those households use to cope with those effects. Thus, while we can say that the spatial segregation and social organisation of low income housing has emerged as a major issue for social inclusion, we are as yet in the early stages of understanding precisely how that is so.

THE ROLE OF LOCAL AUTHORITIES

This brings us to the role of local authorities in dealing with the housing aspects of social exclusion. Because of the limited powers of local government, this role is by no means all-encompassing. Much of the broader framework within which housing is located is beyond the scope of local authorities to tackle. Thus, for example, the residualisation of local authority housing arises from the widespread promotion of owner-occupation in housing policy at the national rather than the local level. Income levels, employment prospects, educational standards and household structure among the kinds of households served by local authority housing are determined by factors which lie largely outside the sphere of housing policy altogether. However, while these factors reflect influences over which local government has no control, there still remains a range of housing issues proper which are within the competence of the local authorities and which are important to any effort to reduce social exclusion among those living in local authority housing.

These issues pose fundamental challenges to the way local government discharges its housing functions. The traditional view of the role of local government in providing housing limited its job to building houses, allocating them to tenants, setting rents on an ability-to-pay basis, collecting the rents and providing a maintenance service. Until the 1980s, debate on how well the local authorities carried out this job was often contentious, but it was largely contained within a frame of reference which directed attention to the material and financial aspects of housing. Usually, the key issue was the *quantity* of housing which the local authorities could provide, with ancillary concerns focused on related issues such as the cost and build quality of that housing, allocations policy and rent levels.

In the 1980s, this traditional approach to their housing remit among local authorities came under question as social difficulties in local authority housing estates came into public view. In the Dublin area, these difficulties coincided with the eruption of drug abuse as a serious problem in a number of Dublin corporation housing estates in the early 1980s. Increasing rates of vandalism, petty crime and joy-riding also signalled a decline in social order within lower-class housing areas in a number of urban centres. Although local authority housing areas always had a reputation for "roughness", especially in new estates with high proportions of young people, these developments signalled a new level of difficulty in the social problems encountered.

These difficulties exposed weaknesses in the capacity of local authorities to cope with the new challenges posed by the changing social circumstances of their housing clientele. Instances of dereliction and decline in public housing estates increased, frequently in cases where the underlying building quality of the housing was quite good. Questions emerged about the competence and commitment of local authority housing departments. By the early 1990s, this had given rise to an increasingly widespread view that, in general, despite their venerable record, local authorities were bad landlords. They seemed to know little or nothing about good housing management, lacked professional housing management skills, wasted public

funds on a massive scale, were remote, rigid and uncaring in their
dealings with tenants and seemed content to preside over the housing disaster zones they had created in the larger urban areas in the
previous decades. (For a blandly phrased but nevertheless damning
statement of such a view, see the opening pages of the Department of
the Environment's *Memorandum on the Preparation of a Statement of
Policy on Housing Management,* issued in 1993.)

Since the early 1990s, criticisms such as these have edged the
housing function in local government towards the kind of institutional reform which has been evident in other parts of the government system (as referred to elsewhere in this volume). Some of this
drive is evident at the national policy level, as reflected in policy
documents such the Department of the Environment's *Plan for Social
Housing* (1991) and *Social Housing — the Way Ahead* (1995). However,
some of its most important manifestations have emerged from the
bottom up. The Ballymun Task Force, a pioneering instance of
housing renewal in the local authority sector, is a case in point. It
emerged from local community activity in the mid-1980s and provided the driving force behind the working out of a comprehensive
regeneration plan for the Ballymun area, involving Dublin Corporation and other agencies. Similar creative initiatives have emerged in
other local authority housing areas around the country, often reflecting *ad hoc* adaptations to local circumstances. The common
thread they share is a greater degree of involvement by local communities in shaping the housing services they receive, and thus a
move from a dependent relationship with housing authorities to a
partnership relationship.

These developments are as yet too piecemeal to amount to a
transformation in the way local government operates in the housing
field, but they are pointing in that direction. They could be characterised as an attempt to bring the principles of local partnership into
local government. Local partnerships, of which the PAUL Partnership in Limerick, the Tallaght Partnership and the South Kerry Development Partnership were early examples, have flourished in
recent years (they now number upwards of 100 nationwide — Walsh
et al., 1997). They have been characterised as "the conduit for a radical new localism in public policy" and as "an innovative form of local governance" which brings together state agencies, the social
partners and local community groups in an effort to combat social

exclusion through community development (Walsh et al., 1997: 175–6; see also OECD, 1996). For the most part, these partnerships have had little connection with existing local government — something which could be counted simultaneously as a strength (as it enables flexibility and innovation) and a weakness (as it raises questions about sustainability and accountability).

It is in this context that housing acquires a particular significance. Community development through local partnerships frequently acquires a housing dimension, while local authority responses to the new social problems in housing are now acquiring a partnership dimension. Housing thus provides a focus where the traditional approach of local government and the new local partnerships have met and bounced off each other, sometimes to beneficial effect. The resulting developments in tenant participation, estate management and inter-agency co-operation on issues connected with housing show much of the improvisation and diversity which has marked the partnership process in other areas of local development. Their eventual impact and long-term development have yet to work themselves out. In the meantime, however, they are generating a great deal of local activity, are introducing new ways of conducting business to housing officials and may yet amount to a major transformation in the way public housing is administered. They mark the beginning at least of a serious attempt to tackle the forms of social exclusion which have been built into housing provision to date.

CONCLUSION

As the century draws to a close, the appalling housing conditions found in Ireland in the early part of the century are largely a thing of the past. We now have nothing like the city slums of the 1930s, and the general physical standard of housing enjoyed by Irish people is reasonably adequate. Certain groups such as the homeless and Travellers on the roadside are an exception to this picture, but for the vast majority of Irish people, the basic physical condition of housing has been transformed beyond recognition in recent decades.

However, housing has social as well as physical dimensions — it locates people in communities and influences the way communities operate. Improvement in physical housing conditions has not always been matched by an advance in these social dimensions of housing.

The housing system is strongly marked by social and spatial seg-regation, and this has resulted in the creation of large clusters of socially deprived housing in urban areas. Some of these areas have experienced a marked decline in social conditions since the early 1980s. This in turn has put pressure on the physical as well as the social fabric of estates, although the different ways and degrees to which this has occurred are as yet poorly understood and open to exaggeration.

Awareness of these social dimensions of housing and the way they have contributed to social exclusion has begun to be reflected in housing policy in the 1990s. Since local authority housing is at the centre of these concerns, the traditional approach of the local authorities to their housing responsibilities has been judged to be lacking. Pressures for a reform of that approach have mounted, both from local communities and central government. That pressure has begun to yield results, though instances of effective change are still sporadic. The potential of the present drive for reform is not just that social and physical conditions in poorer housing areas will improve, but also that valuable lessons in new methods of local governance will be learned in the process.

REFERENCES

Blackwell, J. (1988), *A Review of Housing Policy*, Dublin: National Eco-nomic and Social Council, Report No. 87.

Bourke, J. (1993), *Husbandry to Housewifery: Women, Economic Change and Housework in Ireland, 1890–1914*, Oxford: Clarendon Press.

Callan, T., B. Nolan, B.J. Whelan, D.F. Hannan, with S.F. Creighton (1989), *Poverty, Income and Welfare in Ireland*, Dublin: Economic and Social Research Institute.

Department of the Environment (1991), *Plan for Social Housing*, Dublin: Stationery Office.

Department of the Environment (1993), *Memorandum on the Prepara-tion of a Statement of Housing Management*, Dublin: Department of the Environment.

Department of the Environment (1995), *Social Housing — the Way Ahead*, Dublin: Stationery Office.

Department of the Environment (1996), *Annual Housing Statistics Bulletin 1996*, Dublin: Stationery Office.

Fraser, M. (1996), *John Bull's Other Homes: State Housing and British Policy in Ireland, 1883–1922*, Liverpool: Liverpool University Press.

Kaim-Caudle, P. (1965), *Housing in Ireland: Some Economic Aspects*, Dublin: Economic and Social Research Institute.

NESC (1988) "Council's Comments on A Review of Housing Policy", in J. Blackwell, *A Review of Housing Policy*, Dublin: National Economic and Social Council, Report No. 87.

Nolan, B., and C.T. Whelan (1996), *Resources, Deprivation and Poverty*, Oxford: Clarendon Press.

Nolan, B., C.T. Whelan and J. Williams (1998), *Where Are Poor Households Found? The Spatial Distribution of Poverty and Deprivation in Ireland*, Dublin: Oak Tree Press.

Northern Ireland Annual Abstract of Statistics, No. 13 (1995), Belfast: Department of Finance and Personnel.

O'Connell, C. (1994), "Housing in the Republic of Ireland: A Review of Trends and Recent Policy Measures", *Administration* Vol. 42, No. 2.

OECD (1996), *Ireland: Local Partnerships and Social Innovation*, Paris: Organisation for Economic Co-operation and Development.

Ó hUiginn, P. (1959–60), "Some Social and Economic Aspects of Housing — an International Comparison" *Journal of the Statistical and Social Inquiry Society of Ireland*, XX, Part III.

Pfretzschner, P.A. (1965), *The Dynamics of Irish Housing*, Dublin: Institute of Public Administration.

Power, A. (1997), *Estates on the Edge: The Social Consequences of Mass Housing in Northern Europe*, London: Macmillan.

Social Trends, No. 27 (1997), London: HMSO.

Threshold (1997), *As Safe as Houses? The Nature, Extent and Experience of Debt in the Irish Housing System*, Dublin: Threshold.

Walsh, J., S. Craig and D. McCafferty (1997), "The Role of Local Partnerships in Promoting Social Inclusion", typescript, Dublin: European Foundation for the Improvement of Living and Working Conditions.

Chapter 15

BEYOND IRELAND'S JOBS CRISIS

Charles M.A. Clark *and* Terrence McDonough

THE ECONOMICS OF EMPLOYMENT AND UNEMPLOYMENT

While unemployment would at first appear to be a relatively straightforward phenomenon, it is in fact conceived in radically different ways, even within the field of economics. Following on the Keynesian revolution, economics textbooks have presented unemployment as one of the twin demons of macroeconomics, pairing it with the problem of inflation. Further, as in a folk tale, the weakening of one demon is inevitably accomplished by the proportionate increase in the power of the other. The hero, the modern economist, is both powerful in his ability to arbitrate the strength of the two demons, but helpless in that the complete submission of one demon can only be purchased at the price of unleashing the full fury of the other. Unemployment is primarily conceived as a loss of potential output, a falling short of the full employment GDP. Thus, establishing the proper level of unemployment is both a technical matter of fine-tuning the economy and a political question of how much of either macroeconomic problem the society is willing to tolerate. More microeconomic approaches to unemployment, emphasising rigidities in the labour market as the source of unemployment, still concern themselves largely with improving the terms of this technical and political trade-off. Lost in this balancing act is the basic reality that an increase in the price level is being played off against the accumulation of the personal tragedy of unemployment.

Economists have not been completely blind to this inadequacy in their approach. In moving beyond this rather cold characterisation of unemployment, economists have recognised unemployment as more than a technical question. However, true to the utilitarian tradition, they have seen unemployment as a problem which inheres in individuals, a deduction in total well-being either for the unemployed themselves, or for the rest of the population due to the presence of the unemployed. The well-known studies of M.H. Brenner (Brenner, 1987) have argued a close statistical relationship between levels of unemployment and the incidence of disease, alcoholism, suicide, homicide and crime.

A different, and we believe, healthier conception of unemployment has been gaining at least a rhetorical currency. This developing point of view sees unemployment as a form of social exclusion. This conception has been employed by the National Economic and Social Forum and the National Economic and Social Council and has been developed in the Conference of Religious of Ireland's approach to social issues (CORI, 1997: 13). From this point of view, the unemployed are denied effective participation in society through poverty, a lack of meaningful work, and the opportunity to participate fully in the political and social decisions which affect their lives. Furthermore, this exclusion is, for the most part, inherited by the children of the unemployed, the poor and the marginalised.

It is still possible to regard social exclusion as primarily a problem of the unemployed. The unemployed are disadvantaged because they are socially excluded. Nevertheless, the conception of unemployment as social exclusion has the potential to refocus radically the problem of unemployment, seeing it not as a problem of the unemployed but rather as a problem of society. If unemployment is a contributing factor to social exclusion, it is the manifestation of a failure of our social organisation. The inclusion of all of its members is the first and most fundamental task of society. The existence of unemployment then is not a problem primarily for the unemployed, but one of the basic fabric of our social existence.

When approached from this angle, the solutions to unemployment emerge as not merely the provision of jobs for the unemployed. Beyond job provision, CORI has identified ways of tackling social exclusion through the elimination of poverty, the provision of meaningful work, and the development of participative structures which allow all citizens a measure of self-determination. This alternative approach must realign the economist's traditional ideal of full employment. The goal is not the full mobilisation of resources by the market but the full participation of each citizen in society. Such participation will often involve the acquisition of a traditional "job", but is necessarily broader than this. Meaningful work must be seen in a family and society, as well as market, context. The real issue is not the "jobs crisis"; it is the "social exclusion" crisis.

THE POSSIBILITY OF FULL EMPLOYMENT IN IRELAND

It is a cherished article of faith among orthodox economists that an unhindered market economy has a natural tendency towards full employment. This has led many economists to view Irish unemployment as a malfunction of the labour market; specifically, that rigidities have prevented the labour market from making the necessary adjustments to bring about full employment. Thus, much of the work on Irish unemployment in the 1980s and 1990s has centred on labour market flexibilities and other labour market failures. Labour market imbalances are due to some market imperfection or failure; something must be preventing the market mechanism from performing its market clearing function. The usual suspects are labour unions, government regulation and taxation. Labour unions cause wages to be rigid (as does government intervention, such as minimum wages and national wage agreements), thus preventing a fall in wages that would allow the labour market to clear, while government tax and benefit systems cause individuals to rationally "choose" to be unemployed.[1] The policy conclusions of this view of unemployment are to increase labour market flexibility and to reduce government interference in the economy.[2]

Can Flexibility Solve the Unemployment Problem?

Flexibility in labour markets is something that just about all economists can claim to be in favour of, for the simple reason that labour market flexibility can mean different things. There are four types of flexibility in labour markets:

---

[1] Specifically, these are the issues of replacement rates and the tax wedge, both to be discussed below.

[2] See Paul Tansey (1991) for an extended argument that Ireland's unemployment problem is caused by wages and taxes being too high.

1.   Labour costs

2.   Labour mobility

3.   Labour adaptability

4.   Working time and scheduling.

Orthodox economists typically emphasise the first two aspects, looking to a ruthless labour market to reduce costs and achieve labour mobility. They seek to achieve the third and fourth goals through increasing the power of capital within firms. Heterodox economists, by contrast, emphasise labour adaptability, seeing wage cuts and high mobility as interfering with the achievement of this kind of flexibility.

Following the orthodox line, the main conclusion of the OECD jobs study, the largest and most comprehensive empirical investigation into the recent rise in unemployment, was that:

> much unemployment is the unfortunate result of societies' failure to adapt to a world of rapid change and intensified global competition. Rules and regulations, practices and policies, and institutions designed for an earlier era have resulted in labour markets that are too inflexible for today's world. (OECD, 1994)

These inflexibilities are mainly:

1.   Rigid wages which prevent wage rates from falling in the face of high unemployment

2.   Generous social protection of unemployed workers and the poor, leading them to rationally choose poverty and unemployment over work.

The policy suggestions derived from this view are to let wage rates fall and to make work more attractive by cutting benefits to those out of work (that is, making poverty less attractive).

The argument for cutting wages to reduce unemployment is one that was very popular with economists during the Great Depression, even though wage rates fell significantly and employment failed to respond. The weakness of the wage rigidity argument was first demonstrated by Keynes in *The General Theory* (Keynes, 1936) when he showed how a reduction in wage rates increased unemployment, primarily through a fall in demand. For all its insights and evidence (which are considerable), the *OECD Jobs Study* could not produce any definitive evidence to support the wage flexibility argument.

Related to the flexible labour market argument is the social protection argument. Various forms of social protection are seen as insulating workers from the discipline of the forces of supply and demand. Orthodox economists have developed two indices which measure how government benefits and taxes influence the labour supply and demand decision: the "replacement ratio" and the "tax wedge," both of which have played a prominent role in the discussion on unemployment in Ireland. We shall look at each briefly.

The "replacement ratio" is the ratio of out-of-work earnings to net earnings. The argument is that, if it is high, the unemployed have less of an incentive to take up employment and thus choose to remain unemployed. As the recent ESRI study on the Irish labour market (O'Connell and Sexton, 1997) demonstrates, there is little agreement as to how one should measure the replacement ratio, with many studies giving Ireland one of the lowest in Europe (OECD, 1994) while others find higher replacement ratio values (such as the Department of Enterprise and Employment's "Growing and Sharing our Employment", 1996). Whatever the actual rate may be, its significance as a useful cause of unemployment must be seriously questioned. The replacement ratio goes up when wages fall and benefits increase and goes down when wages rise and benefits fall. An increase in unemployment will tend to cause wages to stagnate or fall, and will also prompt the government to increase benefits, with a fall in the unemployment rate having the reverse effect. Thus we should expect the replacement ratio to move with the rate of unemployment to a certain extent — but the rate of unemployment is the cause, while the replacement ratio is an effect.

The "tax wedge" is the gap between the cost to the employer of employing a person and the take-home pay of the employee. Whereas the replacement ratio attempts to explain unemployment via the effects that tax and benefits have on the decision to work (labour supply), the "tax wedge" analysis shifts the responsibility for unemployment onto the effect of government policy on the demand for labour. The argument runs like this: a rise in taxes causes a reduction in the take-home pay of workers. The workers then demand higher wages from their employer (to keep their take home pay from falling), causing wages to rise. This rise in wages reduces the employers' demand for labour, thus causing unemployment. Again we have cause being mixed up with effect. Falling unemployment tightens the labour market, allowing wages to increase, thus lowering the tax wedge (also, falling unemployment in Ireland has allowed for lowering tax rates, further lowering the tax wedge). Like the replacement ratio, there are numerous measures of the "tax wedge", with empirical studies on the role of the tax wedge in the rise in unemployment in Ireland being inconclusive.

The levels of social spending and social protection have generally fallen in the 1980s and 1990s, the same time as European unemployment was rising. Furthermore, Ireland's social protection was increasing in the 1990s, at the same time as its unemployment rate was falling. The case for social spending and tax policy as the cause of unemployment in Europe and Ireland must be seen as very weak indeed.

Can Economic Growth Solve the Jobs Crisis?

The recent dramatic growth in the Irish economy has led some Irish economists to look towards economic growth as the solution to the problem of unemployment. The latest *Medium-Term Review: 1997–2003* by the ESRI (1997) argues that if Ireland continues its current growth path, all but long-term (structural) unemployment will be eliminated by 2003 (8.4 per cent) with very near full employment achieved in 2005–2010 (5.9 per cent). This "sustained reduction in unemployment" (Duffy et al., 1997: vii) will be achieved through an average growth in GNP of between 4.2 and 5.5 per cent through 2010, as well as a rise in educational attainments. This reduction comes about partly through the demographic shift of the older long-term unemployed to the ranks of the retired (thus no longer statistically unemployed). For the first time in a generation, something resembling full employment is being envisioned by Irish economists.

The short-term unemployment rate is determined by the level of aggregate demand. This is as true today as it was when Keynes first proposed his theory of employment. Both the rise of Ireland's unemployment rate in the 1980s and its recent fall in the mid- to late

1990s can be shown to be caused by variations in aggregate demand (Clark, 1998). The key questions are: what factors have promoted a high level of aggregate demand in recent years; and will these conditions persist into the future? Five factors are typically credited with promoting Ireland's recent success:

1. World economic growth

2. National wage agreements

3. EU investments in Ireland (structural funds)

4. Foreign investment

5. Convergence.[3]

If the authors of the ESRI's *Medium-Term Review* were to write their report today (December 1997), a mere eight months after it was published, they might not have been so rosy in their forecast of world economic growth. Recent developments in the Pacific Rim nations are demonstrating once again how unstable capitalism can be, and how the possibility of an era of deflation and global slow-down are now very real. What is particularly frightening is not the instability in the global stock markets (everyday proving the accuracy of Keynes's description of casino capitalism) but the age-old problem of excess capacity and over-production/under-consumption. The same investment activity which has promoted this boom, mostly in high technology and improved efficiency, has also generated surplus capacity and deflationary pressures. Ireland's recent performance has been greatly enhanced by its strong international trade performance, which will be hit very hard in a world economic slowdown. World economic growth cannot be relied upon to pull the Irish economy indefinitely. Furthermore, a world slowdown will also greatly affect the level of foreign investment. The daily news informs us of how quickly foreign capital can leave a country, even in the best of times, with employment at the Seagate plant in Clonmel going from zero to 1400 to zero within a two-year period. Paradoxically, Ireland's

---

[3] Increase in the "human capital" of the labour force and fiscal stabilisation were also contributing factors, yet their contributions are more in the line of laying the basic conditions for economic growth.

economic growth threatens to disqualify her for structural funds beyond 1999. The failure of the present government to deliver on promised tax cuts for the low-paid has put Partnership 2000 and subsequent wage agreements in jeopardy. Lastly, once Ireland fully catches up, growth from convergence must necessarily disappear.

Ireland's Success So Far

The problem of unemployment is global and any discussion of it must not confine itself to a single country. Ireland's recent success (which entails bringing the rate of unemployment down to the European average) is a classic example of what Cambridge economist Joan Robinson used to call "exporting unemployment". The most significant generators of growth in aggregate demand for Ireland during the "Celtic Tiger" period have been exports, foreign investment and structural funds. All three of these create jobs in Ireland at the expense of jobs elsewhere. Ireland's trade surplus is, however, a very recent phenomenon and reflects advantages which can be quickly erased. Thus sustained full employment in Ireland will necessitate sustained full employment in the world capitalist system, something that is without historical precedent. Global unemployment stems from the fact that the advanced capitalist economies are "demand-constrained" and not, as the classical and neo-classical economists assumed, "supply constrained". In a "demand-constrained" economy, the central economic problem is that the ability of the economy to produce goods and services far exceeds the ability of the society to consume. In a demand-constrained economy, unemployment is the rule rather than the temporary exception, because the economy is only at full capacity in exceptional circumstances (such as war time). Unemployment is useful, however, for keeping wages down and fighting inflation.

THE STRUCTURAL ROOTS OF IRISH UNEMPLOYMENT

Beyond these very short-term threats to continued Irish growth, there are three fundamental sources of the Irish unemployment problem which will necessarily persist into the future, each of them rooted in the deep structure of the current economy. The first is the failure of the monetarist dream of transcending the business cycle, the reasons for which are to be found in the basic dynamics of the capitalist economy itself. The second is the passing of the post-war Golden Age of international capitalist expansion. The third is the historic end of the opportunity for balanced growth.

Behind the neo-classical economic story of a flexible labour market eliminating unemployment is the hidden assumption that the labour market should exhibit the same behaviour as any other commodity market. This ignores the fact that what is being traded in the labour market is not beans or cricket bats, but the human capacity to work. This capacity is embodied in human beings, with all the needs, aspirations and complexity that this implies. The neo-classical story says that when the supply of labour equals the demand for labour (full employment), wages should settle at an equilibrium rate. But this is no more than an assumption and is not backed by the historical evidence. On the contrary, workers' bargaining power is substantially increased under conditions of full employment when lines outside of personnel offices have disappeared and workers leaving positions can easily find work at comparable wages and conditions. As a result of this increased bargaining power at full employment, wages tend to rise, and rise faster than increases in productivity. These wage increases necessarily eat into profitability. Falling profits lead to falling investment. Falling investment leads to falling demand and the re-emergence of unemployment. At positive levels of unemployment, the bargaining power of labour is weakened and wages stabilise or fall. Profits recover and the business cycle turns up again. The economy potentially grows until destabilised again by the approach of full employment. This cyclical movement is reinforced by similar dynamics around other cost factors, including the cost of raw materials and the cost of capital. It is further strengthened by the pro-cyclical behaviour of inflation and by the development of financial fragility in periods of expansion (Bowles and Edwards, 1985: 231–296; Sherman, 1991).

In addition to the short-run business cycle, capitalist economies are subject to longer-run dynamics. Investment on a large scale cannot take place in the absence of secure long-run profit expectations. Any long-run expectations are, however, necessarily problematic. This is due to class conflict over distribution and working conditions and to the destabilising effects of competition between capitals. For this reason, long-run growth demands a set of stable institutions which can moderate conflict and competition and steer these factors into non-destructive channels (see Kotz et al., 1994).

Such a set of stable institutions emerged in the period after the Second World War. These institutions prominently included an international order organised economically and militarily by the dominant position of the United States. Also included was a system of stable and long-term collective bargaining between strong unions and basic industry. This bargaining system guaranteed a large section of labour a secure job and an income which rose in line with both prices and, crucially, productivity. The state took responsibility for guaranteeing the health of the economy and long-term growth through Keynesian techniques of demand management. This institutional framework of accumulation worked so well that some economic analysts of this period have begun to refer to it as the "Golden Age" of post-war capitalism (Marglin and Shor, 1990).

By the mid-1970s, the Golden Age had come to an end. The rise of the European and Japanese economies had eroded US international dominance. This loss was manifested in the end of the Bretton Woods monetary system. The Third World had entered a period of revolution and increased independence, illustrated most dramatically by the US defeat in Vietnam and two successive oil crises. Faced with secularly rising real wages and inadequate productivity growth, business counterattacked with what United Auto Workers president Douglas Frasier labelled "a one-sided class war". Aided by rising levels of unemployment and an increasingly sympathetic government, corporations drastically weakened union power and succeeded in stalling and reversing the growth in real wages. Keynesianism had met its Waterloo in the stagnation of the 1970s and the turn to monetarism was evident in President Carter's appointment of Paul Volker to the US Federal Reserve Board in 1978, before the elections of Reagan and Thatcher. The international capitalist economy entered a period of stagnation and crisis. Among other things, this stagnation was evident by rising rates of unemployment.[4]

It may be the case that we are emerging from this period of stagnation and entering a period of renewed growth. If so, this renewed growth must be based in the construction of a new institutional

---

[4] For a similar analysis, see Bowles et al. (1990).

structure which moderates the capitalist tendencies toward instability. This new structure may be based on the emergence of a global
regime of trade and the free movement of capital and the consequent
increased leverage that capitalism gains both on the shopfloor and in
relations with the nation state. But this new regime of accumulation
will not usher in a new Golden Age. The reason is quite straightforward.

The tendency of a growing capitalism to increase productivity
must be balanced by either increasing standards of consumption or
increasing leisure time for the working class. Increases in the productivity of labour mean that more goods can be produced with the
same amount of labour. The basic Keynesian insight holds that this
increased amount of product needs to find a market. The post-war
Golden Age included mechanisms to ensure a market for its rising
productivity in its wage bargaining system and in the Keynesian
state.

A Kaleckian approach, borrowing the notion of class from Marx,
observes that the income generated by production is divided between capital and labour (Sawyer, 1985: 72–73). Thus, increasing
productivity must be accompanied by an increase in the real income
of either capital or labour or both. If the increase in production ac-
crues to capital, it must be absorbed into the increased capitalist consumption or invested. On the one hand, there is a limit to how much
capitalist consumption can be further increased. On the other, the
money can be invested in increased production. To the extent that
this is pursued through labour-saving means, the problem of con-
suming the increased production is merely reproduced in the next
production period at a higher intensity.

The necessary conclusion from these observations is that a substantial portion of the increasing production must in some way accrue to labour. This can take the form of an increased standard of
living. Alternatively, the increasing productivity of labour can express itself in producing the same quantity of goods and services, but
accomplishing this task in a shorter period of time. Collectively then,
the labouring class would experience a shorter working week or
working year.

Neither of these beneficial effects of increasing productivity can
be universally observed. The new world order is founded on an increase in competition between capitals and regions of the world.

Both firms and governments seek to increase competitiveness through the control of labour costs (Bryan, 1995: 170–8). While it is hard to make generalisations for the developed world as a whole, real wages in the developed world have generally been either stagnant or have lagged behind productivity growth since the mid-1970s. The entry of women into the labour force has tended to increase or slow the decline of the working week on a household basis.[5]

The inevitable result of rising productivity, stagnant working class standards of living, and a constant or rising length of working time is unemployment. The creation of potential free time is inherent in raising the productivity of work time. In the emerging international regime, it tends to concentrate in a few hands — those of the long-term unemployed. It is ironic that the advance of the productive forces which Marx saw as narrowing the realm of necessity and increasing the realm of freedom has instead frequently resulted in social exclusion and the grinding necessity of poverty for those expelled from the labour market, while returning precious little to those remaining at work.

The resolution of this situation can only come from an increase in the standard of living of the working class or from the sharing of the available work and its consequent income. The increasing globalisation of the world economy forestalls the first solution. While it may be in the interests of the capitalist system viewed collectively to raise incomes and so increase demand in step with increases in productivity, it is in the interest of no single firm, unprotected from international competition, to accede unilaterally to increased wage demands. In the post-war era, union organisation and social democratic government in the industrialised nations were able to force on the system a steady increase in both the private and social wage. In the present era, the balance of class forces has tipped in favour of international capital. The international market and the search for "competitiveness" guarantees strong resistance to the raising of wages and social benefits. Indeed, the most that can be hoped for in the short run is to forestall a "race to the bottom" in the standard of living in

---

[5] Bluestone and Rose (1997) provide an excellent review of these issues for the United States. For a discussion of the complicated relationship between wages and productivity growth, as well as on work hours and the unemployment rate, see Gordon (1997: 144–171).

the several Western economies stemming from increasing competition for international capital investment.

Since we cannot hope for a substantial increase in working class standards of consumption, this situation can be rescued through the creation of increased leisure for working people. This can only be achieved through the redistribution of the available leisure away from those who have involuntarily hoarded it, the long-term unemployed. Of course, this implies sharing the available work.

The third reason why unemployment will continue to be a problem is the passing of the historic opportunity for balanced growth. In the case of auto-centric development (Amin, 1972), the initial industrial sector generates domestic demand. This growing demand inaugurates the mass production of consumer goods. The consumer goods industries reciprocally generate demand for the capital goods sector and further consumer goods production. A virtuous circle of continued growth ensues which is not fundamentally dependent on participation in world markets. The further integration of the international marketplace, however, may have made auto-centric development obsolete.

This obsolescence arises from two sources. The first is that international competition places an upper limit on wage growth. This limits the rate at which prosperity in a leading sector can be spread to other sectors through the emergence of mass consumption. Secondly, participation in the international economy increasingly demands the opening of domestic markets to international foreign competition. This means that much of the demand generated by employment in the export sector is in turn directed overseas. This seems to be at least partially the case for Ireland, where foreign investment in general has not substantially increased domestic investment or developed backward or forward linkages. But it is precisely this kind of local economic integration which is increasingly obsolete in the global economy.

Ireland's recent experience as the "Celtic Tiger" only serves to highlight the problem. Ireland has experienced high rates of growth in a few sectors but has been unable to extend this development across the bulk of the economy. As a result, the unemployment rate has remained high in the face of record growth.

CREATIVE SOLUTIONS TO MASS UNEMPLOYMENT

Mass unemployment means that a significant portion of the population is not being allowed to fully participate in society. This is an affront to both human dignity and the common good, and cannot be tolerated by any society that considers itself civilised. Furthermore, many social and individual needs are not being fulfilled that could be if the unemployed were provided with the opportunity to contribute to society. Yet, under capitalist rules, employment is based on fulfilling needs which can be met profitably. Meeting these other needs must come through the government sector or through the social economy — household and volunteer production. Currently, only paid employment is considered an important form of social participation, in that it is the only one which is extensively validated and rewarded by society. What is necessary is to expand the forms of useful social participation, thus allowing unmet needs to be fulfilled, and allowing expanded social participation. Social participation is an essential part of citizenship. It is a good in and of itself, and not just because it might contribute to output. All means must be used to maximise it.

Irish Times columnist John Waters tells a fable of a neighbourhood with two unemployed men and a wall to be built. The first man is hired to build the wall. After working long hours, his income is taxed to provide welfare payments to the second man who remains idle. Not only has the second man been socially excluded, but the seeds of a bitter division have been sown in the community. The solution is simple: divide the available work between the two men.

At a societal level this can be pursued quite simply by shortening the working week. It is often forgotten that a shorter working week has been a common way of coping with increased productivity in the past. It was the primary demand of many of the great labour movements of the nineteenth and early twentieth centuries. Later in the twentieth century, it expressed itself in the demand for a family wage, freeing all but one of the family members from the labour market. Continuing productivity growth eventually places the hours of work on the social agenda again. The penalty for not taking up this question will be continued high levels of unemployment and social exclusion.

Much of the service work of maintaining the social and community infrastructure cannot be provided on the private market. This social economy or "civil sector" (Rifkin, 1994) runs the gamut from social services to health care, education, research, the arts, religion and public advocacy. A pool of labour unutilised by the private market is an invaluable resource in addressing these kinds of community needs. This is partially recognised in the various existing community work training schemes. It would be important not to see such jobs as "make work", but rather as a career, providing an important and necessary service to the community.

The problem of uneven development of the national economy, in the context of an increasingly global world, forces us to recognise that even with our best efforts not all of the labour in society will be effectively allocated. Jobs exposed to the vagaries of the international market may be especially insecure. It is thus necessary to make provisions for those members of society who are, for shorter or longer periods, out of work. If we come to see work as solidaristically allocated among the citizenry, the social stigma must be lifted from those who are out of work. The best way of accomplishing this is to vest a right to income in all citizens. With everyone entitled to a minimum income, the invidious distinction between the dole recipient and the ordinary citizen is at least partially lifted. CORI has developed a detailed proposal laying out how such a guaranteed income might be implemented (Reynolds and Healy, 1995; 1996; CORI, 1997; Clark and Healy, 1997).

These changes cannot be instituted merely through economic policy or through the market mechanism. A change in attitudes towards income, work and the value of non-market contributions to society must be undertaken. These changes in attitudes are not as dramatic as one might expect, for in most countries it is merely the asserting of values which exist in those countries' religious and moral traditions and values which have been eroded by the "market values" of greed and self-interest. It will not be easy, but it is not impossible. "Our problem," John Maynard Keynes wrote, "is to work out a social organisation which shall be as efficient as possible without offending our notions of a satisfactory way of life" (1963: 321).

REFERENCES

Amin, S. (1972), "Accumulation and Development. A Theoretical Model", *Review of African Political Economy*, No. 1.

Bluestone, B. and S. Rose (1997), "Overworked and Underemployed: Unraveling an Economic Enigma", *The American Prospect*, No. 31, March–April, pp. 58–69.

Bowles, S. and R. Edwards (1985), *Understanding Capitalism*, New York: Harper and Row.

Bowles, S., D.M. Gordon and T.E. Weisskopf (1990), *After the Wasteland*, Armonk, NY: M.E. Sharpe.

Brenner, M.H. (1987), "Economic Change, Alcohol Consumption and Heart Disease Mortality in Nine Industrial Countries", *Social Science and Medicine*, Vol. 25, pp. 119–32.

Bryan, D. (1995), *The Chase across the Globe: International Accumulation and the Contradictions for Nation States*, Boulder: Westview.

Clark, C.M.A. (1998), "Unemployment in Ireland: A Post-Keynesian Perspective" in C.M.A. Clark and C. Kavanagh (ed.), *Unemployment in Ireland*, Aldershot, UK: Avebury Publishing Limited.

Clark, C. M. A. and C. Kavanagh (1996), "Basic Income, Inequality, and Unemployment: Rethinking the Linkages Between Work and Welfare" *Journal of Economic Issues*, Vol. 30, June, pp. 399–406.

Clark, C.M.A. and J. Healy (1997), *Pathways to a Basic Income*, Dublin: Conference of Religious of Ireland.

CORI, (1997), *Planning for Progress: Tackling Poverty, Unemployment and Exclusion*, Dublin: Conference of Religious of Ireland.

Department of Enterprise and Employment (1996), *Growing and Sharing Our Employment*, Dublin: Stationery Office.

Duffy, D., J. Fitz Gerald, I. Kearney and F. Shortall (1997), *Medium-Term Review: 1997–2003*, Dublin: The Economic and Social Research Institute.

Gordon, D. (1997), *Fat and Mean: The Corporate Squeeze of Working Americans and the Myth of Managerial "Downsizing"*, New York: The Free Press.

Gray, A.W. (1997), *International Perspectives on the Irish Economy*, Dublin: Indecon Economic Consultants.

Kalecki, M. (1969), *Theory of Economic Dynamics*, New York: Augustus M. Kelley.

Keynes, J.M. (1936), *The General Theory of Employment Interest and Money*, London: Macmillan.

Keynes, J.M. (1963), *Essays in Persuasion*, New York: Norton.

Kotz, D., T. McDonough, and M. Reich (eds.) (1994), *Social Structures of Accumulation: The Political Economy of Growth and Crises*, Cambridge: Cambridge University Press.

Marglin, S.A. and J.B. Shor (eds.) (1990), *The Golden Age of Capitalism: Reinterpreting the Post-war Experience*, Oxford: Oxford University Press.

O'Connell, P.J. and J.J. Sexton (eds.) (1997), *Labour Market Studies: Ireland*, Luxembourg: Office for Official Publications of the European Communities.

OECD (1994), *Jobs Study*, Paris: OECD.

Reynolds, B. and S. Healy (eds.) (1995), *An Adequate Income Guarantee for All: Desirability, Viability, Impact*, Dublin: Conference of Religious of Ireland.

Reynolds, B. and S. Healy (eds.) (1996), *Progress, Values and Public Policy*, Dublin: Conference of Religious of Ireland.

Rifkin, J. (1994), *The End of Work*, New York: Putman.

Sawyer, M.C. (1985), *The Economics of Michal Kalecki*, Basingstoke: Macmillan.

Schor, J.B. (1992), *The Overworked American: The Unexpected Decline of Leisure*, New York: Basic Books.

Sherman, H. (1991), *The Business Cycle*, Princeton: Princeton University Press.

Tansey, P. (1991), *Making the Irish Labour Market Work*, Dublin: Gill and Macmillan.

Chapter 16

THE STATUS OF CHILDREN AND YOUNG PERSONS: EDUCATIONAL AND RELATED ISSUES

Kathleen Lynch[1]

PERSPECTIVES ON CHILDREN AND CHILDHOOD

The model of childhood which has dominated research to date is that of developmentalism. It is essentially an evolutionary model which supposes that rationality is the mark of adulthood and that childhood is basically an apprenticeship for its development. Adulthood and childhood are presented as binary opposites; being a child is presented as the antithesis of being an adult.

The developmentalist view found elaborate expression in Piaget's work. His conceptual framework dominated thinking on cognition, and granted scientific validity to the claim that children develop in predetermined stages, moving eventually to a stage where they achieve logical competence, which is the mark of adult rationality. Within sociology, socialisation theory borrowed heavily from the developmentalist view. Children were generally defined as passive subjects being socialised in schools and families into predefined social roles (Prout and James, 1990).

Underpinning this dominant discourse on children were a range of assumptions about the status and rights of children. Basically, a "caretaking", protectionist model dominated intellectual thought (Archard, 1993). Within the caretaking perspective, children are

---

[1] I would like to express my thanks to Dympna Devine of the Education Department, and Niamh Hardiman of the Politics Department in UCD for their helpful comments and suggestions on an earlier draft of this paper.

denied the right to self-determination on the grounds of under-developed rationality and lack of autonomy. Children are denied rights to self-determination now, on the grounds that they will only be able to exercise them in adulthood if they are denied them in childhood. This is especially evident in arguments about education. It is assumed that going to school is necessary "for maturation into a rational autonomous human being. Present compulsion is a pre-condition of subsequent choice" (ibid: 55).

Children are defined therefore as a homogenous group generally incapable of exercising rational choice; no allowance is made for dif-ferences in terms of intellectual, emotional, physical or social capac-ity, despite the empirical evidence that children (like adults) vary greatly in these abilities, not only with age, but also with the vagaries of culture and individual experience. Neither is the problematic na-ture of children's subordinate status subjected to critical analysis within the protectionist framework. Universalistic assumptions about children's subordination underpin both theory and research. By failing to engage in a reflexive analysis of its own hierarchical as-sumptions, researchers have therefore contributed to the domination of children through intellectual discourse.

The last ten years, however, have witnessed the rise of a growing body of critical research and theory on children (Alanen, 1988; James and Prout, 1990; Archard, 1993; O'Neill, 1994; Qvortrup, 1994; Butler and Shaw, 1996). Just as feminist analysis has begun to uncover the unspoken word of women, and disability studies has begun to name the world from the perspective of disabled people themselves, so too there is a growing movement in the social sciences which challenges "the politics of mutism" which silenced children's voices in the name of protecting them. The reasons why it has taken the intellectual community so long to listen to children is, Ambert (1986) suggests, no different to the reason why it has taken powerful disciplines so long to listen to women (or, I would add, other marginalised groups). The lowly status of children in society made them a lowly subject of research in the academy. Moreover, children were not, and are not, a mobilised political voice in most societies. There was no social movement by children demanding a place for themselves at the policy table, or challenging established perspectives in the academy.

Set in the light of recent critical work in the field, what this chapter attempts to do is to examine the position of children within a number of our public institutions in Ireland using an equality-oriented perspective. The chapter does not purport to present a "children's view" on such policies and practices, however, as this would require empirical research involving children themselves.[2]

While children are different from adults, difference does not necessitate subordination or lack of respect. The economic dependency, and the smaller stature of young children in particular, can be recognised and accommodated without institutionalising systems of subordination and lack of respect. Granting equality of respect demands changes in the organisational practices of many of our public institutions; most conspicuously, it requires a greater democratisation of schooling for all age groups, and of other health and welfare services that care for children. It also means protecting the individual rights of children within families.

What the chapter also recognises is that equality between children and adults is only part of the equation. We also need to promote equality between children in different social contexts. And if there is to be equality *between* children, this necessitates greater equality between adults. The health, welfare and educational rights of all children can only be fully protected in a society in which every child can exert those rights both as individuals, and in association with adults on whom they are dependent. As long as wealth and power differentials persist, between individuals and between households, both intranationally and internationally, then many children will merely experience a weak liberal, rather than a radical form of equality of opportunity at best (see Baker's paper in this volume for a discussion on these concepts).

THE STATUS OF CHILDREN AND YOUNG PERSONS IN IRELAND

During the Presidential campaign of 1997, Adi Roche made repeated proposals for the setting up of a Children's Commission to examine

---

[2] Anne Lodge and I have been working on taking a children's perspective on equality in education in research being undertaken in UCD. A paper based on this work will be published later this year (see Lynch, forthcoming, 1998).

the many issues that affect children in our society. The proposal pro-
voked little public debate, and was, at times, treated with derision.
The level of public disinterest in the proposal gives some indication
of how children's rights are viewed in our society. There appeared to
be little public concern about the status of children (among voting
adults at least, although the views of children themselves were not
canvassed on the issue); children's rights were not regarded as a high
political priority. The level of public indifference to issues relating to
children's rights is not a temporary phenomenon. It is reflected in
numerous public institutions and systems.

This chapter will address two separate but interrelated equality
issues in relation to children in our society. First, it will briefly review
the status of children vis-à-vis adults, and the extent to which children are accorded equality of respect with adults in our key public
institutions and systems. Second, it will examine the question of inequality between children themselves. It will focus especially on the
inequalities of opportunity *between* children from different social
class backgrounds in the field of education.

A central claim of the chapter is that the inalienable rights which
are given to the family *qua* institution in the Constitution (Article 41),
and to parents (Article 42), has created a situation in which children's
rights have been subordinated to those of the family and parents, at
times of conflict. Moreover, the constitutional protection of the family has exonerated the State from intervening at times to protect children's welfare within families, and to guarantee them equality of
opportunity in education. Within the field of education, the State is
only obliged to ensure that "children receive *minimum* education,
moral, intellectual and social" (Article 42.3 (2), *my emphasis*). At best,
our treatment of children is welfarist and patronising; at worst, it is
indifferent, condescending and lacking in respect.

The Constitution and the Status of Children

The constitutional status of children is of paramount importance in
terms of understanding their position within the family, and within
other public institutions such as schools, where they spend a very

large part of their early working[3] lives. Articles 41 and 42 of the Irish Constitution of 1937 pertain to the family and education respectively and are the Articles with the most direct bearing on the lives of children. In line with other policy initiatives in the post-Independence years, these articles were strongly influenced by Roman Catholic social teaching, in particular by the principle of subsidiarity (Duncan, 1987). The role of the State in relation to the family and children was defined in minimalist terms; the State's right to intervene in the family was largely confined to when there were "compelling reasons" for intervention based on the welfare needs of the child (Duncan, 1996: 617). The family *qua* family was duly accorded a range of rights in relation to children which are very strong indeed. Article 41.1 (1) endorses the view that the family is "the natural primary and fundamental unit of Society, and a moral institution possessing inalienable and imprescriptible rights, antecedent and superior to all positive law". Article 42.1 defines the family as the "primary and natural educator of the child" and guarantees that the State will "respect the inalienable right and duty of parents to provide, according to their means, for the religious and moral, intellectual, physical and social education of their children".

The authority granted to parents over their children cannot be understood simply in terms of Catholic social teaching, however. The Constitution also reflected deeply held traditional values about the subordinate status of children. In their review of ethnographic research on children in rural Ireland, Curtin and Varley noted that "Children are not wanted as an end in themselves, but always as a means of providing generational continuity on the farm, of supplying farm labour, or of acting as a hedge against old age" (1984: 42). Moreover, silence and passivity were highly valued qualities in young farm children (ibid: 43).

---

[3] I use the term "working" here deliberately to denote the fact that schooling is work for children. It involves application, effort and engagement that is no different in substance to what is required of adults at work. The principal differences between children's school work and adults' work is that children do not get paid for theirs!

The Family in the Constitution

The principle of "family autonomy" which is endorsed in the Irish Constitution has had a number of important implications for children. The granting of autonomy to the family as a social institution has meant that the most vulnerable members of the family household (most especially children, but also economically dependent women) can and are open to manipulation, exploitation and even abuse by those who are economically and physically dominant within the family itself. Only in the more extreme cases does the State intervene to protect those who are vulnerable, and then it is required to intervene in as minimal a way as is necessary to protect the child (O'Cinnéide and O'Daly, 1980). The empirical evidence available confirms that the abuse of children and women, by men especially, has been taking place over a long time, although much of this abuse has only been publicly recognised and addressed in the last 10 years (McKeown and Gilligan, 1991; Gilligan, 1992–93; Women's Aid, 1995a; 1995b). One of the indirect effects of granting high autonomy to the family as a social institution is that it has resulted in a *"laissez faire"* approach to the enactment of legislation and policies in relation to the protection of children in families until very recent times. It is truly remarkable that the Child Care Act (1991) was the first piece of child welfare legislation enacted since the foundation of the State. Yet other European jurisdictions including England and Wales, Finland, France and Germany, each introduced a number of legislative provisions to protect children over the same period (Gilligan, 1992–93: 367).

A second question which arises in relation to the status of children under the Constitution is the protection of children's interests. While children's interests are taken into account in welfare cases in Ireland, it is generally assumed that parents know what is in the child's best interests and will act on these. The logic of this thinking is that parents' rights over children derive from their natural instinct to act always in the child's best interest. If this logic were followed, of course, it would mean that in the case of conflict, the interests of the child would prevail. This is not the case in Ireland, however, or indeed in other jurisdictions. "There is still a sense in which the laws in most jurisdictions confer property interests on parents in respect of their children" (Duncan, 1996: 622). There is a very real sense, therefore, in which children in Ireland, and in many other jurisdictions, are not accorded equality of respect with adults.

This is not to suggest that children in Ireland do not have rights which are protected under the Constitution; they have all the relevant personal rights enjoyed by adults under Article 40. However, because there is no specific clause in the Constitution which guarantees the rights of children, when there is a conflict of interest between parent and/or family rights, and the individual rights of particular children, the former are most likely to prevail. Both the *Report of the Constitution Review Group* (1996), and the *Report on the Kilkenny Incest Investigation* (1993), recommended that a specific and overt declaration of the rights of children be inserted into the Constitution. The *Report of the Constitution Review Group* (1996: 337) also recommended that the Constitution contain "an express requirement that in all actions concerning children, whether by legislative, judicial or administrative authorities, the best interests of the child shall be the paramount consideration".

Education and the Constitution

Not alone are the parents defined as the primary and natural educators of the child in Ireland, the State is only obliged to ensure that "children receive *minimum* education, moral, intellectual and social" (Article 42.3 (2), *my emphasis*).[4] In addition, the State is required to

> provide for free primary education and [shall] endeavour to supplement and give reasonable aid to private and corporate educational initiative, and, where the public good requires it, provide other educational facilities or institutions with due regard, however, for the rights of parents . . . (Article 42.4).

The freedom given to parents in relation to the education of their children would appear to be a desirable provision in certain respects. In theory, it allows parents great choice in the education of their children. The reality is, however, that choice in education is realistically only open to those with the means to exercise choice. Parents are constrained in their choices, most especially by limited means,

---

[4] Interestingly, and regrettably, there is no obligation on the State to ensure that child receive any physical education.

but also by the practical exigencies of time, geographical location and the availability of accessible schools and services. One of the indirect outcomes of granting autonomy to people in a situation where little choice exists is that they must "choose" what is currently available. Because the Catholic Church controls well over 90 per cent of the primary and second-level schools within the State, this effectively means that most people have no choice but to send their children to Catholic schools, especially at primary level.[5]

Another indirect effect of "free choice" in a strongly stratified and unequal society like ours (regardless of how desirable the principle of choice may be in its own right), is that only those in positions of relative privilege can exercise choice. This has become very evident in Britain, especially in the post-Thatcher era; real choices in schools are only open to those with the means to choose. Although this has been the situation in Ireland for a long period of time, it has never been made problematic. Many middle class, and better-off working class families can and do choose to send their children to schools outside their own areas; they have access to transport and/or financial resources which allow this. For others, there is no real choice. Thus, there is quite a strong degree of class stratification *across* schools, especially in larger towns and cities where choice is possible. Children in schools serving low-income communities are especially disadvantaged in such a system, as they have to attend the schools which have the least capacity for fund-raising but the greatest need.

---

[5] It would be wrong to assume, however, that there is a simple causal relationship between ownership of schools and influence on children. The reality of life in schools is such that no simple causal relationship can be assumed between administrative control and influence, especially in highly mobile, literate and culturally diverse societies. The curricula, the examination systems and much of the organisation of learning is under the control of the State and its agents, directly or indirectly. In this sense, young people are subjected to a range of ideological influences in schools other than the influence of the Churches (Drudy and Lynch, 1993). Indeed the hidden curriculum of school life would suggest that the dominant norm in second-level schools is that of competitive individualism (Lynch, 1989) and there is scant evidence of strong religiosity among young people in Catholic-run schools at the present time (McDonnell, 1995). There are a whole confluence of influences determining the values of young people in our society, including the media, cultural institutions such as music, and of course the peer group.

The fact that the Constitution: (a) grants great autonomy to parents in relation to the education of their children; (b) combines this with a minimalist approach to education provision (primary education only); and (c) does not guarantee any independent *rights* to children to free education; means that children and young people are subject to the wishes and interests of their parents in matters of education. Parental resources, as well as attitudes to education, can and do determine the type and nature of education to which young people have access. The lack of any State-guaranteed right to education, beyond the compulsory age, means that the economic needs of the family *qua* family, can and do take precedence over the educational needs of any given individual. While parents generally do not want their young daughters or sons to leave school early, the economic realities often force that decision in the absence of viable alternatives (Lynch and O'Riordan, 1996). Proof that this happens in low-income working class families is evident from the school-leaver surveys. These show that, while over 90 per cent of students from upper socio-economic groups reach Leaving Certificate level, only a little over half (53 per cent) of the children from unskilled manual backgrounds reach this stage (Technical Working Group Report, 1995: Table 8.2).

Legislation and Children

Recent legislative provisions and proposals indicate that there is no great advance towards a "rights" perspective in relation to children at the public policy level. Apart from the Education (No. 2) Bill (1997) (which we will discuss below), the two most recent pieces of legislation directly concerned with children are the Child Care Act (1991) and the Children Bill[6] (1997). These are concerned respectively with children in care, and with children involved in custody disputes. The Child Care Act (1991, Section 18 (1) (b)) does grant children negatively defined rights, such as the right to protection from abuse and other adversity "seriously threatening to the child's health, development or welfare". Moreover, both the Children Bill (1997, Part IV) and the Child Care Act (1991, Section 3 (2)) also give some protection

---

[6] This Bill was passed by both houses of the Oireachtas at the time of writing (January, 1998), although it was not yet enacted.

to the interests of children in custody disputes, and in issues of care. The Children Bill, for example, obliges the court to "take into account the child's wishes" in custody disputes "as it thinks appropriate and practicable, having regard to the age and understanding of the child, in the matter" (Part IV, Section 11 (25)). A similar provision exists in the Child Care Act, Section 3 (2) (b) (ii). These provisions, while most welcome, are far from being statements protecting children's rights. Neither piece of legislation addresses the status of children generally in our society.

The minimal advances in the legislative sphere noted here are not accompanied by public debate about the empowerment of children. A paternalistic, caretaking ideology underpins the recent legislative proposals and provisions, and these have not been publicly contested in any systematic manner. The discourse *about* children has not changed, and there is very little public discourse *with* children.

INEQUALITIES BETWEEN CHILDREN

Policy Issues: Children and the Risk of Poverty

Economic indicators show that Ireland is a relatively wealthy country (Atkinson et al., 1995). Yet, despite this, a very sizeable minority of people, especially of children, live in poverty (Callan et al., 1996). While this is as incredible as it is unacceptable, it indicates clearly how it is impossible to separate the debate about equality for children from debates about equality between adults. Children's dependent economic status means that their welfare is tied to that of their adult parents. Inequalities between adults impinge directly on children, no matter how questionable that dependency is, especially for older children and young people.

The 1994 *Living In Ireland* Survey by the ESRI found children[7] to be at a higher risk of poverty than adults at each of the relevant poverty lines. While 18 per cent of adults were at risk of being below the 50 per cent poverty line[8] in 1994, 29 per cent of children were living

---

[7] A child is defined in the study as a person under 18 years of age in the Children Bill (1997) and in the Child Care Act (1991).

[8] This means living on 50 per cent or less of the income of the average person. Average income is measured in terms of average disposable income (Callan et al., 1996: 67–8).

at this level. Almost 8 per cent of children were actually at risk of living on less than 40 per cent of the average income. This pattern is not new, although the gap between children and adults has widened greatly over the 23 years from 1973 to 1994. In 1973, just 16 per cent of children were at risk of being below the 50 per cent poverty line; by 1994 the proportion had nearly doubled to 29 per cent. The comparable risk for adults only increased slightly, from 15 per cent to 18 per cent between 1973 and 1994 (Callan et al., 1996: 88–94). When poverty is measured in terms of deprivation indicators, rather than income lines, there is evidence from the ESRI study that the depth of poverty (how far below the average people live) has been reduced, for adults at least, between 1987 and 1994. It is not possible to determine from the data presented, however, whether or not there was an improvement in the situation of children over that time.[9]

While almost 30 per cent of Irish children have a high risk of living in poverty, the risk is not evenly spread; it is especially acute among the unemployed, and where there is a lone parent (in practice, mostly women). Children in larger families (those with more than four children) are also at greater risk.

The ESRI study did not specifically include Traveller children living in non-permanent accommodation. People living in refuges and those who are homeless were also excluded (Callan et al.: 34). While one can understand the logistical reasons for this, it does mean that the experiences of those children who are often most vulnerable and poor in our society are not documented in the study. As numerous reports over the years have noted, Traveller children are at a high risk of living in extreme poverty (Report of the Task Force, 1995). Moreover, their poverty is exacerbated by high levels of discrimination, which exaggerate the effects of poverty itself. Children of other homeless families are also very vulnerable. If the position of all of these children was documented, and if the levels of marginalisation, powerlessness, domination and exploitation which children can experience were assessed, then the position of a significant minority of Irish children would be even worse than it appears by

---

[9] In this, as in most poverty studies, children are not studied separately from their parents. This is unacceptable, especially if one wishes to understand fully the position of children. It means that we lack basic data on children's lives (Qvortrup, 1994).

simply using income measures of poverty (see Lynch, 1997 for a discussion of this issue).

While we now have extensive data documenting the extent of
poverty in our society, we do not appear to have the political will to
eliminate poverty. Poverty management, rather than poverty elimination, seems to be the guiding principle. Despite the availability of
extensive evidence, for example, that certain policies are more effective at eliminating poverty than others, governments persistently fail
to base policies on these (see Sara Cantillon's paper in this volume on
this point). The December 1997 Budget is a particular case in point.
Policies were openly enacted (and vehemently defended) in that
Budget which would benefit the better-off in society to a disproportionate degree — most notably the 50 per cent reduction in capital
gains tax, the reduction in corporation profit tax, and the lowering of
the top tax rate for high earners — while only minor concessions
were made to the most vulnerable, including children. This is a
deeply disturbing development politically, as it implies a growing
detachment and indifference to those who are most vulnerable in our
society. It represents a move away from principles of solidarity
within and between generations and social groups, and a victory for
the principles of possessive individualism.

The way in which budgetary allocations are made, however, does
give a clear indication of how wealth and income differentials are
perpetuated in our society. Those who are central to the executive
and legislative decision-making machinery of the State, and those
who have the corporate and/or legal or collective power to influence
the elected and appointed State Managers (namely the government
of the day and the civil servants) are strategically located to direct the
course of major public decisions about investment, production, taxation, employment, interest rates and wages, even though their political constituency may be relatively small. Major structural inequalities
are not accidental, therefore; neither are they the outcome of some
hidden market forces which are outside public control (Fischer, Hout
et al., 1996). The so-called free market does not operate according to
some hidden rules of economic rationality. The market is embedded
in a set of laws, policies and practices which are extensively regu-
lated and managed by the State. Major structural inequalities between groups are the outcome of legal, financial and strategic

decisions taken over many years. Such inequalities are not inevitable; they can be reversed by different policies and legislative provisions.

Subsidiarity, Voluntary Schools, Private Markets and the Perpetuation of Inequality between Children

The Implications of Subsidiarity

There is a very real sense in which the Constitutional principle of subsidiarity underwrites inequalities of various kinds, most especially by the way in which it allows essential services to be offered in the private market, often making it impossible for those without sufficient means to access them and use them on equal terms with others. Education is one sphere where the voluntarism emanating from the principle of subsidiarity is especially problematic.

It is widely known that there are serious inequalities in the quality of educational services available to different children within the State, especially in terms of access to sports and other extracurricular facilities (Lynch, 1989), but also in terms of school buildings and extra-educational supports such as grinds and education-related resources (Lynch and O'Riordan, 1996; Lynch and Lodge, 1997). Inequalities in the quality of the education service provided are effectively permitted by Article 42, which enshrines the principle of subsidiarity in terms of State aid for private and corporate educational institutions. While this principle, in itself, does not promote inequality, what it does is to exonerate the State from having the defining responsibility for the quality of the educational service offered to all classes of students. The State is only required to act "when the public good requires it".

Only a small proportion of pupils attend publicly controlled school in Ireland. All primary (national) schools are privately owned but publicly funded. Some 60 per cent of second-level schools, namely "voluntary" secondary schools, are also private institutions. Thus the education services attended by most Irish children are mostly privately administered, while relying heavily on State funding for both current and capital expenditure.

What happens in effect with education is that the widely agreed principle of equality of educational opportunity for all (and there have been numerous statements by various Ministers of Education since the late 1960s declaring their support for greater equality in education) are neither constitutionally nor legislatively grounded. There is no compunction on successive governments, from a constitutional point of view, to ensure that there is equality of provision in the educational service and supports offered to all students.

One of the indirect outcomes of the ongoing "symbiotic" relationship between Church and State in education[10] is that voluntary contributions play an increasingly important role in influencing the kind of educational services and facilities (beyond the common core) which are available in many schools. A survey by the ASTI (1996) of 365 secondary schools in 1996 found that 80 per cent of these were involved in fund-raising. Moreover, the clear majority of both parents' and teachers in the schools were involved in contributing in some way to the process. Where parental incomes are such that they can sustain a consistent level of voluntary contributions, the quality of the education service in schools can be improved accordingly, and this is true at both primary and secondary level. Where parents are poor and cannot sustain significant contributions, the quality of the service is adversely affected. Although it is clear that parents' "voluntary contributions" are a relatively small element in the funding of schools, they are a significant source of income, if both the direct and indirect (such as fund-raising events for new buildings) contributions are counted. Moreover, State support for private fee-paying schools in the secondary sector, which is effectively endorsed in the Constitution in the subsidiarity principle, ensures that inequalities in provision arising from differential access to resources in particular communities are compounded by inequalities arising from differentials in the resources of individual families.

Although the voluntarism which underpins some of the funding in Irish education is not intended to operate as a mechanism for the perpetuation of inequalities between schools, one of its unintended consequences is the development of inequalities in the quality of the

---

[10] This is a relationship which is mutually beneficial in several respects. The Churches have provided the original premises and some small proportion of ongoing expenditure in return for the control of "ethos"; the State benefits not only from the Churches' investment and free labour (up to now) but also from the legitimating role which the Churches bring to the entire educational process. The State controls curricula to a large degree, however, and lays down regulations in relation to the appointment of teachers (see Drudy and Lynch, 1993: 73–89 for further discussion of this point).

educational environments in which students are educated. At one end of the continuum stand the fee-paying schools where fees are often more than 20 times the modal (typical) voluntary contribution in most other secondary schools (reported as being between £25 and £50 in 264 of the schools surveyed by the ASTI in 1996). A stage below these stand those free scheme secondary schools which can raise substantial moneys through voluntary contributions and fund-raising, although these are in the minority. While the community/comprehensive and vocational sectors receive grant aid which compensates them for the fee/voluntary contribution element in secondary school income, they cannot solicit voluntary contributions. There is public provision for basic facilities in these schools, but it is far from adequate in many cases. Schools that are free to raise funds through fees and voluntary subscriptions, and that service a clientele who can contribute to these, are clearly advantaged in this situation. Schools that cannot raise voluntary contributions locally, on the other hand, are distinctly disadvantaged.[11] The indirect effect of the subsidiarity principle in education, and the voluntarism flowing from it, is the development of significant difference in the quality and range of resources and facilities across schools (Lynch and Lodge, 1997). Schools serving low-income working class or small farm communities are increasingly disadvantaged, as they simply cannot compete in the "voluntary market" for funds.

While the merits of the principle of subsidiarity are self-evident in a pluralist society, whether it should be the defining constitutional principle governing the provision of such basic services as education (and indeed health) is most questionable. We are in the midst of what can truly be called a "knowledge revolution", as historically important as the industrial revolution. The Irish economy itself is heavily dependent on such knowledge-based industries, and the central role which education can play in our economic development is recognised in a number of policy documents in recent years (White Paper on Education, 1995; White Paper on Science, Technology and Innovation, 1996). Education is not an optional extra in such a society. It is both a fundamental individual right and a public necessity.

---

[11] The inequalities arising from differences in local capacity to pay voluntary contributions and engage in fund-raising also applies at primary level.

Private Markets in Education

What is compounding the differences between schools is the ongoing development of a parallel system of private education which is being funded outside public institutions by parents and students themselves. The most conspicuous example of this parallel system of private education are the so-called "grind schools", the primary purpose of which is to offer an educational advantage to those who can pay for the service. These private institutions are, however, but one element in the private education market. It is not unreasonable to suggest (although it has not been systematically researched) that there are thousands of second-level students who also pay for private tuition (grinds) on a one-to-one basis. In addition, there is also a growing private extracurricular education market in Ireland in music, art, elocution, drama, certain sports, summer camps, etc., all of which are offered outside of school for those who can afford to pay.

What the development of private markets in education indicates is that those with access to higher incomes have the resources to subvert attempts by the State to equalise opportunities in the publicly controlled sector of education. As long as people own and control significantly different levels of wealth and income, then it is almost inevitable that they will be advantaged in education. They have the freedom to use their excess resources to buy extra educational services on the market as required. The under-resourcing of public education greatly exaggerates the impact of the private market, not least because more and more expenditure is required by any given individual to make good the deficit in the publicly controlled sectors of education.

THE EDUCATION (NO. 2) BILL (1997): THE STATUS OF STUDENTS AND OTHER EQUALITY ISSUES

The Rights of Students

Children are accorded some consultative rights in schools in the recent Education Bill (No. 2) 1997. This is a welcome development. Section 27 (1, 2) of the Bill gives students of all ages certain rights to information about school activities, and requires the Board of Management to "facilitate the involvement of the students in the operation of the school having regard to the age and experience of the students". The Board is also obliged, in the case of second-level schools only, to "encourage the establishment by students of a student council and give all reasonable assistance to (a) students who wish to set up a council, and (b) student councils when they have been established" (Section 27 (3)). In addition, Section 23 (2) (d) obliges all school principals to consult with students "to the extent appropriate to their age and experience" in setting and monitoring school objectives.

The fact that students' democratic rights are set out on conditional terms, and that the board of management or the principal can determine when students are of an age, or of sufficient experience to be consulted, has the potential to weaken the impact of these provisions considerably. The provision in Section 27 (5) which states that: "The rules for the establishment of a student council shall be drawn up by the board and such rules *may* provide for the election of members and the dissolution of a student council" (*my emphasis*) seems to be very undemocratic, and to effectively enable the School Board to appoint a student council of their own choosing, superseding the wishes of the students if they so desire. There is, regrettably, no provision for student councils at the primary level.

The rights which are granted to students in terms of appeals against teachers or staff are also very limited. The relevant section of the Bill (28) does not require the Minister or the school authorities to put grievance procedures in place; it merely allows for it to happen. Even then it only applies to those of 18 years and over. As most students are in the final year of second-level education at this age, or have left school, this is a rather empty provision.

The Education Bill also gives other parties in education far more rights and control over schools, and education generally, than it gives to students. As it stands, the Bill will copper-fasten the interests of a given set of corporate bodies in education at a given point in time, without any recognition of the fact that the partners in education may change or should change. The Bill is replete with references to the requirement that various decision-making authorities must consult with patrons, national associations of parents, recognised teacher unions, and school management organisations. These provisions throw into sharp relief the absence of other voices, most notably those of students, but also those of community interests, be these community groups, women's representative bodies, the unemployed, disabled people, older people, etc.

The Treatment of Inequality and Disadvantage in the Education (No. 2) Bill (1997)

The Education Bill makes a number of references to various forms of disadvantage, and to equality issues. Section 15 (2) (g) requires the School Board "within the resources provided to the school" to "make reasonable provision and accommodation for students with special educational needs"[12]. Section 15 (2) (d) requires the Board to publish its policy "concerning admission to and participation in the school and ensure that as regards that policy principles of equality . . . are respected". Section 32 deals specifically with educational disadvantage. This section states that:

> The Minister *may* by order, following consultation with patrons, national associations of parents, recognised school management organisations, recognised trade unions and staff associations representing teachers and such other persons as the Minister considers appropriate, establish and maintain a committee to advise him or her on policies and strategies to be adopted to identify and to correct impediments to education arising from social and economic disadvantage which prevent students from deriving appropriate benefit from education in schools (Section 32 (1), *my emphasis*).

Finally, the National Council for Curriculum and Assessment (NCCA), in carrying out its functions, is to "have regard to the desirability of achieving equality of access to and participation in education" (Section 40 (3) (b)).

It is clear from the above that the Education Bill is not designed to promote equality in education, in any substantive sense, between advantaged and disadvantaged students. Calling on school boards and the NCCA to "respect" or "have regard to" equality principles is welcome. But it begs the question as to which equality principle they will adopt. If they adopt a basic, or even a liberal approach to equality, then nothing will change in terms of the relative advantage of particular students (see John Baker's chapter in this volume on this). Moreover, many educational inequalities occur *between* schools, and between students across different schools. These cannot be

---

[12] Special educational need is defined in Part 1 (2) as applying to students with mental and physical disability and exceptionally able students.

addressed by a provision which is only addressed to the Board of Management of a single school, or even by the NCCA, whose sole remit is curriculum and assessment.

The provision for students with physical and learning disabilities is made conditional on having resources available; it does not guarantee extra moneys for them, hence it is difficult to see how it could promote equality. Any school is free to say it lacks resources, if it decides to prioritise out special-needs students in the first place.

The Bill gives the Minister permission to set up a committee to examine and correct disadvantage, but this is not mandatory; neither is there any guarantee that funds will be made available to the Committee to achieve its goals. This contrasts with the position taken in relation to the body which is to be set up to plan and research the teaching of Irish (a welcome development in its own right). Section 31 (4) of the Act specifies that the Minister *shall* set up a body for this purpose. She or he may use part of the annual budget to grant aid the latter. No provision is made for funding the committee on disadvantage, should it be set up. (Quite amazingly also, there is no requirement in the Bill for the Minister to fund research on education. Research is only mentioned in two places: where it is stated to be one of the functions of inspectors (Section, 13 (3) (c)), and where it is stated to be one of the functions of the body overseeing the teaching of Irish. Hopefully this will change before the Bill is enacted, otherwise there will be no requirement on the Minister to fund broad-based independent research on education, which is needed for policy planning on an on-going basis).

What is most striking about this Bill in relation to equality is that the Minister for Education has no particular role in relation to the promotion of equality in education generally. Responsibility for promoting equality, limited though it may be, has been left with relatively powerless (and relatively penniless) authorities — notably, Boards of Management in individual schools. As the resources required to promote equality of education for disadvantaged groups are considerable — be these people who are socio-economically disadvantaged, people with disabilities, older students, or ethnic minorities such as Travellers — this means that the Bill is likely to have very little impact on the promotion of greater equality in education.

Indeed, the Bill makes no reference at all to the promotion of gender equality or equality for Travellers. While it can be assumed that these are covered under general provisions, such as those applying to Boards of Management or the NCCA, it is notable that they are not named as target groups under any of the provisions of the Bill.

The failure to include a strong equality provision in the Education Bill, which would guarantee all children equality of access to, participation in, or benefit from, education, shows that the issue of equality *between* different children is not being taken seriously. Hopefully, the Bill will be changed before it is enacted to take account of these issues; otherwise a great opportunity to promote equality in education through legislative reform will be missed.

OTHER POLICIES IN EDUCATION: THE PERSISTENCE OF INEQUALITY BETWEEN CHILDREN

Ireland is rightly proud of its overall educational achievements over the last 30 years. There have been very significant increases in overall retention up to Leaving Certificate level. Over 80 per cent of the age cohort complete second-level education, with approximately 40 per cent transferring to higher education. Aggregate data conceal very significant differences in patterns of achievement across social groups, however. While the overall level of education in the population has risen, social-class relativities in terms of achievement, especially beyond the non-compulsory level, have remained remarkably stable over time.

Literacy Issues

There are now numerous Irish studies documenting the extent of social-class and socio-economically related inequality in education (Clancy, 1988, 1995; O'Neill, 1992; Callan, Nolan and Whelan, 1994; Kellaghan et al., 1995) although there are far fewer studies examining the causes of inequality (Lynch and O'Riordan, 1996). One of the more recent studies which shows quite clearly the ways in which inequality is persisting is the OECD study of literacy (Morgan, Hickey, Kellaghan et al., 1997). Although it has received relatively little public attention, this report is a major indictment of our education system in many respects. The report shows that 17 per cent of the 16–25 age group are operating at the minimum level of literacy (ibid.: Table 3.5, p. 31). In the numeracy area, the situation is no better, with 18 per cent operating at the lowest level (ibid.: Table 3.9, p.

36). Moreover, our young people are significantly less literate than those in comparator countries, with the exception of Poland. The proportion of 16 to 25-year-olds in Ireland who are functioning at the lowest literacy (17 per cent) level is more than five times higher than that in Sweden (3 per cent), more than three times that in Germany (5 per cent), and approximately twice than in Switzerland (it varies in the two main regions from 9 to 7 per cent) (ibid.: Table 4.4, p. 48). Given the relative cultural and linguistic homogeneity of our society, this must be a matter of grave concern.

Literacy and other educational differences are not evenly spread across the population, however. Low-income working class groups are disproportionately represented among those who have the lowest literacy levels (ibid.: Table 4.6, p. 50). One longitudinal study of sixth-class primary school pupils in inner-city schools found that 25 per cent of the pupils were judged by teachers as being unlikely to be able to cope with the reading demands of post-primary schooling (Archer and O'Flaherty, 1986). This is almost twice the national average for reading difficulty at this age, which has been estimated at between 12.5 and 16 per cent (Morgan and Martin, 1994).

Early Drop-out, Retention Rates and Attainment Levels

Literacy levels are one measure of differences in educational opportunities. Early drop-out and lower rates of educational attainment are also indicators of the level of inequality in education. There is clear evidence that early school-leaving is disproportionately high among the low-income working class groups (NESC, 1993; European Social Fund, 1996). Research on public examinations at second level gives even clearer indications of the social class differences in educational retention rates and attainment. Analysis of school-leaver surveys show that, while over 90 per cent of students from upper socio-economic groups reach the Leaving Certificate level, only a little over half (53 per cent) of the children of unskilled backgrounds reach this stage. Moreover, of those who stay on to complete the Leaving Certificate, just 29 per cent and 28 per cent of the unskilled and semi-skilled respectively attain at least two Cs in higher level papers, while between 62 per cent and 80 per cent of the four higher socio-economic groups attain these grades (Technical Working Group Report, 1995: Table 8.2).

Despite the increased participation by all social groups in education over the last 30 years, therefore, there are still major differences in both access to and participation within education, based on social class. Clancy's (1995) study, *Access to College: Patterns of Continuity and Change*, shows that while there has been an increase in the rate of participation in higher education by all social groups in the last 12 years, disparities in participation based on social class are still considerable. Thirty-eight per cent of all higher education entrants come from the four highest socio-economic groups, although these only constitute 21 per cent of the relevant population, while just 35 per cent of entrants come from the five lowest socio-economic groups, although these constitute almost 56 per cent of the relevant age cohort. The contrast between participation rates at the upper and lower end of the class continuum is, however, much greater, with 89 per cent of the children of higher professional parents going on to higher education, compared with just 14 per cent of those from unskilled and semi-skilled manual backgrounds (Clancy, 1995: 154–155).

The failure to provide adequate grants and income supports for students from low-income families who stay in school beyond the compulsory age (including adequate maintenance grants for higher education) has been identified as one of the major barriers to equality of participation in higher education in particular (Clancy, 1995; Lynch and O'Riordan, 1996). Moreover, there are no real supports to meet the opportunity costs of staying on in education beyond the compulsory age for second-level students from low income families (ibid.). The push to leave is much greater than the pull to stay, and successive governments have ignored this problem.

While there has been a serious attempt to equalise *access to* education (in the sense of giving people the right to benefit from all levels of education by eliminating fees for second-level and higher education, for example), what has been lacking is a coherent national plan to equalise *participation* rates and *benefits* from education for all social groups. Having equal rights to access, without ensuring equal rights to participation and benefits, guarantees the perpetuation of inequality. Programmes such as "Early Start", "Breaking the Cycle" and "Youthreach" are welcome developments, and such programmes and others[13] do make an important contribution within the resources available to them. However, given the depth of inequality in our society, such programmes alone can do no more than ameliorate the worst effects of inequality for a relatively small group of children and young people. They are too small in scale and lacking in scope to address the root causes of much inequality in education, a good deal of which emanates from the serious economic inequalities which are allowed to persist in our society. Any policy to promote equality in education *between social classes* can only succeed if it is accompanied by economic policies aimed at eliminating the income and wealth differentials which perpetuate educational inequality in the first place.

As long as there are huge income and wealth differentials in our society (and the *Living in Ireland* Survey of 1994 has shown that the number of children and adults living in poverty increased between 1987 and 1994 (Callan et al., 1996)), then it will not be really possible for socially and economically disadvantaged to avail of education services on equal terms with more advantaged groups. While the question of income and wealth differentials is not strictly speaking an educational concern, it is a simple fact that it has a direct bearing on educational outcomes. If there is a serious intent to eliminate social and economic inequalities, as opposed to managing them, then our economic policies must not be such that they offset the positive gains of educational initiatives designed to overcome inequalities. Economic policies also need to be gender-proofed, to take account of the very particular wealth and income differentials which exist between men and women.

Inequality in Education as a Relational Phenomenon

Much of the discussion on educational inequality tends to focus on what are defined as "the problems" of the so-called "disadvantaged". There has been a tendency in educational research to explain

---

[13] The initiatives include increased financial aid and extra teachers in both primary and second-level schools in need; free books and meals; the Home-School-Community Liaison programme; curriculum changes such as the introduction of the Vocational and Preparation and Training Programme (VPT) and the Leaving Certificate Applied Programme (LCAP). The preventive actions in relation to disadvantage are reviewed in the report of the European Evaluation Unit (1997).

social class differences in education by pathologising working class culture and lifestyle. A cultural deficit model of educational inequality has been normalised in much of educational thinking. This implies that the reason low-income working class groups (school-leavers and adults) are not well represented in the non-compulsory education sector is because they have socially and culturally problematic backgrounds. In a very real sense, the cause of class inequality is located in the subject of that inequality.

This is both a damaging and an inaccurate representation of social reality, as it pathologises and stereotypes whole social groups, while depressing expectations among educators, and among the groups themselves, when they are exposed to such images. Moreover, it misrepresents the nature of social causality, as disadvantage can only be understood in the context of advantage. What creates inequality in education is not simply the financial, educational, social and cultural experiences of any particular group in and of itself. What creates the disadvantage is the fact that upper socio-economic groups have superior access to resources, incomes, wealth and power which enables them to avail of the opportunities presented in education in a relatively more successful manner than other groups. This holds true for younger and older students. In a market situation in which educational success is defined in relative terms, those with superior access to valued resources and culture are inevitably positioned to be the major beneficiaries of educational investment.

It is not only at the level of ideology that inequalities have become legitimated, it is also happening through a host of institutional practices, including wage, wealth and welfare bargaining. Various "Programmes for Government" and national agreements reinforce rather than challenge structural inequality (Partnership 2000, while it is not quite as inegalitarian as other agreements, is no exception). Change is permitted, but only on the fringes. The core differentials of power, wealth and income are not altered. Undoubtedly one of the major reasons for this is the political marginality of the groups most affected by poverty (Hardiman, 1998).

As the superordinate-subordination relations are built into the structures of institutions and systems, they become normalised and habituated. The relational character of inequality becomes invisible as it is experienced and presented as inevitable. One of the problems faced in challenging the inequality experienced by disadvantaged

children and students, therefore, is the widespread cultural acceptance of inequality itself. That cultural acceptance is learned both
through the habitual practice and experience of inequality, as well as
through the formal articulation of inegalitarian ideologies in opinion
formation institutions. Unfortunately, we have also learned to accept
inequality because of the public silence of so many people who possess knowledge and understanding of inequality. Many of those who
know of injustice and poverty do not speak out to challenge it in a
public fashion as much as they could. What comes to mind is a piece
written by Bertram Russell, "The Harm that Good Men *(sic)* Do",
written in the context of World War II. He notes that silence is dangerous in the face of injustice; by wanting to remain pure, "above
controversy", or "above politics", many of us contribute to the very
injustices and inequalities which we may abhor in privacy. This is
especially problematic for intellectuals and academics who have the
training and the tools to speak, or who can assist and support others
to speak of their injustice in their own voice.

CONCLUSION

Listening to Children

It has been relatively easy to ignore children in the documentation of
inequality; and researchers have been as "child-blind" as others. We
rarely collect data on issues such as poverty directly from children
themselves. Adults are allowed to speak for children and to name
their world. We see nothing wrong with organising conferences,
meetings and conventions about children without involving them as
partners. The National Education Convention (1994) is perhaps one
of the best examples of a democratic forum on education from which
most of the principal education players, namely children, were excluded. While we have learned not to discuss or plan for other
groups, including women, Travellers or people with disabilities,
without at least consulting with them, we have not yet begun to take
children sufficiently seriously to establish structures whereby they
can exercise control and influence over institutions which affect them
directly. Although our failure to establish structures for listening to
children is not unique to Ireland, our institutions are, in several re-

spects, less respectful of children that they are in other countries (Nic Ghiolla Phadraigh, 1991; Qvortrup, 1994).

Children's structurally generated political powerlessness has guaranteed that they are neither organised nor resourced to be heard in the first place. Moreover, children cannot influence the political process directly, as they lack the franchise. Even at the more basic level of consultation, children are not counted as partners in most institutions that affect them directly, such as schools and welfare institutions (although, as I have noted above, the principle of partnership has received some limited support in the Education Bill (No. 2) 1997)). If children are to be heard, and if their voices are to be taken seriously, then institutions for consultation with children need to be established (including some forum in the research field), and children themselves need to be trained and educated as to how to use the democratic system in their own interests. We must not assume, as has often happened with women and other groups that were structurally excluded from the exercise of public power, that they know how to use power effectively without education and training.

If we are to give children equality of respect, we need to begin with our Constitution. We must take up the recommendations of both the *Report of the Constitution Review Group* (1996), and the *Report on the Kilkenny Incest Investigation* (1993), that a specific and overt declaration of the rights of children be inserted into the Constitution. The recommendation of the *Report of the Constitution Review Group* (1996: 337) that the Constitution should contain a provision guaranteeing that "the best interests of the child shall be the paramount consideration" in all actions concerning children, also needs to be implemented.

We need to review many of our current policies and practices in relation to children and young people, not least of which is the age at which young people can exercise their vote. We need to examine options such as having a Charter of Children's Rights or having a Children's Parliament where views can be heard. Setting up a Commission on the Status of Children is one of the most effective ways in which to explore all of these issues, and to arrive at effective and acceptable proposals for action.

The democratisation of structures for children is not only a rights issue for the children themselves, it is also an educational issue. As Archard (1993: 164) observes, "Active democratic citizens are not born overnight when a certain age is reached". If we want young people to know, appreciate and involve themselves in the democratic institutions of our society, we cannot forestall democratic engagement until they are past their most formative years. Yet this is effectively what has happened to date (apart from some minimal education about civic society through texts alone), with the attendant evidence that many young people are deeply disillusioned with the political institutions of our society. One of the most effective ways in which to learn the value and purpose of democratic participation is through practice. By participating in democratic processes at home, in schools, and in other public places, children can learn the principles of democratic engagement at a young age. The self-confidence and sense of responsibility that comes from real democratic involvement is of benefit to young people, both as private individuals and as citizens.

Education as a Key to Work and Full Participation in Society

For a variety of historical and other reasons, the creation of wealth in Irish society is heavily dependent, for the foreseeable future, on the quality of education provided across all sectors of the economy. Moreover, knowledge, and increasingly the *credentialised knowledge* provided by formal education, is a major form of capital in its own right. Because of the central role which knowledge plays in determining the generation of wealth, it is extremely important that all people have access to education, and can participate and benefit from it on equal terms so that they are not excluded from the process of wealth generation in society. As the *Annual School Leavers Surveys* show that there is a positive correlation between the level of education attained and employment opportunities, people who leave school without any formal credentials are severely disadvantaged in the labour market. Equality of educational opportunity is therefore important from an individual labour market standpoint, as access to paid employment is increasingly tied to level of education attained (Breen, 1991).

Education is also of crucial importance both for personal development and for the development of civil society. It is essential for the development of all the social, cultural and political institutions that contribute to the creation of an inclusive, dynamic and integrated democratic state. Also, the failure to equalise access to, participation in and benefit from education means that much of the talent and ability available in society is under-utilised, and alienation and detachment develops among those who are excluded from participation.

Legislating for Equality in Education

In view of both the importance of education in determining access to the labour market, and its crucial importance for the personal development of the individual and the social, cultural and political development of society, there is a need for a provision promoting equality in education in the Constitution and, more immediately, in legislation, notably in the Education Bill. The absence of a strong equality provision in legislation means that there is no clear requirement on the government to disburse funds in a manner which will promote substantive equality of opportunity in education.

At present, those who have the greatest private resources can benefit most from all forms of education because their families can bear both the direct and indirect costs that prolonged participation in education demands. What this means in effect is that those with the greatest private resources benefit most from State education investment, as both the direct costs and opportunity costs of education provision rises as one moves from first to third level (Tussing, 1981). In addition, those with greater financial resources can also avail of the wide range of services in the private education market outside of schools and colleges themselves. The economic inequalities which allow such differences in opportunities to develop, especially at extreme ends of the wealth and incomes spectrum, must be addressed.

We also need to recognise, however, that childhood is *part of* life, not a preparation for life. Young people in Ireland spend approximately 14 years of their life in school, and almost half continue in education for a further two to three years. The quality of the educational experience matters, not simply in terms of career or economic outcomes, but as an experience in and of itself. Given its lengthy duration, schooling must be meaningful for young people and respectful of their rights and interests at that time in their life. When we think of equality in education, we must not view schooling as some type of unproblematic good, where more is better (Connell, 1993).

There is much that needs to be changed in terms of curricula and assessment in our schools, but time and space does not allow for a discussion of these issues here.[14] No matter what the content of schooling, it must not be simply evaluated in terms of some long, and often uncertain, future job goals. What is offered in the name of education in schools must be meaningful to young people, and the way school life, and other institutions, are organised and administered must be respectful of them, regardless of age.

REFERENCES

Alanen, L. (1988), "Rethinking Childhood", *Acta Sociologica*, Vol. 31, No. 1, pp. 53–67.

Ambert, A.M. (1986), "The Place of Children in North American Sociology", in P. Alder and P. Alder (eds.), *Sociological Studies in Child Development*, Greenwich, Connecticut: JAI Press.

Archard, D. (1993), *Children: Rights and Childhood*, London: Routledge.

Archer, P. and B. O'Flaherty (1986), "A Home Intervention Programme for Pre-school Disadvantaged Children", *Irish Journal of Education*, Vol. 9, pp. 28 43.

Association of Secondary Teachers, Ireland, (ASTI) (1996), *Staffing, Funding and Facilities in Irish Second Level Schools: Survey Commissioned by the ASTI*, Dublin: ASTI.

Atkinson, A., L. Rainwater and T. Smeeding (1995), *Income Distribution in OECD Countries: The Evidence from the Luxembourg Study (LIS)*, Paris: OECD.

Breen, R. (1991), *Education, Employment and Training in the Youth Labour Market*, Dublin: ESRI, Paper No. 152.

Butler, I. and I. Shaw (1996), *A Case of Neglect: Children's Experiences and the Sociology of Childhood*, Aldershot: Avebury.

---

[14] It will be discussed in more detail in a forthcoming publication (Lynch, 1998).

Callan, T., B. Nolan and C. Whelan (1994), "Who are the Poor?" in B. Nolan and T. Callan (eds.), *Poverty and Policy in Ireland*, Dublin: Gill and Macmillan, pp. 63–77.

Callan, T., B. Nolan, B.J. Whelan, C.T. Whelan and J. Williams (1996), *Poverty in the 1990s: Evidence from the 1994 Living in Ireland Survey*, Dublin: Oak Tree Press.

Clancy, P. (1988), *Who Goes to College*, Dublin: Higher Education Authority.

Clancy, P. (1995), *Access to College: Patterns of Continuity and Change*, Dublin: Higher Education Authority.

Connell, R.W. (1993), *Schools and Social Justice*, Philadelphia: Temple University Press.

Curtin, C. and T. Varley (1984), "Children and Childhood in Rural Ireland: A Consideration of the Ethnographic Literature", in C. Curtin et al. (eds.), *Culture and Ideology in Ireland*, Galway: Galway University Press.

Drudy, S., and K. Lynch (1993), *Schools and Society in Ireland*, Dublin: Gill and Macmillan.

Duncan, W. (1987), "Child, Parent and State: Balance of Power" in W. Duncan (ed.), *Law and Social Policy: Some Current Problems in Irish Law*, Dublin University Law Journal.

Duncan, W. (1996), "The Constitutional Protection of Parental Rights", in *Report of the Constitution Review Group*, Dublin: Government Publications Office, pp. 612–626.

European Social Fund (1996), *Evaluation Report: Early School Leavers Provision*, Dublin: ESF Programme Evaluation Unit, Davitt House.

European Social Fund (1997), *Preliminary Evaluation: Preventive Actions in Education*, Dublin: ESF Programme Evaluation Unit, Davitt House.

Fischer, C., M. Hout et al. (1996), *Inequality By Design: Cracking the Bell Curve Myth*, Princeton, NJ: Princeton University Press.

Gilligan, R. (1992–93), "The Child Care Act 1991: An Examination of its Scope and Resource Implications", *Administration*, Vol. 40, No. 4, pp. 347–370.

Government of Ireland (1995), *Charting Our Education Future, White Paper on Education*, Dublin: Government Publications Office.

Government of Ireland (1996), *Science, Technology and Innovation: The White Paper*, Dublin: Government Publications Office.

Government of Ireland (1997), *International Adult Literacy Survey: Results for Ireland*, Dublin: Government Publications Office.

Hardiman, N. (1998), "Inequality and the Representation of Interests", in W.F. Crotty and D. Schmitt (eds.), *Ireland and the Politics of Change*, New York: Addison Wesley Longman.

Higher Education Authority (1995), *Report of the Steering Committee on the Future of Higher Education*, Dublin: Higher Education Authority.

INTO (Irish National Teachers' Organisation) (1994), *Poverty and Educational Disadvantage: Breaking the Cycle*, Dublin: INTO.

James, A. and A. Prout (eds.) (1990), *Constructing and Reconstructing Childhood: Contemporary Issues in the Sociological Study of Childhood*, London: Falmer Press.

Kellaghan, T., S. Weir, S. Ó hUallachain and M. Morgan (1995), *Educational Disadvantage in Ireland*, Dublin: Department of Education and The Combat Poverty Agency.

Lynch, K. (1989), *The Hidden Curriculum: Reproduction in Education, a Reappraisal*, London: Falmer Press.

Lynch, K. (1997), "Inequality, Social Exclusion and Poverty" in The Combat Poverty Agency, *A Selection of Papers from the Combat Poverty Agency Policy and Research Conference, "Prioritising Poverty"*, Dublin, April, pp. 51–68.

Lynch, K. (1998 forthcoming), *Equality in Education*, Dublin: Gill and Macmillan.

Lynch, K. and A. Lodge (1997), *Equality and The Social Climate of Schools: Report of Findings From Student Essays and Focus Groups*,

Research Report submitted to the Research and Development Committee, Department of Education, Spring.

Lynch, K. and C. O'Riordan (1996), *Social Class, Inequality and Higher Education: Barriers to Equality of Access and Participation Among School Leavers*, Dublin: University College Dublin, Registrar's Office.

McKeown, K. and R. Gilligan (1991), "Child Sexual Abuse in the Eastern Health Board Region of Ireland in 1988: An Analysis of 512 Confirmed Cases", *Economic and Social Review*, Vol. 22, No. 2, pp. 101–134.

Morgan, M. and M. Martin (1994), *Literacy Problems among Irish Fourteen-year-olds, ALCE Evaluation, Vol. III*, Dublin: Educational Research Centre.

Morgan, M., B. Hickey, T. Kellaghan et al. (1997), (see Government of Ireland, 1997 *International Adult Literacy Survey* above).

National Economic and Social Council (1993), *Education and Training Policies for Economic and Social Development*, Dublin: The National Economic and Social Council.

Nic Ghiolla Phadraigh, M. (1991), *Childhood as a Social Phenomenon: National Report — Ireland*, Vienna, European Centre for Social Research.

O'Cinnéide, S. and N. O'Daly (1980), *Supplementary Report* to the First Report of the Task Force on Child Care Services, Dublin: Government Publications Office.

O'Neill, C. (1992), *Telling It Like It Is*, Dublin: Combat Poverty Agency.

O'Neill, J. (1994), *The Missing Child in Liberal Theory: Towards a Covenant Theory of Family, Community, Welfare and the Civic State*, Toronto: University of Toronto Press.

Prout, A. and A. James (1990), "A New Paradigm for the Sociology of Childhood?", in A. James and A. Prout (eds.), *Constructing and Reconstructing Childhood: Contemporary Issues in the Sociological Study of Childhood*, London: Falmer Press, pp. 7–34.

Qvortrup, J. (1994), *Childhood Matters: Social Theory, Practice and Politics*, Aldershot: Avebury.

Report of the Constitution Review Group (1996), Dublin: Government Publications Office.

Report of the Task Force on the Travelling Community (1995), Dublin: Government Publications Office.

Report on the Kilkenny Incest Investigation (1993), Dublin: Government Publications Office.

Technical Working Group to the Steering Committee on the Future of Higher Education (1995), *Interim Report to the Steering Committee on the Future of Higher Education*, Dublin: Higher Education Authority.

Tussing, D. (1981) "Equity in the Financing of Education 2" in S. Kennedy (ed.), *One Million Poor*, Dublin: Turoe Press.

Women's Aid (1995), *Domestic Violence: The Social Context*, Dublin: Women's Aid.

Women's Aid (1995), *The Effects of Violence in the Home on Children*, Dublin: Women's Aid.

Chapter 17

WOMEN, EQUALITY AND PUBLIC POLICY

Ursula Barry[1]

Assessing public policy towards women in Ireland is a complex and often contradictory process. Since the early 1970s, women have gradually pushed themselves onto the policy agenda of Irish society, backed up in some instances (for example, in relation to employment) by a wider European Community/Union policy framework. But Irish women continue to experience systematic disadvantage in economic, social and political life. Economic dependency and political marginalisation remain fundamental features of the position of Irish women — a status too frequently reinforced by public policy. This article will examine some of the key changes which have taken place in public policy towards women, encompassing legislation, new organisational structures, the decision-making process and the content of policy. It will also analyse the current economic and social position of Irish women in order to draw some conclusions on the impact of these policy changes.

LEGAL AND POLICY FRAMEWORK

The fundamental legal position of women, as defined by the Irish Constitution, is one of economic dependence, encapsulated by a key clause which prescribes a very particular role for women in the private sphere of the family. This clause commits the State to "endeavour to ensure that mothers shall not be obliged by economic

[1] Some of the information in this article has appeared in *Women in Development: Europe Bulletin 1998, Women's Economic and Social Rights*, Brussels: WIDE.

necessity to engage in labour to the neglect of their duties in the home" (Irish Constitution, Art. 41.2.2) — a statement which is more an ideological position than a practical reality. It does, however, serve as a sharp reminder of the restrictive and discriminatory attitudes and practices towards women inherent in Irish institutional structures.

The Irish Constitution does establish the right of all adults to be "treated equally before the law", but it lacks a specific commitment to non-discrimination or to equal opportunities between women and men. When it was introduced in 1937, it reflected the dominance of Roman Catholic ideology within the State, in its attribution of a "special position" to the Roman Catholic Church, in its definition of women's primary role as in the family, of the "family based on marriage" as the basic unit of society and in its explicit prohibition on divorce legislation. Over more recent years it has become a key battleground in the process of social change as, on the one hand, the "special position" of the Roman Catholic Church and the divorce prohibition were finally removed, while on the other, a new clause was introduced, amidst bitter and sustained controversy, establishing a constitutional "right to life" of a foetus equal to that of a pregnant woman.

While the Constitution establishes the basic legal framework of the State, detailed legal provisions which cover a wide range of aspects of social and economic life are contained in statute law. Two important pieces of equality legislation were introduced in the 1970s, bringing Irish employment legislation into line with EU Directives on equal pay and anti-discrimination and establishing an Employment Equality Agency to monitor, investigate cases of discrimination and promote equality between women and men in employment. While these laws provide key rights and protections for Irish women in employment, their impact has been limited. Equal pay legislation, for example, applies to very specific employment circumstances and, although its introduction did bring with it some narrowing of the pay gap between women and men, the high level of occupational segregation on the labour market has restricted its effect.

New amended employment equality legislation, currently going through the legislative process, is intended to extend existing provisions to cover other sectors of the population. For example, anti-discrimination legislation will in future cover a range of new grounds in addition to gender and marital status (racial and ethnic origin, political and religious beliefs, disability and sexual orientation). To date, equality legislation in Ireland has only covered employment. Another new bill (also going through the legislative process) provides protection against discrimination in the provision of services (for example, accommodation, credit, leisure and education services). If this bill finally becomes law, it will mean that the Irish government will be in a position to remove its main reservation inserted when it signed CEDAW (United Nations Convention on the Elimination of all forms of Discrimination against Women). Other areas of legislative change have been equally important, such as the eventual legalisation of contraception in 1981, the introduction of the Domestic Violence Act in 1995 (which provided greater protection to women experiencing abuse from known men) and the introduction of divorce legislation in 1997.

Recent Policy Initiatives

As well as legislative change, a number of important policy developments took place over the same period. The establishment of a Commission on the Status of Women in 1971 provided the first real opportunity to examine the position of women in Irish society and to review the prevailing legal and policy framework. Twenty years later, in 1992, a Second Commission was set up to review progress and to make a series of recommendations aimed at enhancing the status of Irish women. This has led to a more effective emphasis on equality in the whole policy-making process, including, for example, a decision that 40 per cent of the positions on all State Boards should be filled by women. In practice, however, this refers to new appointments or newly established Boards and operates only as a guideline, without any mechanism for enforcement. Recent research published by the National Women's Council of Ireland showed that, six years after this policy had been adopted, although the percentage of women on national and regional Boards had risen, it was still only 28 per cent (National Women's Council of Ireland, 1997).

Over the last five years, a number of important additional initiatives have been taken by government. New policy proposals coming into Cabinet must now be accompanied by a "gender impact statement". However, the effect of this decision is limited by the fact that

Cabinet confidentiality has prevented gender impact statements being made public. EU Structural Fund expenditure within the economy must also be assessed from a "gender impact" perspective. A new "Gender Monitoring Committee" has been set up in the last few months whose terms of reference are to monitor the implementation of the Report of the Second Commission on the Status of Women and the Beijing Platform of Action. In parallel developments, the National Women's Council of Ireland has been brought into key national policy arenas (such as the National Economic and Social Forum) as well as into the negotiations for the current National Agreement (Partnership 2000). Working Parties on Violence Against Women, on Women's Access to Labour Market Opportunities and on a National Policy Framework for Childcare Provision have been set up. These are very new initiatives, significant in themselves, but whose impact can only be judged over time.

At a local development level, a new policy orientation has led to the establishment of Local Area Partnerships in areas of particular disadvantage, supported by EU Structural Funds. This has created a new and more progressive approach to economic and social development, bringing together statutory agencies, traditional social partners (trade unions and employer organisations) and representatives of the voluntary and community sector focused on combating social exclusion at local level. This has meant that women have become increasingly involved in a structured manner in the planning and implementation of local development initiatives, including training, enterprise and other community support activities. A number of the Local Area Partnerships have focused on the central role of women in community development and have developed systems of childcare support and other programme activities aimed at improving the situation of women at local area level.

At the level of governmental structures, the direction of change is less clear. The government Department with specific responsibility for Equality and Law Reform, established in 1992, was abolished in 1997 and turned into a section of the Department of Justice. This Department, although small and under-resourced, had full representation at Cabinet level, something which has now been lost.

The Strategic Management Initiative (SMI), aimed at reform of the public service in terms of structures, procedures and delivery of services, was produced and began to be implemented in 1996 by the

Co-ordinating Group of Secretaries chaired by the Department of the Taoiseach. Its emphasis is on efficiency and quality in the delivery of public services and on the use of performance measurement techniques in the civil and public sector. Quality and efficiency are put forward as the core criteria in assessing public services. There is, however, no reference to equality or gender equality in service delivery — equality of opportunity is only dealt with in relation to employment policy and structures.

In a similar vein, proposals for local government reform were also produced in 1996 and stated a commitment to equal opportunities within local government organisations. But once again, these proposals restrict equal opportunities policy to staffing issues. Quality of services, financial efficiency and democratisation of local government structures are discussed without reference to equality issues or gender equality. Core principles (enhancing local democracy; serving the customer better; developing efficiency; providing proper resources) do not include any reference to equal opportunities.

In contrast, the development of the National Anti-Poverty Strategy, with the stated aim of achieving greater social and economic equality, does include a specific commitment to gender equality, but suffers from a lack of any additional resource allocation to achieve its aims.

Weaknesses in the Process of Reform

It is evident from the above that there have been a number of important new initiatives taken in Ireland over recent years which have placed increased emphasis on gender equality. These initiatives have created more gender-aware and women-focused policies in a number of areas. But their scope and effect are limited due to a number of factors, particularly the piecemeal and uneven nature of the process of change, and also the lack of specific commitments and agreed timescales for its achievement. What tends to be missing is a strong and clear framework for assessing the actual effect of these measures and a specific process for changing and modifying policies. There are few examples of procedures to monitor and review current policies and there are also, critically, no established indicators or criteria by which the outcome of these kinds of policies can be measured and evaluated. There is a tendency for equality to be referred to as a general aspiration rather than a definite objective, backed up with specific policies, targets and procedures, subject to systematic monitoring and review.

While there have been some welcome moves towards measuring the gender impact of policy proposals, these are either unavailable to public scrutiny (for example, Cabinet memoranda) or else largely driven by EU policy (for example, Structural Fund expenditure review). Such gender impact assessment tends to be partial, however, and in the absence of specific targets remains a weak mechanism for achieving greater gender equality. In the case of Structural Fund expenditure, a joint Report from the Community Workers Co-operative (CWC) and the Northern Ireland Council for Voluntary Action (NICVA), "Equality and the Structural Funds", concluded:

> The principal failure of the funds, insofar as women, people with disabilities, minority ethnic groups and people living in poverty are concerned, is the failure of the national authorities to mainstream the principles of equality. Equality is seen as something which should be promoted in training, human resources and local development. There are specific programmes for women, for people with disabilities and Travellers. While such programmes and targeting are important aspects of the structural funds, the meeting of the needs of these four categories is essentially confined to these discrete areas. (CWC and NICVA 1996)

Another important concern is the way in which gender equality is increasingly placed alongside other equality issues, such as the rights of Travellers or of people with disabilities. While this has the positive effect of creating a broad basis for social change, it is happening without a framework for addressing gender equality as a separate and distinct question — although one which is closely inter-linked with other kinds of direct and indirect discrimination. Equality for women is too often approached as an issue of sectoral or minority rights, without taking into account the existence of overlapping discriminations. In practice, specific sectors and groups of women are faced with issues of minority rights as well as gender equality (for example women of racial or ethnic minorities and older women).

ECONOMIC AND SOCIAL POSITION OF IRISH WOMEN

Having considered the way in which the policy framework has developed over recent years, it is important to turn now to an assessment of the changes which have taken place in the economic and social situation of women in Irish society. Probably the least talked about aspect of the current strong GNP growth in the Irish economy is the crucial central role which women are playing. Almost all of the employment growth which has taken place over recent years has been female. In effect, it is women who are fuelling the "Celtic Tiger" despite a clear lack of support services, no provision for family and parental leave and continuing barriers to the full and equal participation of women in key State-supported training and employment schemes. A comprehensive and fully resourced public policy towards women's labour market opportunities has yet to be developed and applied. To be effective, such a policy would need to recognise past discriminations against and the consequent marginalisation of women on the Irish labour market and aim to ensure equality of access and participation for the future.

The huge growth in the numbers of women in paid employment over the last 25 years has resulted in a situation in which nearly half a million women (41 per cent of all adult women) are now in employment. While the numbers of women in paid work has risen by over 200,000 over the period 1971–96, male employment grew by only 23,000 over the same period. The sharp rise in women's employment has been particularly strong in the 1990s when the increase in women's employment was over 100,000. In that five-year period, 1991–96, the growth in women's employment equalled that of the previous 20 years (Central Statistics Office, 1997).

TABLE 17.1: IRISH LABOUR FORCE ('000S) 1987, 1994 AND 1996

	1987	1994	1996
Total labour force	1,319.0	1,399.3	1,475.2
No. of women in labour force	408.0	485.8	540.2
Female % of labour force	30.9	34.7	36.6
Married women as % of female labour force	39.6	46.1	51.0

Source: Labour Force Survey 1987, 1994, 1996, Central Statistics Office.

As more and more women enter, re-enter and remain in the labour force, the profile of women in paid employment has changed. Half of all married women and over a third of women with children are now in the workforce. However, women workers still tend to be crowded into a narrow range of occupations and make up the majority of part-time workers and low-paid workers. Eighty per cent of women are employed in the services sector where job opportunities for women are severely restricted: clerical, retail, personal services and certain kinds of public sector jobs account for the vast majority of women workers. Given the current concern with skills shortages in the Irish economy, which may act as a barrier to future growth, policies aimed at reskilling and upskilling existing and potential women workers could play an important role in effectively addressing this issue. There is a particular opportunity at the present time to pursue policies promoting greater equality for women on the labour market, which will simultaneously produce a direct, significant and beneficial effect within the wider economy.

While problems of access to employment, the quality of jobs women do, the level of pay and the lack of support services remain acute, the evidence indicates that this process of change is largely irreversible. The emerging economic situation of women is characterised by a shift from the private to the public domain — a shift paralleled in social, cultural and political spheres of Irish life. Irish women now constitute a large and growing part of the official, registered and measured formal economy and this transition has brought with it changes and tensions in family structure, in social attitudes and in public policy. But as well as regular paid employment, large numbers of Irish women move between paid work, under-employment, unpaid work, illegal work and what is categorised as "inactivity" — home-making. This fluidity characterises the economic situation of women everywhere, linked to women's multiple roles and to the often marginal economic value attached to women's work.

Fertility Decline

One of the key factors which has influenced changes in the pattern of participation of Irish women on the labour market has been a decline in the fertility rate. Irish women today are having considerably fewer children than they had a decade ago and this process of change has been extremely rapid. Family size and household size have fallen as a result, as women have fewer children within a shorter period of their life cycle. Over the twenty-year period from 1975 to 1995, women's fertility in Ireland fell by 50 per cent. The Total Period Fertility Rate (TPFR)[2] has also shown a continuous decline over recent years, particularly during the 1980s, falling from 3.55 in 1975, to 3.23 in 1980 to 2.08 in 1989 — by 1995 it had fallen further to 1.87 (below the replacement rate). The percentage of births outside marriage has been increasing steadily over recent years from a level of one in ten a decade ago to just one in five of all births today. There is no breakdown available, however, of the distribution of these births between single mothers and mothers cohabiting outside marriage (McCarthy and Murphy-Lawless, 1997).

Fertility decline has not occurred evenly across the different age categories of women of child-bearing years. The fertility rate among women in the 40–44 age group has fallen the fastest — this age group now account for just 3 per cent of all births — while in the younger age group 15–24 years the fertility rate has also declined consistently from a peak in the early 1970s. Increasingly, the key age group for giving birth is the 25–34 age group whose rate of fertility decline has been the lowest. Fertility decline is linked to other changes: fewer Irish women are marrying; those who do tend to marry at an older age; and child-rearing occurs over a shorter period of women's lives.

Lack of Care Services

As lifestyles and social attitudes change, motherhood, rather than marriage, has become the key factor in the differing rates of paid employment among different groups of women. Although generational differences are very marked, statistical data consistently demonstrate the striking negative impact of motherhood on participation rates of Irish women — stronger in Ireland than in other EU economies. Strong evidence of the impact of motherhood on Irish women's participation in the formal economy may be found in the Report of the European Commission Childcare Network, "Mothers, Fathers

---

[2] The TPFR projects the number of children a woman would have during her child-bearing years based on current age-specific fertility rates — a value of 2.1 is generally considered the population "replacement rate".

and Employment 1985–1991". This Report showed that the lowest level of participation by mothers in the formal economy anywhere in the European Community was in Ireland, at 38 per cent. The range across the Community was recorded as varying between 38 per cent and 75 per cent. Of the 38 per cent of Irish mothers who are active in the formal economy, 21 per cent are employed full-time, 9 per cent are employed part-time and the remaining 8 per cent are un-employed. This Report also highlighted the situation of lone mothers in Ireland, only 20 per cent of whom were in employment — a figure which represents the lowest level of employment of lone mothers anywhere in Europe.

A critical barrier to accessing paid employment among mothers in Ireland is the lack of State support for childcare services. Ireland has the lowest rate of publicly funded pre-school childcare facilities within the EU — only a tiny percentage of pre-school children have access to such services, which are generally confined to "children at risk" categories. There is no tax relief for childcare costs and only a small number of large employers provide subsidised facilities. Private childcare is costly for working mothers, although childcare work itself is generally badly paid and often unregistered.

> At present, Ireland has a low level (two per cent) of publicly funded nursery provision, for less than two per cent of children; no nursery education; and a heavy reliance on playgroups offering short hours of attendance and with little public funding. Many children (64 per cent of four-year olds and 99 per cent of five-year olds) begin at primary school before the compulsory school starting age of six; yet resources in many schools do not adequately meet the needs of these young children. (McKenna, 1992)

Despite the image which Ireland cultivates as a child and family-oriented society, there is an abysmally low level of support in terms of back-up services for families where women wish to secure and maintain paid employment. Together with the almost total lack of publicly supported childcare services, Ireland has no provisions for parental leave, restricted maternity leave and no statutory provisions for family leave. The emphasis on the family is ideological rather than economic and serves to restrict opportunities and choices for women and to reinforce economic dependency.

As a consequence, gender patterning on the Irish labour market is pervasive. A particularly strong feature of this kind of segregation in Ireland is the link between the kind of jobs women are crowded into — such as nursing, teaching, personal services, clothing, retailing and catering — and the roles which women have been traditionally confined to in the domestic or private spheres of Irish society. Women also account for the vast majority (70 per cent) of all those in part-time employment in Ireland — around three times as many women as men are engaged in regular part-time work.

> Of the 137,000 part-time workers in 1994, some 98,000 or over seven in ten were women. Over one in four females in employment were working part-time compared to just one in twenty men. Just over one half of female part-time employees were in the prime 25–44 age group whereas male part-time employment was much more evenly distributed by age. Seven in ten female part-time employees were married whereas half of all male part-time workers were single. (National Economic and Social Forum, 1995)

Part-time employment among women is carried out mainly by married women in the middle to older age groups. It occurs predominantly in the services sector, such as retailing, catering, cleaning and also professional and commercial services. Together with occupational segregation, which confines women to a small number of employment areas, this is another aspect of job segregation on the Irish labour market: women account for most of the low-paid, casual, part-time and precarious employment (Employment Equality Agency, 1995). A key reason for this is that where women have established access to paid employment, they continue to carry the primary caring responsibilities in the home, and social support systems for women in employment are very limited. Over-representation of women among the low paid is a characteristic of all EU countries, but the majority operate a safety net based on minimum wage protection. Ireland and the UK are the only two EU countries without a statutory minimum wage, and are also the two countries with the highest incidence of low pay.

Economic Dependency and Poverty

Despite the current focus on the rate of GNP growth in Ireland, deepening inequalities in income distribution are increasingly evident. One in three people live at or below the poverty line in Ireland and the gap between the lowest and the highest income groups is widening. Analysis of the statistical data indicates that the level of poverty is rising and that there are specific groups within the population which are particularly vulnerable to poverty. Certain groups of women are particularly affected by and at risk of poverty: women rearing children on their own; those in low-paid work; Traveller women; homeless women; elderly women (frequently living alone); women full time carers of elderly or ill relatives; women dependent on social welfare or partners of low-paid workers and social welfare claimants; women with disabilities; women who have suffered violence or abuse; and lesbian women. It is estimated that around 300,000 women live in poverty today in Ireland — and many are involved in rearing children, carrying the burden of their protection and care in situations of disadvantage (Daly, 1993).

A particular feature of the economic situation of women in Ireland is the way in which women are structured into economic dependency by their exclusion and marginalisation from paid employment, by the fact that the majority of unpaid work in Ireland is done by women and by the way in which State structures, together with legal and cultural systems, operate to reinforce and reproduce that economic dependency. Only a minority of Irish women have access to an independent earned income. Others are reliant on earnings and welfare payments which are received by the male in the household. Fifty-eight per cent of women receiving child benefit have no other source of income. Fifty-three per cent of Irish women working full-time in the home are totally economically dependent on their partners (*Magill*, November 1997).

Dependency and inequality between women and men can be linked directly to violence against women — a widespread reality in contemporary Ireland not confined to any particular social class or geographical area. Recent research published by Women's Aid revealed that 18 per cent of women in this country have experienced abuse — over two-thirds of whom have never reported the abuse to the police, a doctor or a solicitor. Economic dependency and having "nowhere to go" are the most frequently cited reasons by women as to why they do not leave violent and abusive relationships (Women's Aid, 1996). Despite legislative and policy change, little has been done to provide adequate accommodation for women experiencing abuse, or to develop a public awareness campaign against domestic violence (as has been done in relation to drug use, AIDS, speeding, drink driving, litter, etc.).

But dependency is not just something which results from the different positions of power occupied by women and men; dependency is something that is produced and reinforced by virtue of the kind of policies being pursued by the State and its various agencies. Economic activity is still organised on the basis that there is a full-time, unpaid adult in the home, and therefore for the one in two women who work outside the home (on only 61 per cent of male average earnings) the task of juggling home/school/work/care falls on the woman.

The household-based nature of the social welfare system in Ireland (linked to a "male bread-winner" model) has traditionally categorised women as "dependants". This discriminatory practice has prevented women establishing themselves as welfare claimants in their own right (in households claiming unemployment payments, for example) thus excluding many from important training and employment schemes. Policies of switching household claimant status from men to women or splitting welfare payments (where agreement between partners is secured) in order to establish such access has had some limited effect, but is not an option for many women, such as those living in situations of violence.

Support Systems

Support systems of different kinds are critical to the attainment of greater equality in access to and participation in economic and social life by women. Women in Ireland continue to carry the burden of care responsibilities in the home and, in the absence of "family-friendly" employment policies, experience systematic disadvantage as a consequence. As has been detailed above, the employment rate of women with dependent children is significantly lower in Ireland than in most other EU countries and is particularly low among lone mothers and mothers with three or more dependent children.

There is no provision in Ireland for family leave for those in employment. While a few individual employers do provide for such leave, there is no statutory entitlement for women (or men) to take time off work to care for sick children or other family members. As a result, the majority of women are vulnerable to enormous pressures in work, which can discourage them from seeking employment and/or disadvantage them in the workplace.

In addition, there is no provision for paternity or parental leave in Ireland, which when added to a restricted provision for maternity leave forces many women off the labour market and can be the basis for discriminatory treatment on their return. Women's interrupted work histories, which are largely not provided for in employment policy, have the longer-term effect of disadvantaging women in promotional and career development opportunities in employment, and make it particularly difficult for women to maintain and upgrade their skills and qualifications. It is hardly surprising that women find themselves crowded into the lower levels of the jobs hierarchy, paid significantly less than their male counterparts and, in many instances, discouraged from employment in the first place. Compared to countries which provide for extended periods of leave as well as publicly supported care services, Irish society demonstrates a serious lack of commitment to the needs of women (and men) who wish to combine family and work responsibilities.

CONCLUSION

Key issues remain to be addressed in Ireland if the legislative and policy framework and the economy are to provide for and promote equality of opportunity and outcome for Irish women. It is clear from this analysis of the various new developments in policy that, while gender equality has become a point of reference within certain parts of the policy-making process, equality issues, and gender equality in particular, are still not being centrally addressed in critical areas of public policy. There is a marked tendency to set equality at the margins of structural change and policy development. Key proposals for the long-term reorganisation of both public services and local government services are being put forward and implemented without any reference to equality of access and opportunity — only in employment policy is the question of gender equality specifically addressed. The national policy framework for gender equality has evolved significantly over recent years but it still lacks the necessary comprehensive, systematic and measurable application across the policy spectrum.

Constitutional reform, together with the enactment of the proposed wider equality framework in statute law, need to be accompanied by specific policies, backed up with adequate resources, on childcare, combating violence against women, access to appropriate training, education and employment, reproductive choice, entitlements to family and parental leave, individualisation of the social welfare system, closing of the pay gap, protection of those in casual and low paid jobs and the valuing of unpaid work. Such policies must be implemented within specific time-scales, aim to achieve specific outcomes and be subject to systematic monitoring and review. Women in situations of acute and multiple disadvantage need to be targeted at local and central policy level in a manner aimed at establishing economic independence based on an adequate income level and respect for the dignity, choices and desire by Irish women to control their lives.

REFERENCES

Barry, U. (1992), "Occupational Segregation on the Irish Labour Market", UMIST Working Papers, University of Manchester.

Barry, U. (1996), "Trends and Prospects for Women's Employment in Ireland in the 1990s", UMIST Working Papers, University of Manchester.

Callan, T. and Farrell, T. (1991), "Women's Participation in the Irish Labour Market", Dublin: Economic and Social Research Institute.

Central Statistics Office (1987, 1992, 1995), Labour Force Surveys, Dublin: Government Publications Office.

Commission of the European Communities (1992), *Report of the Childcare Network*, Luxembourg: CEC Publications Office.

Commission of the European Communities (1995), "Employment Report", Luxembourg: CEC Publications Office.

Daly, M. (1993), "The Relationship Between Women's Work and Poverty", in Ailbhe Smyth (ed.), *Irish Women's Studies Reader*, Dublin: Attic Press.

Employment Equality Agency (1995), *Women on the Irish Labour Market*, Dublin: EEA.

Irish Constitution 1937, Dublin: Government Publications Office.

Magill, November 1997.

McCarthy, J. and J. Murphy-Lawless (1997), *Recent Fertility Change in Ireland and the Future of Irish Fertility*, Columbia University and Trinity College Dublin, Unpublished Paper.

McKenna, A. (1992), "Developing Area Partnerships" in *European Commission Network on Childcare Report 1992*, European Commission.

National Economic and Social Forum (1995), *Job Potential of Work Sharing*, Dublin: Government Publications Office.

National Women's Council of Ireland (1997), *Who Makes the Decisions in 1997?* Dublin: NWCI.

Women's Aid (1996), *Making the Links*, Dublin: Women's Aid.

Chapter 18

INSTITUTIONAL REFORM

Donal de Buitléir,
Donal O'Brolcháin *and* John Roden

INTRODUCTION

In this chapter, we examine the progress made in Ireland to reform the way we govern ourselves in the light of proposals we made over a decade ago (Roden et al., 1986). In particular, we look at two of the most important developments in the area of institutional reform in the past decade. These are the analysis and recommendations of the Constitution Review Group which reported in May 1996, and the new Freedom of Information legislation which was enacted in 1997. We conclude by suggesting the way forward for those interested in achieving better and more accountable government in Ireland.

BACKGROUND

Over ten years ago, we argued the case for substantial reform of our institutions to make Government more effective. Our central proposal was that there should be a full separation of the Taoiseach, Cabinet and Civil Service (the Executive) from the Dáil and Seanad (the elected representatives). We argued that this would improve Irish government in several key areas. These were: the Executive's capacity to deal with the complex tasks required of a modern government; the need for effective control by the Dáil over the Executive; and, crucially, citizens' access to information to allow voters to exercise adequate control over both.

We will consider later whether our idea is still useful and whether we would modify our views in the light of ten years' experience. First, a brief summary of the original thesis. A decade ago, we were struck by the inability of the Executive to use the best organisational talents to run major Departments of State unless they had been elected to the Oireachtas. On the other hand, the Dáil was unable to exercise adequate control in the public interest, because both Government and Opposition sides were relatively powerless on matters of real importance; one by being essentially an appendage of the Executive, the other by being in the minority. One could argue that this delicate balance of a weak Executive and a weaker Dáil provided protection against the abuse of power. However, its shortcoming is that the Executive is unable to deal satisfactorily with difficult issues.

We proposed a directly elected Taoiseach with special measures to prevent any hidden transactions between the Executive and the Representatives. These measures included: rules to prevent serving Dáil Deputies and Senators being part of the Executive; rules to ensure that all transactions between the Representatives and the Executive would be public; and finally, complete freedom for the elected Representatives to investigate the affairs of the Executive. This would require a major extension of the powers of Oireachtas Committees.

Later, one of us (de Buitléir, 1992) looked at the question of institutional reform from a perspective of citizens' participation. In that paper, it was argued that the changes necessary to make government more effective would also increase the participation of citizens in decision-making by creating reforms designed to promote greater visibility, accountability and subsidiarity. The causes of the failures in Irish Government were complex. They stemmed from too much secrecy, which resulted in low visibility and accountability. Our system was over-centralised and did not facilitate the placing of options before the people. To rectify this, increased separation of powers was again recommended. A list of the other changes which were thought necessary are given in Appendix 1.

IMPROVED PERFORMANCE

Some may argue that our 1986 analysis was clearly flawed in that Ireland has become the fastest growing economy in Europe — yet our institutions of Government are broadly unchanged.

However, a number of considerations may challenge any sense of complacency.

First, much of the improvement in economic policy has been driven by external constraints imposed by financial markets and EU obligations.

Second, the people still appear to be dissatisfied, insofar as they have declined to return the same Government in every election since 1969.

Third, a major problem has emerged over the last decade in making the executive arm of government competent and accountable. Well-documented cases are set out in the Beef Tribunal (1994) and BTSB (1997) Reports. In addition, the performance of the Revenue Commissioners in certain areas is now being considered by a Tribunal. Judicial tribunals are an exceptional method of ensuring accountability. Indeed, the establishment of a tribunal is an indication of failure of the normal means of achieving accountability.

Fourth, the need to draw in additional skills to the Executive became apparent to us in the performance of the old Department of Posts and Telegraphs in the 1970s. The great improvement arising from its transformation to State-sponsored bodies is strong proof of this need. Despite some improvement, policy failure is still apparent in important areas such as transport, the criminal justice system and the environment. Increased prosperity is only now exposing the weaknesses in the government's ability to provide the levels of service needed, for example, in the area of infrastructure.

In the light of these considerations, we believe that our thesis is still valid.

WHAT HAPPENED?

In the last decade, some institutional changes have improved the performance of Government. Since 1986, Oireachtas Committees have been strengthened, though considerable scope exists for further development. Limited freedom of information legislation has been introduced, which opens up important opportunities for the future. Some progress has been made in local government. The *ultra vires* rule was repealed. The influence of local councillors in individual planning cases was reduced following the Report of the Barrington Committee (1991). In addition, the appointment of Ministerial advisors has allowed new skills to be brought to the higher levels of Government. The new system of appointing senior civil servants under the Top Level Appointments Committee has improved the quality of public service management.

Our most radical proposal was the direct election of the Taoiseach. This has not yet surfaced as a political possibility, but the character of the 1997 Presidential election suggests that there may be an appetite on the electorate's part for this proposal. One of us, de Buitléir, in an addendum to the Barrington Report (1991), proposed that the Chief Executive of local authorities could be elected directly.

THE WHITAKER REPORT

A Committee to review the Constitution was set up in March 1995, under the chairmanship of Dr T.K. Whitaker. It excluded all elected politicians and met in private. The present and former Attorney Generals were members, as was a former Secretary to the Government and the retiring Permanent Representative of Ireland at the United Nations, in addition to legal officials in both the Office of the Attorney General and the Department of Foreign Affairs. The Committee published its report in May 1996.

The Whitaker Report made a number of recommendations suggesting amendments to the Constitution of those articles (12 to 28) which concern the machinery of Government in Ireland. The main issues which arise and the Report's approach to them are considered under the following headings.

Separation of Powers

The Committee appears to have considered only briefly the issue of changing from a parliamentary system to one based on the full separation of powers. It deserves to be quoted in full on this point:

> Unlike the systems in some other democratic countries such as France and the United States, our system provides for common membership of the legislature and the executive. In fact, under the Constitution, the Government must consist wholly of members of the legislature. The Government is, in this sense, a committee of the Houses. But since the Constitution vests the executive power of the State in the Government, it differentiates it fundamentally from other Committees of the Houses, which must of their nature be legislative, supervisory or advisory rather than executive, in purpose and operation.

The fact that members of the executive must be members of the legislature keeps government in touch with the disposition of the legislature, in a practical way, and the legislature in touch with the realities of government; it also promotes cohesiveness of Irish policy in the European Union, where the legislative function is shared between the Commission, the Council of Ministers and the European Parliament.

The Review Group does not recommend any change in the present constitutional arrangements governing relations between President, Dáil and Seanad or between legislature and government although such change might become necessary in the light of the comprehensive review of Seanad Éireann that the Review Group recommends.

Earlier, in its discussion of the Presidency, the Report states that:

A total re-structuring of our governmental structure so that it becomes a presidential rather than a cabinet kind would result in a major expansion of the President's powers. The Review Group notes that there is no demand for such a radical change. (p. 29)[1]

Increased Participation

The Report noted the deliberate attempt by Governments in recent years to seek the active participation of the community and voluntary sectors as partners with Government organisations, departmental committees and Government-supported organisations. It considered the fact that so many new participatory structures have been established to be itself an indication of the weaknesses of the existing systems of representation. It recommended the amendment of the Constitution to incorporate a reference to community and voluntary groups.

The high ratio of (Dáil) Deputies to population, which offers the possibility of a high level of proportionality, has been justified by reference to the need for a sufficient pool of talent

---

[1] Donal O'Brolcháin made a submission to the Whitaker Review Group seeking increased separation of powers.

and expertise from which to form a Government and appoint Ministers of State, given the requirement in Ireland that all Government Ministers, except two, be members of the Dáil. This argument is strengthened by the development of the Oireachtas committee system which makes further calls on the time and energy of Deputies. (p. 51)

Electoral Reform

There have been calls for electoral reform in recent years, mainly from politicians. In particular, former Education Minister, Gemma Hussey, and current Environment and Local Government Minister, Noel Dempsey, TD, have advocated change. De Buitléir (1987) has drawn attention to the electoral consequences of this and questioned if there was any need for reform in this area. The Whitaker Report contains an excellent analysis of this issue and is rightly sceptical of the case for change:

> the effects of introducing a new electoral system in a particular country are unpredictable, being a complex interaction of electoral law and political culture in the country concerned. This means that, while changing the electoral system may seem on the face of things to be an attractive cure for some malaise in the political system, such change may well not have the predicted effect. The ingenuity of political parties and the subtlety of voters allow systems to be worked in unforeseen ways. Several salutary examples of a change of the electoral system can be found in modern Europe. The most recent is in Italy, where much was hoped for from a change in the electoral system but where, despite radical electoral reform, the same problems remain and reform of the reformed system is now high on the agenda. (p. 58)

The Report concludes that our present system has had popular support and should not be changed without careful advance assessment of the possible effects.

Seanad Éireann

The Report considered the Seanad and clearly felt that radical reform was necessary. If the two main criteria for retention of the Seanad — the desirability of a system of checks and balances and of representation of as wide a cross-section of society as possible — cannot be satisfied by suitable reforms, then the case for a Seanad would fail and it should be abolished.

> As constituted, the Seanad does not appear to satisfy the criteria for a relevant, effective and representative second house. There are fundamental political problems to be answered before a solution can be prescribed for the problem presented by the Seanad; moreover, there is a wide range of solutions that might be prescribed. Given the time and the resources available, the Review Group cannot undertake a comprehensive and authoritative investigation of the Seanad's composition and role . . . [and] recommends a separate, comprehensive, independent examination of all issues relating to Seanad Éireann. (p. 71)

The Government

The Whitaker Report favoured a strong Executive and was anxious to enhance the ability of Government to decide and act in the public interest, subject to full democratic check (p. 91).

The Report considered whether persons who are not members of either the Dáil or Seanad might be appointed to the Government. It noted that Governments in some countries contain "executive experts" and that it is argued that, since executive capacity is not invariably a concomitant of electoral popularity, the facility to draw on experts who are not elected would be useful. Against that, it is argued that democracy is best served by a situation where the people control the Dáil and Seanad, and through them the Government.

The Report concluded that the present system represents a reasonable balance between these arguments. It did not recommend any provision for non-elected members of Government beyond that already available through the Taoiseach's discretion to appoint members whom he or she has nominated as Senators.

Local Government

The Report concluded by a majority that a form of recognition in principle of local government should be inserted in the Constitution.

Citizens' Initiative

The Whitaker Report recommended that there should be no provision to allow constitutional change to be proposed either directly or indirectly by means of a citizens' initiative. It believed such an initiative involves the "dual risks of effecting inadequate or undesirable amendments to the Constitution and of leading to many fruitless and expensive referendums" (p. 401).

Conclusion

The elegance of its writing and the clarity of its presentation cannot disguise the fact that the Whitaker Report is a deeply conservative document, at least insofar as it deals with the institutions of Government.

It recommends no change of substance to our institutions of Government, other than the possible abolition of the Seanad. It dismisses the full separation of powers model without analysis of its strengths and weaknesses — in particular, its acknowledged strengths in achieving accountability (Ward, 1997). Its endorsement of the existing parliamentary model is very weak. (This endorsement hinges on the belief that, because members of the executive must be members of the legislature, government remains in touch with the disposition of the legislature, in a practical way, and the legislature stays in touch with the realities of government.)

De Buitléir (1992) proposed the establishment of a public forum, along the lines of the New Ireland Forum, to carry out the task of institutional renewal. He argued that there was little point in establishing an independent Commission to carry out the task. He noted that:

> Such a body has two defects. First, it meets in private and secondly, by tradition it excludes politicians. It is essential that politicians are involved in and achieve ownership of any proposals to change the institutions of Government. It is also important that any such Forum meets in public to begin the process of informing the public on the changes that are necessary and the options that are available.

This analysis has unfortunately been amply justified. The Whitaker Report Group has set back rather than advanced much needed reforms. The observation of the late Professor John Kelly, TD, that "Ireland's political and official rulers have largely behaved like a crew of maintenance engineers, just keeping a lot of old British structures and plant ticking over"[2] comes to mind.

The role of "a group of experts" is to devise and examine options which prime public debate on difficult issues. The Report's justification of a conservative position on the grounds that "there is no demand for such a radical change" indicates a lack of appreciation of this role.

THE ALL-PARTY OIREACHTAS COMMITTEE ON THE CONSTITUTION

The Whitaker Report was referred to a joint Oireachtas Committee. Following the change of Government in July 1997, a new Committee under the chairmanship of Mr Brian Lenihan, TD, has been established to pursue the matter. The Oireachtas Committee published two reports in April 1997 and we now review the proposals in these insofar as they relate to institutions of Government.

Local Government

The Committee agreed that there should be a general constitutional recognition of local government. It recommended that the Constitution should specify that "elections to local authorities shall be held at least once every five years".

The necessity for this latter change has been amply demonstrated by the decision towards the end of 1997 to postpone the 1998 local elections for a year. This is the latest in a series of such postponements over the years.

Seanad Éireann

In our original paper, we recommended the abolition of the Seanad. In its second report (1997) the Oireachtas Committee considered the question of Seanad Éireann. It agreed that the Seanad does make a useful contribution to the democratic life of the State. It mentioned in particular that the loss of Senators would make the task of manning

---

[2] John Kelly, TD, *Sunday Tribune*, 19 October 1986.

the committee system extremely difficult. It concluded that the Seanad "should be a consultative body where people with knowledge, experience and judgement over the whole spectrum of public affairs should be available in a broadly non-partisan way to help the Dáil to carry out its function more effectively and more efficiently" (p. 7).

To do so, it recommended:

- The direct election of 15 members from the European Parliament constituencies on the same day as the general election

- The indirect election of 28 members (14 by the incoming Dail and 14 elected by the members of county councils and county borough councils) from two sub-panels, one for men and one for women, with an equal number elected from each

- Six third-level representatives from six single seat constituencies, each centred on a major institution.

It is not at all clear that such a system would result in a non-partisan body consisting of "people with knowledge, experience and judgement over the whole spectrum of public affairs". Rather, it is likely that we would get more of the same; an assembly which, with a few honourable exceptions, is an ante-room to the Dáil where those coming from and going to the Lower House spend a few years.

Citizens' Initiative

The Oireachtas Committee (1987, First Report, p. 20) also considered the introduction of a citizens' or popular initiative. It agreed that this would increase the capacity of the political system to increase democratic value. However, it concluded against the introduction of such a provision on the grounds that modern Irish governments find the management of their legislative programme "a stretching one. Provision for a popular initiative would, in the Committee's view, exacerbate a government's legislative difficulties and reduce its efficiency".

FREEDOM OF INFORMATION

The Freedom of Information (1997) Act, introduces a large degree of openness and transparency in many areas of our public administration, which will have far-reaching implications.

The Act provides the public with three fundamental rights:

- The right to access information

- The right to correct inaccurate personal information

- The right to request reasons for decisions which have been made relating to themselves.

The Act will come into force in a number of stages over the next year or so, covering Government Departments and certain State Agencies (April 1998) and local government authorities, including Health Boards (October 1998).

Access to information will only be enforced to the extent that is "consistent with the public interest and the right to privacy". The head of a public body may refuse to grant access to certain categories of information such as Government meetings and commercially sensitive information.

The head of a public body also has the power to refuse a request for information based on administrative grounds. If a request relates to so many records, or to records which would require so much searching or examination that the work of the body would be severely and unreasonably disrupted, then it may be refused. A request may also be refused if the head is of the opinion that it is frivolous or vexatious.

It is important to note that many of the exclusions set out above may be set aside where the public interest would, on balance, be better served by the disclosure rather than the withholding of the records in question.

If a public body refuses a request for information, it must give reasons for the refusal. Where a request for information is refused or delayed, or the information received is edited, there is a right of appeal to an independent Information Commissioner, who has the power to issue binding decisions and is also charged with the task of reporting on the operation of the Act in general. The decisions of the Commissioner can only be set aside by the High Court. For the time being, the Ombudsman will act as the Information Commissioner.

WHERE DO WE GO FROM HERE?

While there has been some progress in the last decade, much remains to be done. It is clear that the proposals emanating from the major review of the Constitution will do little either to enhance the competence of the Executive for action or to increase accountability. The most that can be expected is a mild reform of Seanad Éireann to remove some anachronistic features.

The Oireachtas Committee offers some hope of progress, but that remains to be seen. In its reports to date, the Committee has shown potential to go further than the Whitaker Report in its recommendations on local elections. It should be encouraged not to confine itself to the limited changes suggested by the Whitaker Report.

The question arises: What should citizens who are concerned about the performance and accountability of our institutions of Government do now? The most important thing the ordinary citizen can do is to use the new freedom of information legislation. We now have in place a means which will enable people to examine key issues of public administration. We believe that it is important that the Act be extended to include Government memoranda (de Buitléir, 1995). Cabinet confidentiality need not be infringed in any way. The result would be that the options and arguments put to Cabinet are in the public domain. The public should see all the options that are being considered.

Another impact of freedom of information could be the disclosure of more failures of public administration. The focus of attention should be the improvement of systems to try to ensure that lapses do not recur. In the light of recent experience, the confidence of the Whitaker Report that all is well is likely to have been misplaced.

Resources to support the Representative function should be increased greatly. Dáil Deputies acting singly or Oireachtas Committees should have the capacity to research and investigate the options open to Government and its capability to carry these out. We believe that the ability of Dáil Deputies to protect the interests of the community will be limited until the Executive is fully separated from the Dáil. Until that time, Dáil Deputies will be unable to make the Executive fully accountable.

We are proposing major changes, which are unlikely to be brought about by the political system itself. A well-designed citizens' initiative would provide an alternative mechanism which would enable these changes to occur, if the people could be convinced of their merits. Many politicians are wary of increased participation by the public in the making of laws. We believe, however, that the people of Ireland have learned from their attempts to formulate constitutional law and there is no reason to think that they would not continue to learn if they were given the opportunity to exercise this power.

Ten years ago, we suggested radical changes to the central structures of our government. Developments since then have reinforced our opinion that these changes are necessary. Politicians seem unwilling to propose the required degree of change, which has led us to the conclusion that the citizens' initiative is an essential bridge to further progress. One of the cornerstones of our original proposal was our trust in the ability of the electorate to choose wisely when offered reliable information about the options facing it. We continue to believe that this is an essential basis for advancing the structures of our democracy.

APPENDIX

Summary of Institutional Changes Necessary

National Government

- Introduce Freedom of Information Act

- Abandon Westminster model of Government in favour of one based on the Separation of the Legislature and the Executive

- Provide that Cabinet Officers are served by a Cabinet consisting of a group of personal advisors who would cease to hold office when the Minister whom they serve leaves office.

Local Government

- Give constitutional recognition to local government

- Give all citizens the option of voting for effective sub-county tiers of local government in their areas

- Allow local electors the option of choosing to have an elected Chief Executive of their local authority in place of an appointed manager

- Provide for a proper system of local taxation so that each local authority would have independent access to sufficient resources raised from local electors.

European Community

- Press for increased powers for the European Parliament

- Support the democratic election of the Commission

- Press for meetings of the Council of Ministers to be held in public

- Support the extension of the principle of majority voting in the Council

- Provide that the Irish appointees to the Committee of the Regions are elected by local representatives, rather than being appointed by Government.

Irish Constitution

- Provide for a power to call a referendum by citizen's initiative

- Provide constitutional recognition for the principle of subsidiarity and following its approval introduce a Devolution Bill

- Resist any attempt to change our electoral system in a direction which would reduce its proportionality or weaken the link between deputies and individual constituencies

- Enact a law prohibiting dual mandates.

Source: de Buitléir, 1992.

REFERENCES

Barrington. T.J. (1982), "Whatever Happened to Irish Government", in *Unequal Achievement*, Dublin: Institute of Public Administration.

de Buitléir, Donal (1987), "Electoral Reform — a Red Herring?", *Administration*, Vol. 35, No. 2, pp. 95–106.

de Buitléir, Donal (1992), "Institutional Reform: A Participation Perspective", in Brigid Reynolds and Sean Healy (eds.), *Power, Participation and Exclusion*, Dublin: CORI.

de Buitléir, Donal (1995), "Lessons for Irish Policy-making" in Dermot Keogh (ed.), *Irish Democracy and the Right to Freedom of Information (Ireland: A Journal of History and Society)*, Vol. 1, No. 1, Department of History, University College Cork.

Doyle, John (1997), "Freedom of Information: Lessons from the International Experience ", *Administration*, Vol. 44, No. 4, pp. 64–82.

O'Brolcháin, Donal (1987), "Need Government Fail?", *Business and Finance*, 21 May 1987.

Report of Advisory Expert (Barrington) Committee (1991), "Local Government Re-organisation and Reform", Dublin: Stationery Office.

Report of the Constitution Review Group, (Whitaker Report) (1996), Dublin: Stationery Office, May.

Report of the Tribunal of Inquiry into the Blood Transfusion Services Board (1997), Dublin: Stationery Office, March.

Report of the Tribunal of Inquiry into the Beef Processing Industry (1994), Dublin: Stationery Office, July.

Roden, John, Donal de Buitléir and Donal O'Brolcháin (1986), "Design for Democracy", *Administration*, Vol. 34, No. 2, pp. 147–163.

The All-Party Oireachtas Committee on the Constitution, First Progress Report (1997), Dublin: Stationery Office, April.

The All-Party Oireachtas Committee on the Constitution, Second Progress Report (1997), Dublin: Stationery Office, April.

Ward, Alan J. (1997), "Constitution Review Group and the 'Executive State' in Ireland", *Administration*, Vol. 44, No. 4, pp. 42–63.

Chapter 19

MORE POWER TO THE PEOPLE? THE POLITICS OF COMMUNITY ACTION IN LATE TWENTIETH-CENTURY IRELAND

Tony Varley

INTRODUCTION

We can begin with two wildly different views about community action in present-day Ireland. The view of the optimists is that community action has three things going for it. It can reasonably hope to be participative, effective and sufficiently dynamic to sustain itself over time. By virtue of it being participative (in the sense of being membership- as against leadership-led and controlled), effective (in realising its goals) and dynamic, our optimists find themselves concluding that community action can be "empowering". By this is meant that not only community activists and collective actors but ordinary members of communities can reasonably expect to experience empowerment, at least to the extent that they see themselves acquiring a capacity to take greater control over their own affairs.

Against this optimism, the pessimists may concede that while collective action can be organised in the name of "communities", it is unlikely to be participative, effective, dynamic and empowering in the senses indicated above. In the first place, because only a small minority is ever likely to participate, the chances are that control by elites will quickly set it. On top of elitism, community action may also be viewed as frequently ineffective and ridden with organisational crises and discontinuities. Control by elites, ineffectiveness and organisational weakness imply that community action is likely to be a frustrating rather than empowering experience for ordinary individuals.

My intention is to see how well these two simplified and diverging visions shed light on community action in the Republic of Ireland. Before proceeding further, it might be worth locating our optimists and pessimists in their wider traditions. The optimistic position can be identified as "communitarian populist" or communitarian, that of our pessimists as "elitist populist" or just elitist.

Communitarians suggest that the people, in the form of a myriad of communities, possess the potential to take control over their own destinies through collective action. The motivation to participate in collective action and public affairs is seen as grounded in a sense of individual obligation which may vary in strength, but can be expected to be stronger as the individual comes to identify and share a sense of solidarity with other community members. When they belong to basic communities (as in families or among friends, neighbours and workmates), individuals are viewed as naturally inclined to identify with others, and see themselves as interdependent and as ready to participate in collective action for the good of the group.

The ethical ideal behind participatory democracy calls for an equal distribution of decision-making power among rank-and-file members (Goodin, 1996: 352; Baker, 1997). Yet the demand of participatory democrats "is not for everyone to be eligible to participate but rather for everyone to be actively participating" (Goodin, 1996: 353). In gravitating toward participatory democracy, communitarians do not confine themselves to calling for a reform of democracy in the formal political sphere. Their desire is to see a robust civil society in which active citizenship can thrive in a context where voluntary associations, run on a democratic basis in harmony with the principles of equality and participation, form dense clusters (Hirst, 1994). Where collective action is both participative and effective, empowerment can be expected to materialise.

The radically different contention of the elitist position is that the ideals of participatory democracy and popular empowerment tend to be eclipsed once pre-existing distributions of power cause community-centred collective action to fall into the hands of elites,[1] rampant apathy stemming from the "free rider" phenomenon takes hold[2] and the benefits flow to the few rather than to the many. Community actors, in addition, face a largely hostile wider world, ever more dominated by large-scale, centralising and bureaucratically organised forces.

How is the state's role in initiating and sustaining collective action viewed by communitarians and elitists? The hope of communitarians is that state elites may be drawn to what Midgley (1986: 44) calls a "participatory mode" in which they are willing to countenance "a real devolution of power" to community actors. Possibly the most optimistic scenario here would seem to be where state elites are ideologically committed, and do not simply embrace the participatory mode in response to pressure from below or as a means of defusing crisis conditions. In many parts of the world, however, genuine ideological commitment has been as good as absent. David Lehmann (1990: 198) writes, for instance, that "the political history of Latin America is littered with examples of co-optation disguised as varieties of popular participation, alias empowerment".

COMMUNITY ACTION IN IRELAND

Two broad possibilities can be contemplated in organising community action locally. There are territorial "community groups" that appear as inclusive coalitions of diverse local interests, claiming to speak for and act on behalf of localities. Community councils and local development associations are examples. Then there are more narrowly focused "community-based groups", tied to the constitution and representation of particular interests.

Community-based groups derive some of their identity from being rooted in a "local community", but their memberships are primarily constituted on the basis of some other conception of

---

[1] To say the least, participative ideologies and unequal social, political and economic structures sit uneasily together. Thus, John Baker (1997: 17) can observe how "there will always be opportunities for the privileged to exert unequal power in democracies, even participatory ones".

[2] Free rider analysis assumes that individuals are naturally self-centred and unwilling to pay the costs of collective action, particularly if they can get away with it and can expect to benefit anyway (see Olson, 1968).

community. Class, gender, ethnicity and religion are just some of the social differences around which community-based groups may form. The list of Irish community-based groups can be lengthened with ease to include local women's groups, local unemployed groups, local sporting clubs, the local units of nationally organised voluntary associations (local party branches included), all of which can plausibly claim to have a local as well as some other "community" dimension to their activities. One suggestion is that community-based groups have tended to eclipse community groups in the Ireland of the 1980s (Crickley and Devlin, 1990: 54). Even if this is so, different tendencies are to be found within specific types of community-based groups, as the case of women's groups well illustrates (Ward and O'Donovan, 1996; Dorgan and McDonnell, 1997).

Community action "from above", which is stimulated by states or even supranational entities, can also be distinguished in type from community action "from below", which takes shape autonomously, possibly in opposition to the state or other external forces which are perceived to pose some sort of threat. With the appearance of area partnerships, LEADER projects and the Department of Social Welfare's Community Development Programme, the 1990s have proved to be busy years for community action from above. On the other hand, what the pothole, post office and hospital campaigns that have appeared over the past decade or so in rural Ireland have in common with the numerous local environmental groups is a belief that collective action is required to defend communities from misguided state policy. These groups have sought — sometimes with considerable success — to mobilise local populations to fight the degradation of local services and physical infrastructure as well as the pollution associated with dumping and dirty or potentially dangerous industries.

In light of these distinctions, we can expect that community action in Ireland will be anything but uniform; it is likely to encompass a number of divergent, even rival, tendencies (Ó Cinnéide and Walsh, 1990). Beyond the local level, community actors may combine together in regional or national networks and alliances. These groupings, in turn, may seek to forge a grand alliance or "sector", capable of developing its own identity and capacity for collective action. To consider further how Irish community action is organised and operates at these different levels, I propose to focus on three distinctive strands. These are the community councils of Muintir na Tíre, community actor involvement in the local area-based partnerships and the recent emergence of a community and voluntary "sector" in its own right.

MUINTIR-STYLE COMMUNITY DEVELOPMENT

Since the 1930s, Muintir na Tíre (People of the Land) has been appealing to the ideals of neighbourliness and co-operation as the basis of building community groups — first through the mainly vocationally organised parish guild/council and later through the "representative" community council (CC). Today, Muintir has about 120 affiliated CCs. Rural populations, according to Muintir's early social analysis, were far from homogeneous, but local people, by virtue of inhabiting the same place and sharing the same history, were taken to possess certain common values (especially a capacity for co-operation and neighbourliness) and interests (principally a desire to see their own localities prosper). Professing itself non-political and non-sectarian, Muintir's pre-1960s programme aimed at building a new rural society in which destructive civil war politics would hold no sway, agriculture would be rejuvenated by means of the "parish plan" and village populations would be stabilised with the creation of small-scale manufacturing.[3]

It has been contended that Muintir's democratic and participatory impulses quickly disappeared once local notables take charge of parish guilds. Certainly a leading theme in the ethnographic accounts is the extent to which control was exerted by local elites (propertied and professional classes including the Catholic clergy) (McNabb, 1964: 208; Bax, 1976: 94, 152). Eipper's (1986: 104) depiction of the Bantry guild in the mid-1960s, for instance, suggests that it was "successful because it had the active support of the town's business influentials and because it made good use of politicians —

---

[3] The recent suggestion by Fred Powell and Donal Guerin (1997: 80–1) that Muintir "valiantly sought to defend the traditional, cultural values of rural Ireland against the forces of modernisation and industrialisation" overlooks the extent to which Muintir's leadership saw the movement as a progressive force. Fr Hayes, for instance, spoke of taking the parishes of Ireland as the bricks to be used "in the *reconstruction* of a nation" (Rynne, 1960: 225, my emphasis).

but it was a priest who gave the organisation its unity, drive and focus".[4]

The culture of Muintir's contemporary organisation is projected as participatory and open to all. Participation is seen to be achievable in a number of ways. CCs are urged to hold regular elections aimed at providing the various localities within the council's territory with geographical representation. Electors either write preferences on a blank ballot or choose from a list of pre-selected candidates (Muintir na Tíre, n.d.: 6). Besides having elected councillors represent spatial constituencies, local voluntary groups (excluding party branches) are invited to nominate a representative to sit on the council. A few places may also be created for co-opted members. Once CCs have been formed, popular participation is welcomed in the "surveys of needs" which Muintir recommends be conducted to help a CC set (or re-set) its agenda. Major decisions are expected to be taken only after the public has been given a chance to participate in the CC's decision-making process.

Representativeness is believed to count for little if local groups are ineffective. CCs are therefore encouraged to take on a mix of long and short-term projects that reflects a locality's "social, cultural, economic, educational and recreational needs" (Muintir na Tíre, n.d.: 4–5). Effectiveness is also seen to require CCs working closely with the state.

How have CCs performed in practice? Many CCs, to judge from a mid-1980s western survey, would appear to be weakly organised and to find themselves stuck at a low stage of development (Ó Cearbhaill and Varley, 1986). Typically, organisational growth has been elusive. There is a tendency, in the absence of paid staff, for activity in the larger CCs to slump after a big effort. CCs would seem to have been at their most effective in providing social amenities (such as community centres), recreational facilities and in lobbying the local authorities and other state bodies to supply or improve infrastructural facilities or services.

---

[4] Seeking popular endorsement when large, important decisions were to be made might seem to provide some defence against domination by elites. Eipper (1986: 148–9) argues, however, that dominant elites had become skilful at manipulating appearances to create an "illusion of consensus".

Poor public support was a leading reason given by western Muintir activists to account for the difficulties their CCs had experienced in trying to live up to Muintir's participatory ideals. The tendency for the write-in ballot to return locally popular but poorly motivated CC members had become a serious problem. Nor, in a majority of cases, had the system of providing local, community-based groups with CC representation worked well either.

Improvisation has been central to the manner in which CCs have adapted to these difficulties. A tendency to abandon elections in favour of recruiting what essentially were volunteer councillors had become established by the mid-1980s. Dispensing with formal elections and reliance on volunteers may produce more committed members, but it may also leave CCs dangerously dependent on a handful of activists, while contributing to a view of CCs as under the control of cliques, thus possibly diminishing their legitimacy in the eyes of locals and outsiders alike. The stepping-down of veteran activists may precipitate crippling transition crises, as strong no less than weak CCs have found to their cost. In their defence, surveyed western CC activists pointed out that, without an activist core, nothing of any consequence would ever happen. They also maintained that, while only a few may be actively involved, the benefits of CC activities are nonetheless spread widely.

It would be a mistake to assume that the activist core always forms a uniform bloc or that its members necessarily see eye-to-eye. For one thing, "personality differences" between core activists have been known to become so acute as to bring all CC activity to a stop. Contentious issues — environmental ones most recently — are another potential source of division or even factionalisation. Trouble may also develop when rivalries between different places become disruptive or when a CC unwillingly has to cede control of some part of its activity.

External forces may pose further difficulties for CC representativeness and effectiveness. The weakening and eventual disappearance of a number of the surveyed western CCs was due to local competition.[5] Politicians who regard their own standing as public

---

[5] Bax (1976) provides an early account of how factions, organised around the local GAA and a priest who favoured Muintir, struggled to speak for and control resources in the small Munster town of "Patricksville". More recently, only

representatives to be superior to all others may see community groups claiming to speak for localities as rivals (Roche, 1982: 303–4).[6]

Can the weakness of CCs be partly attributed to the inadequate back-up support Muintir's national organisation provides? Muintir's national leadership accepts that the servicing of its affiliated CCs is severely limited by field staff and other shortages, all of which are related to the low level of state support. Over recent years, the Muintir leadership has looked to "partnership" as a means of remedying these difficulties. The "Community Alert" programme, organised by community actors in association with the Gardaí as a form of community policing, is now seen to represent the best chance that has come the national movement's way to develop part-nership ties with the state. Muintir's national leadership views Community Alert as a means of boosting the movement's national profile, demonstrating its practical relevance, and giving local CCs a new focus and lease of life.

AREA PARTNERSHIPS AND THE
EMPOWERMENT OF COMMUNITY ACTORS

By taking three cases — LEADER I (1992–94), the PESP Pilot Initia-tive on Long-term Unemployment (1991–93) and the Forum partner-ship (1990–94) of north-west Connemara — I will now look at how well the area-based partnerships have empowered Irish community actors. Lying behind these three partnerships is the official aim of bringing together a range of collective actors in a formalised division of labour capable of tacking problems such as rural decline, long-term unemployment and "social exclusion".[7]

How might community actors be empowered through in-volvement in these area-based partnerships? We might expect, at a

---

five of 37 community actors, considered in a late 1980s review of a Gaeltacht community development competition, were free of local competition (Ó Conghaile and Ó Cinnéide, 1991: 215).

[6] Local politicians, when they find themselves excluded and see these bodies being resourced at the expense of local government, may similarly feel threat-ened by the area-based partnerships (See *Irish Times*, 27 September 1994; Gov-ernment of Ireland, 1996: 26–32; Sabel, 1996: 85–6; NESF, 1997: 28).

[7] For a discussion of the tradition of social analysis out of which notions of "social exclusion" have come, see Room (1995).

minimum, that not only should community actors stand formally equal with other partners, but that they should perceive themselves as equal in practice. Obviously any such perception implies active participation. Community actors should also be able to use the partnerships as an effective means both of improving their own position and of pursuing the community (however understood) dimension of local development more broadly.

How central have community actors been to the partnerships during their implementation phases? It seems a great deal depended in LEADER I on who was to emerge as the "leading partner", a position occupied by "voluntary community organisations" in six of the 17 partnership areas (Kearney et al., 1994: 109). Where community actors occupied the leading role, much emphasis was placed on "training and improving the capacity of the community to promote an integrated strategy for the benefit of all inhabitants of the area" (ibid.: 109). When, on the other hand, commercial interests became the leading partner, "the main objectives related to encouraging new enterprises and helping existing businesses" (ibid.: 109). As often powerful actors possessing weighty resources and a preference for "a 'top-down' approach to planning", the statutory partners tended to shy away from developing a "partnership process" and the power-sharing this entailed, though some individual officials could be well disposed (ibid.: 110). "In a number of cases", the LEADER I evaluators note, "the inflexibility of agency representatives was a cause of deep frustration for other partners" (Kearney et al., 1994: 110; Frazer, 1996: 41–2).

As conceived under the Programme for Economic and Social Progress (PESP), the area-based initiative was viewed as a "community response" with "local communities as the primary movers" (Craig, 1994: 31). With each of the three strands having six representatives sitting on the boards of the 12 original PESP partnerships on average, the local community found itself in a position of formal equality with state and social partners (ibid.: 3). Numerical equality, however, did not enable the community representatives to participate on anything like equal terms in practice.

The organisers of the PESP partnerships soon found that each of the 12 local partnership areas was home to numerous community actors, frequently divided by "intra-community rivalry and competition for scarce resources" (ibid.: 32). The guidelines did not address the issue of which type of community actor should be admitted. Nor did they provide for a system to select individuals to represent them. Consequently, identifying the community constituency, the procedures for selecting representatives and democratic accountability were all destined to become troublesome issues (see Craig, 1994: 20, 31–32; CPA, 1995: 4, 9–24).

In attempting to account for why community representatives should view themselves as the weakest link in the partnership chain,[8] Sarah Craig (1994: 90) draws our attention to how the experience of "community directors" did not prepare them for participation in the PESP pilot initiative. A basic difficulty was that "power structures at local level have not changed. Statutory agencies still maintain control over resources and there has been considerable resistance to any proposal that might alter this" (Craig, 1994: 63; Webster, 1991: 58). An in-depth study of one of the 12 PESP cases highlights how the general dominance of commercial interests in the wider society could be carried over into the local partnerships (O'Reilly, 1994: 137).[9]

Differences between community and other partners also found expression in the clash that could occur between the slow, consensual mode of decision-making favoured by some of the community representatives and the more executive and command styles of leadership and decision-making found in state administration and private enterprise (Craig, 1994: 90; see Sabel, 1996: 82–4).

As a result of what transpired, two inter-related policy problems presented themselves: to improve the standing of the community sector's representation on the PESP partnership boards and to strengthen the capabilities of community actors in the districts covered by the partnerships. As a solution to the first of these problems, Craig (1994: 129) called for "a review of representative community structures" and for attention to be paid to the "development of na-

---

[8] This perception, however, was hardly universal. In Tallaght and in the Dublin Inner City Partnership, the evaluator suggests, "it is quite easy to distinguish the leading role played by community activists on the board and within the sub-board structures of partnership" (Craig, 1994: 31).

[9] It appears that nine of the 12 partnership board chairpersons had business backgrounds (Craig, 1994: 22).

tional and local structures in order to improve community sector participation in decision-making".[10]

The task of building organisational capacity among community actors in order to make them more effective lies at the heart of the second problem. Given its weak capacity in disadvantaged areas and the inadequacy of resourcing (technical assistance, information and funding), the "community sector" was viewed as sustaining "participation in partnership activity over a long period" only with great difficulty (Craig, 1994: 31). The more systematic and professional approach that community actors were urged to adopt implied moving toward a full-time commitment, greater dependence on paid staff and therefore a shifting of the balance away from amateurism and voluntarism. As things turned out, the community development dimension of the PESP partnerships expanded significantly with the advent of Area Development Management Ltd. (ADM) in 1992. Funds, under the provisions of the Global Grant (1992–95), could now be allocated to "capacity building among local organisations" (Craig, 1994: 95; Haase et al., 1996: 51).[11]

The Forum project, organised under the auspices of the EU's Poverty 3 (1990–94) programme, offered the members and representatives of excluded social categories the opportunity to participate in the project's work. Changes to the composition of the Forum board and to its programme of work were to embody the wishes of community actors as much as those of state partners.[12] Again, it was realised early on that local community actors would have to undergo significant "capacity building" if the collective dimension to combating social exclusion was ever to realise its potential locally.

An important dynamic of change in Forum — one indeed that ran, to some degree, through all of the local partnerships (especially

---

[10] Similarly the evaluators of the Global Grant in Ireland (1992–95) suggest that "Mechanisms which ensure effective community representation and participation need to be established and it is critical that partnership development and capacity-building activities take place throughout the community, and not just at board, committee or sub-group level" (Haase et al., 1996: 87).

[11] Building from the 12 pilot PESP partnerships, the number of ADM-financed Local Development Partnerships stood at 38 by 1997.

[12] There was, however, also a local perception that "the management of the project reflected the statutory sector's organisational culture rather than that of community groups" (Varley and Ruddy, 1996: 78).

the paid staff) — was the tension between two contrasting styles of approaching community work. What marks off the first of these styles is the importance attached to the process of building up the capacity and awareness of local actors in line with democratic and emancipatory ideals, a process that is normally a lengthy affair and one that cannot be speeded up unduly. Demonstrating effectiveness by being able to deliver "end product" expeditiously is the distinctive feature of the second style. In Forum, as in the other partnerships, both the experimental and temporal nature of the area-based partnerships generated intense pressure to demonstrate effectiveness in the short term.

ORGANISING A COMMUNITY SECTOR

The fragmentation of community action can be regarded as either a weakness or a strength. As a strength, it reflects the extent to which the presence and power of community actors is unmistakably local in character, centred in a large number of places, each with its own complex of community actors engaged in locally based struggles. Yet at a time when "social partnership", conceived to stimulate participation from the top down, is making strides, fragmentation may leave community actors lacking that sense of collective identity required if the state is to regard them as worthy of national partnership status.

Conditions in the 1990s have become much more sympathetic to the idea of the community sector as social partner. For one thing, some nationally organised bodies (such as the Community Workers Co-operative) have taken up the idea.[13] Simultaneously, the official climate has begun to change in a way that has left some sections of the state better disposed to viewing community actors as partnership material (see CORI, 1996: 86–9; NESF, 1997: 12–14).[14] In a number of national level policy-making institutional sites, a place is now being

---

[13] The consensus at the Community Workers Co-operative's 1994 conference in Kilkenny was that "if the Government was committed to partnership, then the community sector must be accorded social partner status and included in bodies from which the sector had been so far excluded" (Watt, 1997: 67).

[14] Much the same would appear to apply in Northern Ireland (see Kearney, 1997; Rolston, 1997).

reserved for the so-called "community and voluntary sector".[15] The cases of the National Economic and Social Forum (NESF) and the Community Platform's involvement in the Partnership 2000 negotiations can serve to illustrate an evolving pattern.

In 1993, the community and voluntary sector joined Oireachtas members and the established social partners (employers/business, trade unions and agricultural/farming organisations) as the "third strand" of the National Economic and Social Forum (NESF).[16] Within this third strand, eight constituencies are recognised: women's organisations, the unemployed, the disadvantaged, youth, the elderly, people with a disability, environmental interests and academics. Each constituency selects its own representatives. In the "disadvantaged" constituency's case, for instance, three representatives are elected by groups such as the Community Workers Co-operative, the European Anti-Poverty Network, the One-Parent Exchange Network, the Irish Traveller Movement, the Irish Rural Link, the Women's Regional Networks and the Community Development Projects. Provision for three alternates extends the range of available representation. The disadvantaged constituency's representatives are answerable to an assembly (composed of five representatives drawn from the constituency's member associations); this meets regularly to hear reports from its representatives and to review its agenda. As well as being kept informed, the rank-and-file of constituent associations have a chance at regular intervals to give voice to their concerns.

The influence of the community and voluntary sector, in Niall Crowley's (1997: 66) view, is already to be seen in the topics prioritised by NESF, the substance of its reports and opinions, as well as in its working practices. The experience of NESF involvement, in turn,

---

[15] These sites include the Structural Fund Operational Programme monitoring committees, the National Economic and Social Forum, the Advisory Committee for the Local Employment Service, the Partnership 2000 agreement, the Task Force on the Travelling Community, the Commission on the Status of People with Disabilities, the Irish National Committee for the European Year Against Racism and the National Anti-Poverty Strategy.

[16] The official brief given to NESF has been to "develop economic and social policy initiatives, particularly initiatives to combat unemployment, and to contribute to the formation of a national consensus on social and economic matters" (NESF, 1997: 63).

is shaping the community and voluntary sector. A sense of common identity among the constituencies is being forged "on the basis of generating solidarity and co-operation around policy agendas without forcing any form of consensus" (ibid.: 65). Participation, as Crowley (1997: 66) observes it, has called for

> . . . new skills, approaches and tactics. It requires a combination of work within the NESF based on negotiation and work outside of the NESF based on lobbying and protest. This can be difficult to sustain not least because of time constraints. However, the combination is crucial to our effective impact . . . . Participation within the NESF has enhanced co-ordination and co-operation within the sector.

In the run-up to the Partnership 2000 negotiations in 1996, the Community Platform (CP) was put together as an alliance of 15 community-based national networks and organisations.[17] While "acknowledging diversity and even disagreement", the CP has so far succeeded in assembling a motley coalition around "a common commitment to development, equality and justice in Irish society" (CP, 1997: 7). The CP lists as its specific aims: "empowerment, employment, equality, participatory democracy, human rights, elimination of poverty, reversal of rural decline and depopulation, and new models of development" (CP, 1997: 8). CP activists see "governance", now developing in Ireland "to include a more balanced mix of representative and participative democracy", as an issue central to social partnership (CP, 1979: 8).

As one of the four pillars of partnership, the CP took its place alongside employer, trade union and farmer organisations in the Partnership 2000 negotiations. Some hard negotiating on the "Community Room's" part was to result in the government's last-minute acceptance of the minimum payments rates recommended by the

---

[17] CP members involved in the Partnership 2000 negotiations were as follows: the Community Action Network; the Community Workers Co-operative; the Conference of Religious of Ireland; the European Anti-Poverty Network; Focus on Children; the Forum of People with Disabilities; the Gay and Lesbian Equality Network; the Irish Commission for Prisoners Overseas; the Irish National Organisation of the Unemployed; Irish Rural Link; Irish Traveller Movement; the National Women's Council of Ireland; the One Parent Exchange Network; Pavee Point and the Society of St. Vincent de Paul (CP, 1997: 5).

1986 Commission on Social Welfare. Once the Partnership 2000 document had been produced, the individual networks and organisations "sought opinion and debate on ratification" from their memberships, typically by holding national and regional meetings (Watt, 1997: 68).

At the close of this process, the CP, with some significant reservations, was prepared to ratify Partnership 2000 "as providing a basis on which to further progress a social inclusion agenda" (Watt, 1997: 68). As well as providing "sector participation", the CP's existence, as Philip Watt (1997: 69) sees it, has "helped to create a stronger sense of solidarity within the community sector itself".

While substantive gains were made in shaping some of the distinctive elements of Partnership 2000 (CP, 1997: 12–13) and the CP did attain "full social partnership status" (ibid.: 18), a number of "limiting parameters" served nonetheless to put a brake on progress. The negotiations on tax and pay, for instance, were to take precedence over those surrounding "social inclusion/equality". Nor was the Community Room able to ensure that the chapters relating to tax, enterprise promotion, agriculture and the public sector in Partnership 2000 contained "a clear social inclusion/equality dimension". The fact that many of Partnership 2000's commitments relating to social inclusion and equality "are couched in vague terms" has provided the CP with both an immediate challenge and opportunity (ibid.: 16, 19). A third limitation was that the CP had to accept, as a precondition of participation, the broad macroeconomic framework which had been agreed by NESC (ibid.: 15).

EMPOWERMENT OR DISEMPOWERMENT?

Behind the communitarian world-view lies an ethical ideal which celebrates a more people-centred world in which ordinary individuals stand to be empowered by organising themselves as community actors, participating in decision-making and advancing their collective projects. But how well is the promise of empowerment realised in our three cases? To answer this question, I now return to consider the optimistic and pessimistic reading of community action under the headings of participation, effectiveness and empowerment.

The Muintir CCs risk being over-ambitious in trying to represent everyone. They can also run into difficulty in relying on the recommended selection procedures to recruit motivated councillors. The ideal of "everyone . . . participating actively" (Goodin, 1996: 353), so dear to the hearts of participatory theorists, can lose its lustre when this occurs. Elitists might read this as indicating how differentiated social structures allow elitism to rear its head. Equally, they might see it as underlining how pervasive free-riding tends to be. Other possible explanations of low levels of popular participation, such as those pointing to the weakness of civic culture (Lee, 1989) or the strength of authoritarianism (Chubb, 1971), assume contrastingly that the obstacles to greater participation, far from being embedded in human nature as free-rider analysis supposes, can be cleared away with the arrival of conditions more favourable to participation.

The optimistic view of the area-based partnerships is that they are opening up "a potential arena of participative democracy"[18] by attracting the participation of historically excluded social categories: the poor, the unemployed, Travellers, women and the physically disabled, to name but some. Active participation implies that not alone do community actors take the initiative,[19] but that agendas can be reviewed and power-holders held accountable on a continuing basis. Conceivably, many positive benefits for community actors — such as broadening their perspective and acquiring experience (see Haase et al., 1996: 87) — can follow from participation in the area partnerships.

Our pessimists, mindful of power imbalances and free riders, would tend to see community actors being in danger of co-optation in the partnerships, decision-making power falling into the hands of elites and the community interest losing out in the distribution of benefits. An observation of Haase et al. (1996: 87) is that while there is "invariably a healthy demand for seats on Boards and Committees" within the community sector, some concern does arise from "the lack of movement of personnel . . . and the fact that new people do not seem to be emerging". Representatives of the long-term un-

---

[18] This phrase was used by Siobhán Lynam in her presentation to the conference on "New Roles, New Responsibilities: Enhancing Local Democracy to Eliminate Poverty", Galway, 24 November 1997.

[19] Under the Global Grant in Ireland (1992–95), it seems that "In many cases [the community] sector was the prime mover, bringing in the others after a certain amount of groundwork had been completed" (Haase et al., 1996: 87).

employed were conspicuous by their absence from most of the original PESP directorates (Craig, 1994: 120; Frazer, 1996: 48–9). A recent study of women's involvement in the area partnerships relates how, "overall, women said they felt peripheral to partnership structures rather than central to establishing priorities and making decisions" (Faughnan et al., 1997: 8).

A remarkable feature of the recent appearance of a distinct "community and voluntary sector" spread across different institutional sites has been how well a wide span of associations have united around the promotion of an agenda of social inclusion.[20] Unlike the conventional pattern of social partnership, the emerging community and voluntary sector, far from being "hierarchically organised and concentrated" (NESF, 1997: 37), is being mobilised as a series of overlapping alliances.

Turning to effectiveness, a dilemma faced by all-purpose groups such as Muintir's CCs is that, in attempting to do too much, they risk ending up ineffective. This risk is obviously greater when CCs are weak to begin with and when what assistance the state makes available is channelled heavily toward job and enterprise creation, areas where CCs have found it hard historically to blaze a trail. Muintir may have found a niche in the expanding complex of state/voluntary partnerships through its involvement in Community Alert. So far, however, new CCs are not being born out of Community Alert groups and Muintir is in danger of being distracted ever more from its core activity of organising and servicing CCs.

It is clear that the area partnerships can supply opportunities to advance community action in new and significant ways. It is equally clear, however, that the participation of community actors can be heavily constrained by the rules and actions of other partners. Even if other forces do not have complete power over them, community actors have at a minimum come under pressure to adopt a more formalised approach to how they represent themselves and to what they do. There is always the possibility that increased rationalisation and reliance on paid community workers may marginalise or even

---

[20] It might be argued, of course, that the range of internal difference is just too great and that it might therefore be better in the long run to think in terms of building separate though interrelated community and voluntary sectors (see McInerney, 1998).

squeeze out the principle of voluntarism and so give rise to a new form of elitism.[21]

Still very much in its infancy, the appearance of the community and voluntary sector on the national partnership scene does represent a watershed in Irish community politics. Yet effective participation at this level, as the recent NESF report (1997) makes plain, can present acute difficulties for frequently resource-strapped community alliances and networks.[22] Among the obstacles NESF identifies are the gap that can open up between the national and local levels, perceptions that participation cannot effect "real change", and "the drain on resources which arises from the proliferation of partnership bodies" (NESF, 1997: 45, 24). In discussing the proliferation of partnerships, NESF (1997: 26) suggests that "disempowerment rather than empowerment" may occur if popular participation was to drop in consequence of roles being "taken over by the professional staff of the organisation".

If we take empowerment to be subjectively defined by people themselves, we must view it as something that flows and ebbs in response to a large number of contingent circumstances, rather than something achieved once and for all. This is not to suggest, of course, that activists cannot build on achievements or that they must continually start again from scratch. Have our community actors experienced empowerment? While the success of Community Alert may be heartening, Muintir's national leadership has also seen its hopes of building a national network of CCs blighted for want of official support. Together, the discontinuities in public funding for CC promotion and maintenance, and Muintir's preoccupation with Community Alert, illustrate how the state is more interested in programmes than in the aims that organisations or community movements define for themselves. All in all, the potential for community action to be empowering remains largely to be realised in Muintir's case.

---

[21] Grist to the mill of the pessimists here would be Proinnsias Breathnach's (1986) account of the Gaeltacht community development co-operatives, where paid managers come to be almost beyond membership control and effectively the dominant force in the 1970s and 1980s.

[22] Significantly, the CP's participation in the Partnership 2000 negotiations benefited crucially from the technical support (including the costing of proposals) supplied by the Combat Poverty Agency (Watt, 1997: 68).

Can community actors use the area partnerships to progress their own agendas, or is their room to manoeuvre always constrained by what other partners take to be their priorities? Support can in fact be found for both these possibilities. Some community actors have undoubtedly been adroit and skilful in playing the cards they have been dealt. On the other hand, and similar to Muintir's experience, community representatives and actors may be viewed by others in purely instrumental terms, as a means to achieving the partnership's ends rather than as entities with their own concerns and priorities (see Frazer, 1996: 53).

Can support for empowerment be found at the national level? While the advances made by the community and voluntary interest as a social partner have inspired confidence among national-level community activists, there is still a considerable distance to go. NESC, for instance, remains as yet largely out of bounds (NESF 1997: 53). Many limitations remain to be overcome. The nature of social partnership, as NESF recently argues, may in fact have to change radically if further progress is to be made. Currently, the community sector faces the challenges of spreading its meagre resources across several institutional sites and of convincing a numerous and diverse membership that national level participation can make a concrete difference to ordinary people. As with all such undertakings, it also has to guard against the danger of an "inner circle" of national-level activists, insulated from membership control, becoming overly dominant.

REFERENCES

Baker, J. (1997), "What is Participatory Democracy?" in K. Fahy (ed.), *Strategies to Encourage Participation*, Galway: Community Workers Co-operative.

Bax, M. (1976), *Harpstrings and Confessions: Machine-style Politics in the Irish Republic*, Assen/Amsterdam: Van Gorcum.

Breathnach, P. (1986), "Structural and Functional Problems of Community Development Co-operatives in the Irish Gaeltacht" in D. Ó Cearbhaill (ed.), *New Approaches to the Development of Marginal Regions: The Organisation and Development of Local Initiative*, Vol. 2,

Galway: 8th International Seminar on Marginal Regions in association with University College Galway.

Chubb, B. (1971), *The Government and Politics of Ireland*, London: Oxford University Press.

Combat Poverty Agency (1995), *Community Participation: A Handbook for Individuals and Groups in Local Development Partnerships*, Dublin: Combat Poverty Agency.

Community Platform (1997), *Achieving Social Partnership: The Strategy and Proposals of the Community Platform at the Partnership 2000 Negotiations*, Dublin: The Community Platform.

CORI (1996), *Planning for Progress: Tackling Poverty, Unemployment and Exclusion (Socio-economic Review 1997)*, Dublin: Justice Commission, Conference of Religious of Ireland.

Craig, S. (1994), *Progress Through Partnership: Final Evaluation Report on the PESP Pilot Initiative on Long-term Unemployment*, Dublin: Combat Poverty Agency.

Crickley, A. and M. Devlin (1990), "Community Work in the Eighties — An Overview" in *Community Work in Ireland: Trends in the '80s, Options for the '90s*, Dublin: Combat Poverty Agency.

Crowley, N. (1997), "Participating in the National Economic and Social Forum" in K. Fahy (ed.), *Strategies to Encourage Participation*, Galway: Community Workers Co-operative.

Dorgan, M. and O. McDonnell (1997), "Conversing on Class Activism: Claiming Our Space in Feminist Politics", *Irish Journal of Feminist Studies*, Vol. 2, No. 1, pp. 67–85.

Eipper, C. (1986), *The Ruling Trinity: A Community Study of Church, State and Business in Ireland*, Aldershot: Gower.

Faughnan, P. et al. (1997), *Gender Equality in the Partnerships: Women's Experience*, Dublin: CAN (Community Action Network).

Frazer, H. (1996), "The Role of Community Development in Local Development" in P. Conroy et al., *Partnership in Action: The Role of Community Development and Partnership in Ireland*, Galway: The Community Workers' Co-operative.

Goodin, R.E. (1996), "Inclusion and Exclusion", *European Journal of Sociology*, Vol. 37, No. 2, pp. 343–371.

Government of Ireland (1996), *Better Local Government: A Programme for Change*, Dublin: The Stationery Office.

Haase, T. et al. (1996), *Local Development Strategies for Disadvantaged Areas: Evaluation of the Global Grant, 1992–1995*, Dublin: Area Development Management Limited.

Hirst, P. (1994), *Associative Democracy: New Forms of Economic and Social Governance*, Oxford: Polity Press.

Kearney, B. et al. (1994), *EU LEADER I Initiative in Ireland; Evaluation and Recommendations*, Dublin: Department of Agriculture, Food and Forestry.

Kearney, J. (1997), "Achieving Equality for the Voluntary and Community Sector in Policy-making" in K. Fahy (ed.), *Equality Policies and Social Change*, Galway: Community Workers Co-operative and Northern Ireland Council for Voluntary Action.

Lee, J.J. (1989), *Ireland 1912–1985: Politics and Society*, Cambridge: Cambridge University Press.

Lehmann, D. (1990), *Democracy and Development in Latin America*, Cambridge: Polity Press.

McInerney, C. (1998), "A Test of Partnership: Defining the Relationship between the Community and Voluntary Sectors and the State", *Poverty Today*, December 1997/January 1998, No. 38, pp. 4–5.

McNabb, P. (1964), "Social Structure" in Newman, J. (ed.), *The Limerick Rural Survey*, Tipperary: Muintir na Tíre Publications.

Midgley, J. (1986), *Community Participation, Social Development, and the State*, London: Methuen.

Muintir na Tíre (n.d.), *Community Development and the Representative Community Council*, Tipperary: Muintir na Tíre.

NESF (1997), *A Framework for Partnership — Enriching Strategic Consensus through Participation, Forum Report No. 16*, Dublin: National Economic and Social Forum.

Ó Cearbhaill, D. and A. Varley (1986), "A Longitudinal Study of Twenty-five West of Ireland Community Councils" in D. Ó Cearbhaill (ed.), *New Approaches to the Development of Marginal Regions: The Organisation and Development of Local Initiative, Vol. 2*, Galway: 8th International Seminar on Marginal Regions in association with University College Galway.

Ó Cinnéide, S. and J. Walsh (1990), "Multiplication and Divisions: Trends in Community Development in Ireland since the 1960s", *Community Development Journal*, Vol. 25, No. 4, pp. 326–336.

Ó Conghaile, M. and M. Ó Cinnéide (1991), "Competition as a Means of Promoting Local Development: An Assessment of a Community Development Scheme in the Irish *Gaeltacht*" in T. Varley et al. (eds.), *Rural Crisis: Perspectives on Irish Rural Development*, Galway: Centre for Development Studies, University College, Galway.

Olson, M. (1968), *The Logic of Collective Action: Public Goods and the Theory of Groups*, New York: Schocken Books.

O'Reilly, P. (1994), "Who's Plan Is It Anyway? Struggles over the Attribution of Meaning in the Planning Process", Unpublished MA thesis, Galway: University College Galway.

Powell, F. and D. Guerin (1997), *Civil Society and Social Policy: Voluntarism in Ireland*, Dublin: A. and A. Farmar.

Roche, D. (1982), *Local Government in Ireland*, Dublin: Institute of Public Administration.

Rolston, B. (1997), "Overview of Community Development in Northern Ireland", *Inishowen Development Journal*, Summer, pp. 15–19.

Room, G. (1995), "Poverty in Europe: Competing Paradigms of Analysis", *Policy and Politics*, Vol. 23, No. 2, pp. 103–13.

Rynne, S. (1960), *Father John Hayes*, Dublin: Clonmore and Reynolds.

Sabel, C. (1996), *Ireland: Local Partnerships and Social Innovation*, Paris: OECD.

Varley, T. and M. Ruddy (1996), "Partners Worthy of the Name? The State and Community Groups in the Forum Project" in P. Conroy et al., *Partnership in Action: The Role of Community Development and*

Partnership in Ireland, Galway: The Community Workers' Co-operative.

Ward, E. and O. O'Donovan (1996), "Networks of Women's Groups and Politics in Ireland: What (Some) Women Think", *UCG Women's Studies Centre Review*, Vol. 4, pp. 1–20.

Watt, P. (1997), "The Community Platform" in K. Fahy (ed.), *Strategies to Encourage Participation*, Galway: Community Workers Co-operative.

Webster, C.M. (1991), "How Far Can You Go? The Role of the Statutory Sector in Developing Community Partnership", Unpublished MA thesis, Galway: University College Galway.

Chapter 20

THE CATHOLIC CHURCH AND SOCIAL POLICY

Tony Fahey

INTRODUCTION

The influence of the Catholic church on social policy in Ireland can be identified under two broad headings: a *teaching* influence, derived from Catholic social thought; and a *practical* influence, which arose from the church's role as a major provider of social services. Historically, the second of these was the most important. The church developed a large practical role in the social services before it evolved anything approaching a formal body of social teaching, and its formal teaching in the social field never matched the inventiveness or impact of its social provision. Today, this order is being reversed. The church's role as service provider is dwindling, mainly because falling vocations have left it without the personnel to sustain that role. Its teaching role in the social field, however, while lacking the aura of authority it claimed in the past, is nevertheless finding new content and new forms of expression, and may well offer a means by which the church can play an important part in the development of social policy in the future.

Drawing on this distinction between the church's teaching and provider roles, the present chapter gives a brief overview of the evolution of the church's influence in social policy in Ireland, assesses the present situation and offers some brief comments on possible directions for future development. The chapter adopts the conventional, though rather arbitrary, definition of "social policy", which links it to questions of distribution of material resources and services in society. It thereby excludes a whole range of social issues (such as family and sexual matters) on which the Catholic church has for long exerted an influence. In Catholic circles, these latter issues are often classified as "moral" rather than "social", and while this is a forced distinction, I will follow it here in order to reduce the field of reference to manageable dimensions.

CHURCH AS SOCIAL PROVIDER

Throughout the western world in the nineteenth century, the Catholic church's survival and expansion in the face of social revolution, industrialisation and the spread of secularism rested in part at least on its success in developing a powerful, far-reaching role as a social service provider. Catholic schools, hospitals, orphanages and other similar institutions multiplied and flourished in the course of the nineteenth century and in many instances anticipated the development of similar services by emergent welfare states. In some countries (such as Ireland), the church eventually entered into various forms of partnership with the state in jointly providing social services; in others (such as the United States), it created independent systems which paralleled and in some ways competed with state provision. In any event, no other organisation in the modern western world came as close as did the Catholic church to matching the capacity of the present-day welfare state to fund and deliver mass social services.

A number of institutional devices, which the church either invented in the nineteenth century or took out of its traditional repertoire and brought to new levels of development, enabled it to develop this role to such effect. One such device was the system of clerical recruitment, training and deployment in parish ministry. This was based on a model outlined in the Council of Trent in the seventeenth century but which was fully and properly implemented only in the nineteenth century. Parish clergy were usually not of themselves significant providers of social services, as their dominant role was pastoral ministry (though in Ireland, they acquired a peculiar though important role as managers of schools in the national primary school system). But the ubiquitous, disciplined and tightly organised parish system, which most national churches cultivated and successfully staffed with clergy in the nineteenth century, provided the basic presence of the church in people's lives. This was the foundation of its capacity to develop its social provision.

The Role of the Religious Congregations

While parishes provided the remote framework within which Catholic social provision developed, the real drive and energy came from a different institutional source — the religious congregations. Communal ascetic withdrawal traces its origins in the Catholic tradition back to the sixth-century Benedictines. The male mendicant orders in the Middle Ages developed that tradition by harnessing the ascetic impulse to the evangelising mission of the church. In the sixteenth and seventeenth centuries, the Jesuits added a new dimension through the medium of elite education and scholarship, while new charity orders (exemplified by St Vincent de Paul's Congregation of the Mission in seventeenth-century France) began to develop methods of working among the poor which combined missionary teaching with charitable service. The nineteenth century was an important period of innovation within this tradition. Taking their cue from the active, charitable strand of the tradition typified by St Vincent de Paul, a wave of religious founders emerged at that time and set up scores of new orders and congregations. These were devoted to a mixture of social provision and evangelisation, both for the poor and the bourgeoisie.

The novelty of this movement rested in part on its scale and on the comprehensiveness and extent of the social services which this scale allowed. It also represented a breakthrough in another important respect — in its new openness to *female* religious and in the consequent mushrooming of female congregations which occurred throughout the Catholic world during the nineteenth century. The Irish experience was typical in this respect. A number of new female congregations were founded between 1780 and the mid-nineteenth century (most notably the Presentation Sisters, the Irish Sisters of Charity, the Loreto Sisters and the Sisters of Mercy), geared to practical teaching and social service work rather than cloistered devotion (see Clear, 1987, for an overview). These and a number of other foundations provided the basis for a long-lasting expansion of numbers. In 1800, there were some 200 nuns in Ireland; by 1850, there were 1,500 and by 1900 there were some 9,000. The numbers of male religious and clergy also grew, but less spectacularly — the number of priests almost doubled between 1800 and 1900, reaching 3,500 in the latter year (Fahey, 1987). The Irish church was somewhat exceptional in that growth in personnel continued throughout the first half of the present century (though even this was not unique — Catholic church personnel in the US also continued to grow rapidly up to the 1960s). In Ireland by the mid-1960s, there about 16,000 nuns in Ireland and some 14,000 male religious and clergy — numbers which made the Irish Catholic church the most heavily staffed of any national church in the Catholic world (Inglis, 1987). Parish ministry carried out by clergy occupied less than one-in-five of these. The balance provided the human resources which formed the foundation of the church's massive role in social provision.

Effects on Social Services

What effects did that role have on the social services system in Ireland? One considerable effect was to increase the overall level of provision in education, health and related social services. In Ireland, it is often said that the work of the church in these areas simply displaced the role of the state and meant that the church colonised activities which properly should have been provided by the state. While there may be some truth in this view, it should not be overstated. State investment in social provision in Ireland prior to the rapid expansion which took place in the 1960s was not generous. No reserve existed within the public system which could easily have been drawn upon to fill gaps caused by withdrawal or non-activity on the part of the church. State provision might have been somewhat greater than it actually was had the church not been as active, but on its own it is unlikely to have risen to the levels achieved by the combined church–state provision which actually evolved.[1]

While the church's social services had an effect in raising the overall level of provision, and thus the overall standard of services

---

[1] Tussing (1978) pointed out that, from the 1950s to the 1970s, Ireland had a reasonably high rate of participation in post-compulsory education — one that was higher, for example, than that in Britain and Northern Ireland, despite the higher level of public funding for education in the latter systems. He points to the role of the Catholic church in providing post-primary schools as one of the factors contributing to the Republic's somewhat surprising educational performance.

available to the public, there is little indication that the social services system was more *equitable* as a result. The primary purpose of social service provision for the Catholic church was to disseminate and safeguard the faith, not to combat social inequality or reform society. Arising out of the primary focus on Catholic propagation, Catholic schools and hospitals were structured in such a way as to reflect, and to some extent reinforce, existing social hierarchies. There were elite schools as well as poor schools and exclusive services for the wealthy as well as broadly provided services for the less well-off. The religious congregations themselves incorporated status distinctions into their structures — for example, in the distinction between lay sisters and choir sisters in the female congregations or the status rankings of the elite orders versus the more run-of-the-mill congregations.[2] Many of the religious congregations founded in the nineteenth century to provide services for the poor soon found themselves subject to upward social drift; once their reputations became established, they found it difficult to resist the demand from the Catholic middle classes that they expand their services upwards on the social scale. Any potential they might have had for substantial social distribution down the social scale was thus compromised. Those congregations most associated with populist provision, such as the Sisters of Mercy and the Irish Christian Brothers, eventually found themselves oriented more to the lower middle classes than to those at the very bottom of the social scale.

As Catholic social services matured in the first half of the twentieth century, they became more rather than less associated with social privilege and eventually came to form as much an obstacle to the equitable distribution as a means of promoting it. The lack of a genuine redistributive concern in Catholic social provision tended to create a vacuum in services for those at the bottom of the social scale — or at least did little to narrow gaps between the poor and the better-off. This evolution also tended to develop a vested interest in the existing system of provision among Catholic service providers. The consequence was that, as the state in Ireland began to make

---

[2] Echoing these gradations, a former pupil from a Loreto secondary school in the 1960s recalled to me recently how one of the sisters would reprimand unruly pupils by saying, "Remember girls, you're not factory girls, you're not Mercy girls, you're Loreto girls".

sporadic efforts to move towards welfare state supports and services for the poor, the Catholic church often found itself resisting rather than promoting this kind of reform. (The role of the Catholic church as an obstacle to redistributive policies on the part of the state in Ireland is extensively argued in Breen et al., 1990.) An early instance came in the field of health, as the Catholic church came to the support of vested medical interests in fighting off the extension of public health insurance from Britain to Ireland in the period 1912–18 (Barrington, 1987). It acted similarly in the course of the long-drawn out struggle over the improvement of the health services which eventually resulted in the Health Act of 1953. In the latter instance, the church's conservatism and apparent lack of a social conscience did considerable damage to its credibility as an agent of Christian concern for the poor.

A similar vitiation of the church's claim to serve the cause of social justice occurred in the field of education. For example, the system of vocational education created by the Vocation Education Act 1930 was designed in part to protect the social standing and exclusiveness of Catholic academic secondary schools and thus helped inflict a status inferiority on vocational schools, which blighted their development over succeeding decades. In the 1960s, as the state attempted to rescue the position of vocational education and bridge the gap with secondary education by moving towards a comprehensive, universal system of post-primary education, the Catholic church again played an obstructive role, particularly in the face of the seminal proposals put forward by the then Minister for Education, Dr Patrick Hillery, in 1963 (Ó Buachalla, 1988: 163–66).

A further feature of Catholic social provision which affected its impact on social policy was its overwhelmingly pragmatic character and its consequent lack of an intellectual or theoretical base. Catholic religious congregations which emerged in the nineteenth century were highly successful in developing efficient and effective social services but they neither drew on nor contributed to contemporary developments in social analysis. They added little or nothing to intellectual reflection on social issues and left no mark on emerging academic study in fields like pedagogy or social administration. Out of the thousands of capable men and women who flooded into these congregations over the last century and a half, there were remarkably few who expressed a thought of any lasting intellectual significance about the work they did or the social conditions they confronted. At the level of thought and understanding, therefore, their heritage is strangely empty and this drains their achievement of a progressive, creative dimension, which its sheer scale and practical effectiveness would seem to have warranted.

In sum, the Catholic church's role as social service provider, in Ireland as in other countries, was an extraordinary organisational achievement and exceeded anything provided by any other non-state organisation in the western world in the nineteenth or twentieth centuries. In advance of the expansion of state provision in the last 50 years, it substantially raised the overall level of services enjoyed by Catholic populations and brought real practical benefit to many people. It also played a role in the development of certain social service professions (particularly nursing) which it is beyond our scope to examine here.

However, its larger impact in the development of social policy and social administration was limited and was less than the practical scale of its social service activity would lead one to expect. This was so largely because social service provision was a means rather than an end for the Catholic church — it was an instrument for the dissemination of the faith, not a field of endeavour which was worth pursuing in its own right. This evangelising purpose meant that the concern for social redistribution was relegated to second place, if it was there at all. It also meant that intellectual and creative energies were diverted away from a focus on the purpose, methods and philosophy of the social services and social policy as worthy things in their own right rather than as aids to Catholic propagation.

CATHOLIC SOCIAL THOUGHT

It is a reflection of the disjuncture which ran through the Catholic church's role in social policy that, while it threw itself energetically into social service provision from the early nineteenth century onwards, it was only with the publication of the Pope Leo XIII's encyclical *Rerum Novarum* in 1891 that it acquired anything approaching a formal body of social thought. In the social field, thought thus came long after action, and it referred to social issues at such a general level that it had little bearing on the tradition of social intervention represented by the Catholic social services.

The social analysis presented in *Rerum Novarum* and its main successor, *Quadragessimo Anno* (1931) drew attention to the plight of the poor and showed a new awareness of the importance of social deprivation as a concern in its own right and as a factor in sustaining or undermining faith. However, the impact of this social analysis on social policy in Ireland was limited by a number of factors. The first was that it was a construct of the Vatican rather than of the national church at any level. In contrast to social service provision, which emanated from a bottom-up growth of popular new congregations, Catholic social thought was handed down from the Olympian heights of Rome, quite often reflecting the personal preoccupations of the pope of the day. While the Vatican's concerns about the ravages of unrestrained capitalism and the plight of the poor undoubtedly chimed with popular concerns throughout the Catholic world, it was nevertheless inevitably remote from local issues within national churches.

This remoteness was particularly notable in Ireland. The central thrust of papal social teaching, which directed at finding a middle ground between what the Vatican saw as the extremes of *laissez-faire* capitalism and state socialism, had only limited relevance to social conditions in Ireland. Outside of the industrialised north-east of the island, capitalism had failed to take off in Ireland and the socialist movement scarcely developed beyond the embryonic stage. The main targets of attack for Catholic social teaching were thus either weak or largely absent in Ireland — or were present primarily as external conditioning circumstances. Ireland had evolved as a peripheral agrarian offshoot of the capitalist, industrialised economy in Britain, and in the process had created a distinct smallholder social structure centred on the non-commercial family farm. Cleavages between landlord and tenant, between large farmer and small farmer, and between native and coloniser were more central to Irish concerns than those between employer and worker or between free enterprise and state regulation. While the Irish bent for the rural and the small-scale was highly compatible with the anti-urban, anti-industrial sympathies of papal social teaching, the corresponding forms of social organisation were neither derived in any way from the papal social teaching nor were they adopted as a model of social development which Catholic social thought was prepared to analyse or recommend.

A further feature which conditioned the impact of Catholic social teaching was its tendency towards negativism. It was better at rejecting than recommending, clearer on what it was against than on what it was for. It did not strive to hold out a clear, appealing model of how society should be organised, but rather warned about the threats and dangers which it saw in the current situation. *Quadragessimo Anno* came closest to providing an exception to this oppositional orientation as it flirted with a positive social programme. In that encyclical, Pius XI outlined the main features of Mussolini's corporative state in Italy with what he called "benevolent attention" (Dorr, 1992: 79-80) and spoke at length about the merits of vocational organisation and the principle of subsidiarity. However, the programmatic content in Pius XI's social commentary was limited. He hesitated to adopt corporatism as an officially endorsed Catholic model of society and, in raising positive proposals, as Donal Dorr says, he "carefully avoids details and specific applications" and confines himself instead to "general norms", dealing broadly with vocational organisation and the principle of subsidiarity (Dorr, 1992: 79-80). The latter norms were used more as means to assess and criticise existing social systems rather than as foundations of an alternative social programme.

In keeping with its reluctance to commit itself to any particular social model, Catholic social thought held aloof from technical analyses of existing social systems. Pius XI defined the church's role in social teaching as belonging to the moral rather than the technical sphere. This meant that the specialist competence which the church required in order to enunciate social teaching lay in the field of moral theology rather than social science. In consequence, Catholic social thought took no systematic cognisance of economics or any of the other emerging branches of secular social analysis. It was largely indifferent to the increasingly extensive and rigorous empirical examination of social problems and declined to equip itself with the analytic tools necessary to grapple with such forms of enquiry. It thereby set itself on the margins of major intellectual currents which were then beginning to shape secular thinking about social and economic issues, and lost the opportunity either to draw from them or to influence them in a Catholic direction.

Few places were more willing in principle to embrace Catholic social teaching than Ireland, but its actual impact on social policy was smaller than the level of interest and comment it generated would suggest. This was not entirely surprising, given the generality and lack of positive direction in Catholic social principles, and the lack of relevance to Irish conditions of many of the Vatican's pre-occupations in the social field. Even the Church's activities in social service provision seemed little touched by Catholic social thought — the religious congregations providing such services acted much the same way after *Rerum Novarum* and *Quadragessimo Anno* as they had before.[3] The doctrine of subsidiarity did lead to some resistance on the part of the Catholic church to the expansion of state social service provision, but even that was more intermittent and unsystematic than is often believed.[4]

A rare attempt to define a blueprint for governance based on Catholic vocationalist principles was undertaken by the Commission on Vocational Organisation, which had been appointed by de Valera in 1938 under the chairmanship of the bishop of Galway, Dr Michael Browne. Its report, which was completed in 1943, was strong on criticism of the existing system, but its proposals for an alternative were grandiose, uncosted and lacking an air of realism. A smaller effort in a similar direction was presented by Dr John Dignan, bishop of Clonfert, in his pamphlet, *Social Security: Outlines of a Scheme of National Health Insurance* (1944), which grew out of his experience as chairman of the National Health Insurance Society. While confining its attention to health insurance, Dr Dignan's pamphlet echoed the report of the Commission on Vocational Organisation in being severe in its criticisms of existing provision, while being fanciful and speculative in proposing an alternative. Both documents, in J.H. Whyte's words, were "intellectually undistinguished documents"; they were received unsympathetically both in the Cabinet and the civil service (some

---

[3] Some papal pronouncements in the social field did have a direct bearing on the role of the church in the social services, but the most important of these, such as Pius XI's encyclical *Divini Illius Magistri* (1929) on education, had the effect in Ireland of confirming and shoring up what the church was already doing rather than offering a basis for new developments.

[4] Thus, for example, while the church's role in opposing the government's Mother and Child Scheme in 1950–51 has been dwelt on at length, less attention has been given to the broad welcome (or at least acceptance) which it simultaneously accorded the 1952 Social Welfare Act. See Keogh (1996) for a useful account of the diversity of views within the Catholic church on the state's role in social matters.

ministerial responses to them were scornful) and did more to expose the poverty of Catholic social thought in Ireland than to influence policy (Whyte, 1980: 103-6).

THE 1960S AND AFTER

The 1960s brought a double transition in the Catholic church's role in the social field in Ireland. First, the long expansion in the numbers of Catholic religious personnel came to an end and soon turned into a decline. This turnaround struck earliest and hardest in the religious congregations, both female and male: having begun to fall in the 1960s, vocations to female religious congregations and male orders of brothers quickly collapsed and had dried to a trickle by the 1980s (recruitment to the diocesan clergy held up for a good deal longer — Weafer, 1988). The consequence today is that the religious congregations have dwindling and rapidly ageing memberships, and some have begun to plan for their own demise. The process of disengagement from the schools, hospitals and other services which they built up over the previous hundred years is now well underway. This process typically has two stages — first a withdrawal by religious personnel into administrative and managerial positions and then an orderly exit in which they sometimes strive to retain links or influence of a vestigial kind with the institutions they leave behind. As this movement has become general throughout the Catholic church in Ireland, the consequence is that the role of the church as mass provider of social services is fast coming to an end.

The "Option for the Poor"

As Catholic strength in social service provision began to fade in the 1960s, Catholic social thought entered an extraordinary period of ferment and development. The accession of Pope John XXIII in 1958 and the opening of the Second Vatican Council in 1962 were key markers of the start of this phase. Its high-point was the conference of Latin American bishops in Medellín in Colombia in 1968 and the eruption of liberation theology into the consciousness of the international Catholic church. Concepts of solidarity with the poor and marginalised, of "conscientisation" of the masses and of confrontation with secular authority in the cause of social justice, which were espoused in Medellín, electrified those in the Catholic church who

were impatient with old conservatism. John XXIII had abandoned
traditional Catholic suspicion of the welfare state and had adopted a
hopeful view of what capitalist development could do for human
kind. The Latin American experience took many in the church a step
beyond this optimism, including John's successor, Pope Paul VI.
Paul's encounters with the reality of Third World poverty in Latin
America and with the daring of liberation theology had radicalised
him to a degree previously unknown in Rome. He hesitated to endorse the scepticism about "development", the call to confrontation
and the "option for the poor" with which Medellín had challenged
the church worldwide. But his pronouncements (particularly his ap-
ostolic letter, *Octogesima Adveniens*, which marked the eightieth anniversary of *Rerum Novarum*) did endorse the view that social problems
required political solutions and also required that the church be
guided by local wisdom and the precise nature of local social circumstances in deciding what form local political solutions should take
(Dorr, 1992: 205ff).

The changes in Catholic social teaching wrought by Medellín and
Paul VI's responses to it were as much about method and the nature
of the church's teaching authority as about content. They reflected a
view that social teaching should not emerge from on high by way of
deductions from broad, Vatican-ordained social principles. Rather,
they should emerge from the "signs of the times", as evident in local
or regional circumstances. Since Rome could not read the signs of the
times around the world, this approach also meant that local and regional voices could be authoritative in determining the proper course
for the Catholic social action to follow in particular regions — just as
the Latin American bishops had done at Medellín. Since local and
regional voices from around the world could not all be expected to
say the same thing, this in turn allowed for variation and flexibility
in Catholic teaching in place of the old claim to universal validity.
Thus, a whole new set of principles entered Catholic approaches to
social questions. Attention was directed downwards to local circumstances rather than upward to general doctrines, teaching authority
on social issues devolved to some degree from Rome to those in
touch with local circumstances, and regional diversity was allowed
for in place of the old universality and uniformity. The very notion of
Catholic social thought as a unitary, general and universally valid set
of principles, laid out in Rome and handed down to the faithful

everywhere, was implicitly abandoned and replaced by a more fragmentary, variable and democratically sensitive approach.

SOCIAL JUSTICE AND THE IRISH CATHOLIC CHURCH

While the new departures on social justice which emerged during the pontificate of Paul VI have since generated conservative counter-reaction within the church, they have left their mark everywhere in the Catholic world, not least in Ireland. A noticeable shift towards the left-of-centre took place in the Irish church in the late 1960s and 1970s. The empirical analysis of Irish social conditions, with a particular focus on issues connected with poverty and underdevelopment, began to be pioneered under church auspices (the discipline of sociology was initially established in Ireland by priests), and Irish bishops adopted a more consistent focus on issues of social justice in their pastorals (as reflected especially in the joint pastoral, *The Work of Justice*, 1977).

Two institutional developments in the Irish church can be pointed to as indicative of these developments, both of which in their own way reflect a new growth emerging out of old traditions.

Trócaire

The first was the founding, in 1973, of Trócaire, the Irish Catholic church's agency for Third World development. Set up as a trust by the Irish conference of bishops, this was a response to the call by Paul VI and the Third World church for a concerted Catholic championing of the poor and the marginalised. Trócaire quickly became Ireland's largest non-governmental agency in the field of Third World development and, since non-governmental development aid was relatively strong in Ireland, it became a significant actor in the world of international aid.

Trócaire has a number of strong links with the mainstream Catholic church. As an episcopal trust, it is under the general control of the bishops and is viewed within the diocesan church as an important form of institutional witness to the gospel message. It is also rooted in a very practical fashion in an element of traditional Catholic ritual practice — its main means of fund-raising (and one that has proved highly successful) is the Lenten collection, which is run in conjunction with parishes and Catholic schools throughout the country. This collection gives a new form of expression to the old tradition of ritual self-denial during the Lenten period (and as such appeals especially to children). At the same time it gives Trócaire the life-blood of substantial popular subscription.

While Trócaire is thus clearly a Catholic agency, it nevertheless marks such a radical break with past traditions of Catholic social action that its Catholic identity is blurred, in wider public perception if not within the church itself. For one thing, in its work overseas, it is careful to present itself as a determinedly non-missionary organisation — its purpose is development, not Catholic propagation. In stark reversal of traditional priorities, its work in the field is drained of any overt Catholic message, and its inspiration in Catholic thinking is held firmly in the background. While it works co-operatively with Irish missionary agencies in developing countries, it maintains a strict non-missionary identity.

The secular nature of its mission is reflected in its personnel. It is staffed by lay people, hired for their professional expertise in development work rather than for their devotion to the faith. This in turn reflects the conviction that the organisation's worth lies in its technical competence and commitment, not in its denominational colour.

In all these ways, Trócaire has moved far outside the mould of traditional Catholic provision of social services, and in its day-to-day work has merged in with the style and structures of its secular counterparts. This is not to say that its foundations in Catholic social teaching have been lost, but rather that its work is designed as a form of Christian witness for the existing institutional church, rather than as a means of expanding the reach of the church or winning converts.

CORI

The second institutional development I want to point to here is the collective forum for social action which has been created by the religious congregations under the umbrella of CORI, the Conference of Religious of Ireland. This organisation was founded originally as the Conference of Major Religious Superiors in 1960, at which time it played a largely defensive, obstructive role designed to protect church interests in social provision. Today, it brings together some 135 member congregations incorporating more than 15,000 personnel in 1,400 locations around the country. Some of its members continue to regard it as a rearguard defensive mechanism, designed to protect as much as possible of the congregations' influence in the social services, as their numbers decline and their hold weakens.

For other members, however, it has provided the platform for a re-grouping and re-direction of the congregations' efforts, as required by the dictates of the new Catholic thinking on social justice. This has occurred particularly under the auspices of CORI's Justice Office, for which the cause of solidarity with the poor requires a lesser emphasis on mass social services for a society increasingly well endowed with secular provision, and a more concerted focus on the plight of the marginalised. Furthermore, Christian solidarity with the marginalised requires not simply the provision of services, along the lines of the congregations' traditional role. Rather it requires a challenge to the structural causes of poverty and social exclusion, the articulation of detailed alternatives and peaceful struggle to bring these alternatives into being. This role requires it to maintain an interest in education and health services, the main traditional preserves of it membership. However, this interest is increasingly directed at shaping those services from outside rather than at mainstream involvement in their delivery. It also extends into a wider range of areas such as unemployment, poverty, taxation and public spending, discrimination, community participation in decision-making, and so on.

While this radical wing of CORI might be thought of as the parallel within Ireland of the overseas development work carried on by Trócaire, it differs from Trócaire in a number of respects. First, it is in the form of a conference rather than an active agency, and its main focus is on the development of policy rather than on implementation. Its focus on policy sometimes involves it in devising and testing out new forms of service provision (such as the Part-time Job Opportunities Programme), but these are transitional activities designed to influence state policy rather than to provide new fields of activity for the church itself.

Secondly, as an organisation of religious rather than of the hierarchy, it is somewhat removed from the popular pastoral links of the diocesan church. It has no popular outreach along the lines of Trócaire's Lenten collection, though in recent years it has begun efforts to engage lay people around the country in its work through a system of regional associations. Its material base lies in the resources which have been accumulated by the religious congregations, rather than in direct popular subscription. It is thus somewhat less constrained by popular conservatism in the stances it adopts on social issues (though a degree of conservatism in its own membership means that it is far from entirely free in this regard).

However, despite these differences, many of its operational methods echo those of Trócaire. It relies heavily on technical expertise in the fields of economics, sociology and social administration as a basis of its influence — it aims to speak to policy-makers in their own language and at a level of competence which matches anything the public policy system can throw up. It often draws on lay professionals to provide that expertise, and does so without undue regard for their religious outlooks. The central secretariat which carries out this analytical function is small, and its capacity for technically sophisticated analysis and lobbying is organisationally precarious, given its dependence on certain key individual personnel (measures to increase the number of religious with the necessary skills and experience have been undertaken in recent years). Yet, it is capable of offering a sustained, technically sophisticated critique of social and economic policy. This critique is informed by the new Catholic thinking on social justice, but it relies on detailed technical analysis of real conditions rather than on an appeal to theology as its source of authority.

Effects

The effects of the new Catholic approach to social questions on social policy in Ireland are hard to quantify. This is so in part because the new approach is by no means universal within the church. Strong residues of a defensive stance in regard to the powers and privileges of the church are still present, and these sometimes work at cross-purposes to the social justice mission. However, the authority and standing of the church have been thrown behind a large part of the new agenda and these amount to substantial moral backing for the cause of social justice. At a minimum, this undoubtedly has had an effect in keeping social justice issues on the table in national debates about policy development. Neo-liberal doctrines calling for a freeing of the market and the rolling back of the state have not succeeded in pushing these issues to margins in Ireland, as they have done in some other countries. While there may be many reasons for this, the counterweight offered by church support for a social justice perspective is undoubtedly one.

This effect also operates beyond the level of general doctrine. The technocratic dimension of the church's work on social issues has also given it a role in shaping the details of policy. It is significant in this regard, for example, that CORI is included in the community and voluntary pillar which was added to the national partnership process in September 1996. This gives CORI a direct role in the partnership negotiations which have had played such a central part in shaping both the details and the general evolution of public policy. In this it acts not as a defender of the institutional interests of the church but as a representative of the marginalised groups to which the community and voluntary pillar is intended to give a voice.

CONCLUSION

The Catholic church's role in social policy has experienced a major transformation in the last 30 years. Prior to the Second Vatican Council and the upheavals of the 1960s, it had built up a massive presence in the delivery of social services. However, despite its scale, the impact of Catholic social service provision on the evolution of social policy was more limited than one might expect. This was largely because social services were designed to propagate the faith rather than influence social distribution or shape the secular ordering of society. As a result, the church did not subject them to the continuous quest for improvement in purely social terms, which would have made them into a more dynamic element of social provision.

In contrast to the strength of the church's presence in social service provision, the church's formal social teaching was often vague and didactic and its positive effects on social policy are hard to discern, in Ireland or elsewhere. While serving to maintain a general concern for the poor in Catholic teaching, it was too unwilling to grapple with specifics and recommend solutions to serve as an inspiration to sustained action.

The pre-1960s pattern of strong social provision and weak social thought has been reversed in the decades since then. Catholic social provision has declined in the face of a rapid fall in the numbers of religious, but Catholic social thought has become more assertive, sharp-edged and committed to the cause of social justice (even though there may be less than complete unanimity within the church on the desirability of this development). It has also become more empirical and technocratic in its methods of analysis, and more geared to influencing public policy at a detailed technical level, as well as at the level of general principle. In the past, massive numbers of church personnel were deployed to deliver social services, but they had little creative impact on thinking about social issues. Today, the massive numbers are quickly shrinking, and the system of Catholic social services is in decline. However, the new models of Catholic social action which are now being created suggest that smaller numbers, concentrated and deployed at the cutting edge of social policy, can have an impact on the shape of future developments that matches, and may even exceed, anything achieved in the past.

REFERENCES

Barrington, R. (1987), *Health, Medicine and Politics in Ireland, 1900-1970*, Dublin: Institute of Public Administration.

Breen, R., D.F. Hannan, D.B. Rottman and C.T. Whelan (1990), *Understanding Contemporary Ireland: State, Class and Development in the Republic of Ireland*, Dublin: Gill and Macmillan.

Clear, C. (1987), *Nuns in Nineteenth Century Ireland*, Dublin: Gill and Macmillan.

Dorr, D. (1992), *Option for the Poor: A Hundred Years of Catholic Social Teaching*, Second Edition, Dublin: Gill and Macmillan.

Fahey, T. (1987), "Nuns in Ireland in the Nineteenth Century", in M. Cullen (ed.), *Girls Don't Do Honours: Irish Women in Education in the 19th and 20th Centuries*, Dublin: WEB.

Inglis, T. (1987), *Moral Monopoly: The Catholic Church in Modern Irish Society*, Dublin: Gill and Macmillan.

Keogh, D. (1996), "The Role of the Catholic Church in the Republic of Ireland 1922–1995" in *Building Trust in Ireland: Studies Commissioned by the Forum for Peace and Reconciliation*, Belfast: Blackstaff Press.

Ó Buachalla, S. (1988), *Education Policy in Twentieth-Century Ireland*, Dublin: Wolfhound Press.

Tussing, A.D. (1978), *Irish Educational Expenditures: Past, Present, and Future*, Dublin: Economic and Social Research Institute.

Weafer, J.A. (1988), "Vocations — a Review of National and International Trends", *The Furrow*, August.

Whyte, J.H. (1980), *Church and State in Modern Ireland*, Dublin: Gill and Macmillan.

INDEX